Advance praise for *Sacred Economics*:

"If you want a convincing account of just how deep the shift in our new axial age is and must be, look no further than this brilliant book by Charles Eisenstein, one of the deepest integrative thinkers active today."

—Michel Bauwens, founder of the P2P Foundation

"With his breadth of knowledge, enthusiasm, commitment, diligence, and sensitivity, Eisenstein has become a beacon of hope for others. Your heart and mind will be opened by this treasure of a book that shines with wisdom of crucial importance to our troubled world today."

—Kamran Mofid, PhD in economics; founder of the Globalisation for the Common Good Initiative

Praise for *The Ascent of Humanity*:

"This is an extraordinary book. Eisenstein has put his finger on the core problem facing humanity—namely: separation. All the crises that humanity now faces are grounded in the belief that we are separate—separate from each other, separate from the biosphere that sustains us, separate from the universe that has brought us forth. This is a tour-de-force filled with astounding insight, wit, wisdom, and heart."

—Christopher Uhl, author of *Developing Ecological Consciousness: Paths to a Sustainable Future*

"Quite marvelous, a hugely important work . . . This book is truly needed in this time of deepening crisis."

—John Zerzan, author of *Future Primitive* and *Elements of Refusal*

"A radical awakening as to how we arrived at our current crisis and how we can more effectively redefine the path of our evolutionary journey."

—Bruce Lipton, author of *The Biology of Belief*

"Brilliant and original, with great depth of insight and understanding, Eisenstein's *Ascent of Humanity* easily ranks with the works of such giants of our age as David Bohm, Julian Jaynes, Jean Gebser, and Alfred North Whitehead. It is a profoundly serious, indeed somber portrait of our times, even as it opens a door of honest hope amidst the dark destiny we have woven about us. Accept the challenge of this major accomplishment and discover the light shining within it."

—Joseph Chilton Pearce, author of *The Crack in the Cosmic Egg, Magical Child, Evolution's End,* and *The Biology of Transcendence*

"This is one of those rare books that moves the goal posts. Eisenstein pulls together a wide array of insights to show that what we thought was the solution is also the problem. It is eye-opening fodder for conversations with everyone I meet. As a technologist and a human being, I believe this could well be one of the most important books of the decade."

—Garret Moddel, professor of electrical engineering at UC Boulder; chairman & CTO, Phiar Corporation

Sacred Economics

MONEY, GIFT & SOCIETY
IN THE AGE OF TRANSITION

Charles Eisenstein

EVOLVER
EDITIONS

Berkeley, California

Published by Evolver Editions

Evolver Editions' publications are distributed by
North Atlantic Books
P.O. Box 12327
Berkeley, California 94712

Cover art, "Still Life with Flowers, Fruits, and Poultry"
   by Jan Van Os (courtesy of Rijksmuseum, Amsterdam).
Art direction and cover design by michaelrobinsonnyc.com
Book design by Brad Greene
Printed in the United States of America

Sacred Economics: Money, Gift, and Society in the Age of Transition is sponsored by the
Society for the Study of Native Arts and Sciences, a nonprofit educational corporation whose goals are to develop an educational and cross-cultural perspective
linking various scientific, social, and artistic fields; to nurture a holistic view of
arts, sciences, humanities, and healing; and to publish and distribute literature
on the relationship of mind, body, and nature.

North Atlantic Books' publications are available through most
bookstores. For further information, call 800-733-3000 or visit our
website at www.northatlanticbooks.com.

Library of Congress Cataloging-in-Publication Data

Eisenstein, Charles, 1967–
   Sacred economics : money, gift, and society in the age of transition
/ Charles Eisenstein.
      p. cm.
   Includes bibliographical references.
   ISBN 978-1-58394-397-7 (pbk.)
   1. Money—History. 2. Money—Philosophy. I. Title.
   HG231.E37 2011
   332.4'9—dc22

2011010766

3 4 5 6 7 8 9 SHERIDAN 16 15 14 13 12

Printed on recycled paper

To my parents
and all others who have given me so much
with no thought of return

AUTHOR'S NOTE

I offer this book to you in the spirit of a gift, in keeping with its theme of bringing gift principles into the realm of money. In order to align principles with action, the publisher and I have chosen a Creative Commons copyright, which allows you to freely share this book for any non-commercial purpose. That means you can photocopy material from the book, put it on your blog, and so forth, as long as you don't sell it or use it to carry advertising. We also ask that you provide attribution, in order that people who want to find more of my work can do so. You can find other legal details on the Creative Commons website.

One characteristic of gifts is that the return gift is not specified in advance. If you receive or disseminate this work free of charge, we welcome a voluntary return gift that expresses the gratitude or sense of value that you may feel. You may do so through the websites associated with the author and the book.

Ultimately, I see myself as a steward and channel for the ideas of Sacred Economics. Standing atop the shoulders of thinkers far more illustrious than myself, I absorb, digest, and transmit ideas from our cultural commons. Such is the gift I have received and from which I give in turn. That is why I cannot, in good conscience, consider myself the morally legitimate owner of these ideas. Thankfully, my publisher has had the courage to explore a new model of handling intellectual property. I look forward to the day when artists no longer need to maintain, through intellectual property laws, an artificial scarcity of their work, yet still receive abundant returns borne of the gratitude of those who receive it.

TABLE OF CONTENTS

INTRODUCTION

The purpose of this book is to make money and human economy as sacred as everything else in the universe.

Today we associate money with the profane, and for good reason. If anything is sacred in this world, it is surely not money. Money seems to be the enemy of our better instincts, as is clear every time the thought "I can't afford to" blocks an impulse toward kindness or generosity. Money seems to be the enemy of beauty, as the disparaging term "a sellout" demonstrates. Money seems to be the enemy of every worthy social and political reform, as corporate power steers legislation toward the aggrandizement of its own profits. Money seems to be destroying the earth, as we pillage the oceans, the forests, the soil, and every species to feed a greed that knows no end.

From at least the time that Jesus threw the money changers from the temple, we have sensed that there is something unholy about money. When politicians seek money instead of the public good, we call them corrupt. Adjectives like "dirty" and "filthy" naturally describe money. Monks are supposed to have little to do with it: "You cannot serve God and Mammon."

At the same time, no one can deny that money has a mysterious, magical quality as well, the power to alter human behavior and coordinate human activity. From ancient times thinkers have marveled at the ability of a mere mark to confer this power upon a disk of metal or slip of paper. Unfortunately, looking at the world around us, it is hard to avoid concluding that the magic of money is an evil magic.

Obviously, if we are to make money into something sacred, nothing less than a wholesale revolution in money will suffice, a transformation of its essential nature. It is not merely our attitudes about money that must change, as some self-help gurus would have us believe; rather, we will create new *kinds* of money that embody and reinforce changed attitudes. *Sacred Economics* describes this new money and the new economy that will coalesce around it. It also explores the metamorphosis in human identity that is both a cause and a result of the transformation of money. The changed attitudes of which I speak go all the way to the core of what it is to be human: they include our understanding of the purpose of life, humanity's role on the planet, the relationship of the individual to the human and natural community; even what it is to be an individual, a self. After all, we experience money (and property) as an extension of our selves; hence the possessive pronoun "mine" to describe it, the same pronoun we use to identify our arms and heads. My money, my car, my hand, my liver. Consider as well the sense of violation we feel when we are robbed or "ripped off," as if part of our very selves had been taken.

A transformation from profanity to sacredness in money—something so deep a part of our identity, something so central to the workings of the world—would have profound effects indeed. But what does it mean for money, or anything else for that matter, to be sacred? It is in a crucial sense the opposite of what *sacred* has come to mean. For several thousand years, the concepts of sacred, holy, and divine have referred increasingly to something separate from nature, the world, and the flesh. Three or four thousand years ago the gods began a migration from the lakes, forests, rivers, and mountains into the sky, becoming the imperial overlords of nature rather than its essence. As divinity separated from nature, so also it became unholy to involve oneself too deeply in the affairs of the world. The human being changed from a living embodied soul into its profane envelope, a mere receptacle of spirit, culminating in the Cartesian mote of consciousness observing the world but not participating in it, and the Newtonian watchmaker-God doing the same. To be divine was to be supernatural, nonmaterial. If God participated in the world at all, it was through miracles—divine intercessions violating or superseding nature's laws.

Paradoxically, this separate, abstract thing called spirit is supposed to be what animates the world. Ask the religious person what changes when a person dies, and she will say the soul has left the body. Ask her who makes the rain fall and the wind blow, and she will say it is God. To be sure, Galileo and Newton appeared to have removed God from these everyday workings of the world, explaining it instead as the clockwork of a vast machine of impersonal force and mass, but even they still needed the Clockmaker to wind it up in the beginning, to imbue the universe with the potential energy that has run it ever since. This conception is still with us today as the Big Bang, a primordial event that is the source of the "negative entropy" that allows movement and life. In any case, our culture's notion of spirit is that of something separate and nonworldly, that yet can miraculously intervene in material affairs, and that even animates and directs them in some mysterious way.

It is hugely ironic and hugely significant that the one thing on the planet most closely resembling the forgoing conception of the divine is money. It is an invisible, immortal force that surrounds and steers all things, omnipotent and limitless, an "invisible hand" that, it is said, makes the world go 'round. Yet, money today is an abstraction, at most symbols on a piece of paper but usually mere bits in a computer. It exists in a realm far removed from materiality.

In that realm, it is exempt from nature's most important laws, for it does not decay and return to the soil as all other things do, but is rather preserved, changeless, in its vaults and computer files, even growing with time thanks to interest. It bears the properties of eternal preservation and everlasting increase, both of which are profoundly unnatural. The natural substance that comes closest to these properties is gold, which does not rust, tarnish, or decay. Early on, gold was therefore used both as money and as a metaphor for the divine soul, that which is incorruptible and changeless.

Money's divine property of abstraction, of disconnection from the real world of things, reached its extreme in the early years of the twenty-first century as the financial economy lost its mooring in the real economy and took on a life of its own. The vast fortunes of Wall Street were unconnected to any material production, seeming to exist in a separate realm.

Looking down from Olympian heights, the financiers called themselves "masters of the universe," channeling the power of the god they served to bring fortune or ruin upon the masses, to literally move mountains, raze forests, change the course of rivers, cause the rise and fall of nations. But money soon proved to be a capricious god. As I write these words, it seems that the increasingly frantic rituals that the financial priesthood uses to placate the god Money are in vain. Like the clergy of a dying religion, they exhort their followers to greater sacrifices while blaming their misfortunes either on sin (greedy bankers, irresponsible consumers) or on the mysterious whims of God (the financial markets). But some are already blaming the priests themselves.

What we call recession, an earlier culture might have called "God abandoning the world." Money is disappearing, and with it another property of spirit: the animating force of the human realm.

At this writing, all over the world machines stand idle. Factories have ground to a halt; construction equipment sits derelict in the yard; parks and libraries are closing; and millions go homeless and hungry while housing units stand vacant and food rots in the warehouses. Yet all the human and material inputs to build the houses, distribute the food, and run the factories still exist. It is rather something immaterial, that animating spirit, which has fled. What has fled is money. That is the only thing missing, so insubstantial (in the form of electrons in computers) that it can hardly be said to exist at all, yet so powerful that without it, human productivity grinds to a halt. On the individual level as well, we can see the demotivating effects of lack of money. Consider the stereotype of the unemployed man, nearly broke, slouched in front of the TV in his undershirt, drinking a beer, hardly able to rise from his chair. Money, it seems, animates people as well as machines. Without it we are *dispirited*.

We do not realize that our concept of the divine has attracted to it a god that fits that concept, and given it sovereignty over the earth. By divorcing soul from flesh, spirit from matter, and God from nature, we have installed a ruling power that is soulless, alienating, ungodly, and unnatural. So when I speak of making money sacred, I am not invoking a supernatural agency to infuse sacredness into the inert, mundane objects of nature. I am rather reaching back to an earlier time, a time before the divorce of matter and spirit, when sacredness was endemic to all things.

And what is the sacred? It has two aspects: uniqueness and relatedness. A sacred object or being is one that is special, unique, one of a kind. It is therefore infinitely precious; it is irreplaceable. It has no equivalent, and thus no finite "value," for value can only be determined by comparison. Money, like all kinds of measure, is a standard of comparison.

Unique though it is, the sacred is nonetheless inseparable from all that went into making it, from its history, and from the place it occupies in the matrix of all being. You might be thinking now that really all things and all relationships are sacred. That may be true, but though we may believe that intellectually, we don't always feel it. Some things feel sacred to us, and some do not. Those that do, we call sacred, and their purpose is ultimately to remind us of the sacredness of *all* things.

Today we live in a world that has been shorn of its sacredness, so that very few things indeed give us the feeling of living in a sacred world. Mass-produced, standardized commodities, cookie-cutter houses, identical packages of food, and anonymous relationships with institutional functionaries all deny the uniqueness of the world. The distant origins of our things, the anonymity of our relationships, and the lack of visible consequences in the production and disposal of our commodities all deny relatedness. Thus we live without the experience of sacredness. Of course, of all things that deny uniqueness and relatedness, money is foremost. The very idea of a coin originated in the goal of standardization, so that each drachma, each stater, each shekel, and each yuan would be functionally identical. Moreover, as a universal and abstract medium of exchange, money is divorced from its origins, from its connection to matter. A dollar is the same dollar no matter who gave it to you. We would think someone childish to put a sum of money in the bank and withdraw it a month later only to complain, "Hey, this isn't the same money I deposited! These bills are different!"

By default then, a monetized life is a profane life, since money and the things it buys lack the properties of the sacred. What is the difference between a supermarket tomato and one grown in my neighbor's garden and given to me? What is different between a prefab house and one built with my own participation by someone who understands me and my life? The essential differences all arise from specific relationships that incorporate the uniqueness of giver and receiver. When life is full of such things, made with care, connected by a web of stories to people and places we know, it is a rich life, a nourishing life. Today we live under a barrage of sameness, of impersonality. Even customized products, if mass-produced, offer only a few permutations of the same standard building blocks. This sameness deadens the soul and cheapens life.

The presence of the sacred is like returning to a home that was always there and a truth that has always existed. It can happen when I observe an insect or a plant, hear a symphony of birdsongs or frog calls, feel mud between my toes, gaze upon an object beautifully made, apprehend the impossibly coordinated complexity of a cell or an ecosystem, witness a synchronicity or symbol in my life, watch happy children at play, or am touched by a work of genius. Extraordinary though these experiences are, they are in no sense separate from the rest of life. Indeed, their power comes from the glimpse they give of a realer world, a sacred world that underlies and interpenetrates our own.

What is this "home that was always there," this "truth that has always existed"? It is the truth of the unity or the connectedness of all things, and the feeling is that of participating in something greater than oneself, yet which also *is* oneself. In ecology, this is the principle of interdependence: that all beings depend for their survival on the web of other beings that surrounds them, ultimately extending out to encompass the entire planet. The extinction of any species diminishes our own wholeness, our own health, our own selves; something of our very being is lost.

If the sacred is the gateway to the underlying unity of all things, it is equally a gateway to the uniqueness and specialness of each thing. A sacred object is one of a kind; it carries a unique essence that cannot be reduced to a set of generic qualities. That is why reductionist science seems to rob the world of its sacredness, since everything becomes one or another combination of a handful of generic building blocks. This conception mirrors our economic system, itself consisting mainly of standardized, generic commodities, job descriptions, processes, data, inputs and outputs, and—most generic of all—money, the ultimate abstraction. In earlier times it was not so. Tribal peoples saw each being not primarily as a member of a category, but as a unique, enspirited individual. Even rocks, clouds, and seemingly identical drops of water were thought to be sentient, unique beings. The products of the human hand were unique as well, bearing through their distinguishing irregularities the signature of the maker. Here was the link between the two qualities of the sacred, connectedness and uniqueness: unique objects retain the mark of their origin, their unique place in the great matrix of being, their dependency on the rest of creation for their existence. Standardized objects, commodities, are uniform and therefore disembedded from relationship.

In this book I will describe a vision of a money system and an economy that is sacred, that embodies the interrelatedness and the uniqueness of all things. No longer will it be separate, in fact or in perception, from the natural matrix that underlies it. It reunites the long-sundered realms of human and nature; it is an extension of ecology that obeys all of its laws and bears all of its beauty.

Within every institution of our civilization, no matter how ugly or corrupt, there is the germ of something beautiful: the same note at a higher octave. Money is no exception. Its original purpose is simply to connect human gifts with human needs, so that we might all live in greater abundance. How instead money has come to generate scarcity rather than abundance, separation rather than connection, is one of the threads of this book. Yet despite what it has become, in that original ideal of money as an *agent of the gift* we can catch a glimpse of what will one day make it sacred again. We recognize the exchange of gifts as a sacred occasion, which is why we instinctively make a ceremony out of gift giving. Sacred money, then, will be a medium of giving, a means to imbue the global economy with the spirit of the gift that governed tribal and village cultures, and still does today wherever people do things for each other outside the money economy.

Sacred Economics describes this future and also maps out a practical way to get there. Long ago I grew tired of reading books that criticized some aspect of our society without offering a positive alternative. Then I grew tired of books that offered a positive alternative that seemed impossible to reach: "We must reduce carbon emissions by 90 percent." Then I grew tired of books that offered a plausible means of reaching it but did not describe what I, personally, could do to create it. *Sacred Economics* operates on all four levels: it offers a fundamental analysis of what has gone wrong with money; it describes a more beautiful world based on a different kind of money and economy; it explains the collective actions necessary to create that world and the means by which these actions can come about; and it explores the personal dimensions of the world-transformation, the change in identity and being that I call "living in the gift."

A transformation of money is not a panacea for the world's ills, nor should it take priority over other areas of activism. A mere rearrangement of bits in computers will not wipe away the very real material and social devastation afflicting our planet. Yet, neither can the healing work in any other realm achieve its potential without a corresponding transformation of money, so deeply is it woven into our social institutions and habits of life. The economic changes I describe are part of a vast, all-encompassing shift that will leave no aspect of life untouched.

Humanity is only beginning to awaken to the true magnitude of the crisis on hand. If the economic transformation I will describe seems miraculous, that is because nothing less than a miracle is needed to heal our world. In all realms, from money to ecological healing to politics to technology to medicine, we need solutions that exceed the present bounds of the possible. Fortunately, as the old world falls apart, our knowledge of what is possible expands, and with it expands our courage and our willingness to act. The present convergence of crises—in money, energy, education, health, water, soil, climate, politics, the environment, and more—is a birth crisis, expelling us from the old world into a new. Unavoidably, these crises invade our personal lives, our world falls apart, and we too are born into a new world, a new identity. This is why so many people sense a spiritual dimension to the planetary crisis, even to the economic crisis. We sense that "normal" isn't coming back, that we are being born into a new normal: a new kind of society, a new relationship to the earth, a new experience of being human.

I dedicate all of my work to the more beautiful world our hearts tell us is possible. I say our "hearts," because our minds sometimes tell us it is not possible. Our minds doubt that things will ever be much different from what experience has taught us. You may have felt a wave of cynicism, contempt, or despair as you read my description of a sacred economy. You might have felt an urge to dismiss my words as hopelessly idealistic. Indeed, I myself was tempted to tone down my description, to make it more plausible, more responsible, more in line with our low expectations for what life and the world can be. But such an attenuation would not have been the truth. I will, using the tools of the mind, speak what is in my heart. In my heart I know that an economy and society this beautiful are possible for us to create—and indeed that anything less than that is unworthy of us. Are we so broken that we would aspire to anything less than a sacred world?

PART I

THE ECONOMICS OF SEPARATION

The converging crises of our time all arise from a common root that we might call Separation. Taking many forms—the human/nature split, the disintegration of community, the division of reality into material and spiritual realms—Separation is woven into every aspect of our civilization. It is also unsustainable: it generates great and growing crises that are propelling us into a new era, an Age of Reunion.

Separation is not an ultimate reality, but a human projection, an ideology, a story. As in all cultures, our defining Story of the People has two deeply related parts: a Story of Self, and a Story of the World. The first is the discrete and separate self: a bubble of psychology, a skin-encapsulated soul, a biological phenotype driven by its genes to seek reproductive self-interest, a rational actor seeking economic self-interest, a physical observer of an objective universe, a mote of consciousness in a prison of flesh. The second is the story of Ascent: that humanity, starting from a state of ignorance and powerlessness, is harnessing the forces of nature and probing the secrets of the universe, moving inexorably toward our destiny of complete mastery over, and transcendence of, nature. It is a story of the separation of the human realm from the natural, in which the former expands and the latter is turned progressively into resources, goods, property, and, ultimately, money.

Money is a system of social agreements, meanings, and symbols that develops over time. It is, in a word, a story, existing in social reality along with such things as laws, nations, institutions, calendar and clock time, religion, and science. Stories bear tremendous creative power. Through them we coordinate human activity, focus attention and intention, define roles, and identify what is important and even what is real. Stories give meaning and purpose to life and therefore motivate action. Money is a key element of the story of Separation that defines our civilization.

Part I of this book illuminates the economic system that has arisen on the foundation of the story of Separation. Anonymity, depersonalization, polarization of wealth, endless growth, ecological despoliation, social turmoil, and irremediable crisis are built into our economic system so deeply that nothing less than a transformation of our defining Story of the People will heal it. My intention is that by identifying the core features of the economics of Separation, we may be empowered to envision an economics of Reunion as well, an economics that restores to wholeness our fractured communities, relationships, cultures, ecosystems, and planet.

CHAPTER 1

THE GIFT WORLD

Even after all this time
The sun never says to the earth,
"You owe Me."
Look what happens
with a love like that,
It lights the Whole Sky.

—Hafiz

In the beginning was the Gift.

We are born helpless infants, creatures of pure need with little resource to give, yet we are fed, we are protected, we are clothed and held and soothed, without having done anything to deserve it, without offering anything in exchange. This experience, common to everyone who has made it past childhood, informs some of our deepest spiritual intuitions. Our lives are *given* us; therefore, our default state is gratitude. It is the truth of our existence.

Even if your childhood was horrific, if you are reading this right now, at least you were given enough to sustain you to adulthood. For the first years of life, none of this was anything you earned or produced. It was all a gift. Imagine walking out the door right now and finding yourself plunged into an alien world in which you were completely helpless, unable to feed or clothe yourself, unable to use your limbs, unable even to distinguish where your body ends and the world begins. Then huge beings come and hold you, feed you, take care of you, love you. Wouldn't you feel grateful?

In moments of clarity, perhaps after a narrow brush with death, or upon accompanying a loved one through the death process, we know that life itself is a gift. We experience an overwhelming gratitude at being alive. We walk in wonderment at the riches, undeserved and freely available, that come with life: the joy of breathing, the delights of color and sound, the pleasure of drinking water to quench thirst, the sweetness of a loved one's face. This sense of mixed awe and gratitude is a clear sign of the presence of the sacred.

We feel the same reverence and gratitude when we apprehend the magnificence of nature, the miraculous complexity and order of an ecosystem, an organism, a cell. They are impossibly perfect, far beyond the capacity of our minds to conceive, to create, even to understand more than a tiny part of. Yet they exist, without our ever having to create them: an entire world to sustain and environ us. We don't have to understand exactly how a seed germinates and grows; we don't have to make it happen. Even today, the workings of a cell, an organism, an ecosystem are largely a mystery. Without needing to engineer it, without needing even to understand its inner workings, we still receive nature's fruits. Can you imagine the wonder, the gratitude, of our early ancestors as they contemplated the undeserved provenance the world gave them so freely?

No wonder ancient religious thinkers said that God made the world, and no wonder they said God gave the world to us. The first is an expression of humility, the second of gratitude. Sadly, later theologians twisted this realization to mean, "God gave us the world to exploit, to master, to dominate." Such an interpretation is contrary to the spirit of the original realization. Humility knows that this Gift is beyond our ability to master. Gratitude knows that we honor, or dishonor, the giver of a gift by how we use it.

Modern cosmology also affirms the mythological recognition of universe-as-gift. Is not the Big Bang something (indeed everything) for nothing?[1] This feeling is strengthened by closer examination of the various constants of physics (speed of light, electron mass, relative strengths of the four fundamental forces, etc.), all of which inexplicably have the precise values necessary for a universe containing matter, stars, and life. It is as if the whole universe were constructed for us, so that we might exist.

In the beginning was the Gift: in the archetypal beginning of the world, at the beginning of our lives, and in the infancy of the human species. Gratitude therefore is natural to us, so primal, so elemental that it is very difficult to define. Perhaps it is *the feeling of having received a gift, and the desire to give in turn.* We might therefore expect primitive people, connected with this primal gratitude, to enact it in their social and economic relationships. Indeed, they did. Most accounts of the history of money begin with primitive barter, but barter is a relative rarity among hunter-gatherers. The most important mode of economic exchange was the gift.

Primal though it is, gratitude and the generosity flowing from it coexist with other, less savory, aspects of human nature. While I believe in the fundamental divinity of human beings, I also recognize that we have embarked on a long sojourn of separation from that divinity, and created a world in which ruthless sociopaths rise to wealth and power. This book doesn't pretend such people don't

---

1. Readers of *The Ascent of Humanity* know I prefer non–Big Bang cosmologies such as Halton Arp's dynamic steady-state universe, in which matter is continually born, grows old, and dies. But here, too, it appears spontaneously from nowhere, as if by a gift.

exist, nor that such tendencies don't exist in everyone. Rather, it seeks to awaken the spirit of the gift that is latent within us, and to construct institutions that embody and encourage that spirit. Today's economic system rewards selfishness and greed. What would an economic system look like that, like some ancient cultures, rewarded generosity instead?

Let us begin by better understanding the dynamics of the gift. I referred to economic *exchange* above, but that is generally not an accurate description of gift community. *Circulation* is a better word. Today we often exchange gifts, but gift *exchange* is already a step toward barter. In ancient communities, elaborate customs governed gift giving, customs that persist today in societies that have not completely lost their connection to the past. Usually gift networks are closely tied to kin networks. Customs dictate who gives to whom. To some kin categories you might be expected to give; from others you might expect to receive; and in others the gifts flow in both directions.

While gifts can be reciprocal, just as often they flow in circles. I give to you, you give to someone else . . . and eventually someone gives back to me. A famous example is the *kula* system of the Trobriand Islanders, in which precious necklaces circulate in one direction from island to island, and bracelets in the other direction. First described in depth by the anthropologist Bronislaw Malinowski, *kula*, which literally means "circle," is the lynchpin of a vast system of gifts and other economic exchanges. Marcel Mauss describes it as follows:

> The system of gift-through-exchange permeates all the economic, tribal, and moral life of the Trobriand people. It is "impregnated" with it, as Malinowski very neatly expressed it.

It is a constant "give and take." The process is marked by a continuous flow in all directions of presents given, accepted, and reciprocated."[2]

While the pinnacle of the *kula* system is the highly ritualized exchange of ceremonial bracelets and necklaces by chiefs, the gift network surrounding it extends to all kinds of utilitarian items, food, boats, labor, and so forth. Outright barter, according to Mauss, is unusual. In any event, "Generally, even what has been received and comes into one's possession in this way—in whatever manner—is not kept for oneself, unless one cannot do without it."[3] In other words, gifts flow continuously, only stopping in their circulation when they meet a real, present need. Here is Lewis Hyde's poetic description of this principle of the gift:

> The gift moves toward the empty place. As it turns in its circle it turns toward him who has been empty-handed the longest, and if someone appears elsewhere whose need is greater it leaves its old channel and moves toward him. Our generosity may leave us empty, but our emptiness then pulls gently at the whole until the thing in motion returns to replenish us. Social nature abhors a vacuum.[4]

While today we clearly distinguish between a gift and a commercial transaction, in past times this distinction was by no means clear. Some cultures, such as the Toaripi and Namau, had but a single word to designate buying, selling, lending, and borrowing,[5]

---

2. Mauss, *The Gift*, 29.
3. Ibid., 30.
4. Hyde, *The Gift*, 23.
5. Mauss, *The Gift*, 32.

while the ancient Mesopotamian word šám meant both "buy" and "sell."[6] This ambiguity persists in many modern languages. Chinese, German, Danish, Norwegian, Dutch, Estonian, Bulgarian, Serbian, Japanese, and many others each have but a single term for borrowing and lending, perhaps a vestige of an ancient time when the two were not distinguished.[7] It even persists in English among less-educated speakers, who sometimes use the word "borrow" to mean "lend," as in "I borrowed him twenty dollars." How could this be? How could the same word apply to two opposite operations?

The solution to this puzzle lies in the dynamics of the gift. With the rare, perhaps theoretical, exceptions that Derrida called "free gifts," gifts are accompanied either by some token of exchange or by a moral or social obligation (or both). Unlike a modern money transaction, which is closed and leaves no obligation, a gift transaction is open-ended, creating an ongoing tie between the participants. Another way of looking at it is that the gift partakes of the giver, and that when we give a gift, we give something of ourselves. This is the opposite of a modern commodity transaction, in which goods sold are mere property, separate from the one who sells them. We all can feel the difference. You probably have some treasured items that were given you, that are perhaps objectively indistinguishable from something you might buy, but that are unique and special because of who gave them to you. Thus it was that ancient people recognized that a magical quality, a spirit, circulates along with gifts.

Useless objects like cowry shells, pretty beads, necklaces, and

---

6. Seaford, *Money and the Early Greek Mind*, 323.

7. The Chinese terms for buying and selling have nearly identical pronunciation and similar ideograms as well. The character for buying, 買, originated as a depiction of a cowry shell, an early form of money, while the character for selling, 賣, was developed later, suggesting an earlier nondistinction.

so on were the earliest money. To exchange them for something of utilitarian value is, naively speaking, merely a way to facilitate a gift—something for nothing. They turn it into something-for-something, but that doesn't make it any less a gift, because they are merely giving physical form to the felt sense of obligation; they are tokens of gratitude. From this perspective, the identity of buying and selling, borrowing and lending, is easy to understand. They are not opposite operations at all. All gifts circle back to the giver in another form. Buyer and seller are equal.

Today there is an asymmetry in commercial transactions, which identifies the buyer as the one giving money and receiving goods and the seller as the one receiving money and giving goods. But we could equally say the "buyer" is selling money for goods, and the "seller" is buying money with goods. Linguistic and anthropological evidence indicates that this asymmetry is new, far newer than money. What has happened to money, then, to create this asymmetry? Money is different from every other commodity in the world, and, as we shall see, it is this difference that is crucial in making it profane.

Gifts, on the other hand, we intuitively recognize as sacred, which is why even today we make ceremonies of giving presents. Gifts embody the key qualities of the sacredness I discussed in the introduction. First, uniqueness: unlike the standardized commodities of today, purchased in closed transactions with money and alienated from their origins, gifts are unique to the extent that they partake of the giver. Second, wholeness, interdependency: gifts expand the circle of self to include the entire community. Whereas money today embodies the principle, "More for me is less for you," in a gift economy, more for you is also more for me because those who have give to those who need. Gifts cement the mystical realization of participation in something greater than oneself which, yet, is not separate from oneself. The axioms of rational self-interest change because the self has expanded to include something of the other.

The conventional explanation of how money developed that one finds in economics texts assumes barter as a starting point. From the very beginning, competing individuals seek to maximize their rational self-interest. This idealized description is not supported by anthropology. Barter, according to Mauss, was rare in Polynesia, rare in Melanesia, and unheard of in the Pacific Northwest. Economic anthropologist George Dalton emphatically concurs, "Barter, in the strict sense of moneyless exchange, has never been a quantitatively important or dominant model or transaction in any past or present economic system about which we have hard information."[8] The only instances of barter, says Dalton, were for petty, infrequent, or emergency transactions—just as is the case today. Aside from these, moneyless transactions scarcely resembled the impersonal, utility-maximizing transactions of economists' fantasies, but rather "tended to require lasting (and sometimes ritualized) personal relationships sanctioned by custom and characterized by reciprocity."[9] Such transactions should not be called barter at all, but rather ritualized gift exchange.

Today we put gifts and purchases into separate, exclusive categories; to be sure, different economics and psychology apply to each. But very ancient times bore no such dichotomy, nor was there today's distinction between a business relationship and a personal relationship. Economists, in telling the history of money, tend to project this modern distinction backward, and with it some deep

---

8. Dalton, "Barter," 182.
9. Seaford, *Money and the Early Greek Mind,* 292.

assumptions about human nature, the self, and the purpose of life: that we are discrete and separate selves competing for scarce resources to maximize our self-interest. I won't say that these assumptions are not true. They are part of the defining ideology of our civilization, a Story of the People that is now drawing to a close. This book is part of the telling of a new Story of the People. The transformation of money is part of a larger transformation, founded on very different assumptions about self, life, and world.

Human economy is never very far from cosmology, religion, and the psyche. It was not only ancient economies that were based on gifts: ancient cosmology and religion were too. Today as well, our money with its qualities of standardization, abstraction, and anonymity is aligned with many other aspects of the human experience. What new scientific, religious, or psychological paradigms might arise in the context of a different kind of money?

If money did not arise from the economists' imaginary world of calculated, interest-maximizing barter, then how did it arise? I propose that it arose as a means to facilitate gift giving, sharing, and generosity, or at least that it bore something of that spirit. To recreate a sacred economy, it is necessary to restore to money that original spirit.

At its core, money is a beautiful concept. Let me be very naive for a moment so as to reveal this core, this spiritual (if not historical) essence of money. I have something you need, and I wish to give it to you. So I do, and you feel grateful and desire to give something to me in return. But you don't have anything I need right now. So instead you give me a token of your gratitude—a useless, pretty thing like a wampum necklace or a piece of silver. That token says, "I have met the needs of other people and earned their gratitude." Later, when I receive a gift from someone else, I give them that token. Gifts can circulate across vast social distances, and I can receive from people to whom I have nothing to give while still fulfilling my desire to act from the gratitude those gifts inspire within me.

On the level of a family, clan, or hunter-gatherer band, money is not necessary to operate a gift economy. Nor is it necessary in the next larger unit of social organization: the village or tribe of a few hundred people. There, if I don't need anything from you now, either you will (acting from gratitude) give me something that I need in the future, or you will give to someone else, who gives to someone else, who gives to me. This is the "circle of the gift," the basis of community. In a tribe or village, the scale of society is small enough that those who give to me recognize my gifts to others. Such is not the case in a mass society like ours. If I give generously to you, the farmer in Hawaii who grew my ginger or the engineer in Japan who designed my cell phone display won't know about it. So instead of personal recognition of gifts, we use money: the representation of gratitude. The social witnessing of gifts becomes anonymous.

Money becomes necessary when the range of our gifts must extend beyond the people we know personally. Such is the case when economic scale and the division of labor exceed the tribal or village level. Indeed, the first money appeared in the first agricultural civilizations that developed beyond the Neolithic village: Mesopotamia, Egypt, China, and India. Traditional, decentralized gift networks gave way to centralized systems of redistribution, with the temple, and later the royal palace, as the hub. Quite possibly, these evolved from potlatch-type traditions in which gifts flowed to chiefs and other leaders, and then back from them to their kin and tribe. Starting as centralized nodes for a large-scale flow of gifts, they soon diverged from the gift mind-set as contributions became forced and quantified, and outward disbursement became unequal. Ancient Sumerian documents already speak of economic polarization, haves and have-nots, and wages that were barely at subsistence.[10] While centralized directives, and not market trade, governed the movement of goods,[11] the early agricultural empires also used what some call money: agricultural and metallic commodities in standard measured units that served as media of exchange, units of account, and stores of value. So already, four thousand years ago, money was failing to meet my naive expectation that it would create greater abundance for all by facilitating the meeting of gifts and needs.

By facilitating trade, motivating efficient production, and allowing the accumulation of capital to undertake large-scale projects, money should enrich life: it should bestow upon us ease, leisure, freedom from anxiety, and an equitable distribution of wealth. Indeed, conventional economic theory predicts all of these results. The fact that money has become an agent of the opposite—anxiety, hardship, and polarization of wealth—presents us with a paradox.

If we are to have a world with technology, with cinema and symphony orchestras, with telecommunications and great architecture, with cosmopolitan cities and world literature, we need money, or something like it, as a way to coordinate human activity on the vast scale necessary to create such things. I have therefore written this book, to describe a system that restores to money the sacredness of the gift. I say "restore" because from the earliest times, money has had sacred or magical connotations. Originally, it was the temples where agricultural surpluses were stored and

---

10. Nemat-Nejat, *Daily Life in Ancient Mesopotamia*, 263.
11. Seaford, *Money and the Early Greek Mind*, 123. Seaford adduces persuasive evidence for this claim: early documents that took the form of lists, artwork showing processions of individuals bearing offerings, etc.

redistributed: the center of religious life was also the center of economic life. Some authors claim that the earliest symbolic money (as opposed to commodity money) was issued by temples and could be redeemed for sacred sex with temple prostitutes;[12] in any event, it is certain that temples were deeply involved in issuing early coins, many of which bore the images of sacred animals and deities. This practice continues today with bills and coins bearing the likenesses of deified presidents.

Perhaps someday we won't need money to have a gift economy on the scale of billions of humans; perhaps the money I shall describe in this book is transitional. I am not a "primitivist" who advocates the abandonment of civilization, of technology and culture, of the gifts that make us human. I foresee rather the restoration of humanity to a sacred estate, bearing all the wholeness and harmony with nature of the hunter-gatherer time, but at a higher level of organization. I foresee the fulfillment, and not the abdication, of the gifts of hand and mind that make us human.

Notice how natural it is to describe our uniquely human attributes as gifts. In keeping with the gift's universal principles, our human gifts partake of their Giver as well. In other words, they are divine gifts. Mythology bears this intuition out, from the Promethean gift of fire to the Apollonian gift of music, to the gift of agriculture from the Chinese mythological ruler Shen Nong. In the Bible, too, we are given not only the world, but the breath of life and our capacity to create—for we are made "in the image" of the Creator itself.

---

12. Bernard Lietaer makes this claim in *The Future of Money* for a bronze shekel that he states is the earliest known coin, dating to 3000 BCE. I have found no other mention of this in my research, however. As far as I know, the earliest coins appeared in Lydia and China at about the same time, the seventh century BCE.

On the personal level as well, we all sense that our individual gifts were given to us for a reason, a purpose. Moreover, we have an irrepressible desire to develop those gifts, and from them, to give our own gifts out into the world. Everyone has experienced the joy of giving and the selfless generosity of strangers. Ask for directions in a city, and most people are pleased to take time to help. It is in no one's rational self-interest to give directions to a stranger; this is a simple expression of our innate generosity.

It is ironic indeed that money, originally a means of connecting gifts with needs, originally an outgrowth of a sacred gift economy, is now precisely what blocks the blossoming of our desire to give, keeping us in deadening jobs out of economic necessity, and forestalling our most generous impulses with the words, "I can't afford to do that." We live in an omnipresent anxiety, borne of the scarcity of the money which we depend on for life—witness the phrase "the cost of living." Our purpose for being, the development and full expression of our gifts, is mortgaged to the demands of money, to making a living, to surviving. Yet no one, no matter how wealthy, secure, or comfortable, can ever feel fulfilled in a life where those gifts remain latent. Even the best-paid job, if it does not engage our gifts, soon feels deadening, and we think, "I was not put here on earth to do this."

Even when a job does engage our gifts, if the purpose is something we don't believe in, the same deadening feeling of futility arises again, the feeling that we are not living our own lives, but only the lives we are paid to live. "Challenging" and "interesting" are not good enough, because our gifts are sacred, and therefore meant for a sacred purpose.

That we are indeed here on earth to do *something* is essentially a religious concept, for conventional biology teaches that we have evolved to be able to survive, that any effort toward something outside of survival and reproduction goes against our genetic programming. However, one can make a cogent neo-Lamarckian case that the view of biology as consisting of myriad discrete, separate competing selves—organisms or "selfish genes"—is more a projection of our own present-day culture than it is an accurate understanding of nature.[13] There are other ways of understanding nature that, while not ignoring its obvious competition, give primacy to cooperation, symbiosis, and the merging of organisms into larger wholes. This new understanding is actually quite ancient, echoing the indigenous understanding of nature as a web of gifts.

Each organism and each species makes a vital contribution to the totality of life on earth, and this contribution, contrary to the expectations of standard evolutionary biology, need not have any direct benefit for the organism itself. Nitrogen-fixing bacteria don't directly benefit from doing so, except that the nitrogen they give to the soil grows plants that grow roots that grow fungi, which ultimately provide nutrients to the bacteria. Pioneer species pave the way for keystone species, which provide microniches for other species, which feed yet other species in a web of gifts that, eventually, circle back to benefit the pioneer species. Trees bring up water to water other plants, and algae make oxygen so that animals can breathe. Remove any being, and the health of all becomes more precarious.

You may think me naive, with my "so that" reasoning. You may say it is just good luck that things work out so well: the trees don't care about watering the plants around them—they are in it for themselves, maximizing their chances to survive and reproduce.

---

13. I sum up this argument in Chapter 7 of *The Ascent of Humanity*, drawing on the work of Lynn Margulis, Bruce Lipton, Fred Hoyle, Elisabet Sahtouris, and others.

That they nourish other beings is an unintended side-effect. The same for the algae, for the nitrogen-fixing bacteria, and for the bacteria inside ruminants that allow them to digest cellulose. This world, you might think, is everyone for himself. Nature is a cutthroat competition, and an economy that is the same is natural too.

I do not think it is natural. It is an aberration, a peculiar though necessary phase that has reached its extreme and is now giving way to a new one. In nature, headlong growth and all-out competition are features of immature ecosystems, followed by complex interdependency, symbiosis, cooperation, and the cycling of resources. The next stage of human economy will parallel what we are beginning to understand about nature. It will call forth the gifts of each of us; it will emphasize cooperation over competition; it will encourage circulation over hoarding; and it will be cyclical, not linear. Money may not disappear anytime soon, but it will serve a diminished role even as it takes on more of the properties of the gift. The economy will shrink, and our lives will grow.

Money as we know it is inimical to an economy manifesting the spirit of the gift, an economy we might call sacred. In order to know what kind of money could be a sacred currency, it will help to identify exactly what makes money into the force for greed, evil, scarcity, and environmental pillage that it is today.

Just as science often projects culture onto nature, so economics takes culturally determined conditions as axiomatic. Living in a culture of scarcity (for scarcity is what we are experiencing, when "making a living" dictates the expression of our gifts), we assume it as the basis of economics. As in biology, we have seen the world as a competition among separate selves for limited resources. Our money system, as we shall see, embodies this belief on a deep, structural level. But is this belief true? Do we live in a world, a universe, of basic scarcity? And if not, if the true nature of the universe is abundance and the gift, then how did money become so unnatural?

CHAPTER 2

THE ILLUSION OF SCARCITY

With unabated bounty the land of England blooms and grows;
waving with yellow harvests; thick-studded with workshops,
industrial implements, with fifteen millions of workers, understood
to be the strongest, the cunningest and the willingest our Earth ever
had; these men are here; the work they have done, the fruit they have
realized is here, abundant, exuberant on every hand of us: and
behold, some baleful fiat as of Enchantment has gone forth, saying,
"Touch it not, ye workers, ye master-workers, ye master-idlers; none
of you can touch it, no man of you shall be the better for it; this is
enchanted fruit!"

—Thomas Carlyle, *Past and Present*

It is said that money, or at least the love of it, is the root of all evil. But why should it be? After all, the purpose of money is, at its most basic, simply to facilitate exchange—in other words, to connect human gifts with human needs. What power, what monstrous perversion, has turned money into the opposite: an agent of scarcity?

For indeed we live in a world of fundamental abundance, a world where vast quantities of food, energy, and materials go to waste. Half the world starves while the other half wastes enough to feed the first half. In the Third World and our own ghettos, people lack food, shelter, and other basic necessities and cannot afford to buy them. Meanwhile, we pour vast resources into wars, plastic junk, and innumerable other products that do not serve human happiness. Obviously, poverty is not due to a lack of productive capacity. Nor is it due to a lack of willingness to help: many people would love to feed the poor, to restore nature, and do other meaningful work but cannot because there is no money in it. Money utterly fails to connect gifts and needs. Why?

For years, following conventional opinion, I thought the answer was "greed." Why do sweatshop factories push wages down to the bare minimum? Greed. Why do people buy gas-guzzling SUVs? Greed. Why do pharmaceutical companies suppress research and sell drugs that they know are dangerous? Greed. Why do tropical fish suppliers dynamite coral reefs? Why do factories pump toxic waste into the rivers? Why do corporate raiders loot employee pension funds? Greed, greed, greed.

Eventually I became uncomfortable with that answer. For one thing, it plays into the same ideology of separation that lies at the root of our civilization's ills. It is an ideology as old as agriculture's division of the world into two separate realms: the wild and the domestic, the human and the natural, the wheat and the weed. It says there are two opposing forces in this world, good and evil, and that we can create a better world by eliminating evil. There is something bad in the world and something bad in ourselves, something we must extirpate to make the world safe for goodness.

The war against evil imbues every institution of our society. In agriculture, it appears as the desire to exterminate wolves, to destroy all weeds with glyphosate, to kill all the pests. In medicine it is the war against germs, a constant battle against a hostile world. In religion it is the struggle against sin, or against ego, or against faithlessness or doubt, or against the outward projection of these things: the devil, the infidel. It is the mentality of purifying and purging, of self-improvement and conquest, of rising above nature and transcending desire, of sacrificing oneself in order to be good. Above all, it is the mentality of control.

It says that once final victory over evil is won, we will enter paradise. When we eliminate all the terrorists or create an impenetrable barrier to them, we will be safe. When we develop an irresistible antibiotic and artificial regulation of body processes, we will have perfect health. When we make crime impossible and have a law to govern everything, we will have a perfect society. When you overcome your laziness, your compulsions, your addictions, you will have a perfect life. Until then, you are just going to have to try harder.

In the same vein, the problem in economic life is supposedly greed, both outside ourselves in the form of all those greedy people and within ourselves in the form of our own greedy tendencies. We like to imagine that we ourselves are not so greedy—maybe we have greedy impulses, but we keep them under control. Unlike *some* people! Some people don't keep their greed in check. They are lacking in something fundamental that you and I have, some basic decency, basic goodness. They are, in a word, Bad. If they can't learn to restrain their desires, to make do with less, then we'll have to force them to.

Clearly, the paradigm of greed is rife with judgment of others, and with self-judgment as well. Our self-righteous anger and hatred of the greedy harbor the secret fear that we are no better than they are. It is the hypocrite who is the most zealous in the persecution of evil. Externalizing the enemy gives expression to unresolved feelings of anger. In a way, this is a necessity: the consequences of keeping them bottled up or directed inward are horrific. But there came a time in my life when I was through hating, through with the war against the self, through with the struggle to be good, and through with the pretense that I was any better than anyone else. I believe humanity, collectively, is nearing such a time as well. Ultimately, greed is a red herring, itself a symptom and not a cause of a deeper problem. To blame greed and to fight it by intensifying the program of self-control is to intensify the war against the self, which is just another expression of the war against nature and the war against the other that lies at the base of the present crisis of civilization.

Greed makes sense in a context of scarcity. Our reigning ideology assumes it: it is built in to our Story of Self. The separate self in a universe governed by hostile or indifferent forces is always at the edge of extinction, and secure only to the extent that it can control these forces. Cast into an objective universe external to ourselves, we must compete with each other for limited resources. Based on the story of the separate self, both biology and economics have therefore written greed into their basic axioms. In biology it is the gene seeking to maximize reproductive self-interest; in economics it is the rational actor seeking to maximize financial self-interest. But what if the assumption of scarcity is false—a projection of our ideology, and not the ultimate reality? If so, then greed is not written into our biology but is a mere symptom of the perception of scarcity.

An indication that greed reflects the *perception* rather than the reality of scarcity is that rich people tend to be less generous than poor people. In my experience, poor people quite often lend or give each other small sums that, proportionally speaking, would be the equivalent of half a rich person's net worth. Extensive research backs up this observation. A large 2002 survey by Independent Sector, a nonprofit research organization, found that Americans making less than $25,000 gave 4.2 percent of their income to charity, as opposed to 2.7 percent for people making over $100,000. More recently, Paul Piff, a social psychologist at University of California–Berkeley, found that "lower-income people were more generous, charitable, trusting and helpful to others than were those with more wealth."[1] Piff found that when research subjects were given money to anonymously distribute between themselves and a partner (who would never know their identity), their generosity correlated inversely to their socioeconomic status.[2]

While it is tempting to conclude from this that greedy people become wealthy, an equally plausible interpretation is that wealth makes people greedy. Why would this be? In a context of abundance greed is silly; only in a context of scarcity is it rational. The wealthy perceive scarcity where there is none. They also worry more than anybody else about money. Could it be that money itself *causes* the perception of scarcity? Could it be that money, nearly synonymous with security, ironically brings the opposite? The answer to both these questions is yes. On the individual level, rich people have a lot more "invested" in their money and are less able to let go of it. (To let go easily reflects an attitude of abundance.) On the systemic level, as we shall see, scarcity is also built in to money, a direct result of the way it is created and circulated.

The assumption of scarcity is one of the two central axioms of economics. (The second is that people naturally seek to maximize their rational self-interest.) Both are false; or, more precisely, they are true only within a narrow realm, a realm that we, the frog at the bottom of the well, mistake for the whole of reality. As is so often the case, what we take to be objective truth is actually a projection of our own condition onto the "objective" world. So immersed in

1. Warner, "The Charitable-Giving Divide."
2. Piff et al., "Having Less, Giving More."

scarcity are we that we take it to be the nature of reality. But in fact, we live in a world of abundance. The omnipresent scarcity we experience is an artifact: of our money system, of our politics, and of our perceptions.

As we shall see, our money system, system of ownership, and general economic system reflect the same fundamental sense of self that has, built into it, the perception of scarcity. It is the "discrete and separate self," the Cartesian self: a bubble of psychology marooned in an indifferent universe, seeking to own, to control, to arrogate as much wealth to itself as possible, but foredoomed by its very cutoff from the richness of connected beingness to the experience of never having enough.

The assertion that we live in a world of abundance sometimes provokes an emotional reaction, bordering on hostility, in those of my readers who believe that harmonious human coexistence with the rest of life is impossible without a massive reduction in population. They cite Peak Oil and resource depletion, global warming, the exhaustion of our farmland, and our ecological footprint as evidence that the earth cannot long support industrial civilization at present population levels.

This book offers a response to this concern as part of a vision of a sacred economy. More importantly, it addresses the "how" questions as well—for example, how we will get to there from here. For now I will offer a partial response, a reason for hope.

It is true that human activity is vastly overburdening the earth today. Fossil fuels, aquifers, topsoil, the capacity to absorb pollution, and the ecosystems that maintain the viability of the biosphere are all being depleted at an alarming rate. All the measures on the table are far too little, far too late—a drop in the bucket compared to what is needed.

On the other hand, an enormous proportion of this human activity is either superfluous or deleterious to human happiness. Consider first the armaments industry and the resources consumed in war: some $2 trillion dollars a year, a vast scientific establishment, and the life energy of millions of young people, all to serve no need except one we create ourselves.

Consider the housing industry here in the United States, with the enormous McMansions of the last two decades that again serve no real human need. In some countries a building that size would house fifty people. As it is, the cavernous living rooms go unused, for people feel uncomfortable in their inhuman scale and seek out the comfort of the small den and the breakfast nook. The materials, energy, and maintenance of such monstrosities are a waste of resources. Perhaps even more wasteful is the layout of suburbia, which makes public transportation impossible and necessitates inordinate amounts of driving.

Consider the food industry, which exhibits massive waste at every level. According to a government study, farm-to-retail losses are about 4 percent, retail-to-consumer losses 12 percent, and consumer-level losses 29 percent.[3] Moreover, vast tracts of farmland are devoted to biofuel production, and mechanized agriculture precludes labor-intensive intercropping and other intensive production techniques that could vastly increase productivity.[4]

---

3. Buzby et al., "Supermarket Loss Estimates."

4. You can get some idea of the untapped potential of agriculture by reading F. H. King's fascinating 1911 book, *Farmers of Forty Centuries; Or, Permanent Agriculture in China, Korea, and Japan,* which explains how these regions sustained enormous populations for millennia on tiny amounts of land, without mechanization, pesticides, or chemical fertilizers. Instead, they relied on sophisticated crop rotation, interplanting, and ecological relationships among farm plants, animals, and people. They wasted nothing, including human manure. *(continued on next page)*

Such figures suggest the potential plenty available even in a world of seven billion people—but with a caveat: people will spend much more time (per capita) growing food, in a reversal of the trend of the last two centuries. Few realize that organic agriculture can be two to three times more productive than conventional agriculture—per hectare, not per hour of labor.[5] And intensive gardening can be more productive (and more labor-intensive) still. If you like gardening and think that most people would benefit from being closer to the soil, this is good news. With a few hours' work a week, a typical suburban garden plot of perhaps a thousand square feet can meet most of a family's vegetable needs; double that and it can provide substantial amounts of staples too, like potatoes, sweet potatoes, and squash. Is the vast transcontinental trucking system that brings California lettuce and carrots to the rest of the country really necessary? Does it enhance life in any way?

Another type of waste comes from the shoddy construction and planned obsolescence of many of our manufactured goods. Presently there are few economic incentives, and some disincentives, to produce goods that last a long time and are easy to fix, with the absurd result that it is often cheaper to buy a new appliance than to

---

4. *(continued)* Their farming was extremely labor-intensive, although, according to King, it was usually conducted at a leisurely pace. In 1907 Japan's fifty million people were nearly self-sufficient in food; China's land supported, in some regions, clans of forty or fifty people on a three-acre farm; in the year 1790 China's population was about the same as that of the United States today!

5. LaSalle et al., *The Organic Green Revolution,* 4., citing numerous supporting studies. If you have the opposite impression, consider that many of the studies that show no benefit from organic agriculture are conducted by people with little experience with organic farming and on land that is impoverished from decades of chemical farming. Organic methods are not easily amenable to controlled studies because they properly involve a long-term relationship between farmer and land. It is only after years, decades, or even generations that the true benefits of organic agriculture become fully apparent.

repair an old one. This is ultimately a consequence of our money system, and it will be reversed in a sacred economy.

On my street, every family possesses a lawnmower that is used perhaps ten hours per summer. Each kitchen has a blender that is used at most fifteen minutes per week. At any given moment, about half the cars are parked on the street, doing nothing. Most families have their own hedge clippers, their own power tools, their own exercise equipment. Because they are unused most of the time, most of these things are superfluous. Our quality of life would be just as high with half the number of cars, a tenth of the lawnmowers, and two or three Stairmasters for the whole street. In fact, it would be higher since we would have occasion to interact and share.[6] Even at our current, gratuitously high rate of consumption, some 40 percent of the world's industrial capacity stands idle. That figure could be increased to 80 percent or more without any loss of human happiness. All we would lose would be the pollution and tedium of a lot of factory production. Of course, we would lose a vast number of "jobs" as well, but since these are not contributing much to human well-being anyway, we could employ those people digging holes in the ground and filling them up again with no loss. Or, better, we could devote them to labor-intensive roles like permaculture, care for the sick and elderly, restoration of ecosystems, and all the other needs of today that go tragically unmet for lack of money.

A world without weapons, without McMansions in sprawling suburbs, without mountains of unnecessary packaging, without giant mechanized monofarms, without energy-hogging big-box

---

6. Unfortunately, many of us are so wounded that we prefer not to interact and share, but to retreat farther into the hell of separation and the illusion of independence until its fabric unravels. As various crises converge and this happens to more and more people, the urge to restore community will grow.

stores, without electronic billboards, without endless piles of throwaway junk, without the overconsumption of consumer goods no one really needs is not an impoverished world. I disagree with those environmentalists who say we are going to have to make do with less. In fact, we are going to make do with more: more beauty, more community, more fulfillment, more art, more music, and material objects that are fewer in number but superior in utility and aesthetics. The cheap stuff that fills our lives today, however great its quantity, can only cheapen life.

Part of the healing that a sacred economy represents is the healing of the divide we have created between spirit and matter. In keeping with the sacredness of all things, I advocate an embrace, not an eschewing, of materialism. I think we will love our things more and not less. We will treasure our material possessions, honor where they came from and where they will go. If you have a treasured baseball mitt or fishing rod, you may know what I'm talking about. Or perhaps your grandfather had a favorite set of woodworking tools that he kept in perfect condition for fifty years. That is how we will honor our things. Can you imagine what the world would be like if that same care and consideration went into everything we produced? If every engineer put that much love into her creations? Today, such an attitude is uneconomic; it is rarely in anyone's financial interest to treat a thing as sacred. You can just buy a new baseball mitt or fishing rod, and why be too careful with your tools when new ones are so cheap? The cheapness of our things is part of their devaluation, casting us into a cheap world where everything is generic and expendable.

Amidst superabundance, even we in rich countries live in an omnipresent anxiety, craving "financial security" as we try to keep scarcity at bay. We make choices (even those having nothing to do with money) according to what we can "afford," and we commonly associate freedom with wealth. But when we pursue it, we find that the paradise of financial freedom is a mirage, receding as we approach it, and that the chase itself enslaves. The anxiety is always there, the scarcity always just one disaster away. We call that chase *greed*. Truly, it is a response to the perception of scarcity.

Let me offer one more kind of evidence, for now meant to be suggestive rather than conclusive, for the artificiality or illusory nature of the scarcity we experience. Economics, it says on page one of textbooks, is the study of human behavior under conditions of scarcity. The expansion of the economic realm is therefore the expansion of scarcity, its incursion into areas of life once characterized by abundance. Economic behavior, particularly the exchange of money for goods, extends today into realms that were never before the subject of money exchanges. Take, for example, one of the great retail growth categories in the last decade: bottled water. If one thing is abundant on earth to the point of near-ubiquity, it is water, yet today it has become scarce, something we pay for.

Child care has been another area of high economic growth in my lifetime. When I was young, it was nothing for friends and neighbors to watch each other's kids for a few hours after school, a vestige of village or tribal times when children ran free. My ex-wife Patsy speaks movingly of her childhood in rural Taiwan, where children could and did show up at any neighbor's house around dinner time to be given a bowl of rice. The community took care of the children. In other words, child care was *abundant;* it would have been impossible to open an after-school day care center.

For something to become an object of commerce, it must be made scarce first. As the economy grows, by definition, more and more of human activity enters the realm of money, the realm of goods and services. Usually we associate economic growth with an increase in wealth, but we can also see it as an impoverishment, an increase in scarcity. Things we once never dreamed of paying for, we must pay for today. Pay for using what? Using money, of course—money that we struggle and sacrifice to obtain. If one thing is scarce, it is surely money. Most people I know live in constant low-level (sometimes high-level) anxiety for fear of not having enough of it. And as the anxiety of the wealthy confirms, no amount is ever "enough."

From this perspective, we must be cautious in our indignation at such facts as, "Over two billion people live on less than two dollars a day." A low cash income could mean that someone's needs are met outside the money economy, for example through traditional networks of reciprocity and gifts. "Development" in such cases raises incomes by bringing nonmonetary economic activity into the realm of goods and services, with the resulting mentality of scarcity, competition, and anxiety so familiar to us in the West, yet so alien to the moneyless hunter-gatherer or subsistence peasant.

Ensuing chapters explain the mechanisms and meaning of the centuries-old conversion of life and the world into money, the progressive commodification of everything. When everything is subject to money, then the scarcity of money makes everything scarce, including the basis of human life and happiness. Such is the life of the slave—one whose actions are compelled by threat to survival.

Perhaps the deepest indication of our slavery is the monetization of time. It is a phenomenon with roots deeper than our money system, for it depends on the prior quantification of time. An animal or a child has "all the time in the world." The same was apparently true for Stone Age peoples, who usually had very loose concepts of time and rarely were in a hurry. Primitive languages often lacked tenses, and sometimes lacked even words for "yesterday" or "tomorrow." The comparative nonchalance primitive people had toward time is still apparent today in rural, more traditional parts of the world. Life moves faster in the big city, where we are always in a hurry because time is scarce. But in the past, we experienced time as abundant.

The more monetized society is, the more anxious and hurried its citizens. In parts of the world that are still somewhat outside the money economy, where subsistence farming still exists and where neighbors help each other, the pace of life is slower, less hurried. In rural Mexico, everything is done mañana. A Ladakhi peasant woman interviewed in Helena Norberg-Hodge's film *Ancient Futures* sums it all up in describing her city-dwelling sister: "She has a rice cooker, a car, a telephone—all kinds of time-saving devices. Yet when I visit her, she is always so busy we barely have time to talk."

For the animal, child, or hunter-gatherer, time is essentially infinite. Today its monetization has subjected it, like the rest, to scarcity. Time is life. When we experience time as scarce, we experience life as short and poor.

If you were born before adult schedules invaded childhood and children were rushed around from activity to activity, then perhaps you still remember the subjective eternity of childhood, the afternoons that stretched on forever, the timeless freedom of life before the tyranny of calendar and clocks. "Clocks," writes John Zerzan, "make time scarce and life short." Once quantified, time too could be bought and sold, and the scarcity of all money-linked commodities afflicted time as well. "Time is money," the saying goes, an identity confirmed by the metaphor "I can't afford the time."

If the material world is fundamentally an abundant world, all the more abundant is the spiritual world: the creations of the human mind—songs, stories, films, ideas, and everything else that goes by the name of intellectual property. Because in the digital age we can replicate and spread them at virtually no cost, artificial scarcity must be imposed upon them in order to keep them in the monetized realm. Industry and the government enforce scarcity through copyrights, patents, and encryption standards, allowing the holders of such property to profit from owning it.

Scarcity, then, is mostly an illusion, a cultural creation. But because we live, almost wholly, in a culturally constructed world, our experience of this scarcity is quite real—real enough that nearly a billion people today are malnourished, and some 5,000 children die each day from hunger-related causes. So our responses to this scarcity—anxiety and greed—are perfectly understandable. When something is abundant, no one hesitates to share it. We live in an abundant world, made otherwise through our perceptions, our culture, and our deep invisible stories. Our perception of scarcity is a self-fulfilling prophecy. Money is central to the construction of the self-reifying illusion of scarcity.

Money, which has turned abundance into scarcity, engenders greed. But not money per se—only the kind of money we use today, money that embodies our cultural sense of self, our unconscious myths, and an adversarial relationship with nature thousands of years in the making. All of these things are changing today. Let us look, then, at how money came to so afflict our minds and ways, so that we might envision how the money system might change with them.

CHAPTER 3

MONEY AND THE MIND

When all are isolated by egoism, there is nothing but dust,
and at the advent of a storm, nothing but mire.

—Benjamin Constant

The power to induce a collective hallucination of scarcity is only one of the ways money affects our perceptions. This chapter will explore some of the deep psychological and spiritual effects of money: on the way we see the world, on our religion, our philosophy, even our science. Money is woven into our minds, our perceptions, our identities. That is why, when a crisis of money strikes, it seems that the fabric of reality is unraveling, too—that the very world is falling apart. Yet this is also cause for great optimism, because money is a social construction that we have the power to change. What new kinds of perceptions, and what new kinds of collective actions, would accompany a new kind of money?

Here we are on Chapter 3, and I have not even defined "money" yet! Most economists define money by its functions, such as medium of exchange, unit of account, and store of value. Accordingly, they put a very early date on the origin of money, perhaps five thousand years ago with the emergence of standard commodities such as grain, oil, cattle, or gold that served these functions. But when I speak of money, I am talking about something quite different, something that first appeared in Greece in the seventh century

BCE. That was arguably the first time that money transcended mere commodity to become a distinct category of being. Henceforward, we could speak not only of what money does, but also of what it *is*.

Economists' folklore holds that coins were invented in order to provide a guarantee of weight and purity for the underlying commodity metal. Their value, this story goes, came entirely from the gold or silver from which they were made. In fact, like the barter origin of money, like the assumption of scarcity, this account of the origin of coinage is an economist's fantasy. It is a fantasy with an illustrious lineage to be sure. Aristotle wrote,

> For the various necessaries of life are not easily carried about, and hence men agreed to employ in their dealings with each other something which was intrinsically useful and easily applicable to the purposes of life, for example, iron, silver, and the like. Of this the value was at first measured simply by size and weight, but in process of time they put a stamp upon it, to save the trouble of weighing and to mark the value.[1]

This account seems quite reasonable, but historical evidence seems to contradict it. The very first coins, minted in Lydia, were made of electrum (a silver-gold alloy) that varied widely in consistency.[2] Coinage quickly spread to Greece, where, even though coins were fairly consistent in weight and purity, they often had a value greater than the commodity value of the silver from which they were minted.[3] Indeed, some city-states (including Sparta) minted

---

1. Aristotle. *Politics*, book 1, part 9.
2. Seaford, *Money and the Early Greek Mind*, 132–3.
3. Ibid., 137.

coins from base metals like iron, bronze, lead, or tin: such coins had negligible intrinsic value but still functioned as money.[4] In either case, stamped coins had a value (which, following historian Richard Seaford, we shall call the "fiduciary value") greater than an identical but unstamped disk of metal. Why? What was this mysterious power that inhered in a mere sign? It was not a guarantee of weight and purity, nor was it an extension of the personal power of a ruler or religious authority. Seaford observes, "Whereas seal-marks seem to embody the power of the owner of the seal, coin-marks create no imagined attachment between the coins and their source."[5] Rather, coin-marks

> authenticate the metal as possessing a certain value. And they do so not by transmitting power (magical or otherwise) to the piece of metal, but by imposing on it a form that recognizably assigns it to a distinct category of things, the category of authentic coins.... The coin-mark...operates in effect as a mere sign.[6]

Signs have no intrinsic power, but derive it from human interpretation. To the extent a society holds such interpretations in common, signs or symbols bear social power. The new kind of money that emerged in ancient Greece derived its value from a social agreement, of which the marks on coins were tokens.[7] This agreement

---

4. Ibid., 139–45.

5. Ibid., 119.

6. Ibid.

7. The exception was coins used for foreign trade—coins that circulated outside the range of a social agreement. Such coins indeed depended on the intrinsic value of their underlying metal. Yet even here, a broader social perception of value was necessary to give them value, since silver and gold were not intrinsically very useful as metals.

is the essence of money. This should be obvious today, when most money is electronic and the rest has the approximate intrinsic value of a sheet of toilet paper, but money has been an agreement ever since the days of the ancient Greeks. Those reformers who advocate gold coinage as a way to return to the good old days of "real money" are trying to return to something that never existed, except perhaps for brief historical moments almost as an ideal. I believe that the next step in the evolution of human money will be not a return to an earlier form of currency, but its transformation from an unconscious to an intentional embodiment of our agreements.

Over 5,000 years, money has evolved from pure commodity, to a symbol riding upon a material, to pure symbol today. *Sacred Economics* seeks not to undo this evolution, but to fulfill it. The agreement that is money does not stand in isolation from the other systems of signs and symbols by which our civilization operates. We can embody in our money new agreements about the planet, the species, and what we hold sacred. For a long time we held "progress" sacred, the advancement of science and technology, the conquest of the natural realm. Our money system supported those goals. Our goals are changing now, and with them the great meta-stories of which the agreement called money is a part: the Story of Self, the Story of the People, and the Story of the World.

The purpose of this book is to tell a new story of money; to illuminate what new agreements we might embody within these fiduciary talismans, so that money is the ally, and not the enemy, of the more beautiful world our hearts tell us is possible.

It is no accident that ancient Greece, the place where symbolic money originated, also gave birth to the modern conception of the individual, to the notions of logic and reason, and to the philosophical underpinnings of the modern mind. In his scholarly masterpiece *Money and the Ancient Greek Mind,* classics professor Richard Seaford explores the impact of money on Greek society and thought, illuminating the characteristics that make money unique. Among them are that it is both concrete and abstract, that it is homogeneous, impersonal, a universal aim, and a universal means, and that it is unlimited. The entrance of this new, unique power into the world had profound consequences, many of which are now so deeply woven into our beliefs and culture, psyche and society, that we can barely perceive them, let alone question them.

Money is homogeneous in that regardless of any physical differences among coins, coins qua money are identical (if they are of the same denomination). New or old, worn or smooth, all one-drachma coins are equal. This was something new in the sixth century BCE. Whereas in archaic times, Seaford observes, power was conferred by unique talismanic objects (e.g., a scepter said to be handed down from Zeus), money is the opposite: its power is conferred by a standard sign that wipes out variations in purity and weight. Quality is not important, only quantity. Because money is convertible into all other things, it infects them with the same feature, turning them into commodities—objects that, as long as they meet certain criteria, are seen as identical. All that matters is how many or how much. Money, says Seaford, "promotes a sense of homogeneity among things in general." All things are equal, because they can be sold for money, which can in turn be used to buy any other thing.

In the commodity world, things are equal to the money that can replace them. Their primary attribute is their "value"—an abstraction. I feel a distancing, a letdown, in the phrase, "You can always buy another one." Can you see how this promotes an antimaterialism, a detachment from the physical world in which each person, place, and thing is special, unique? No wonder Greek philosophers of this era began elevating the abstract over the real, culminating in Plato's invention of a world of perfect forms more real than the world of the senses. No wonder to this day we treat the physical world so cavalierly. No wonder, after two thousand years' immersion in the mentality of money, we have become so used to the replaceability of all things that we behave as if we could, if we wrecked the planet, simply buy a new one.

I named this chapter "Money and the Mind." Very much like the fiduciary value of money, mind is an abstraction riding a physical vehicle. Like monetary fiduciarity, the idea of mind as a separate, nonmaterial essence of being developed over thousands of years, leading to the modern concept of an immaterial consciousness, a disembodied spirit. Tellingly, in both secular and religious thought, this abstraction has become more important than the physical vehicle, just as the "value" of a thing is more important than its physical attributes.

In the introduction I mentioned the idea that we have created a god in the image of our money: an unseen force that moves all things, that animates the world, an "invisible hand" that orders human activity, nonmaterial yet ubiquitous. Many of these attributes of God or spirit go back to the pre-Socratic Greek philosophers who developed their ideas at precisely the time that money took over their society. According to Seaford, they were the first to even distinguish between essence and appearance, between the concrete and the abstract—a distinction completely absent (even implicitly) from Homer. From Anaximander's *apeiron* to Heraclitus's *logos* to the Pythagorean doctrine "All is number," the early Greeks emphasized the primacy of the abstract: an unseen principle that orders the world. This ideology has infiltrated the DNA of our civilization to the point where the size of the financial sector dwarfs the real economy; where the total value of financial derivatives is ten times the world's gross domestic product; where the greatest rewards of our society go to the Wall Street wizards who do nothing but manipulate symbols. For the trader at his computer, it is indeed as Pythagoras said: "All is number."

One manifestation of this spirit-matter split that gives primacy to the former is the idea, "Sure, economic reform is a worthy cause, but what is much more important is a transformation of human consciousness." I think this view is mistaken, for it is based on a false dichotomy of consciousness and action, and ultimately of spirit and matter. On a deep level, money and consciousness are intertwined. Each is bound up in the other.

The development of monetary abstraction fits into a vast meta-historical context. Money could not have developed without a foundation of abstraction in the form of words and numbers. Already, number and label distance us from the real world and prime our minds to think abstractly. To use a noun already implies an identity among the many things so named; to say there are five of a thing makes each a *unit*. We begin to think of objects as representatives of a category, and not unique beings in themselves. So, while standard, generic categories didn't begin with money, money vastly accelerated their conceptual dominance. Moreover, the homogeneity of money accompanied the rapid development of standardized commodity goods for trade. Such standardization was crude in preindustrial times, but today manufactured objects are so nearly identical as to make the lie of money into the truth.

As we consider the form of the money of the future, let us keep in mind money's power to homogenize all that it touches. Perhaps money should *only* be used for that which is or should be standard, quantifiable, or generic; perhaps a different kind of money, or no money at all, should be involved in the circulation of those things that are personal and unique. We can only compare prices based on standard quantities; thus, when we receive more than that, something immeasurable, we have received a bonus, something we didn't pay for. In other words, we have received a gift. To be sure, we can buy art, but we sense that if it is mere commodity, we pay too much; and if it is true art, we pay infinitely too little. Similarly, we can buy sex but not love; we can buy calories but not real nourishment. Today we suffer a poverty of immeasurable things, priceless things; a poverty of the things that money cannot buy and a surfeit of the things it can (though this surfeit is so unequally distributed that many suffer a poverty of those things, too).[8]

Just as money homogenizes the things it touches, so also does it homogenize and depersonalize its users: "It facilitates the kind of commercial exchange that is disembedded from all other relations."[9] In other words, people become mere parties to a transaction. In contrast to the diverse motivations that characterize the giving and receiving of gifts, in a pure financial transaction we are all identical: we all want to get the best deal. This homogeneity among human beings that is an effect of money is assumed by economics to be a cause. The whole story of money's evolution from barter assumes that it is fundamental human nature to want to maximize self-interest. In this, human beings are assumed to be identical. When there is no standard of value, different humans want different things. When money is exchangeable for any thing, then all people want the same thing: money.

---

8. This surfeit is reflected in the persistent problem of "overcapacity" that afflicts nearly every industry, which is why solutions to the economic crisis usually involve stimulating demand.

9. Seaford, *Money and the Early Greek Mind,* 151.

Seaford writes, "Stripped of all personal association, money is promiscuous, capable of being exchanged with anybody for anything, indifferent to all nonmonetary interpersonal relationships."[10] Unlike other objects, money retains no trace of its origins and no trace of those through whom it has passed. Whereas a gift seems to partake of its giver, everyone's money is the same. If I have $2,000 in the bank, half from my friend and half from my enemy, I cannot choose to spend my enemy's $1,000 first and save my friend's. Each dollar is identical.

Wisely, perhaps, many people refuse on principle to mix business with friendship, wary of the essential conflict between money and personal relationship. Money depersonalizes a relationship, turning two people into mere "parties to an exchange" driven by the universal goal of maximizing self-interest. If I seek to maximize self-interest, perhaps at your expense, how can we be friends? And when in our highly monetized society we meet nearly all our needs with money, what personal gifts remain from which to build friendship?

That the profit motive is antithetical to any benignant personal motive is nearly axiomatic—hence the phrase, "Don't take it personally; it's just business." Today, an ethical business movement and ethical investment movement seek to heal the opposition between love and profit, but however sincere the motives, such efforts often mutate into public relations, "green-washing," or self-righteousness. This is no accident. In later chapters I will describe a fatal contradiction in the attempt to invest ethically, but for now just note your natural suspicion of it, and in general of any claim to "do well by doing good."

Any time we come across a seemingly altruistic enterprise, we

---

10. Seaford, *Money and the Early Greek Mind,* 155.

tend to think, "What's the catch?" How are they secretly making money from this? When are they going to ask me for money? The suspicion, "He's actually doing it for the money" is nearly universal. We are quick to descry financial motives in everything people do, and we are deeply moved when someone does something so magnanimous or so naively generous that such motive is obviously absent. It seems irrational, even miraculous, that someone would actually give without contrivance of return. As Lewis Hyde puts it, "In the empires of usury the sentimentality of the man with the soft heart calls to us because it speaks of what has been lost."[11]

The near-universality of the suspicion of an ulterior profit motive reflects money as a universal aim. Imagine yourself back in school, speaking to the career counselor, discussing what your gifts are and how you might use them to make a living (i.e., to convert them into money). This habit of thought runs deep: when my teenage son Jimi shows me the computer games he makes, I sometimes find myself thinking about how he might commercialize them and about which programming skills he could develop next to be more marketable. Almost any time someone gets an exciting creative idea, the thought, "How can we make money from this?" follows close behind. But when profit becomes the aim, and not a mere side effect, of artistic creation, the creation ceases to be art, and we become sellouts. Expanding this principle to life in general, Robert Graves warns, "You choose your jobs to provide you with a steady income and leisure to render the Goddess whom you adore valuable part-time service. Who am I, you will ask, to warn you that she demands either whole-time service or none at all?"[12]

---

11. Hyde, *The Gift*, 182.
12. Graves, *The White Goddess*, 15.

Money as a universal aim is embedded in our language. We speak of "capitalizing" on our ideas and use "gratuitous," which literally means received with thanks (and not payment), as a synonym for unnecessary. It is embedded in economics to be sure, in the assumption that human beings seek to maximize a self-interest that is equivalent to money. It is even embedded in science, where it is a cipher for reproductive self-interest. Here, too, the notion of a universal aim has taken hold.

That there is even such a thing as a universal aim to life (be it money or something else) is not at all obvious. This idea apparently arose at about the same time money did; perhaps it was money that suggested it to philosophers. Socrates used a money metaphor explicitly in proposing intelligence as universal aim: "There is only one right currency for which we ought to exchange all these other things [pleasures and pains]—intelligence."[13] In religion this corresponds to the pursuit of an ultimate aim, such as salvation or enlightenment, from which all other good things flow. How like the unlimited aim of money! I wonder what the effect would be on our spirituality if we gave up on the pursuit of a unitary, abstract goal that we believe to be the key to everything else. How would it feel to release the endless campaign to improve ourselves, to make progress toward a goal? What would it be like just to play instead, just to be? Like wealth, enlightenment is a goal that knows no limit, and in both cases the pursuit of it can enslave. In both cases, I think that the object of the pursuit is a spurious substitute for a diversity of things that people really want.[14]

---

13. Plato, Tht. 146d. Cited by Seaford, *Money and the Early Greek Mind*, 242.

14. Among the greatest of unmet needs today is for connection, both to other people and to nature. Ironically, money, with its abstraction and impersonality, attenuates our connections to both. Spirituality, when conceived as an individual pursuit best done apart from the world, does the same. Can we conceive of a different kind of money that bears the opposite effects?

In a fully monetized society, in which nearly everything is a good or a service, money converts the multiplicity of the world into a unity, a "single thing that is the measure of, and exchangeable with, almost anything else."[15] The *apeiron*, the *logos*, and similar conceptions were all versions of an underlying unity that gives birth to all things. It is that from which all things arise and to which all things return. As such it is nearly identical with the ancient Chinese conception of the Tao, which gives birth to yin and yang, and then to the ten thousand things. Interestingly, the semilegendary preceptor of Taoism, Lao Tzu, lived at approximately the same time as the pre-Socratic philosophers—which is also more or less the time of the first Chinese coinage. In any event, today it is still money that gives birth to the ten thousand things. Whatever you want to build in this world, you start with an investment, with money. And then, when you have finished your project, it is time to sell it. All things come from money; all things return to money.

Money is therefore not only a universal aim; it is a universal means as well, and indeed it is largely because it is a universal means that it is also a universal end, of which one can never have too much. Or at least, that is how we perceive it. Many times I've been witness to discussions about creating an intentional community or launching some other project, only for it to end with a disheartening admission that it will never happen because, "Where are we going to get the money?" Money is quite understandably seen as the crucial factor in determining what we can create: after all, it can buy virtually any good, can induce people to perform virtually any service. "Everything has its price." Money can even, it seems, purchase intangibles such as social status, political power,

---

15. Seaford, *Money and the Early Greek Mind*, 150.

and divine goodwill (or if not that, at least the favor of religious authorities, which is the next best thing). We are quite accustomed to seeing money as the key to the fulfillment of all our desires. How many dreams do you have that you assume you could fulfill if only (and only if) you had the money? Thus we mortgage our dreams to money, turning it from means to end.

I will not advocate the abolition of money. Money has exceeded its proper bounds, become the means to attain things that should never be infected by its homogeneity and depersonalization; meanwhile, as we have universalized it as means, those things that money truly cannot buy have become unattainable, and no matter how much money we have, we can obtain only their semblance. The solution is to restore money to its proper role. For indeed there are things that human beings can create only with money, or with some equivalent means of coordinating human activity on a mass scale. In its sacred form, money is the implement of a story, an embodied agreement that assigns roles and focuses intention. I will return to this theme later as I describe what money might look like in a sacred economy.

Because there is no apparent limit to what money can buy, our desire for money tends to be unlimited as well. The limitless desire for money was abundantly apparent to the ancient Greeks. At the very beginning of the money era, the great poet and reformer Solon observed, "Of wealth, there is no limit that appears to man, for those of us who have the most wealth are eager to double it." Aristophanes wrote that money is unique because in all other things (such as bread, sex, etc.) there is satiety, but not of money.

"How much is enough?" a friend once asked of a billionaire he knew. The billionaire was stumped. The reason that no amount of money can ever be enough is that we use it to fulfill needs that money cannot actually fulfill. As such it is like any other addictive substance, temporarily dulling the pain of an unmet need while leaving the need unmet. Increasing doses are required to dull the pain, but no amount can ever be enough. Today people use money as a substitute for connection, for excitement, for self-respect, for freedom, and for much else. "If only I had a million dollars, then I'd be free!" How many talented people sacrifice their youth hoping for an early retirement to a life of freedom, only to find themselves, at midlife, enslaved to their money?

When the primary function of money is as a medium of exchange, it is subject to the same limits as the goods for which it is exchanged, and our desire for it is limited by our satiety. It is when money takes on the additional function of store-of-value that our desire for it becomes unlimited. One idea I will therefore explore is the decoupling of money as medium-of-exchange from money as store-of-value. This idea has ancient roots going back to Aristotle, who distinguished between two kinds of wealth-getting: for the sake of accumulation, and for the sake of meeting other needs.[16] The former kind of wealth-getting, he says, is "unnatural" and, moreover, bears no limit.

Unlike physical goods, the abstraction of money allows us, in principle, to possess unlimited quantities of it. Thus it is easy for economists to believe in the possibility of endless exponential growth, where a mere number represents the size of the economy. The sum total of all goods and services is a number, and what limit is there on the growth of a number? Lost in abstraction, we ignore the limits of nature and culture to accommodate our growth. Following Plato, we make the abstraction more real than the reality, fixing Wall Street while the real economy languishes. The monetary

16. Aristotle, *Politics*, book 1, section 9.

essence of things is called "value," which, as an abstracted, uniform essence, reduces the plurality of the world. All things are reduced to what they are worth. This gives the illusion that the world is as limitless as numbers are. For a price, you can buy anything, even the pelt of an endangered species.[17]

Implicit in the unlimit of money is another kind of limitlessness: that of the human domain, the part of the world that belongs to human beings. What kind of things, after all, do we buy and sell for money? We buy and sell property, things that we own, things that we perceive as belonging to us. Technology has constantly widened that domain, making things available for ownership that were never attainable or even conceivable before: minerals deep within the earth, bandwidth on the electromagnetic spectrum, sequences of genes. Contemporaneous with technological extension of our reach was the progression of the mentality of property, as things like land, water rights, music, and stories entered the realm of the owned. The unlimit of money implies that the realm of the owned can grow indefinitely, and therefore that the destiny of mankind is to conquer the universe, to bring everything into the human domain, to make the whole world ours. This destiny is part of what I have described as the myth of Ascent, part of our defining Story of the People. Today, that story is rapidly becoming obsolete, and we need to invent a money system aligned with the new story that will replace it.[18]

---

17. The reader may have noticed a paradox: we live in a world of abundance, as described in Chapter 2, yet we are also depleting a limited biosphere. To resolve that paradox, consider that most of our excess production and consumption serve no real need, but are driven by the perception of scarcity and the existential loneliness of the separate self cut off from nature and community.

18. The same goes for the other defining story of our civilization, "the discrete and separate self." Our money system reifies this story, too, by dissolving personal ties, setting us into competition, and disconnecting us from both community and nature.

The features of money that I've discussed are not necessarily *bad*. By helping to homogenize or standardize all it touches, by serving as a universal means, money has enabled human beings to accomplish wonders. Money has played a key role in the rise of technological civilization, but perhaps, as with technology, we have barely begun to learn to use this potent creative instrument for its true purpose. Money has fostered the development of standardized things like machine components and microchips—but do we want our food to be homogeneous as well? Money's impersonality fosters cooperation over vast social distances, helping coordinate the labor of millions of people who are mostly strangers to each other—but do we want our relationships with the people in our own neighborhoods to be impersonal too? Money as universal means enables us to do nearly anything, but do we want it to be an exclusive means too, so that without it we can do nearly nothing? The time has come to master this tool, as humanity steps into an intentional, conscious new role on the earth.

CHAPTER 4

THE TROUBLE WITH PROPERTY

What would be the result in heaven itself if those who get there first instituted private property in the surface of heaven, and parceled it out in absolute ownership among themselves, as we parcel out the surface of the earth?

—Henry George

Man did not make the earth, and, though he had a natural right to occupy it, he had no right to locate as his property in perpetuity any part of it; neither did the Creator of the earth open a land-office, from whence the first title-deeds should issue.

—Thomas Paine

THE URGE TO OWN

We have lived in an Age of Separation. One by one, our bonds to community, nature, and place have dissolved, marooning us in an alien world. The loss of these bonds is more than a reduction of our wealth, it is a reduction of our very being. The impoverishment we feel, cut off from community and cut off from nature, is an impoverishment of our souls. That is because, contrary to the assumptions of economics, biology, political philosophy, psychology, and institutional religion, we are not in essence separate beings having relationships. We *are* relationship.

I once heard Martín Prechtel, speaking of his village in Guatemala, explain, "In my village, if you went to the medicine man with a sick child, you would never say, 'I am healthy, but my child is sick.' You would say, 'My family is sick.' Or if it were a neighbor, you might say, 'My village is sick.'" No doubt, in such a society, it would be equally inconceivable to say, "I am healthy, but the forest is sick." To think anyone could be healthy when her family, her village, or indeed the land, the water, or the planet were not, would be as absurd as saying, "I've got a fatal liver disease, but that's just my liver—I am healthy!" Just as my sense of self includes my liver, so theirs included their social and natural community.

The modern self, in contrast, is a discrete and separate subject in a universe that is Other. This self is the Economic Man of Adam Smith; it is the embodied soul of religion; it is the selfish gene of biology. It underlies the converging crises of our time, which are all variations on the theme of separation—separation from nature, from community, from lost parts of ourselves. It underlies all the usual culprits blamed for the ongoing destruction of ecology and polity, such as human greed or capitalism. Our sense of self entails, "More for me is less for you"; hence we have an interest-based money system embodying precisely that principle. In older, gift-based societies, the opposite was true.

The urge to own grows as a natural response to an alienating ideology that severs felt connections and leaves us alone in the universe. When we exclude world from self, the tiny, lonely identity that remains has a voracious need to claim as much as possible of that lost beingness for its own. If all the world, all of life and earth, is no longer me, I can at least compensate by making it mine. Other separate selves do the same, so we live in a world of competition and omnipresent anxiety. It is built into our self-definition. This is the deficit of being, the deficit of soul, into which we are born.

Trapped in the logic of me and mine, we seek to recover some tiny fraction of our lost wealth by expanding and protecting the separate self and its extension: money and property. Those who lack the economic means to inflate the self often inflate the physical self instead, which is one reason why obesity disproportionately afflicts the poor. Addictions to shopping, to money, and to acquisition arise from the same basic source as do addictions to food: both come from loneliness, from the pain of merely existing cut off from most of what we are.

Looking out upon the strip mines and the clear-cuts and the dead zones and the genocides and the debased consumer culture, we ask, What is the origin of this monstrous machine that chews up beauty and spits out money? The discrete and separate self, surveying a universe that is fundamentally Other, naturally treats the natural and human world as a pile of instrumental, accidental *stuff*. The rest of the world is fundamentally not-self.[1] Why should we care about it, beyond our own foreseeable utility? So it was that Descartes, a pioneering articulator of the modern sense of self, articulated as well the ambition to become the "lords and possessors" of nature. As the latter word implies, the idea of property occurs quite naturally to the separate self.

Our rigid, narrow, self/other distinction is coming to an end, victim of its own premises. As the mystics have taught, the separate self

---

1. As above, so below. Having made nature into an adversary, or at best a pile of "resources," it is no surprise that we manifest the same relationship within our bodies. The defining diseases of our time are the autoimmune diseases, the somatization of our self-other confusion. Just as the village, the forest, and the planet are inseparable parts of ourselves that we mistake as other, so our immune systems reject our own body tissues. What we do to nature, we do to ourselves, inescapably.

can be maintained only temporarily, and at great cost. And we have maintained it a long time, and built a civilization upon it that seeks the conquest of nature and human nature. The present convergence of crises has laid bare the futility of that goal. It portends the end of civilization as we know it, and the instauration of a new state of human beingness defined by a more fluid, more inclusive sense of self.

One theory of the origin of property associates it with the notion of autonomy, or self-sovereignty, that emerged slowly out of our communal tribal past. Charles Avila describes the logic this way: "If I am my own, and my labor power belongs to me, then what I make is mine."[2] Here then is an ideological prerequisite for any concept of property, that "I am my own," which is by no means a universal precept in human societies. In other societies, the clan, the tribe, the village, or even the community of all life may have taken priority over the individual conception of the self, in which case your labor power does not belong to you, but to something greater.[3] The institution of property, therefore, is not the root of our present malady, but a symptom of our disconnection and isolation. This book, therefore, does not seek to abolish property (for to do so would address the symptom rather than the cause) but to transform it as part of a larger transformation of human beingness.

Other thinkers, notably Wilhelm Reich and Genevieve Vaughan, link the origin of property to the emergence of male dominance

---

2. Avila, *Ownership*, 5.

3. Even today, we have a spiritual sense that our labor is indeed not our own. It comes through in our desire to work for something greater than ourselves—that is, to dedicate our labor to a cause beyond our rational self-interest. Religious people might describe it as "giving one's life to God." Another way of putting it is that we have a need to make a gift of our labor and its products, and of all the skills and talents that inform it. We then feel fulfilled, serene in the knowledge that we are fulfilling our purpose here on earth. Intuitively, we know that our gifts must be given in turn, and not hoarded for the brief and illusory aggrandizement of the separate self.

and patriarchal society.[4] While I believe these arguments have merit, I have chosen not to explore herein the sexual dimensions of money and property, a subject deserving of its own treatise. Each institution of our Age of Separation is tied to all the others; alienation from nature, the body, and the sacred feminine echoes the alienation from the world that property implies when it makes things detachable objects of commerce.

The urge to own diminishes as our sense of connectedness and gratitude grows, and we realize that our labor power is not our own, and what I make is not properly mine. Is not my ability to labor, and my life itself, a gift too? In that realization, we desire to give our creations to all that have contributed to our being and granted us the gift of life.

Certain socialist philosophers have turned this desire, motivated by gratitude, into an obligation instead, and into a justification for state expropriation of individual labor. We owe a "debt to society," and the state becomes the debt collector. In less extreme form, it justifies the income tax—also an expropriation of individual labor. In both cases, we are compelled through force to give. Can we instead create an economic system that liberates, celebrates, and rewards the innate urge to give? That is what this book describes: a system that rewards flow and not accumulation, creating and not owning, giving and not having.

THE ORIGINAL ROBBERY

The sovereignty of the individual was but a first step toward the modern concept of property, for most things on this earth do not

---

4. See, for example, Reich's *Sex-Pol* and Vaughan's "Gift Giving as the Female Principle vs. Patriarchal Capitalism."

exist through anyone's labor. By the logic of "what I make is mine," anything that existed independent of human effort could belong to no one. To claim ownership of such a thing—the land, the rivers, the animals, the trees—would be tantamount to theft, just as I am a thief if I seize ownership of something you make.

A distinguished line of economic thought has arisen from this realization, whose most notable exponents were P. D. Proudhon, Karl Marx, Henry George, and Silvio Gesell. "Property is robbery," proclaimed Proudhon: tracing back the origin of any piece of property through a succession of "legitimate" transfers, we eventually get to the first owner—the one who simply took it, the one who separated it off from the realm of "ours" or "God's" into the realm of "mine." Usually this happened by force, as in the seizure of the vast lands of all North America in the last three centuries. This story has played itself out in various forms for millennia all over the world. After all, before Roman times there was no such thing as a deed. Land was like the air and water; it could not be owned. The first owners therefore could not have acquired it legitimately. They must have taken it.

It is often argued that land ownership is a natural consequence of agriculture. While the hunter-gatherer has made little investment in her land, the farmer has put labor into making it more productive (of food for humans, that is). It would be patently unjust for the farmer to labor all year only to have "gatherers" come in at harvest time and live off the harvest. Private property is supposed to give people an incentive to make improvements upon the land. But wouldn't it be more just if there were some way to own the improvements, and not the land itself?

Originally, land rights were almost always held in common, accruing to the village or tribe, and not the individual. In the great agrarian civilizations such as Egypt, Mesopotamia, and Zhou Dynasty China, there was little concept of private land ownership. All land was the property of the king, and because the king was the representative of the divine on earth, all land was the property of God.

There is a vast conceptual gulf between having a right to the fruits of one's labor as applied to land and owning the land itself. In the West, the absolute concept of land ownership seems to have originated in Rome, fertilized, perhaps, by the Greek conception of the individual. It was in Rome that land first came under what they called *dominium,* "the ultimate right, the right which had no right behind it, the right which legitimated all others, while itself having no need of legitimation . . . the right 'of using, enjoying, and abusing'—*ius utendi, fruendi, abutendi.*"[5]

In the East, explicit land ownership began somewhat earlier, at least in concept. In China it dates back at least to the reign of Shang Yang in the fourth century BCE and perhaps before, though even then a time prior to land ownership was still a matter of historical memory, as evidenced by Confucian statements that it was improper to sell land in "ancient times."[6] India as well probably knew private ownership of land by the sixth century BCE, though the evidence is somewhat contradictory.[7] In any event, the vast majority of land in India was communally owned up until the time of British rule.[8]

---

5. Avila, *Ownership,* 20.

6. Xu, *Ancient China in Transition,* 112. This book seeks to interpret the Confucian position as a criticism of concentration of ownership. Deng, "A Comparative Study on Land Ownership," 12. Deng maintains that prior to then, alienation of land was forbidden, since it was all the property of the king. Deng also argues that in practice, land was generally not alienable or fungible at least through the medieval Song Dynasty.

7. Altekar, *State and Government in Ancient India,* 273–4.

8. Kuhnen, *Man and Land,* Sec. 2.1.1 and 2.1.2.

In Medieval Europe, the bulk of the land was owned either in common or by feudal lords who did not "own" the land in the full modern sense, as an alienable commodity to freely buy and sell. They had certain rights to the land, which could be transferred to vassals in exchange for various services, shares of crops, and eventually for money. In England, free alienation of land was generally not possible until the fifteenth century.[9] Thereafter, the vast communal lands of England rapidly came under private ownership thanks to the Enclosure Acts, a process paralleled across the continent, for example through the "emancipation" of the serfs. Lewis Hyde writes,

> Whereas before a man could fish in any stream and hunt in any forest, now he found there were individuals who claimed to be the owners of these commons. The basis of land tenure had shifted. The medieval serf had been almost the opposite of a property owner: the land had owned *him*. He could not move freely from place to place, and yet he had inalienable rights to the piece of land to which he was attached. Now men claimed to own the land and offered to rent it out at a fee. While a serf could not be removed from his land, a tenant could be evicted not only through failure to pay the rent but merely at the whim of the landlord.[10]

As with so many social reforms, the freeing of the serfs was another step in the consolidation of economic and political power in the hands of the already powerful. By one means or another, people who had for generations freely grazed their herds, collected fire-

---

9. Deng, "A Comparative Study on Land Ownership," 10.
10. Hyde, *The Gift*, 121.

wood, and hunted on the lands around them could no longer do so.[11] These lands had been a *commons,* the property of all and of none. Forever after, they became property.

If property is robbery, then a legal system dedicated to the protection of private property rights is a system that perpetuates a crime. By making property sacrosanct we validate the original theft. This should not be too surprising if the laws were made by the thieves themselves to legitimize their ill-gotten gains. Such was indeed the case: in Rome and elsewhere, it was the rich and powerful who both seized the land and made the laws.

Lest the reader think I am launching a Marxist diatribe, let me hasten to add that I am not advocating the abolition of private property. For one thing, the whole mentality of *abolition* involves a fervid, abrupt, jarring change imposed forcefully on the unwilling. Secondly, private property is but a symptom of a deeper malady (Separation), and if we address that symptom from the mind-set of Separation, of conquest, of overcoming evil, we will end up with the same iniquities in different forms. Finally, even on the economic level, the problem is not private property per se, but the unfair advantages of owning it. Even though it is wrong for someone to benefit from mere ownership of what was once common, everyone benefits when resources go toward those who will use them the best. These include the land, soil, minerals, aquifers, and capacity of the atmosphere to absorb waste. We need an economic system that disallows profit-by-owning yet rewards the entrepreneur's spirit

---

11. Of course, the peasants resisted their dispossession from the commons, fomenting the bloody struggle known in Germany as the Peasants' War. It is a struggle reenacted time and again around the globe whenever people resist the incursion of property rights into yet another sphere of human relationship. As Hyde puts it, "the Peasants' War was the same war that the American Indians had to fight with the Europeans, a war against the marketing of formerly inalienable properties."

that says, "I know a way to use it better," and allows that spirit free rein. Marxist systems not only eliminate profit from exclusive *control* of scarce capital resources; they also eliminate profit from their efficacious *use*. The result is inefficiency and stagnation. Can we reward those who put resources to best use without rewarding the mere fact of ownership? This book describes a money system that preserves the freedom of private property without allowing its owners to accrue unfair advantages.

Wherever and whenever it happened, the privatization of land soon brought with it a concentration of ownership. In the early days of ancient Rome, land was common (not personal) property, except for a small homestead plot: "The corn land was of public right."[12] As Rome expanded through conquest, the new lands did not stay "public" very long but soon migrated into the hands of the wealthiest families—the patrician class—setting the norm for many centuries to come. Their estates also grew at the expense of the original plebeian freeholds, whose owners were frequently called away to serve in the legions, and which in any case could not compete economically with the cheap slave labor of the patrician estates. They accumulated insurmountable debts and, because land had become an alienable commodity, were forced off their homesteads and into beggary, banditry, or, if they were fortunate, the urban craft professions.

When the fortunes of the Empire turned and the supply of slaves dried up, many large landholders turned to tenant farmers, the *coloni*, to farm their fields. Bound by debt, these tenants eventually became the Medieval serfs. Think of it this way: if you owe

---

12. Avila, *Ownership*, 16, quoting a ancient source from H. F. Jolowicz and Barry Nicholas, *Historical Introduction to the Study of Roman Law*, 139.

me an insurmountable debt, then you are obliged to pay at least as much of it as you can. The proceeds of your labor, forever after, belong to me. How similar this is to the United States bankruptcy laws as promulgated in the Bankruptcy "Reform" Act of 2005, which compel the person declaring bankruptcy to commit a portion of future wages to creditors.[13] How similar as well to the plight of Third World countries, who are compelled to restructure their economies and devote their entire economic surplus toward the perpetual servicing of debt. These are the modern counterparts of the serfs, bound to work for the owners of money just as the serfs worked for the owners of land. Their condition is known as "debt peonage."

The parallel between ancient Rome and the present day is striking. Now as then, wealth is increasingly concentrated in the hands of the few. Now as then, people must go into lifelong debt that they can never pay off just to have access to the necessities of life. Then it was through access to land; today it is through access to money. The slaves, serfs, and tenants gave a lifetime of labor to the enrichment of the landowners; today the proceeds of our labor go to the owners of money.

In the history of radical thought, the realization that property is theft usually accompanies a rage and desire for vengeance against the thieves. Matters are not so simple, though. The owners of wealth, whether inherited or not, are born into a role that is created and necessitated by the great invisible stories of our civilization that compel us to turn the world into property and money whether we are aware of doing so or not.

---

13. Moreover, many types of debt, such as tax debt, alimony debt, and student loans, are not affected by bankruptcy. At the present writing, student loan debt in the United States exceeds credit card debt, posing a huge burden on graduating students.

Let us not waste our psychic energy hating the rich, or even the original plunderers. Cast in their station, we would have enacted the same role. Indeed, most of us participate, in one way or another, in the ongoing theft of the commons. Let us not hate, lest we prolong the Age of Separation even further and lest we, like the Bolsheviks, perpetrate a revolution that is insufficiently deep, and so re-create the old order in a different, distorted form. Still, let us not lose sight of the nature and effects of the unconscious crime of property, so that we may return our world to its original and still-latent abundance.

The transformation from a right to benefit into outright ownership of land was a gradual one, whose terminus is the practice of selling land for money. Let's keep in mind that this was a conceptual transformation (the land doesn't admit to being owned), a human projection onto reality. Land ownership (and indeed all forms of ownership) says more about our perception of the world than about the nature of the thing owned. The transition from the early days, when ownership of land was as unthinkable as ownership of the sky, sun, and moon, to the present day, when nearly every square foot of the earth is subject to ownership of one sort or another, is really just the story of our changing view of ourselves in relation to the universe.

THE GEORGIST TRADITION

The distinction between the right to use and outright ownership echoes the primitive distinction between that which is produced through human effort and that which is there already; it persists today in the distinction between "real" and "personal" property, and it is a basis for thousands of years of reformist thought.

Since the Roman Empire developed the legal basis of property rights as we know them today, it is unsurprising that it also produced some of the earliest critics of property. In the third and fourth centuries, the early leaders of the Christian church were especially clear that the things of the earth were for all to share. Ambrose wrote, "Rich and poor alike enjoy the splendid ornaments of the universe ... The house of God is common to rich and poor," and "The Lord our God has willed this earth to be the common possession of all and its fruit to support all."[14] Elsewhere he writes that private property

> is not according to nature, for nature has brought forth all things for all in common. Thus God has created everything in such a way that all things be possessed in common. Nature therefore is the mother of common right, usurpation of private right.[15]

Others of the Christian Fathers, notably John Chrysostom, Augustine, Basil the Great, and Clement, weighed in with similar views, encouraging followers to follow Jesus's teachings quite literally and give all their possessions to the poor. Theirs was not a detached philosophy: many of these leaders did exactly that. Ambrose, Basil, and Augustine had been men of considerable wealth before entering the clergy, and they gave it all away.

The teachings of its founders notwithstanding, eventually the Church itself acquired considerable property and allied itself with imperial power. The teachings of Jesus became otherworldly ideals that were not seriously recommended to anyone, and the Kingdom of God was transported from earth to Heaven. This was a

---

14. In Psalmum CXVIII Expositio, 8, 22, PL 15:1303, cited by Avila, *Ownership*, 72.
15. Avila, *Ownership*, 74.

major step in the conceptual separation of spirit and matter that has contributed to making materiality, and especially money, profane today. Even more ironically, most people today who profess to follow Christian teachings have turned everything inside out and associate socialism with atheism and private wealth with God's favor.

The early Church fathers made frequent reference to the distinction between what people produce through their own effort and what was given to humanity by God for all to use in common. Many social and economic critics of the last several centuries echoed this early indignation at the appropriation of the commons and developed creative proposals to remedy it. One such early critic, Thomas Paine, wrote,

> And as it is impossible to separate the improvement made by cultivation from the earth itself, upon which that improvement is made, the idea of landed property arose from that parable connection; but it is nevertheless true, that it is the value of the improvement, only, and not the earth itself, that is individual property. . . . Every proprietor, therefore, of cultivated lands, owes to the community a ground-rent (for I know of no better term to express the idea) for the land which he holds.[16]

The first economist to develop this idea fully was Henry George, in his eloquent 1879 classic *Progress and Poverty*. He started with essentially the same premise as Paine and the early Christians:

> But who made the earth that any man can claim such ownership of it, or any part of it, or the right to give, sell or bequeath it? Since the earth was not made by us, but is only a temporary

---

16. Paine, *Agrarian Justice*, par. 11–12.

dwelling place on which one generation of men follow another; since we find ourselves here, are manifestly here with equal permission of the Creator, it is manifest that no one can have any exclusive right of ownership in land, and that the rights of all men to land must be equal and inalienable. There must be exclusive right of possession of land, for the man who uses it must have secure possession of land in order to reap the products of his labor. But his right of possession must be limited by the equal right of all, and should therefore be conditioned upon the payment to the community by the possessor of an equivalent for any special valuable privilege thus accorded him.[17]

Why should someone profit from the use-value of land by the mere fact of owning it, especially when the origin of that ownership is based on ancient injustice? Accordingly, Henry George proposed his famous Single Tax—essentially a 100-percent tax on the "economic rent" deriving from land. This was to be implemented through a tax on the value of land as distinct from improvements upon it; for example, land would be taxed but not buildings or crops. It was called "single" because he advocated the abolition of all other taxes, reasoning that it is just as much theft to tax legitimate private property as it is to profit from something that belongs to all. George's writings sparked a massive political movement that almost got him elected to the New York mayor's office, but of course the established money power fought him at every turn.[18] His ideas have been sporadically adopted around the world (the

---

17. George "The Single Tax."

18. Another reason for his political defeat was that George was rigidly dogmatic, refusing political alliance with anyone who did not uncompromisingly endorse his Single Tax.

two places I've spent most of my life, Taiwan and Pennsylvania, both levy taxes on the underlying value of land) and have greatly influenced economic thought.

One of his admirers, Silvio Gesell, proposed a near-equivalent to George's land tax: the public ownership of all land, available for private leasing at a rate that would approximate the economic rent.[19] Gesell's reasoning is compelling and remarkably prescient in its understanding of ecology and the connected self. Read this extraordinary passage from 1906:

> We frequently hear the phrase: Man has a natural right to the earth. But that is absurd, for it would be just as correct to say that man has a right to his limbs. If we talk of rights in this connection we must also say that a pine-tree has the right to sink its roots in the earth. Can man spend his life in a balloon? The earth belongs to, and is an organic part of man. We cannot conceive man without the earth any more than without a head or a stomach. The earth is just as much a part, an organ, of man as his head. Where do the digestive organs of man begin and end? They have no beginning and no end, but form a closed system without beginning or end. The substances which man requires to maintain life are indigestible in their raw state and must go through a preparatory digestive process. And this preparatory work is not done by the mouth, but by the plant. It is the plant which collects and transmutes the substances so that they may become nutriment in their further progress through the digestive canal. Plants and the space they occupy are just as much a part of man as his mouth, his teeth or his stomach. . . .

---

19. *Economic rent* refers to the proceeds of ownership, such as rents, royalties, dividends, and interest.

How, then, can we suffer individual men to confiscate for themselves parts of the earth as their exclusive property, to erect barriers and with the help of watchdogs and trained slaves to keep us away from parts of the earth, from parts of ourselves— to tear, as it were, whole limbs from our bodies? Is not such a proceeding equivalent to self-mutilation?[20]

Gesell goes on, with great rhetorical flourish, to say that this mutilation is even worse than the amputation of a body part, for wounds of the body heal, but

the wound left ... by the amputation of a piece of land festers forever, and never closes. At every term for the payment of rent, on every Quarter Day, the wound opens and the golden blood gushes out. Man is bled white and goes staggering forward. The amputation of a piece of land from our body is the bloodiest of all operations; it leaves a gaping, festering wound which cannot heal unless the stolen limb is grafted on again.

I think this is a wound we all feel, not only as the rent built into the cost of everything we buy, but also as a spiritual disenfranchise-ment. Some time ago I was driving with a woman from France down the country roads of central Pennsylvania. The gentle moun-tains and broad valleys beckoned to us, so we decided to walk them. It seemed as if the ground was begging for our feet, wanting to be tread. We decided to find a place to pull over and walk. We drove for an hour, but we never did find a field or forest that wasn't fes-tooned with "No Trespassing" signs. Every time I see one I feel a twinge, a loss. Any squirrel is freer than I am, any deer. These signs

20. Gesell, *The Natural Economic Order,* part 2, chapter 5, "The Case for the Nation-alization of Land."

apply to humans only. Herein lies a universal principle: the regime of property, the enclosure of the unowned, has made us all poorer. The promise of freedom inherent in that broad, verdant landscape was a mirage. Woody Guthrie's words ring true:

There was a big high wall there that tried to stop me.
The sign was painted, it said private property.
But on the back side it didn't say nothing.
That side was made for you and me.[21]

After three hundred years of economic expansion, we are so impoverished that we lack the wealth and freedom of a squirrel. The indigenous people who lived here before the Europeans arrived had the run of the land. They had the simple freedom to say, "Let us climb that mountain. Let us swim in that lake. Let us fish that river." Not even the wealthiest among us have that freedom today. Even a billion-dollar landholding is smaller than the domain of the hunter-gatherer.[22]

The situation is different in most of Europe; in Sweden, for instance, the right of *Allemansrätt* allows individuals to walk, pick flowers, camp for a day or two, swim, or ski on private land (but not too near a dwelling). I met a horse enthusiast who described how, in Ireland, all the gates to private farm lanes and pastures are unlocked. "Trespassing" is not a concept; the land is open to all.

---

21. From "This Land is Your Land." This verse is usually omitted from the songbooks.

22. The reader might bring up the territoriality of animals, many of whom are not free to roam. Not all animals are territorial, however, and those that are often exhibit group territoriality, not individual territoriality. So it was with humans for most of our existence. At the very least, each person had the freedom of the entire tribal territory. Shall we today shrink our territory down to the level of the nuclear family? Or shall we expand our tribe to include the whole earth?

The riders are respectful of the farmer and the land in turn, sticking to the perimeters to avoid disturbing animals and pasture. Hearing of this system, I don't think any American can look out upon the vast expanses of this country with their gates, fences, and no-trespassing signs without a feeling of confinement or loss. Can you feel Gesell's "wound"—that the very land has been severed from us?

Gesell's huge contribution beyond George was to apply parallel thinking beyond land to money, inventing a new kind of money system that I will describe, after due groundwork, later in this book as a key element of a sacred economy.

Controversial among progressives of his time, Henry George's insistence on taxing only land makes even less sense today because so many other commons have been brought into the realm of private property.[23] Hyde's "marketing of formerly inalienable properties" has gone far beyond land to encompass nearly everything essential to human existence and human joy. Our connections to nature, to culture, and to community have been riven, separated off and sold back to us. I have so far focused on the land, but nearly every other commons has suffered the same fate. Intellectual property offers the most obvious example, and the royalties that derive from owning it play a role similar to land rent. (If you think intellectual property differs from land because it is created by humans, read on!) But there is one form of ownership that contains

---

23. There are other significant problems with George's program. In particular, it is very difficult to separate the value of land from the value of improvements upon it, especially because the intrinsic value of land is determined not only by its physical characteristics, but also by its location relative to other pieces of land bearing human improvements. By building on your land, you attract others to build nearby, thus raising the value of your own land and creating a disincentive to build in the first place. This is one reason why I prefer Silvio Gesell's leasing approach to solving the problem of economic rent.

and supersedes the rest: the ownership of money. In the realm of finance, interest plays the role of royalties and rents, ensuring that the wealth that flows from human creativity and labor flows primarily to those who own money. Money is just as criminal in its origins as are other forms of property—an ongoing robbery that both impels and embodies the expropriation of the commons.

To restore sacredness to economy, we need to redress this robbery, because it is ultimately a theft and a reduction of a divine gift. It is the conversion of what was once sacred, unique, and personal into the status of commodity. It is not immediately obvious that the right to profit from mere ownership of money is just as illegitimate as the right to profit from the mere ownership of land. After all, money, unlike land, is a human creation. We earn money from the application of our human gifts, our own energy, time, and creativity. Surely the proceeds from this labor rightfully belong to the laborer? Surely, therefore, not all money is illegitimate in its ultimate origin?

This view is naive. In fact, money is deeply and irretrievably implicated in the conversion of the land commons into private property, the final and defining stage of which is its reduction to the status of just another commodity that can be bought and sold. So too have other elements of our natural and cultural bequest been cordoned off, turned into property, and finally, as "goods and services," into money. This is not to say that it is immoral to work for money; it is, rather, immoral for money to work for you. What rental is on land, so interest is on money. Money is the corpse of the commons, the embodiment of all that was once common and free, turned now into property of the purest form. The next several chapters will substantiate this claim, describing exactly how and why interest-bearing money, by nature, usurps the commons, ruins the planet, and reduces the vast majority of humanity to peonage.

CHAPTER 5

THE CORPSE OF THE COMMONS

We cry shame on the feudal baron who forbade the peasant to turn a clod of earth unless he surrendered to his lord a fourth of his crop. We call those the barbarous times. But if the forms have changed, the relations have remained the same, and the worker is forced, under the name of free contract, to accept feudal obligations. For, turn where he will, he can find no better conditions. Everything has become private property, and he must accept, or die of hunger.

—Peter Kropotkin

At the foundation of every great fortune lies a great crime.

—Leo Tolstoy

Despite land's obvious independence of human effort for its existence, land is not so different from any other kind of property. Let us first consider material property—anything made of metal, wood, plastic, plants or animals, minerals, and so on. Are these anything other than pieces of the earth, altered through the application of human effort? The distinction between land and improvements thereupon—the distinction between that which already exists and that which human effort creates—is no more or less valid for land than for any other material good. All that we use and all that we own consists of modified bits of earth. Together they are "natural capital"—the wealth and goodness that nature has bequeathed upon us. Originally none of it was property; it came into that realm as technology lengthened our grasp and the mentality of separation intensified our will to own. Today, forms of natural capital that we barely knew existed have become property: the electromagnetic spectrum, sequences of DNA, and, indirectly, ecological diversity and the earth's capacity to absorb industrial waste.[1]

Whether it has been made into a direct subject of property, as in land, oil, and trees, or whether it is still a commons that we draw on to create other property, such as the open sea, the original Great Commons has been sold off: converted first into property and then into money. It is this final step that confirms that something has indeed completed its metamorphosis into property. To be able to freely buy and sell something means that it has been dissociated from its original matrix of relationships; in other words, that it has become "alienable." That is why money has become a proxy for land and all other property, and why charging rental (interest) for its use bears the same effects and partakes of the same ancient injustice as does charging rent on land.

CULTURAL AND SPIRITUAL CAPITAL

Natural capital is one of four broad categories of the common-wealth that also comprises social, cultural, and spiritual capital.

---

1. Pollution credits and similar schemes seek to convert the earth's absorptive capacity into property. Even without them, however, it is already an invisible, embedded component of every manufactured product, an essential input of which there is a limited supply. Even without explicit property rights, this absorptive capacity is being taken from the commons.

Each consists of things that were once free, part of self-sufficiency or the gift economy, that we now pay for. The robbery then is not from mother earth, but from mother culture.

The most familiar of these other forms of capital in the economic discourse is cultural capital, which goes by the term *intellectual property*. In former times, the vast fund of stories, ideas, songs, artistic motifs, images, and technical inventions formed a commons that everyone could draw upon for pleasure and productivity, or incorporate into yet other innovations. In the Middle Ages, minstrels would listen to each other's songs and borrow new tunes that they liked, modify them, and circulate them back into the commons of music. Today artists and their corporate sponsors scramble to copyright and protect each new creation, and vigorously prosecute anyone who tries to incorporate those songs into their own. The same happens in every creative sphere.[2]

The moral justification for intellectual property is, again, "If I am my own, and my labor power belongs to me, then what I make is mine." But even granting the premise that "I am my own," the implicit assumption that artistic and intellectual creations arise *ex nihilo* from the mind of the creator, independent of cultural context, is absurd. Any intellectual creation (including this book) draws on bits and pieces of the sea of culture around us, and from the fund of images, melodies, and ideas that are deeply imprinted upon the human psyche, or perhaps even innate to it. As Lewis Mumford

---

2. Filmmakers, for instance, need entire "rights clearance" legal departments in order to make sure they haven't inadvertently used some copyrighted image in their movie. These could include images of designer furniture, buildings, brand logos, and clothing—almost everything in the built environment. The result has been to stifle creativity and relegate much of the most interesting art illegal. (This is inevitable when art uses the stuff of life around us for its subject and that stuff is in the realm of property already.)

puts it, "A patent is a device that enables one man to claim special financial rewards for being the last link in the complicated social process that produced the invention."[3] The same is true of songs, stories, and all other cultural innovations. By making them private property, we are walling off something that is not ours. We are stealing from the cultural commons. And because, like land, pieces of the cultural commons are themselves productive of continued wealth, this theft is an ongoing crime that contributes to the divide between the haves and the have-nots, the owners and the renters, the creditors and the debtors. The Russian anarchist Peter Kropotkin made this general point eloquently:

> Every machine has had the same history—a long record of sleepless nights and of poverty, of disillusions and of joys, of partial improvements discovered by several generations of nameless workers, who have added to the original invention these little nothings, without which the most fertile idea would remain fruitless. More than that: every new invention is a synthesis, the resultant of innumerable inventions which have preceded it in the vast field of mechanics and industry.
>
> Science and industry, knowledge and application, discovery and practical realization leading to new discoveries, cunning of brain and of hand, toil of mind and muscle—all work together. Each discovery, each advance, each increase in the sum of human riches, owes its being to the physical and mental travail of the past and the present.

---

3. Mumford, *Technics and Civilization*, 142. Of course, the person at the last stage of the invention process deserves reward for his or her ingenuity and toil, but the social context must also be acknowledged. This is decreasingly the case as patent and copyright periods have expanded from their original decade or two to, in some cases, upwards of a century.

> By what right then can any one whatever appropriate the least morsel of this immense whole and say—This is mine, not yours?[4]

Such considerations inform my desire to make my books freely available online and to forgo some of the normal copyrights. I could not have written this book outside a vast organic matrix of ideas, a commonwealth of cultural capital that I cannot rightfully enclose.[5]

Spiritual capital is more subtle. It refers to our mental and sensuous capacities, for example, the ability to concentrate, to create worlds of the imagination, and to derive pleasure from experiencing life. When I was young, in the very last days before television and video games came to dominate American childhood, we created our own worlds with intricate story lines, practicing the psychic technologies that adults can use to fashion their lives and their collective reality: forming a vision, telling a story around that vision that assigns meanings and roles, playing out those roles, and so on. Today, those worlds of the imagination come prefabricated from TV studios and software companies, and children wander through cheap, gaudy, often violent worlds created by distant strangers. These come with prefabricated images as well, and the ability to form their own images (we call this ability *imagination*) atrophies. Unable to envision a new world, the child

---

4. Kropotkin, *The Conquest of Bread*, chapter 1.

5. A detailed discussion of intellectual property rights is beyond the scope of this book. Certainly, I have made a contribution to this matrix of ideas (at least I think I have!) and deserve to be sustained in my work. However, to prevent other people from incorporating my writing and other creations into new creations of their own feels miserly. Practically speaking, I advocate a broad expansion of the "fair use" doctrine and a dramatic shortening of the term for copyrights and patents.

grows up accustomed to accepting whatever reality is handed her.[6] Could this, perhaps, be contributing to the political passivity of the American public?

Another depletion of spiritual capital comes via the intense sensory stimulation of electronic media. Modern action films, for instance, are so fast-paced, so loud, so grossly stimulating, that older movies seem boring in comparison, not to mention books or the world of nature. Despite my best efforts to limit their exposure to modern excesses, my children can barely stand to watch any film made before 1975. Once habituated to intense stimulation, in its absence we get the withdrawal symptom we call boredom. We become dependent, and therefore must pay to acquire something that was once available simply by virtue of being alive. A baby or a hunter-gatherer will be fascinated by the slow processes of nature: a twig floating on the water, a bee visiting a flower, and other things that are beyond the anemic attentiveness of modern adults. Just as the Roman *coloni* had to pay to use the land they needed to survive, so also must most people today pay the owners of the processes, media, and capital necessary to create the extreme sensory stimulation that they need to feel alive.

It may not be readily apparent that spiritual capital constitutes a commons. What has really been appropriated here is a locus of attention. The capabilities of the human mind that I call spiritual capital do not exist in isolation; it is our upbringing, our nurture, our cultural surroundings that foster and direct them. Our ability to imagine and to obtain sensory fulfillment is to a great degree a collective ability, one today that we can no longer exercise from

---

6. Or she accepts no reality at all, discounting everything as just so many images and symbols. On the one hand, this allows her to "see through the bullshit." On the other hand, it leaves her cynical and jaded.

the freely available sources of mind and nature, but must purchase from their new owners.

The collective attention of the human race is a commons like the land or the air. Like them, it is a raw material of human creativity. To make a tool, to do any work, to do anything at all requires that one place attention on that task rather than on some other. The ubiquity of advertising and media in our society is a co-optation of the collective human attention, and a depletion of our divine bequest. On the road, everywhere my eyes turn, there is a billboard. On the subway, on the internet, on the street, commercial messages reach out to "capture" our attention. They infiltrate our very thoughts, our narratives, our inner dialog, and via these, our emotions, desires, and beliefs, turning all toward the making of product and profit. Our attention is hardly our own anymore, so easily do the powers of politics and commerce manipulate it.

After it has been so long manipulated, chopped up, habituated to intense stimuli, and jerked around from one lurid but empty object to another, our attention is so fragmented we cannot sustain it long enough to create anything independent of the programs that surround us. We lose our capacity to sustain thought, understand nuance, and put ourselves in another person's shoes. Susceptible to any simplistic narrative with immediate emotional appeal, we are easy targets not just for advertising, but for propaganda, demagoguery, and fascism. In various ways, all of these serve the money power.

THE STRIP-MINING OF COMMUNITY

The most important type of capital for purposes of this discussion is social capital. Social capital refers primarily to relationships and skills, the "services" that people once provided for themselves and each other in a gift economy, such as cooking, child care, health care, hospitality, entertainment, advice, and the growing of food, making of clothes, and building of houses. As recently as one or two generations ago, many of these functions were far less commoditized than they are today. When I was a child, most people I knew seldom ate at restaurants, and neighbors took care of each other's children after school. Technology has been instrumental in bringing human relationships into the realm of "services," just as it has brought deeper and more obscure pieces of the earth into the realm of goods. For example, the technology of the phonograph and radio helped turn music from something people made for themselves into something they paid for. Storage and transportation technologies have done the same for food processing. In general, the fine division of labor that accompanies technology has made us dependent on strangers for most of the things we use, and makes it unlikely that our neighbors depend on us for anything we produce. Economic ties thus become divorced from social ties, leaving us with little to offer our neighbors and little occasion to know them.

The monetization of social capital is the strip-mining of community. It should not be surprising that money is deeply implicated in the disintegration of community, because money is the epitome of the impersonal. Convert two distinct forests into money, and they become the same. Applied to cultures, the same principle is fast creating a global monoculture where every service is a paid service. When money mediates all our relationships, we too lose our uniqueness to become a standard consumer of standard goods and services, and a standard functionary performing other services. No personal economic relationships are important because we can always "pay someone else to do it." No wonder, strive as we might, we find it so hard to create community. No wonder we feel so insecure, so replaceable. It is all because of the conversion, driven, as we shall see, by interest, of the unique and sacred into the monetized and generic. In *The Ascent of Humanity* I wrote,

"We don't really need each other." ... What better description could there be of the loss of community in today's world? We don't really need each other. We don't need to know the person who grows, ships, and processes our food, makes our clothing, builds our house, creates our music, makes or fixes our car; we don't even need to know the person who takes care of our babies while we are at work. We are dependent on the role, but only incidentally on the person fulfilling that role. Whatever it is, we can just pay someone to do it (or pay someone else to do it) as long as we have money. And how do we get money? By performing some other specialized role that, more likely than not, amounts to someone paying us to do something for them ...

The necessities of life have been given over to specialists, leaving us with nothing meaningful to do (outside our own area of expertise) but to entertain ourselves. Meanwhile, whatever functions of daily living that remain to us are mostly solitary functions: driving places, buying things, paying bills, cooking convenience foods, doing housework. None of these demand the help of neighbors, relatives, or friends. We wish we were closer to our neighbors; we think of ourselves as friendly people who would gladly help them. But there is little to help them with. In our house-boxes, we are self-sufficient. Or rather, we are self-sufficient in relation to the people we know but dependent as never before on total strangers living thousands of miles away.

The commoditization of social relationships leaves us with nothing to do together but to consume. Joint consumption does nothing to build community because it requires no gifts. I think the oft-lamented vacuity of most social gatherings arises from the inchoate knowledge, "I don't need you." I don't need you to help me consume food, drink, drugs, or entertainment. Consumption calls upon no one's gifts, calls forth none of anyone's true being. Community and intimacy cannot come from joint consumption, but only from giving and cocreativity.

When libertarians invoke the sanctity of private property, they unintentionally create a need for the very Big Government they so despise. For in the absence of community bonds, the atomized individuals that remain depend on remote authority—a legally constituted state—for many of the social functions that community structures once fulfilled: security, dispute resolution, and the allocation of collective social capital. The propertization and privatization of the economic realm leaves us, to coin a phrase, helplessly independent—independent of anyone we know, and dependent on impersonal, coercive institutions that govern from afar.

When I ask people what is missing most from their lives, the most common answer is "community." But how can we build community when its building blocks—the things we do for each other—have all been converted into money? Community is woven from gifts. Unlike money or barter transactions, in which there are no obligations remaining after the transaction, gifts always imply future gifts. When we receive, we owe; gratitude is the knowledge of having received and the desire to give in turn. But what is there now to give? Not the necessities of life, not food, shelter, or clothing, not entertainment, not stories, not health care: everyone buys these. Hence the urge to get away from it all, to return to a more self-sufficient life where we build our own houses and grow our own food and make our own clothes, in community. Yet while there is value in this movement, I doubt that many people will start doing things the hard way again just in order to have community. There is another solution besides reversing the specialization of labor and the machine-based efficiency of the modern age, and it springs from the fact that money does not meet many of our needs at all. Very important needs go unmet today, and money, because of its impersonal nature, is incapable of meeting them. The community of the future will arise from the needs that money inherently cannot meet.

You can see now why I call money "the corpse of the commons." The conversion of natural, cultural, social, and spiritual capital into money is the fulfillment of its power, described by Richard Seaford, to homogenize all that it touches. "In reducing individuality to homogeneous impersonality," he writes, "the power of money resembles the power of death."[7] Indeed, when every forest has been converted into board feet, when every ecosystem has been paved over, when every human relationship has been replaced by a service, the very processes of planetary and social life will cease. All that will be left is cold, dead money, as forewarned by the myth of King Midas so many centuries ago. We will be dead—but very, very rich.

THE CREATION OF NEEDS

Economists would say that such things as phonographs and bulldozers and the rest of technology have enriched us, creating new goods and services that did not exist before. On a deep level,

---

7. Seaford, *Money and the Early Greek Mind*, 157.

though, the human needs these things meet are nothing new. They just meet them in a different way—a way that we must now pay for.

Consider telecommunications. Human beings do not have an abstract need for long-distance communication. We have a need to stay in contact with people with whom we share emotional and economic ties. In past times, these people were usually close by. A hunter-gatherer or fourteenth-century Russian peasant would have had little use for a telephone. Telephones began to meet a need only when other developments in technology and culture spread human beings farther apart and splintered extended families and local communities. So the basic need they meet is not something new under the sun.

Consider another technological offering, one to which my children, to my great consternation, seem irresistibly attracted: massively multiplayer online fantasy role-playing games. The need these meet is not anything new either. Preteens and teenagers have a strong need to go exploring, to have adventures, and to establish an identity via interactions with peers that reference this exploration and adventure. In past times, this happened in the actual outdoors. When I was a child we had nothing like the freedom of generations before us, as you might read about in *Tom Sawyer,* yet still my friends and I would sometimes wander for miles, to a creek or an unused quarry pit, an undeveloped hilltop, the train tracks. Today, one rarely finds groups of kids roaming around, when every bit of land is fenced and marked with no-trespassing signs, when society is obsessed with safety, and when children are overscheduled and driven to perform. Technology and culture have robbed children of something they deeply need—and then, in the form of video games, sold it back to them.

I remember the day I realized what was happening. I happened to watch an episode of the Pokémon television show, which is basically about three kids roaming around having magical adventures. These on-screen, fictitious, trademarked characters were having the magical adventures that real children once had but now must pay (via advertising) for the privilege of watching. As a result, GDP has grown. New "goods and services" (by definition, things that are part of the money economy) have been created, replacing functions that were once fulfilled for free.

A little reflection reveals that nearly every good and service available today meets needs that were once met for free. What about medical technology? Compare our own poor health with the marvelous health enjoyed by hunter-gatherers and primitive agriculturalists, and it is clear that we are purchasing, at great expense, our ability to physically function. Child care? Food processing? Transportation? The textile industry? Space does not permit me to analyze each of these for what necessities have been stolen and sold back to us. I will offer one more piece of evidence for my view: if the growth of money really were driving the technological and cultural meeting of new needs, then wouldn't we be more fulfilled than any humans before us?

Are people happier now, more fulfilled, for having films rather than tribal storytellers, MP3 players rather than gatherings around the piano? Are we happier eating mass-produced food rather than that from a neighbor's field or our own garden? Are people happier living in prefab units or McMansions than they were in old New England stone farmhouses or wigwams? Are we happier? Has any new need been met?

Even if it has not, I won't discard the entire corpus of technology, despite all the ruin it has wrought upon nature and humanity. In fact, the achievements of science and technology do meet important needs, needs that are key drivers of sacred economics. They include the need to explore, to play, to know, and to create what we in the New Economy movement call "really cool stuff." In a sacred economy, science, technology, and the specialization of labor that goes along with them will continue to be among the agents for the meeting of these needs. We can see this higher purpose of science and technology already, like a recessive gene that crops up irrepressibly in spite of its endless commercialization. It is in the heart of every true scientist and inventor: the spirit of wonder, excitement, and the thrill of novelty. Every institution of the old world has a counterpart in the new, the same note at another octave. We are not calling for a revolution that will eradicate the old and create the new from scratch. That kind of revolution has been tried before, with the same results each time, because that mentality is itself part of the old world. Sacred economics is part of a different kind of revolution entirely, a transformation and not a purge. In this revolution, the losers won't even realize they have lost.

Up until today, very few of the products of our economy and technology have served the aforementioned needs. Not only are our needs for play, exploration, and wonder underfulfilled, but great anxiety and struggle accompany even the meeting of our physical needs. This contradicts economists' assertion that even if no new needs have been met, technology and the division of labor allow us to meet existing needs more efficiently. A machine, it is said, can do the work of a thousand men; a computer can coordinate the work of a thousand machines. Accordingly, futurists since the eighteenth century have predicted an imminent age of leisure. That age has never arrived, and indeed has seemed in the last thirty-five years to recede even farther into the distance. Something obviously is not working.

One of the two primary assumptions of economics is that human beings normally act in their rational self-interest and that this self-interest corresponds to money. Two people will only make an exchange (e.g., buying something for money) if it benefits both to do so. The more exchanges that are happening, then, the more benefits are being had. Economists therefore associate money with Benthamite "utility"—that is, the good. That is one reason why economic growth is the unquestioned holy grail of economic policy—when the economy grows, the world's supposed goodness level rises. What politician wouldn't want to take credit for economic growth?

Economic logic says that when a new good or service comes into being, the fact that someone is willing to pay for it means that it must be to someone's benefit. In a certain narrow sense, this is true. If I steal your car keys, it may be to your benefit to buy them back from me. If I steal your land, it may be to your benefit to rent it back so you can survive. But to say that money transactions are evidence of an overall rise in utility is absurd; or rather, it assumes that the needs they meet were originally unmet. If we are merely paying for something once provided through self-sufficiency or the gift economy, then the logic of economic growth is faulty. Herein lies a hidden ideological motivation for the assumption that primitive life was, in Hobbes's words, "solitary, poor, nasty, brutish, and short." Such a past would justify the present, which actually bears all of Hobbes's qualities in various ways. What is life in the Great Indoors of suburbia, if not solitary? What is life in equatorial Africa, if not short?[8] And has any age rivaled the last century

---

8. Modern life is short, too: despite relatively long life spans, life seems short to a busy, hurried person.

in its nastiness and brutality? Perhaps the Hobbesian view that the past was a harsh survival struggle is an ideological projection of our own condition.

For the economy to grow, the realm of money-denominated goods and services must grow too. Money must meet more and more of our needs. Gross domestic product, after all, is defined as the sum total of the goods and services a nation produces. Only those exchanged for money count.

If I babysit your children for free, economists don't count it as a service or add it to GDP. It cannot be used to pay a financial debt; nor can I go to the supermarket and say, "I watched my neighbors' kids this morning, so please give me food." But if I open a day care center and charge you money, I have created a "service." GDP rises and, according to economists, society has become wealthier. I have grown the economy and raised the world's level of goodness. "Goods" are those things you pay money for. Money = Good. That has been the equation of our time.

The same is true if I cut down a forest and sell the timber. While it is still standing and inaccessible, it is not a good. It only becomes "good" when I build a logging road, hire labor, cut it down, and transport it to a buyer. I convert a forest to timber, a commodity, and GDP goes up. Similarly, if I create a new song and share it for free, GDP does not go up and society is not considered wealthier, but if I copyright it and sell it, it becomes a good. Or I can find a traditional society that uses herbs and shamanic techniques for healing, destroy their culture and make them dependent on pharmaceutical medicine that they must purchase, evict them from their land so they cannot be subsistence farmers and must buy food, and clear the land and hire them on a banana plantation—and I have made the world richer. I have brought various functions, relationships, and natural resources into the realm of money.

Any time someone pays for anything she once received as a gift or did herself, the world's "goodness" level rises. Each tree cut down and made into paper, each idea captured and made into intellectual property, each child who uses video games instead of creating worlds of the imagination, each human relationship turned into a paid service, depletes a bit of the natural, cultural, spiritual, and social commons and converts it into money.

It is true that it is more efficient (in terms of labor-hours) for day care professionals to care for three dozen kids than for a bunch of stay-at-home parents to do it themselves. It is also more efficient to farm thousand-acre fields with megatractors and chemicals than it is to raise the same amount of food on a hundred small holdings using hand tools. But all this efficiency has neither given us more leisure nor met any fundamentally new need. The efficiency ends up meeting the old needs in endless, obscene elaboration, eventually reaching the extreme of closets full of clothes and shoes that are barely worn before entering the landfill.

The limited character of human needs presented problems from the very beginning of the industrial era, appearing first in the textile industry. After all, how many garments does one person really need? The solution to the looming crisis of overproduction was to manipulate people into overfulfilling their need for clothes. Enter the fashion industry, which, in a surprisingly conscious and cynical way, encouraged would-be dandies to stay up with the fashions. Part of the reason that people embraced this is because clothing occupies a special place in all cultures, fulfilling various sacred, joyful, somber, and playful needs and contributing greatly to the deeper need for social identity. It is as natural to adorn our bodies as it is to spice our food. The point is that no new need was being fulfilled. More and more production is devoted toward meeting the same need, endlessly elaborated.

Moreover, the same industrialization that brought the mass production of textiles also caused the social disintegration that shattered traditional communities and made people susceptible to the fashion industry. I described this in a somewhat broader context in *The Ascent of Humanity:*

> To introduce consumerism to a previously isolated culture it is first necessary to destroy its sense of identity. Here's how: Disrupt its networks of reciprocity by introducing consumer items from the outside. Erode its self-esteem with glamorous images of the West. Demean its mythologies through missionary work and scientific education. Dismantle its traditional ways of transmitting local knowledge by introducing schooling with outside curricula. Destroy its language by providing that schooling in English or another national or world language. Truncate its ties to the land by importing cheap food to make local agriculture uneconomic. Then you will have created a people hungry for the right sneaker.

The crisis of overproduction that occurs when one need has been generally fulfilled is resolved by exporting it onto some other need. An equivalent way of looking at it is that one type after another of natural, social, cultural, and spiritual commonwealth is converted into property and money. When the social capital of clothesmaking (i.e., the skills and traditions and the means for their transmission) is turned into a commodity, and no one is making clothes outside the money economy any more, then it is time to sell even more clothes by destroying other identity-sustaining social structures.

Identity becomes a commodity, and clothes and other consumer items its proxy.

The social ecology of the gift—the shared skills, customs, and social structures that meet each other's needs—is just as rich a source of wealth, and bears just as many veins of treasure, as do the natural ecology and the earth underlying it. The question is, what happens when all of these forms of common capital are tapped out? What happens when there are no more fish to turn into seafood, no more forests to turn into paper, no more topsoil to turn into corn syrup, no longer anything people do for each other for free?

On the face of it, this should not be a crisis at all. Why must we keep growing? If all our needs are met with increasing efficiency, why can't we just work less? Why has the promised age of leisure never arrived? As we shall see, in our present money system, it will never arrive. No new technological wonder will be enough. The money system we have inherited will always compel us to choose growth over leisure.

One might say that money *has* met one need that was truly unmet before—the need for the human species to grow and to operate on a scale of millions or billions. Our need for food, music, stories, medicine, and so forth may be no more satisfied than in the Stone Age, but we can, for the first time, create things that require the coordinated efforts of millions of specialists around the globe. Money has facilitated the development of a metahuman organism of seven billion cells, the collective body of the human species. It is like a signaling molecule, coordinating the contributions of individuals and organizations toward purposes that no smaller grouping could ever achieve. All the needs that money has created or transferred from the personal to the standard and generic have been part of this organismic development. Even the fashion industry has been part of it, as a means for creating identity and a sense of belonging extending across vast social distances.

Like a multicellular organism, humanity as a collective being needs organs, subsystems, and the means to coordinate them. Money, along with symbolic culture, communication technology, education, and so forth, has been instrumental in developing these. It has also been like a growth hormone, both stimulating growth and governing the expression of that growth. Today, it seems, we are reaching the limits of growth, and therefore the end of humanity's childhood. All of our organs are fully formed; some, indeed, have outlived their usefulness and may revert to vestigial form. We are maturing. Perhaps we are about to turn our newfound creative power of billions towards its mature purpose. Perhaps, accordingly, we need a different kind of money, one that continues to coordinate the vastly complex metahuman organism but no longer compels it to grow.

THE MONEY POWER

All of the myriad forms of property today have one defining feature in common: all of them can be bought and sold for money. All are the equivalent of money, for whoever owns money can own any other form of capital and the productive power that goes along with it. And each of these forms, remember, arose from the commons, was once unowned by any person, and was eventually stripped from the commons and made property. The same thing that happened to land has happened to everything else and has brought the same concentration of wealth and power in the hands of those who own it. As the early Christian fathers, Proudhon, Marx, and George knew, it is immoral to rob someone of his property and then make him pay you to use it. Yet that is what happens any time you charge rent on land or interest on money. No accident, then, that nearly all world religions impose prohibitions on usury. Someone should not benefit from merely owning what existed before ownership, and money today is the embodiment of all that existed before ownership, the distilled essence of property.

However, the anti-interest money systems I will propose and describe in this book are not motivated by mere morality. Interest is more than just the proceeds of a crime, more even than the ongoing income from a crime already committed. It is also the engine of continued robbery; it is a force that compels us all, however kind in our intentions, into willing or unwilling complicity in the strip-mining of the earth.

In my travels, firstly my inward journeying and then as a speaker and writer, I have oft encountered a deep anguish and helplessness borne of the ubiquity of the world-devouring machine and of the near-impossibility of avoiding participation in it. To give one example among millions, people who rage against Wal-Mart still shop there, or at other stores equally a part of the global predation chain, because they feel they cannot afford to pay double the price or to do without. And what of the electricity that powers my house—coal ripped out of the tops of mountains? What of the gas that gets me places and gets deliveries to me if I go "off-grid"? I can minimize my participation in the world-devouring machine, but I cannot avoid it entirely. As people become aware that merely living in society means contributing to the evils of the world, they often go through a phase of desiring to find a completely isolated and self-sufficient intentional community—but what good does that do, while Rome burns? So what, if you are not contributing your little part to the pollution that is overwhelming the earth? It proceeds apace whether you live in the forest and eat roots and berries or in a suburb and eat food trucked in from California.[9] The desire for personal exculpation from the sins of society is a kind of fetish, akin to solar panels on a 4,000-square-foot house.

Laudable though the impulse may be, movements to boycott Wal-Mart or reform health care or education or politics or anything else quickly become exercises in futility as they run up against the money power. To make any impact at all feels like a grueling upstream swim, and as soon as we rest, some new outrage, some new horror sweeps us away again, some new stripping of nature, community, health, or spirit for the sake of money.

What, exactly, is this "money power"? It is not, as it sometimes may seem, an evil cabal of bankers controlling the world through the Bilderberg Council, the Trilateral Commission, and other instruments of the "Illuminati." In my travels and correspondence, I sometimes run into people who have read books by David Icke and others that make a persuasive case for an ancient global conspiracy dedicated to a "New World Order," symbolized by the all-seeing eye atop the pyramid, controlling every government and every institution, and run behind the scenes by a small, secret coterie of power-hungry monsters who count even the Rothschilds and Rockefellers among their puppets. I must be very naive, or very ignorant, not to comprehend the true nature of the problem.

While I confess to being naive, I am not ignorant. I have read much of this material and come away unsatisfied. While it is clear

---

9. Nonetheless, the efforts people are making to reduce their complicity in the wrecking of the world are very important on the level of ritual. Ritual consists of the manipulation of symbols in order to affect reality—even money is an implement of ritual—and therefore wield great practical power. So please don't allow my words to dissuade you from boycotting Wal-Mart. For a deeper discussion, see my essay "Rituals for Lover Earth" online, preferably after having read through Chapter 8 of this book.

that there is much more to such events as 9/11 and the Kennedy assassinations than we have been told, and that the financial industry, organized crime, and political power are closely interlinked, I find that generally speaking, conspiracy theories give too much credit to the ability of humans to successfully manage and control complex systems. Something mysterious is certainly going on, and the "coincidences" that people like Icke cite defy conventional explanation, but if you'll allow a moment's indulgence in metaphysics, I think ultimately what is happening is that our deep ideologies and belief systems, and their unconscious shadows, generate a matrix of synchronicities that looks very much like a conspiracy. It is in fact a conspiracy with no conspirators. Everyone is a puppet, but there are no puppet-masters.

Moreover, the appeal of conspiracy theories, which are usually nonfalsifiable, is just as much psychological as it is empirical. Conspiracy theories have a dark allure because they tap into our primal outrage and identify something onto which to channel it, something to blame and something to hate. Unfortunately, as numerous revolutionaries have discovered when they topple the oligarchs, our hatred is misplaced. The true culprit is much deeper and much more pervasive. It transcends conscious human agency, and even the bankers and oligarchs live under its thrall. The true culprit is the alien overlords that rule the world from their flying saucers. Just kidding.[10] The true culprit, the true puppet-master that manipulates our elites

---

10. Well, not entirely. The imputation of nefarious control to extraterrestrial or demonic entities encodes a valid insight: that the source of evil in our world is beyond conscious human agency. There are puppet-masters, but they are systems and ideologies, not people. As for extraterrestrials, I have trouble answering the question of whether I "believe in them." Perhaps the question of whether they "exist" smuggles in ontological assumptions that aren't true, especially that there is an objective backdrop in which things objectively either exist or do not exist. So usually I just say "yes."

from behind the scenes, is the money system itself: a credit-based, interest-driven system that arises from the ancient, rising tide of separation; that generates competition, polarization, and greed; that compels endless exponential growth; and, most importantly, that is coming to an end in our time as the fuel for that growth—social, natural, cultural, and spiritual capital—runs out.

The next few chapters describe this process and the dynamics of interest, reframing the current economic crisis as the culmination of a trend centuries in the making. Thus revealed, we can better understand how to create not just a new money system, but a new *kind* of money system, one that has the opposite effects of ours today: sharing instead of greed, equality instead of polarization, enrichment of the commons instead of its stripping, and sustainability instead of growth. As well, this new kind of money system will embody an even deeper shift that we see happening today, a shift in human identity toward a connected self, bound to all being in the circle of the gift. Any money that is part of this Reunion, this Great Turning, surely deserves to be called sacred.

CHAPTER 6

THE ECONOMICS OF USURY

In spite of the holy promises of people to banish war once and for all, in spite of the cry of millions "never again war" in spite of all the hopes for a better future I have this to say: If the present monetary system based on interest and compound interest remains in operation, I dare to predict today that it will take less than twenty-five years until we have a new and even worse war. I can foresee the coming development clearly. The present degree of technological advancement will quickly result in a record performance of industry. The buildup of capital will be fast in spite of the enormous losses during the war, and through the oversupply [of money] the interest rate will be lowered [until the money speculators refuse to lower their rates any further]. Money will then be hoarded [causing predictable deflation], economic activities will diminish, and increasing numbers of unemployed persons will roam the streets . . . within these discontented masses, wild, revolutionary ideas will arise and with it also the poisonous plant called "Super Nationalism" will proliferate. No country will understand the other, and the end can only be war again.

—Silvio Gesell (1918)

We are faced with a paradox. On the one hand money is properly a token of gratitude and trust, an agent of the meeting of gifts and needs, a facilitator of exchanges among those who otherwise could make none. As such it should make us all richer. Yet it does not.

Instead, it has brought insecurity, poverty, and the liquidation of our cultural and natural commons. Why?

The cause of these things lies deep within the very heart of today's money system. They are inherent in the ways money today is created and circulated, and the centerpiece of that system is usury, better known as interest. Usury is the very antithesis of the gift, for instead of giving to others when one has more than one needs, usury seeks to use the power of ownership to gain even more—to take from others rather than to give. And as we shall see, it is just as contrary to the gift in its effects as it is in its motivation.

Usury is built into the very fabric of money today, from the moment of its inception. Money originates when the Federal Reserve (or the ECB or other central bank) purchases interest-bearing securities (traditionally, Treasury notes, but more recently all kinds of mortgage-backed securities and other financial junk) on the open market. The Fed or central bank creates this new money out of thin air, at the stroke of a pen (or computer keyboard). For example, when the Fed bought $290 billion in mortgage-backed securities from Deutsche Bank in 2008, it didn't use existing money to do it; it created new money as an accounting entry in Deutsche Bank's account. This is the first step in money creation. Whatever the Fed or central bank purchases, it is always an interest-bearing security. In other words, it means that the money created accompanies a corresponding debt, and the debt is always for more than the amount of money created.

The kind of money just described is known as the "monetary base," or M0. It exists as bank reserves (and physical cash). The second step occurs when a bank makes a loan to a business or individual. Here again, new money is created as an accounting entry in the account of the borrower. When a bank issues a business a $1 million loan, it doesn't debit that amount from some other account; it simply writes that amount into existence. One million dollars of new money is created—and *more* than one million dollars of debt.[1] This new money is known as M1 or M2 (depending on what kind of account it is in). It is money that actually gets spent on goods and services, capital equipment, employment, and so forth.

The above description of how money is created, while widely accepted, is not fully accurate. I discuss the subtleties in the appendix. It will suffice for now because it is accurate enough for the purpose of describing the effects of usury.

AN ECONOMIC PARABLE

Usury both generates today's endemic scarcity and drives the world-devouring engine of perpetual growth. To explain how, I will begin with a parable created by the extraordinary economic visionary Bernard Lietaer entitled "The Eleventh Round," from his book *The Future of Money*.

> Once upon a time, in a small village in the Outback, people used barter for all their transactions. On every market day, people walked around with chickens, eggs, hams, and breads, and engaged in prolonged negotiations among themselves to exchange what they needed. At key periods of the year, like harvests or whenever someone's barn needed big repairs after a storm, people recalled the tradition of helping each other out

---

1. I have purposely left out issues such as margin reserve requirements, capital requirements, and so forth that limit a bank's ability to extend loans because they are not directly relevant to the discussion of interest in this chapter.

that they had brought from the old country. They knew that if they had a problem someday, others would aid them in return.

One market day, a stranger with shiny black shoes and an elegant white hat came by and observed the whole process with a sardonic smile. When he saw one farmer running around to corral the six chickens he wanted to exchange for a big ham, he could not refrain from laughing. "Poor people," he said, "so primitive." The farmer's wife overheard him and challenged the stranger, "Do you think you can do a better job handling chickens?" "Chickens, no," responded the stranger, "But there is a much better way to eliminate all that hassle." "Oh yes, how so?" asked the woman. "See that tree there?" the stranger replied. "Well, I will go wait there for one of you to bring me one large cowhide. Then have every family visit me. I'll explain the better way."

And so it happened. He took the cowhide, and cut perfect leather rounds in it, and put an elaborate and graceful little stamp on each round. Then he gave to each family 10 rounds, and explained that each represented the value of one chicken. "Now you can trade and bargain with the rounds instead of the unwieldy chickens," he explained.

It made sense. Everybody was impressed with the man with the shiny shoes and inspiring hat.

"Oh, by the way," he added after every family had received their 10 rounds, "in a year's time, I will come back and sit under that same tree. I want you to each bring me back 11 rounds. That 11th round is a token of appreciation for the technological improvement I just made possible in your lives." "But where will the 11th round come from?" asked the farmer with the six chickens. "You'll see," said the man with a reassuring smile.

Assuming that the population and its annual production

remain exactly the same during that next year, what do you think had to happen? Remember, that 11th round was never created. Therefore, bottom line, one of each 11 families will have to lose all its rounds, even if everybody managed their affairs well, in order to provide the 11th round to 10 others.

So when a storm threatened the crop of one of the families, people became less generous with their time to help bring it in before disaster struck. While it was much more convenient to exchange the rounds instead of the chickens on market days, the new game also had the unintended side effect of actively discouraging the spontaneous cooperation that was traditional in the village. Instead, the new money game was generating a systemic undertow of competition among all the participants.

This parable begins to show how competition, insecurity, and greed are woven into our economy because of interest. They can never be eliminated as long as the necessities of life are denominated in interest-money. But let us continue the story now to show how interest also creates an endless pressure for perpetual economic growth.

There are three primary ways Lietaer's story could end: default, growth in the money supply, or redistribution of wealth. One of each eleven families could go bankrupt and surrender their farms to the man in the hat (the banker), or he could procure another cowhide and make more currency, or the villagers could tar-and-feather the banker and refuse to repay the rounds. The same choices face any economy based on usury.

So imagine now that the villagers gather round the man in the hat and say, "Sir, could you please give us some additional rounds so that none of us need go bankrupt?"

The man says, "I will, but only to those who can assure me they will pay me back. Since each round is worth one chicken, I'll lend new rounds to people who have more chickens than the number of rounds they already owe me. That way, if they don't pay back the rounds, I can seize their chickens instead. Oh, and because I'm such a nice guy, I'll even create new rounds for people who don't have additional chickens right now, if they can persuade me that they will breed more chickens in the future. So show me your business plan! Show me that you are trustworthy (one villager can create 'credit reports' to help you do that). I'll lend at 10 percent—if you are a clever breeder, you can increase your flock by 20 percent per year, pay me back, and get rich yourself, too."

The villagers ask, "That sounds OK, but since you are creating the new rounds at 10 percent interest also, there still won't be enough to pay you back in the end."

"That won't be a problem," says the man. "You see, when that time arrives, I will have created even more rounds, and when those come due, I'll create yet more. I will always be willing to lend new rounds into existence. Of course, you'll have to produce more chickens, but as long as you keep increasing chicken production, there will never be a problem."

A child comes up to him and says, "Excuse me, sir, my family is sick, and we don't have enough rounds to buy food. Can you issue some new rounds to me?"

"I'm sorry," says the man, "but I cannot do that. You see, I only create rounds for those who are going to pay me back. Now, if your family has some chickens to pledge as collateral, or if you can prove you are able to work a little harder to breed more chickens, then I will be happy to give you the rounds."

With a few unfortunate exceptions, the system worked fine for a while. The villagers grew their flocks fast enough to obtain the additional rounds they needed to pay back the man in the hat. Some, for whatever reason—ill fortune or ineptitude—did indeed go bankrupt, and their more fortunate, more efficient neighbors took over their farms and hired them as labor. Overall, though, the flocks grew at 10 percent a year along with the money supply. The village and its flocks had grown so large that the man in the hat was joined by many others like him, all busily cutting out new rounds and issuing them to anyone with a good plan to breed more chickens.

From time to time, problems arose. For one, it became apparent that no one really needed all those chickens. "We're getting sick of eggs," the children complained. "Every room in the house has a feather bed now," complained the housewives. In order to keep consumption of chicken products growing, the villagers invented all kinds of devices. It became fashionable to buy a new feather mattress every month, and bigger houses to keep them in, and to have yards and yards full of chickens. Disputes arose with other villages that were settled with huge egg-throwing battles. "We must create demand for more chickens!" shouted the mayor, who was the brother-in-law of the man in the hat. "That way we will all continue to grow rich."

One day, a village old-timer noticed another problem. Whereas the fields around the village had once been green and fertile, now they were brown and foul. All the vegetation had been stripped away to plant grain to feed the chickens. The ponds and streams, once full of fish, were now cesspools of stinking manure. She said, "This has to stop! If we keep expanding our flocks, we will soon drown in chicken shit!"

The man in the hat pulled her aside and, in reassuring tones, told her, "Don't worry, there is another village down the road with plenty of fertile fields. The men of our village are planning to farm out chicken production to them. And if they don't agree ... well, we outnumber them. Anyway, you can't be serious about ending growth. Why, how would your neighbors pay off their debts? How would I be able to create new rounds? Even I would go bankrupt."

And so, one by one, all the villages turned to stinking cesspools surrounding enormous flocks of chickens that no one really needed, and the villages fought each other for the few remaining green spaces that could support a few more years of growth. Yet despite their best efforts to maintain growth, its pace began to slow. As growth slowed, debt began to rise in proportion to income, until many people spent all their available rounds just paying off the man in the hat. Many went bankrupt and had to work at subsistence wages for employers who themselves could barely meet their obligations to the man in the hat. There were fewer and fewer people who could afford to buy chicken products, making it even harder to maintain demand and growth. Amid an environment-wrecking superabundance of chickens, more and more people had barely enough on which to live, leading to the paradox of scarcity amidst abundance.

And that is where things stand today.

THE GROWTH IMPERATIVE

I hope it is clear how this story maps onto the real economy. Because of interest, at any given time the amount of money owed is greater than the amount of money already existing. To make new money to keep the whole system going, we have to breed more chickens—in other words, we have to create more "goods and services." The principal way of doing so is to begin selling something that was once free. It is to convert forests into timber, music into product, ideas into intellectual property, social reciprocity into paid services.

Abetted by technology, the commodification of formerly non-monetary goods and services has accelerated over the last few centuries, to the point today where very little is left outside the money realm. The vast commons, whether of land or of culture, has been cordoned off and sold—all to keep pace with the exponential growth of money. This is the deep reason why we convert forests to timber, songs to intellectual property, and so on. It is why two-thirds of all American meals are now prepared outside the home. It is why herbal folk remedies have given way to pharmaceutical medicines, why child care has become a paid service, why drinking water has been the number-one growth category in beverage sales.

The imperative of perpetual growth implicit in interest-based money is what drives the relentless conversion of life, world, and spirit into money. Completing the vicious circle, the more of life we convert into money, the more we need money to live. Usury, not money, is the proverbial root of all evil.

Let's examine how this happens in a bit more detail. Just like the man in the hat, a bank or any other lender will ordinarily agree to lend you money only if there is a reasonable expectation you will pay it back. This expectation could be based on expected future income, collateral, or a good credit rating. Serious consequences for default enforce this expectation. The repayment of debt depends not only on the ability to do so, but on various forms of social, economic, and legal pressure. Courts can order the seizure of assets to meet contractual debt obligations, and, while we don't have debtors' prisons any more,[2] delinquent debtors suffer endless harassment at the hands of collection agencies, as well as denial of apartments, employment, and security clearances. Many people also feel a moral obligation to repay their debts. This is natural: in gift economies as well, those who have received are under social and moral pressure to give.

The money to repay principle and interest comes from selling goods and services, or it could come from further borrowing. Any time you use money, you are essentially guaranteeing, "I have performed a service or provided a good of equivalent value to the one I am buying." Any time you borrow money, you are saying that you will provide an equivalent good/service in the future. In theory, this should be to everyone's benefit, because it allows the connecting of gifts and needs not only across space and profession, but across time as well. Credit-based money exchanges goods now for goods in the future. This is not inconsistent with gift principles. I receive now; later I give.

The problems start with interest. Because interest-bearing debt accompanies all new money, at any given time, the amount of debt exceeds the amount of money in existence. The insufficiency of money drives us into competition with each other and consigns us to a constant, built-in state of scarcity. It is like a game of musical chairs, with never enough room for anyone to be secure. Debt-pressure is endemic to the system. While some may repay their debts, overall the system requires a general and growing state of indebtedness.

---

2. Actually, they are making a covert comeback in some U.S. states as people are incarcerated for failing to heed court summons for nonpayment of debts. See White, "America's New Debtor Prison."

Constant, underlying debt-pressure means there will always be people who are insecure or desperate—people under pressure to survive, ready to cut down the last forest, catch the last fish, sell someone a sneaker, liquidate whatever social, natural, cultural, or spiritual capital is still available. There can never be a time when we reach "enough" because in an interest-based debt system, credit exchanges not just "goods now for goods in the future," but goods now for *more* goods in the future. To service debt or just to live, either you take existing wealth from someone else (hence, competition) or you create "new" wealth by drawing from the commons.

Here is a concrete example to illustrate how this works. Suppose you go to the bank and say, "Mr. Banker, I would like a $1 million loan so I can buy this forest to protect it from logging. I won't generate any income from the forest that way, so I won't be able to pay you interest. But if you need the money back, I could sell the forest and pay you back the million dollars." Unfortunately, the banker will have to decline your proposal, even if her heart wants to say yes. But if you go to the bank and say, "I'd like a million dollars to purchase this forest, lease bulldozers, clear-cut it, and sell the timber for a total of $2 million, out of which I'll pay you 12 percent interest and make a tidy profit for myself, too," then an astute banker will agree to your proposal. In the former instance, no new goods and services are created, so no money is made available. Money goes toward those who create new goods and services. This is why there are many paying jobs to be had doing things that are complicit in the conversion of natural and social capital into money, and few jobs to be had reclaiming the commons and protecting natural and cultural treasures.

Generalized, the relentless pressure on debtors to provide goods and services is an organic pressure toward economic growth (defined as growth in total goods and services exchanged for money). Here's another way to see it: because debt is always greater than money supply, the creation of money creates a future need for even more money. The amount of money must grow over time; new money goes to those who will produce goods and services; therefore, the volume of goods and services must grow over time as well.

So it is not just that the apparent limitlessness of money, observed since ancient Greek times, allows us to believe in the possibility of eternal growth. In fact, our money system necessitates and compels that growth. Most economists consider this endemic growth-pressure to be a good thing. They say that it creates a motivation to innovate, to progress, to meet more needs with ever-increasing efficiency. An interest-based economy is fundamentally, unalterably a growth economy, and except for a very radical fringe, most economists and probably all policy makers see economic growth as a demonstration of success.

The whole system of interest-bearing money works fine as long as the volume of goods and services exchanged for money keeps pace with its growth. But what happens if it doesn't? What happens, in other words, if the rate of economic growth is lower than the rate of interest? Like the people in the parable, we must consider this in a world that appears to be reaching the limits of growth.

THE CONCENTRATION OF WEALTH

Because economic growth is almost *always* lower than the rate of interest, what generally happens in such conditions is no mystery. If debtors cannot, in aggregate, make interest payments from the new wealth they create, they must turn over more and more of their existing wealth to their creditors and/or pledge a greater and greater proportion of their current and future income to debt service. When their assets and discretionary income are exhausted, they must go into default. It can be no other way, when the average return on investment is lower than the average interest rate paid to obtain the capital invested. Defaults are inevitable for a certain proportion of borrowers.

In theory at least, defaults are not necessarily a bad thing: they bring negative consequences for decisions that don't further the general good—that is, that don't result in more efficient production of goods that people want. Lenders will be cautious not to lend to someone who is unlikely to contribute to the economy, and borrowers will be under pressure to act in ways that do contribute to the economy. Even in a zero-interest system, people might default if they make dumb decisions, but there wouldn't be a built-in, organic *necessity* for defaults.

Aside from economists, no one likes defaults—least of all creditors, since their money disappears. One way to prevent a default, at least temporarily, is to lend the borrower even more money so she can continue making payments on the original loan. This might be justified if the borrower is facing a temporary difficulty or if there is reason to believe that enough higher productivity is around the corner to pay back all the loans. But often, lenders will throw in good money after bad just because they don't want to write down the losses from defaults, which could indeed send them into bankruptcy themselves. As long as the borrower is still making payments, the lender can pretend that everything is normal.

This is essentially the situation the world economy has occupied for the last several years. After years, or even decades, of interest rates far exceeding economic growth, with no compensatory rise in defaults, we face an enormous debt overhang. The government, at the behest of the financial industry (i.e., the creditors, the owners of money), has done its best to prevent defaults and keep the full value of the debts on the books, hoping that renewed economic growth will allow them to continue to be serviced.[3] We will "grow our way out of debt," they hope.

At the political level, then, the same pressure exists to create "economic growth" as it does on the level of the individual or business. The debtor is under pressure to sell something, if only his labor, in order to obtain money to pay debt. That is essentially what growth-friendly policies do as well—they make this "selling something" easier; that is, they facilitate the conversion of natural, social, and other capital into money. When we relax pollution controls, we ease the conversion of the life-sustaining atmosphere into money. When we subsidize roads into old-growth forests, we ease the conversion of ecosystems into money. When the International Monetary Fund (IMF) pressures governments to privatize social services and cut spending, it pushes the conversion of social capital into money.

That is why, in America, Democrats and Republicans are equally eager to "open new markets," "enforce intellectual property rights," and so on. That is also why any item of the commons that is unavailable to exploitation, such as oil in the Alaskan Wildlife Refuge, local food economies protected by tariffs, or nature preserves in Africa, must endure constant assault from politicians, corporations, or poachers. If the money realm stops growing, then the middle passage between defaults and polarization of wealth narrows to nothing, resulting in social unrest and, eventually, revolution.

---

3. Even after it is obvious that these debt-based assets are junk and the debts will never be repaid, the authorities do their best to hide this fact and maintain them at face value.

Without growth, there is no other alternative when debts increase exponentially in a finite world.

If this growth, this conversion of commonwealth into money, happens at a rate faster than the rate of interest, then everything is fine (at least from the financial perspective, if not the human or ecological perspective). If there is enough demand for chickens and enough natural resources to feed them, villagers can borrow at 10 percent to increase their chicken flock by 20 percent. To use conventional language, capital investment brings a return in excess of the cost of capital; therefore, the borrower gains wealth beyond the portion that goes to the creditor. Such was the case in frontier days, when there was plenty of the unowned ripe for the taking. Such is still the case in a society where social relationships are not fully monetized—in economic parlance this is called an "undeveloped market." Only with economic growth can "all boats rise"—the creditors get richer and richer, and the borrowers can prosper as well.

But even in good times, growth is rarely fast enough to keep pace with interest. Imagine now that the villagers can only increase their flocks by 5 percent a year. Instead of paying a portion of new growth to the bankers, now they have to pay (on average) *all* of it, plus a portion of their existing wealth and/or future earnings. Concentration of wealth—both income and assets—is an inescapable corollary of debt growing faster than goods and services.

Economic thinkers since the time of Aristotle have recognized the essential problem. Aristotle observed that since money is "barren" (i.e., it does not leave offspring like cattle or wheat do), it is unjust to lend it at interest. The resulting concentration of wealth had been seen many times already by 350 BCE, and it would happen many times thereafter. It happened again in Roman times. As long as the empire was expanding rapidly, acquiring new lands and new tribute, everything worked passably well, and there was no extreme concentration of wealth. It was only when the growth of the empire slowed that concentration of wealth intensified and the once-extensive class of small farmers, the backbone of the legions, entered debt peonage. It was not long before the empire became a slave economy.

I need not belabor the parallels between Rome and the world today. As growth has slowed, many today, both individuals and nations, are entering a state similar to Roman debt peonage. A larger and larger proportion of income goes toward the servicing of debt, and when that does not suffice, preexisting assets are collateralized and then seized until there are none left. Thus it is that U.S. home equity has declined without interruption for half a century, from 85 percent in 1950 to about 40 percent today (including the one-third who own their houses free and clear). In other words, people don't own their own homes anymore. Most people I know don't own their own cars either but essentially rent them from banks via auto loans. Even corporations labor under an unprecedented degree of leverage, so that a large proportion of their revenue goes to banks and bondholders. The same is true of most nations, with their ballooning debt-to-GDP ratios. On every level we are, increasingly, slaves to debt, the fruits of our labors going to our creditors.

Even if you carry no debt, interest costs factor into the price of nearly everything you buy. For example, around 10 percent of U.S. government spending (and tax dollars) is devoted to interest on the national debt. If you rent your home, most of the rental cost goes to cover the landlord's highest expense—the mortgage on the property. When you eat a meal at a restaurant, the prices reflect in part the cost of capital for the restaurateur. Moreover, the costs of the restaurant's electricity, food supply, and rent also include the interest that *those* suppliers pay on capital, too, and so on down the line. All of this money is a kind of a tribute, a tax on everything we buy, that goes to the owners of money.

Interest comprises about six components: a risk premium, the cost of making a loan, an inflation premium, a liquidity premium, a maturation premium, and a zero-risk interest premium.[4] A more sophisticated discussion of the effects of interest might distinguish among these components, and conclude that only the latter three— and particularly the last—are usurious. Without them, concentration of wealth is no longer a given because that portion of the money doesn't stay in the hands of the lenders. (Growth pressure would still exist, though.) In our present system, however, all six contribute to prevailing interest rates. That means that those who have money can increase their wealth simply by virtue of having money. Unless borrowers can increase their wealth just as fast, which is only possible in an expanding economy, then wealth will concentrate in the hands of the lenders.

Let me put it simply: a portion of the interest rate says, "I have money and you need it, so I am going to charge you for access to it—just because I can, just because I have it, and you don't." In order to avoid polarization of wealth, this portion must be lower than the economic growth rate; otherwise, the mere ownership of

---

4. Actually, interest doesn't consist of "components"—this is an analytic fiction—but we can pretend it does. Most authorities list only three or five components of interest. I won't offer definitions here—you can look them up yourself—except for the most relevant, the zero-risk interest premium. That is equivalent to the rate on short-term U.S. government securities (T-bills), which have essentially zero risk and full liquidity. One might say that there is risk here too, but if things unravel to the point where the U.S. government is incapable of printing money, then no asset class would be safe.

money allows one to increase wealth faster than the average marginal efficiency of productive capital investment. In other words, you get rich faster by owning rather than producing. In practice, this is nearly *always* the case, because when economic growth speeds up, the authorities push interest rates higher. The rationale is to prevent inflation, but it is also a device to keep increasing the wealth and power of the owners of money.[5] Absent redistributive measures, the concentration of wealth intensifies through good times and bad.

As a general rule, the more money you have, the less urgent you are to spend it. Ever since the time of ancient Greece, people have therefore had what Keynes called a "liquidity preference": a preference for money over goods, except when goods are urgently needed. This preference is inevitable when money becomes a universal means and end. Interest reinforces liquidity preference, encouraging those who already have money to keep it. Those who need money *now* must pay those who do not, for the use of their money. This payment—interest on the loan—must come from future earnings. This is another way to understand how interest siphons money from the poor to the rich.

One might be able to justify paying interest on long-term, illiquid, risky investments, for such interest is actually a kind of compensation for forgoing liquidity. It is in keeping with gift principles, in that when you give a gift you often receive a greater gift in return (but not always and never with absolute assurance; hence, risk). But in the present system, even government-insured demand deposits

---

5. The new means of keeping interest rates above growth is the Fed's new power to offer interest on bank reserves. Currently at near zero, the Fed plans to raise these rates when the economy starts growing (see, e.g., Keister and McAndrews, "Why Are Banks Holding So Many Excess Reserves?"). This will ensure that any new wealth created through economic growth will accrue to the banks and bondholders who benefited from the Fed's liquidity facility giveaways.

and short-term risk-free government securities bear interest, allowing "investors" to profit while essentially keeping the money for themselves. This risk-free component is added as a hidden premium to all other loans, ensuring that those who own will own more and more.[6]

The dual pressures I have described—toward growth of the money realm, and toward the polarization of wealth—are two aspects of the same force. Either money grows by devouring the nonmonetized realm, or it cannibalizes itself. As the former is exhausted, the pressure of the latter increases, and concentration of wealth escalates. When that happens, another pressure arises to rescue the system: redistribution of wealth. After all, ever-increasing polarization of wealth and misery is not sustainable.

WEALTH REDISTRIBUTION AND CLASS WAR

Without wealth redistribution, social chaos is unavoidable in an interest-bearing, debt-based money system, especially when growth slows. Nonetheless, wealth redistribution always happens against the resistance of the wealthy, for it is their wealth that is being redistributed. Economic policy therefore reflects a balancing act

---

6. The situation has grown far worse in recent years, as the category of risk-free investments has expanded to include all kinds of financial junk that the government has decided to back up. By ensuring the solvency of risk-taking financial institutions and the liquidity of their financial offerings, the government has effectively increased the risk-free rewards of owning money and accelerated the concentration of wealth. No longer is the Fed Funds rate or T-bill rate the benchmark of risk-free interest. The concept of moral hazard that has come up in the context of "too big to fail" financial institutions isn't just a moral issue. When risky, high-interest bets are not actually risky, then those with the money to make such bets will increase their wealth far faster than (and at the expense of) everyone else. Moral hazard is a shortcut to extreme concentration of wealth.

between the redistribution and preservation of wealth, tending over time toward the minimum amount of redistribution necessary to maintain social order.

Traditionally, liberal governments seek to ameliorate concentration of wealth with redistributive policies such as progressive income taxes, estate taxes, social welfare programs, high minimum wages, universal health care, free higher education, and other social programs. These policies are redistributive because while the taxes fall disproportionately on the wealthy, the expenditures and programs benefit all equally, or even favor the poor. They counteract the natural tendency toward the concentration of wealth in an interest-based system. In the short term at least, they also run counter to the interests of the wealthy, which is why, in the present conservative political climate, such policies are characterized as class warfare.

In opposing redistributive policies, conservative governments seem to see concentration of wealth as a good thing. You might too, if you are wealthy, because concentration of wealth means more you for and less for everyone else. Hired help is cheaper. Your relative wealth, power, and privilege are greater.[7] Governments serving the (short-term) interests of the wealthy therefore advocate the opposite of the aforementioned distributive policies: flat-rate income taxes, reduction of estate taxes, curtailment of social programs, privatized health care, and so forth.

In the 1930s, the United States and many other countries faced a choice: either redistribute wealth gently through social spending

---

7. The conservative argument that putting money in the hands of the wealthy will spur increased investment, more jobs, and prosperity for all holds only if the rate of return on capital so invested exceeds the prevailing interest rate on risk-free financial investment. As the relentless concentration of wealth in the absence of redistribution demonstrates, such circumstances are rare, and they will become rarer if not extinct as we near the limits of growth.

and taxing the rich, or let the concentration of wealth proceed to the point of revolution and violent redistribution. By the 1950s, most countries had adopted the social compromise forged in the New Deal: the rich got to stay on top, but they had to give up through taxation an amount offsetting the profits of ownership of capital. The compromise worked for a while, as long as growth stayed high as it did through the early 1970s.

However, even this gentle solution bears many undesirable consequences. High income taxes penalize those who earn a lot rather than those who merely own a lot. They also set up an unending battle between tax authorities and citizens, who usually end up finding ways to avoid paying at least some of their taxes, employing tens of thousands of lawyers and accountants in the process. Is this a good use of our human resources? Moreover, it is a system in which we are giving with one hand to the owners of money and taking away with the other.

In an interest-based system, class war is inevitable, whether in muted or explicit form. The short-term interests of the holders of wealth oppose the interests of the debtor class. At the present writing, the balance has swung to the wealthy, as their political representatives have dismantled the mosaic of redistributive social programs assembled in the 1930s in most Western countries. For a while, in the post–World War II era, high growth obscured the inherency of class warfare, but that era is over. Until the money system undergoes a fundamental change, we can expect class warfare to intensify in coming years. This book aims to change the basic ground rules and remove the basis of class warfare entirely.

As the social contract forged in the 1930s breaks down and debt levels reach crisis proportions, more radical measures may become necessary. In ancient times, some societies addressed the polarization of wealth with a periodic nullification of debts. Examples include the Solonic *Seisachtheia,* the "shaking off of burdens," in which debts were canceled and debt peonage abolished, and the jubilee of the ancient Hebrews. "At the end of every seven years thou shalt make a release. And this is the manner of the release: Every creditor that lendeth ought unto his neighbor shall release it; he shall not exact it of his neighbor, or of his brother; because it is called the Lord's release" (Deuteronomy 15:1–2). Both of these ancient practices were much more radical than bankruptcy because the debtor got to keep his possessions and collateral. Under Solon, lands were even restored to their original owners.

A more recent example of debt nullification has been the partial annulment of the foreign debts of impoverished, disaster-stricken nations. For example, the IMF, World Bank, and Inter-American Development Bank canceled Haiti's foreign debt in 2008. A broader movement has existed for decades to cancel Third World debt generally but so far has gained little traction.

A related form of redistribution is bankruptcy, in which a debtor is released from obligation, usually after the forfeiture to creditors of most of his property. This is nonetheless a nominal transfer of wealth from creditor to debtor, since the amount of the property is less than the debt owed. In recent times, it has become much more difficult in the United States to declare true personal bankruptcy, as the laws (rewritten at the behest of credit card issuers) now force the debtor onto a payment plan that assigns a portion of her income to the creditor far into the future.[8] Increasingly, debts become inescapable, a lifelong claim on the labor of the debtor, who occupies a state

---

8. Moreover, some types of debts, such as student loans and tax debts, cannot be discharged through bankruptcy.

of peonage. Unlike the *Seisachtheia* and Jubilee, bankruptcy transfers assets to the creditor, who then controls both physical and financial capital. The former debtor has little choice but to go into debt again. Bankruptcies are a mere hiccup in the concentration of wealth.

More extreme is outright debt repudiation—refusal to pay a debt or transfer collateral to the creditor. Ordinarily, of course, the creditor can sue and employ the force of the state to seize the debtor's property. Only when the legal system and the legitimacy of the state begin to fall apart is personal debt repudiation possible.[9] Such unraveling reveals money and property as the social conventions that they are. Stripped of all that is based on the conventional interpretation of symbols, Warren Buffett is no wealthier than I am, except maybe his house is bigger. To the extent that it is his because of a deed, even that is a matter of convention.

At the present writing, debt repudiation is not much of an option for private citizens. For sovereign nations it would seem to be a different matter entirely. In theory, countries with a resilient domestic economy and resources to barter with neighbors can simply default on their sovereign debts. In practice, they rarely do. Rulers, democratic or otherwise, usually ally themselves with the global financial establishment and receive rich rewards for doing so. If they defy it, they face all kinds of hostility. The press turns against them; the bond markets turn against them; they get labeled as "irresponsible," "leftist," or "undemocratic"; their political opposition receives support from the global powers that

---

9. There are signs of the beginnings of such an unraveling, in the U.S. mortgage documentation crisis of 2010. Here, the web of agreements that constitutes a mortgage came under question. Mortgages had been split into so many pieces that it became difficult to prove who actually owned the property. The corpus of contracts, laws, regulations, and documentation practices began to crumble under the weight of its own complexity.

be; they might even find themselves the target of a coup or invasion. Any government that resists the conversion of its social and natural capital into money is pressured and punished. That is what happened in Haiti when Aristide resisted neoliberal policies and was overthrown in a coup in 1991 and again in 2004; it happened in Honduras in 2009; it has happened all over the world, hundreds and hundreds of times. (It failed in Cuba and more recently in Venezuela, which has so far escaped the invasion stage.) Most recently, in October 2010 a coup barely failed in Ecuador as well—Ecuador, the country that repudiated $3.9 billion in 2008 and subsequently restructured it at 35 cents on the dollar. Such is the fate of any nation that resists the debt regime.

Ex-economist John Perkins describes the basic strategy in *Confessions of an Economic Hit Man:* first bribes to rulers, then threats, then a coup, then, if all else fails, an invasion. The goal is to get the country to accept and make payments on loans—to go into debt and stay there. Whether for individuals or nations, the debt often starts out with a megaproject—an airport or road system or skyscraper, a home renovation or college education—that promises great future rewards but actually enriches outside powers and springs the debt trap. In the old days, military power and forced tribute were the instruments of empire; today it is debt. Debt forces nations and individuals to devote their productivity toward money. Individuals compromise their dreams and work at jobs to keep up with their debts. Nations convert subsistence agriculture and local self-sufficiency, which do not generate foreign exchange, into export commodity crops and sweatshop production, which do.[10] Haiti has

---

10. It is no accident that World Bank policy permits agricultural loans only for the development of export crops. Crops that are consumed domestically do not generate foreign exchange with which to service the loans.

been in debt since 1825, when it was forced to compensate France for the property (i.e., slaves) lost in the slave revolt of 1804. When will it pay off its debt? Never.[11] When will any of the Third World pay off its debt and devote its productivity to its own people? Never. When will most of you pay off your student loans, credit cards, and mortgages? Never.

Nonetheless, whether on the sovereign or personal level, the time of debt repudiation may be closer than we think. The legitimacy of the status quo is wearing thin, and when just a few debtors repudiate their debt, the rest will follow suit. There is even a sound legal basis for repudiation: the principle of odious debt, which says that fraudulently incurred debts are invalid. Nations can dispute debts incurred by dictators who colluded with lenders to enrich themselves and their cronies and built useless megaprojects that didn't serve the nation. Individuals can dispute consumer and mortgage loans sold them through deceptive lending practices. Perhaps a time is soon coming when we will shake off our burdens.

INFLATION

A final way to redistribute wealth is through inflation. On the face of it, inflation is a covert, partial form of debt annulment because it allows debts to be repaid in currency that is less valuable than it was at the time of the original loan. It is an equalizing force, reducing the value of both money and debt over time. However, matters are not as simple as they might seem. For one thing, inflation is usually accompanied by rising interest rates, both because monetary

---

11. Since the writing of this chapter, Haiti's foreign debt was annulled by a world sympathetic to its plight following the earthquake. Now the country has uncommitted income and assets—perfect targets for collateralization as the basis for renewed debt.

authorities raise rates to "combat inflation" and because potential lenders would rather invest in inflation-proof commodities than lend their money at interest below the inflation rate.[12]

Standard economics says inflation results from an increase in the money supply without a corresponding increase in the supply of goods. How, then, to increase the money supply? In 2008–2009, the Federal Reserve cut interest rates to near zero and vastly increased the monetary base without causing any appreciable inflation. That was because the banks did not increase lending, which puts money in the hands of people and businesses who would spend it. Instead, all of the new money sat as excess bank reserves or sloshed into equities markets; hence the rise in stock prices from March to August 2009.[13]

It is no wonder, given the lack of creditworthy borrowers and economic growth, that low interest rates have done little to spur lending. Even if the Fed bought every treasury bond on the market, increasing the monetary base tenfold, inflation still might not result. To have inflation, the money must be in the hands of people who will spend it. Is money that no one spends still money? Is money a miser buries in a hole and forgets still money?[14] Our Newtonian-Cartesian intuitions see money as a thing; actually, it is a relationship. When it is concentrated in few hands, we become less related, less connected to the things that sustain and enrich life.

The Fed's bailout programs mostly put money into the hands of

---

12. Moreover, many loans today have variable interest rates, often indexed to inflation (there are now even inflation-indexed treasury bonds.)

13. Moreover, many loans today have variable interest rates, often indexed to inflation (there are now even inflation-indexed treasury bonds.)

14. Economists try to deal with this question through the concept of "velocity of money." As the Appendix describes, the distinction between money supply and money velocity breaks down under close scrutiny.

the banks, where it has remained. In times of economic recession, to get money to people who will spend it, it is necessary to bypass the private credit-creation process that says, "Thou shalt have access to money only if you will produce even more of it." The main way to do that is through fiscal stimulus—that is, government spending. Such spending is indeed potentially inflationary. Why is inflation bad? No one likes to see rising prices, but if incomes are rising just as fast, what harm is done? The harm is done only to people who have savings; those who have debts actually benefit. What ordinary people fear is price inflation without wage inflation. If both prices and wages rise, then inflation is essentially a tax on idle money, redistributing wealth away from the wealthy and counteracting the effects of interest.[15] We will return later to this beneficial aspect of inflation when we consider negative-interest money systems.

Standard theory says that government can fund inflationary spending either through taxation or deficit spending. Why would tax-funded spending be inflationary? After all, it just takes money from some people and gives it to others. It is inflationary only if it takes from the rich and gives to the poor—to those who will spend it quickly. By the same token, deficit spending is only inflationary if the money goes to those who will spend it and not, for example, to large banks. In either case, inflation is more a consequence or symptom of wealth redistribution than a means to achieve it.[16]

---

15. There are some other negative effects of inflation, such as "menu costs" (from the need to keep changing prices), accounting difficulties, and others. In the case of very high inflation—above the carry cost of commodities—it can result in hoarding. These considerations play a role in envisioning negative-interest money systems.

16. The only kind of inflation that does not result from wealth redistribution arises from shortages of goods caused by war or embargo. In this scenario, which some-times leads to hyperinflation, there is no equalizing effect since the rich simply hoard inflation-proof commodities.

Inflation, then, cannot be seen as separate from more basic forms of wealth redistribution. It is no accident that political conservatives, traditionally guardians of the wealthy, are the keenest "deficit hawks." They oppose deficit spending, which tends to put money in the hands of those who owe, not those who own. Failing that, once deficit spending has already happened, they argue for retrenchment, the raising of interest rates and the repayment of public debts, which is essentially wealth redistribution in reverse. Invoking the specter of inflation, they make their arguments even when there is no sign whatever of actual inflation.

In principle, any government with a sovereign currency can create unlimited amounts of money without need for taxation, simply by printing it or forcing the central bank to buy zero-interest bonds. Yes, it would be inflationary—wages and prices would rise, and the relative worth of stored wealth would fall. That governments instead use the mechanism of interest-bearing bonds to create money is a key indicator of the nature of our money system. Here, at the very heart of a government's sovereign powers, a tribute to the owners of money is rendered.

Why should government pay interest to the wealthy for the sovereign privilege of issuing currency? Since ancient times, the right to issue coinage was considered a sacred or political function that established a locus of social power. It is clear where that power rests today. "Permit me to issue and control the money of a nation, and I care not who makes its laws," said Meyer Rothschild. Today, money serves private wealth. That indeed is the fundamental principle of usury. Yet the age of usury is coming to an end; soon, money shall serve another master.

MORE FOR YOU IS LESS FOR ME

The systemic causes of the greed, competition, and anxiety so prevalent today contradict some of the New Age teachings I regularly come across—that "Money is just a form of energy," that "Everyone can have monetary abundance if they simply adopt an attitude of abundance." When New Age teachers tell us to "release our limiting beliefs around money," to "shed the mentality of scarcity," to "open to the flow of abundance," or to become rich through the power of positive thinking, they are ignoring an important issue. Their ideas draw from a valid source: the realization that the scarcity of our world is an artifact of our collective beliefs, and not the fundamental reality; however, they are inherently inconsistent with the money system we have today.

Here is a well-articulated example of this kind of thinking, from *The Soul of Money* by Lynn Twist:

> Money itself isn't bad or good, money itself doesn't have power or not have power. It is our interpretation of money, our interaction with it, where the real mischief is and where we find the real opportunity for self-discovery and personal transformation.[17]

Lynn Twist is a visionary philanthropist who has inspired many to use money for good. But can you imagine how these words might sound to someone who is destitute for want of money? When I was broke a couple years ago, I remember feeling annoyed at well-meaning spiritual friends who told me my problem was "an attitude of scarcity." When the economy of an entire country like Latvia or Greece collapses and millions go bankrupt, shall we blame it all on their attitudes? What about poor, hungry children—do they have scarcity mentality too?

---

17. Twist, 19.

Later in the book, Twist describes toxic scarcity attitudes as follows: "It's like the child's game of musical chairs, with one seat short of the number of people playing. Your focus is on not losing and not being the one who ends up at the end of the scramble without a seat."[18]

But as I have described, the money system *is* a game of musical chairs, a mad scramble in which some are necessarily left out. On a deep level, though, Twist is right. She is right insofar as the money system is an outgrowth of our attitude of scarcity—an attitude that rests on an even deeper foundation: the basic myths and ideologies of our civilization that I call the Story of Self and Story of the World. But we can't just change our attitudes about money; we must change money too, which after all is the embodiment of our attitudes. Ultimately, work on self is inseparable from work in the world. Each mirrors the other; each is a vehicle for the other. When we change ourselves, our values and actions change as well. When we do work in the world, internal issues arise that we must face or be rendered ineffective. Thus it is that we sense a spiritual dimension to the planetary crisis, calling for what Andrew Harvey calls "Sacred Activism."

The money system we have today is the manifestation of the scarcity mentality that has dominated our civilization for centuries. When that mentality changes, the money system will change to embody a new consciousness. In our current money system, it is mathematically impossible for more than a minority of people to live in abundance, because the money creation process maintains a systemic scarcity. One man's prosperity is another man's poverty.

One of the principles of "prosperity programming" is to let go

---

18. Ibid., 49.

of the guilt stemming from the belief that you can only be wealthy if another is poor, that more for me is less for you. The problem is that under today's money system it is true! More for me *is* less for you. The monetized realm grows at the expense of nature, culture, health, and spirit. The guilt we feel around money is quite justified. Certainly, we can create beautiful things, worthy organizations, and noble causes with money, but if we aim to earn money with these goals in mind, on some level we are robbing Peter to pay Paul.

Please understand here that I do not mean to deter you from opening to the flow of abundance. To the contrary—because when enough people do this, the money system will change to conform to the new belief. Today's money system rests on a foundation of Separation. It is as much an effect as it is a cause of our perception that we are discrete and separate subjects in a universe that is Other. Opening to abundance can only happen when we let go of this identity and open to the richness of our true, connected being. This new identity wants no part of usury.

Here is an extreme example that illustrates the flaw in "prosperity programming" and, indirectly, in the present money system. Some years ago, a woman introduced me to a very special organization she had joined, called "Gifting." Basically, the way it worked is that first, you "gift" $10,000 to the person who invites you. Then you find four people to each "gift" you with $10,000, and then each of them goes out and brings the gifting concept to four more people, who each "gift" them with $10,000. Everyone ends up with a net $30,000. The program literature explained this as a manifestation of universal abundance. All that is required is the right expansive attitude. Needless to say, I jumped at the opportunity. Just kidding. Instead I asked the woman, "But aren't you just taking money from your friends?"

"No," she replied, "because they are going to end up making $30,000 too, as long as they fully believe in the principles of gifting."

"But they are going to make that money from *their* friends. Eventually we're going to run out of people, and the last ones who joined will lose $10,000. You are essentially taking it from them, stealing it, and using a language of gifting to do so."

You may be surprised to learn that I never heard from that woman again. Her indignation and denial mirror that of the beneficiaries of the money economy as a whole, which itself bears a structural similarity to her pyramid scheme. To see it, imagine that each $10,000 entrance fee were created as an interest-bearing debt (which in fact it is). You *have* to bring in more people under you, or you lose your property. The only way those "at the bottom" can avoid penury is to find even more people to draw into the money economy, for example through colonization—ahem, I mean "opening up new markets to free trade"—and through economic growth: converting relationship, culture, nature, and so on into money. This delays the inevitable, and the inevitable—an intensifying polarization of wealth—rears its ugly head whenever growth slows. The people who have been left holding the debt bag have no way to pay it off: no one else to take the money from, and nothing to convert into new money. That, as we shall see, is the root of the economic, social, and ecological crisis our civilization faces today.

CHAPTER 7

THE CRISIS OF CIVILIZATION

We have bigger houses but smaller families;
more conveniences, but less time.
We have more degrees but less sense;
more knowledge but less judgment;
more experts, but more problems;
more medicines but less healthiness.
We've been all the way to the moon and back,
but have trouble in crossing the street to meet our new neighbor.
We built more computers to hold more copies than ever,
But have less real communication;
We have become long on quantity,
but short on quality.
These are times of fast foods but slow digestion;
Tall men but short characters;
Steep profits but shallow relationships.
It's a time when there is much in the window
But nothing in the room.

 —Authorship unknown

The financial crisis we are facing today arises from the fact that there is almost no more social, cultural, natural, and spiritual capital left to convert into money. Centuries of near-continuous money creation have left us so destitute that we have nothing left to sell. Our forests are damaged beyond repair, our soil depleted and washed into the sea, our fisheries fished out, and the rejuvenating capacity of the earth to recycle our waste saturated. Our cultural treasury of songs and stories, of images and icons, has been looted and copyrighted. Any clever phrase you can think of is already a trademarked slogan. Our very human relationships and abilities have been taken away from us and sold back, so that we are now dependent on strangers, and therefore on money, for things few humans ever paid for until recently: food, shelter, clothing, entertainment, child care, cooking. Life itself has become a consumer item.

Today we sell away the last vestiges of our divine endowment: our health, the biosphere and genome, even our own minds. Pythagoras's dictum, "All things are number," has nearly come true: the world has been converted into money. This is the process that is culminating in our age. It is almost complete, especially in America and the "developed" world. In the "developing" world (notice how these terms assume our own economic system as the destination of other societies) there still remain people who live substantially in gift cultures, where natural and social wealth is not yet the subject of property. Globalization is the process of stripping away these assets, to feed the money machine's insatiable, existential need to grow. Yet this strip-mining of other lands is running up against its limits too, both because there is almost nothing left to take and because of growing pockets of effective resistance.

The result is that the supply of money—and the corresponding volume of debt—has for several decades outstripped the production of goods and services that it promises. It is deeply related to the problem of overcapacity in classical economics. To defer the Marxian crisis of capital—a vicious circle of falling profits, falling wages, depressed consumption, and overproduction in mature industries—into the future, we must constantly develop new, high-profit industries and markets. The continuation of capitalism as we know it depends on an infinite supply of these new industries, which essentially must convert infinite new realms of social, natural, cultural, and spiritual capital into money. The problem is that these resources are finite, and the closer they come to exhaustion, the more painful their extraction becomes. Therefore, contemporaneous with the financial crisis we have an ecological crisis and a health crisis. They are intimately interlinked. We cannot convert much more of the earth into money, or much more of our health into money, before the basis of life itself is threatened.

An ancient Chinese myth helps illuminate what is happening. There was a monster, it is said, called the *tao tie*, which was possessed of an insatiable appetite. It consumed every creature around it, even the earth itself, yet it was still hungry. So it turned finally to its own body, eating its arms, legs, and torso, leaving nothing but the head.

A head cannot live without its body. Faced with the exhaustion of the nonmonetized commonwealth that it consumes, financial capital has turned to devour its own body: the industrial economy that it was supposed to serve. If income from production of goods and services is insufficient to service debt, then creditors seize assets instead. This is what has happened both in the American economy and globally. Mortgages, for example, were originally a path toward owning your own home free and clear, starting with 20 percent equity. Today few ever dream of actually one day repaying their mortgage, but only of endlessly refinancing it, in effect renting the house from the bank. Globally, Third World countries find themselves in a similar situation, as they are forced to sell off national assets and gut social services under IMF austerity programs. Just as you might feel your entire productive labor is in the service of debt repayment, so is their entire economy directed toward producing commodity goods to repay foreign debt.

IMF austerity measures are exactly analogous to a court-imposed debt-payment plan. They say, "You are going to have to make do with less, work harder, and devote a greater proportion of your income to debt payments. You will give me everything you own and turn over all your future earnings to me!" Worker pensions, teacher salaries, minerals, oil—all are turned to debt service. The forms of slavery have changed over the years, but not the essential directive. The irony is that in the long term, austerity measures don't even benefit the creditors. They choke off economic growth by reducing consumption, demand, and business investment opportunities. Jobs evaporate, commodity prices fall, and the debtor people and nations are less able than ever to make their payments.

Incapable of thinking beyond the short term, the money interests love austerity because the debtor is essentially saying, "We will devote more of our labor and resources toward the servicing of debt." It allows unserviceable debts to be serviced just a little while longer. This is what is happening in Europe at the time of this writing (2010), as governments slash pensions and agree to privatize social services so that they can assure bondholders that they will be paid. The rumblings of austerity are audible here in America too, in the form of alarums about the federal deficit. From within the logic of bond markets and budget deficits, the case for greater fiscal responsibility is unassailable. From outside that logic, it is absurd: are we to be forced by mere numbers, mere interpretation of bits, to erode the standard of living of the many for the sake of preserving the wealth of the few?

Eventually, debtors run out of disposable income and seizable assets. The crash underway today should have actually happened many years ago, except that various phony and inflated assets were created to keep it going a little longer as the financial *tao tie* cannibalized itself, covering debt with more debt. The efforts to shore up this edifice cannot work, because it must keep growing—all those debts bear interest. Yet the authorities keep trying. When you hear the phrase "rescue the financial system," translate it in your mind into "keep the debts on the books." They are trying to find a way for you (and debtor nations too) to keep paying and for the debt to keep growing. A debt pyramid cannot grow forever, because eventually, after all the debtors' assets are gone, and all their disposable income devoted to debt payments, creditors have no choice but to lend debtors the money to make their payments. Soon the outstanding balance is so high that they have to borrow money even to pay interest, which means that money is no longer flowing, and can no longer flow, from debtor to creditor. This is the final stage, usually short, though prolonged in our day by Wall Street's financial "wizardry." The loans and any derivatives built on them begin to lose their value, and debt deflation ensues.

Essentially, the proximate financial crisis and the deeper growth crisis of civilization are connected in two ways. Interest-based debt-money compels economic growth, and a debt crisis is a symptom that shows up whenever growth slows.

The present crisis is the final stage of what began in the 1930s. Successive solutions to the fundamental problem of keeping pace with money that expands with the rate of interest have been applied, and exhausted. The first effective solution was war, a state that has been permanent since 1940. Unfortunately, or rather fortunately, nuclear weapons and a shift in human consciousness have limited the solution of endless military escalation. War between the great powers is no longer possible. Other solutions—globalization, technology-enabled development of new goods and services to replace human functions never before commoditized, technology-enabled plunder of natural resources once off limits, and finally financial autocannibalism—have similarly run their course. Unless there are realms of wealth I have not considered, and new depths of poverty, misery, and alienation to which we might plunge, the inevitable cannot be delayed much longer.

The credit bubble that is blamed as the source of our current economic woes was not a cause of them at all, but only a symptom. When returns on capital investment began falling in the early 1970s, capital began a desperate search for other ways to maintain its expansion. When each bubble popped—commodities in the late 1970s, S&L real estate investments in the 1980s, the dotcom stocks in the 1990s, and real estate and financial derivatives in the 2000s—capital immediately moved on to the next, maintaining an illusion of economic expansion. But the real economy was stagnating. There were not enough needs to meet the overcapacity of production, not enough social and natural capital left to convert into money.

To maintain the exponential growth of money, either the volume of goods and services must be able to keep pace with it, or imperialism and war must be able to escalate indefinitely. All have reached their limit. There is nowhere to turn.

Today, the impasse in our ability to convert nature into commodities and relationships into services is not temporary. There is little more we can convert. Technological progress and refinements to industrial methods will not help us take more fish from the seas—the fish are mostly gone. It will not help us increase the timber harvest—the forests are already stressed to capacity. It will not allow us to pump more oil—the reserves are drying up. We cannot expand the service sector—there are hardly any things we do for each other that we don't pay for already. There is no more room for economic growth as we have known it; that is, no more room for the conversion of life and the world into money. Therefore, even if we follow the more radical policy prescriptions from the left, hoping by an annulment of debts and a redistribution of income to ignite renewed economic growth, we can only succeed in depleting what remains of our divine bequest of nature, culture, and community. At best, economic stimulus will allow a modest, short-lived expansion as the functions that were demonetized during the recession are remonetized. For example, because of the economic situation, some friends and I cover for each other's child care needs, whereas in prosperous times we might have sent our kids to preschool. Our reciprocity represents an opportunity for economic growth: what we do for each other freely can be converted into monetized services. Generalized to the whole society, this is only an opportunity to grow back to where we were before, at which point the same crisis will emerge again. "Shrink in order to grow," the essence of war and deflation, is only effective, and decreasingly so, as a holding action while new realms of unmonetized social and natural capital are accessed.

The current problem is therefore much deeper than today's conventional wisdom holds. Consider this typical example from a financial journal:

[Paul] Volcker is right. The collateralized debt obligations, collateralized mortgage-backed securities, and other computer-spawned complexities and playthings were not the solutions to basic needs in the economy, but to unslaked greed on Wall Street. Without them, banks would have had no choice but to continue to devote their capital and talents to meeting real needs from businesses and consumers, and there would have been no crisis, no crash, and no recession."[1]

This describes only the most superficial level of a deeper problem of which the collateralized debt obligations (CDOs) and so forth are mere symptoms. The deeper problem was that there were insufficient "real needs" to which banks could devote their capital, because only those needs that will generate profits beyond the interest rate constitute valid lending opportunities. In an economy plagued by overproduction, such opportunities are rare. So, the financial industry played numbers games instead. The CDOs and so on were a symptom, not a cause, of the financial crisis that originated in the impossibility of economic growth keeping pace with interest.

Various pundits have observed that Bernard Madoff's Ponzi scheme was not so different from the financial industry's pyramid of mortgaged-based derivatives and other instruments, which themselves formed a bubble that, like Madoff's, could only sustain itself through an unceasing, indeed exponentially growing, influx of new money. As such, it is a symbol of our times—and even more than people suppose. It is not only the Wall Street casino economy that is an unsustainable pyramid scheme. The larger economic system, based as it is on the eternal conversion of a finite commonwealth into money, is unsustainable as well. It is like a bonfire that must burn higher and higher, to the exhaustion of all available fuel. Only a fool would think that a fire can burn ever-higher

---

1. Coxe, 13.

when the supply of fuel is finite. To extend the metaphor, the recent deindustrialization and financialization of the economy amount to using the heat to create more fuel. According to the second law of thermodynamics, the amount created is always less than the amount expended to create it. Obviously, the practice of borrowing new money to pay the principal and interest of old debts cannot last very long, but that is what the economy as a whole has done for ten years now.

Yet even abandoning this folly, we still must face the depletion of fuel (remember, I mean not literal energy sources, but any bond of nature or culture that can be turned into a commodity). Most of the proposals for addressing the present economic crisis amount to finding more fuel. Whether it is drilling more oil wells, paving over more green space, or spurring consumer spending, the goal is to reignite economic growth—that is, to expand the realm of goods and services. It means finding new things for which we can pay. Today, unimaginably to our forebears, we pay even for our water and our songs. What else is left to convert into money?

As far as I know, the first economist to recognize the fundamental problem and its relation to the money system was Frederick Soddy, a Nobel laureate and pioneer of nuclear chemistry who turned his attention to economics in the 1920s. Soddy was among the first to debunk the ideology of infinite exponential economic growth, extending the reasoning of Thomas Malthus beyond population to economics. Herman Daly describes Soddy's view succinctly:

> The idea that people can live off the interest of their mutual indebtedness . . . is just another perpetual motion scheme—a vulgar delusion on a grand scale. Soddy seems to be saying that what is obviously impossible for the community—for everyone

to live on interest—should also be forbidden to individuals, as a principle of fairness. If it is not forbidden, or at least limited in some way, then at some point the growing liens of debt holders on the limited revenue will become greater than the future producers of that revenue will be willing or able to support, and conflict will result. The conflict takes the form of debt repudiation. Debt grows at compound interest and as a purely mathematical quantity encounters no limits to slow it down. Wealth grows for a while at compound interest, but, having a physical dimension, its growth sooner or later encounters limits.[2]

This association of economic growth with resource consumption is especially common today among Peak Oil theorists, who forecast economic collapse as oil production begins its "long descent." Their critics contend that economic growth can and does happen independent of energy use, thanks to technology, miniaturization, efficiency improvements, and so on. Since 1960, U.S. economic growth has outstripped energy use, a trend that accelerated in the 1980s (see Figure 1). Germany has done even better, having essentially flat energy use since 1991 despite considerable economic growth. However, this objection only illustrates a larger point. Yes, it is possible to maintain economic growth by displacing it from the consumption of one part of the commons to another—by burning gas instead of oil or by commoditizing human services or intellectual property instead of the cod fishery—but aggregated over the totality of the social, natural, cultural, and spiritual commons, the basic argument of Peak Oil remains valid. Instead of Peak Oil, we are facing Peak Everything.

---

2. Daly, "The Economic Thought of Frederick Soddy," 475.

When the financial crisis hit in 2008, the first government response, the bailout and monetary stimulus, was an attempt to uphold a tower of debt upon debt that far exceeded its real economic foundation. As such, its apparent success was temporary, a postponement of the inevitable: "pretend and extend," as some on Wall Street call it. The alternative, economic stimulus, is doomed for a deeper reason. It will fail because we are "maxed out": maxed out on nature's capacity to receive our wastes without destroying the ecological basis of civilization; maxed out on society's ability to withstand any more loss of community and connection; maxed out on our forests' ability to withstand more clear-cuts; maxed out on the human body's capacity to stay viable in a depleted, toxic world. That we are also maxed out on our credit only reflects that we have nothing left to convert into money. Do we really need more

GDP and Energy Consumption 1949–1999

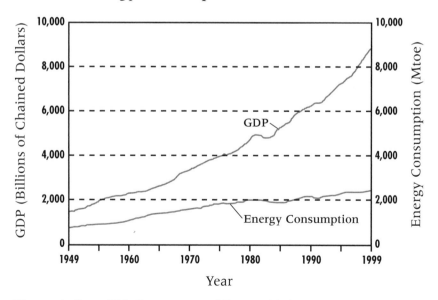

Figure 1. *Source:* U.S. Department of Energy, 2000.

roads and bridges?[3] Can we sustain more of them, and more of the industrial economy that goes along? Government stimulus programs will at best prolong the current economic system for two or three years, with perhaps a brief period of growth as we complete the pillage of nature, spirit, body, and culture. When these vestiges of the commonwealth are gone, then nothing will be able to stop the Great Unraveling of the money system.

Although the details and timeline of this unraveling are impossible to predict, I think we will first experience persistent deflation, stagnation, and wealth polarization, followed by social unrest, hyperinflation, or currency collapse. At that moment, the alternatives we are exploring today will come into their own, offering an opportunity to build a new and sacred economy. The farther the collapse proceeds, the more attractive the proposals of this book will become.

In the face of the impending crisis, people often ask what they can do to protect themselves. "Buy gold? Stockpile canned goods? Build a fortified compound in a remote area? What should I do?" I would like to suggest a different kind of question: "What is the most beautiful thing I can do?" You see, the gathering crisis presents a tremendous opportunity. Deflation, the destruction of money, is only a categorical evil if the creation of money is a categorical good. However, you can see from the examples I have given that the creation of money has in many ways impoverished us all. Conversely, the destruction of money has the potential to enrich us. It

---

3. Some might say that Third World countries do need more roads and bridges to raise their standard of living. Consider, however, that big infrastructure projects, exemplary of World Bank investment, are key to the integration of formerly autonomous economies into the global commodity economy. Perhaps what they need is not more roads and bridges. Perhaps what they need is protection from the depredations of the global commodity economy, of which roads and bridges are an agent.

offers the opportunity to reclaim parts of the lost commonwealth from the realm of money and property.

We see this happening every time there is an economic recession. People can no longer pay for various goods and services, and so have to rely on friends and neighbors instead. Where there is no money to facilitate transactions, gift economies reemerge and new kinds of money are created. Ordinarily, though, people and institutions try to hang on to the old ways as long as possible. The habitual first response to economic crisis is to make and keep more money—to accelerate the conversion of anything you can into money. On a systemic level, the debt surge is generating enormous pressure to extend the commodification of the commonwealth. We can see this happening with the calls to drill for oil in Alaska, commence deep-sea drilling, and so on. The time is here, though, for the reverse process to begin in earnest—to remove things from the realm of goods and services and return them to the realm of gifts, reciprocity, self-sufficiency, and community sharing. Note well: this is going to happen anyway in the wake of a currency collapse, as people lose their jobs or become too poor to buy things. People will help each other, and real communities will reemerge.

Even if you care mostly about the security of your own future, community is probably the best investment you can make. When the financial system unravels, most investments become mere pieces of paper or electronic data files. They derive value only from the web of social agreements that contains and interprets them. Even physical gold doesn't provide much security when things get really bad. In times of extreme crisis, governments typically confiscate private gold holdings—Hitler, Lenin, and Roosevelt all did so. If even the government falls apart, then people with guns will come and take your gold or any other store of wealth.

I sometimes read the financial website Zero Hedge for its remarkable insight into the pretenses and machinations of the financial power elite. In that website's dim view, no asset class except physical gold and other physical commodities is safe today. I agree with its logic as far as it goes, but it does not go far enough. If the system breaks down to the point of hyperinflation, then the institution of property—as much a social convention as money is—will break down too. In times of social turmoil, I can't imagine anything more dangerous than possessing a few hundred ounces of gold. Really the only security is to be found in community: the gratitude, connections, and support of the people around you. If you have wealth now, I recommend, as your investment advisor, that you use it to enrich the people around you in lasting ways.

In the meantime, before the collapse of the current system, anything we do to protect some natural or social resource from conversion into money will both hasten the collapse *and* mitigate its severity. Any forest you save from development, any road you stop, any cooperative playgroup you establish; anyone you teach to heal themselves, or to build their own house, cook their own food, or make their own clothes; any wealth you create or add to the public domain; anything you render off-limits to the world-devouring Machine will help shorten the Machine's life span. And when the money system collapses, if you already do not depend on money for some portion of life's necessities and pleasures, then the collapse of money will pose much less of a harsh transition for you. The same applies on the social level. Any form of natural wealth, whether biodiversity, fertile soil, or clean water, and any community or social institution that is not a vehicle for the conversion of life into money, will sustain and enrich life *after* money.

I am referring to money as we know it. I will soon describe a money system that does not drive the conversion of all that is good, true, and beautiful into money. It enacts a fundamentally different human identity, a fundamentally different sense of self, from what dominates today. No more will it be true that more for me is less for you. On a personal level, the deepest possible revolution we can enact is a revolution in our sense of self, in our identity. The discrete and separate self of Descartes and Adam Smith has run its course and is becoming obsolete. We are realizing our own inseparability, from each other and from the totality of all life. Usury belies this union, for it seeks growth of the separate self at the expense of something external, something other. Probably everyone reading this book agrees with the principles of interconnectedness, whether from a spiritual or an ecological perspective. The time has come to live it. It is time to enter the spirit of the gift, which embodies the felt understanding of nonseparation. It is becoming abundantly obvious that less for you (in all its dimensions) is also less for me. The ideology of perpetual gain has brought us to a state of poverty so destitute that we are gasping for air. That ideology, and the civilization built upon it, is what is collapsing today.

Resisting or postponing the collapse will only make it worse. Finding new ways to grow the economy will only consume what is left of our wealth. Let us stop resisting the revolution in human beingness. If we want to outlast the multiple crises unfolding today, let us not seek to *survive* them. That is the mind-set of separation; that is resistance, a clinging to a dying past. Instead, let us shift our perspective toward reunion and think in terms of what we can give. What can we each contribute to a more beautiful world? That is our only responsibility and our only security.

I will develop this theme—right livelihood and right investing—later in this book. We can engage in conscious, purposeful money destruction in place of the unconscious destruction of money that happens in a collapsing economy. If you still have money to invest, invest it in enterprises that explicitly seek to build community, protect nature, and preserve the cultural commonwealth. Expect a zero or negative financial return on your investment—that is a good sign that you are not unintentionally converting even more of the world to money. Whether or not you have money to invest, you can also reclaim what was sold away by taking steps out the money economy. Anything you learn to do for yourself or for other people, without paying for it; any utilization of recycled or discarded materials; anything you make instead of buy, give instead of sell; any new skill or new song or new art you teach yourself or another will reduce the dominion of money and grow a gift economy to sustain us through the coming transition. The world of the Gift, echoing primitive gift societies, the web of ecology, and the spiritual teachings of the ages, is nigh upon us. It tugs on our heartstrings and awakens our generosity. Shall we heed its call, before the remainder of earth's beauty is consumed?

CHAPTER 8

THE TURNING OF THE AGE

For at least another hundred years we must pretend to ourselves and to everyone that fair is foul and foul is fair; for foul is useful and fair is not. Avarice and usury and precaution must be our gods for a little longer still.

—John Maynard Keynes (1931)

MONEY: STORY AND MAGIC

As the economic meltdown proceeds to its next phase, we begin to see the unreality of much we thought real. The verities of two generations become uncertain, and despite a lingering hope that a return to normalcy is just around the corner—"by the middle of 2012" or "more slowly than expected"—the realization is dawning that normal isn't coming back.

When faced with an abrupt shift in personal reality, whether the death of a loved one, or the Gestapo coming into town, human beings usually react first with denial. My first response when tragedy hits is usually, "I can't believe this is happening!" I was not surprised, then, that our political and corporate leaders spent a long time denying that a crisis was underway. Consider some quotes from 2007: "The country's economic fundamentals are sound," said George W. Bush. "I don't see subprime mortgage market troubles imposing a serious problem. I think it's going to be largely contained," said Secretary of the Treasury Henry Paulson. "A recession is unlikely." "We are experiencing a correction in the housing sector." "America is not in recession." "It is likely that housing prices won't recover until early 2009." Today, as well, the authorities are "predicting" (but really, trying to speak into existence) economic growth of over 5 percent over the period 2010–2015.[1]

Of course, many of these pronouncements were insincere efforts at perception management. The authorities hoped that by controlling the public perception of reality, they could control reality itself—that by the manipulation of symbols they could manipulate the reality they represent. This, in essence, is what anthropologists call "magico-religious thinking." It is not without reason that our financial elites have been called a priesthood. Donning ceremonial garb, speaking an arcane language, wielding mysterious inscriptions, they can with a mere word, or a mere stroke of a pen, cause fortunes and nations to rise and fall.

You see, magico-religious thinking normally works. Whether it is a shamanic rite, the signing of an appropriations bill, or the posting of an account balance, when a ritual is embedded in a story that people believe, they act accordingly, playing out the roles the story assigns to them, and responding to the reality the story establishes. In former times, when a shamanic rite was seen to have failed, everyone knew this was a momentous event, signaling the End of the World, a shift in what was real and what was not, the end of the old Story of the People and the beginning, perhaps, of a new. What, from this perspective, is the significance of the accelerating failure of the rites of finance?

---

1. U.S. Department of the Treasury, "Annual Report on the Public Debt," June 2010.

Some would scoff at primitive cave-dwellers who imagined that their representations of animals on cave walls could magically affect the hunt. Yet today we produce our own talismans, our own systems of magic symbology, and indeed affect physical reality through them. A few numbers change here and there, and thousands of workers erect a skyscraper. Some other numbers change, and a venerable business shuts its doors. The foreign debt of a Third World country, again mere numbers in a computer, consigns its people to endless enslavement producing commodity goods that are shipped abroad. College students, ridden with anxiety, deny their dreams and hurry into the workforce to pay off their student loans, their very will subject to a piece of paper with magical symbols ("Account Statement") sent to them once every moon, like some magical chit in a voodoo cult.[2] These slips of paper that we call money, these electronic blips, bear a potent magic indeed!

How does magic work? Rituals and talismans affirm and perpetuate the consensus stories we all participate in, stories that form our reality, coordinate our labor, and organize our lives. Only in exceptional times do they stop working: the times of a breakdown in the story of the people. We are entering such times today. The economic measures enacted to contain the crisis that began in 2008 have worked only temporarily. They don't go deep enough. The only reform that can possibly be effective will be one that embodies, affirms, and perpetuates a new story of the people. To see what that story might be, let us dig down through the layers of failing realities and their relationship to money.

---

2. This is not to denigrate voodoo cults or to cite them as an example of primitive mumbo jumbo. In fact, I don't want to denigrate mumbo jumbo either. Whether it is the modern financial system or voodoo ritual, symbolic magic works by the same essential principles. Our modern system of ritual differs little from the primitive.

When the government's first response to the 2008 crisis—denial—proved futile, the Federal Reserve and Treasury Department tried another sort of perception management. Deploying their arsenal of mystical incantations, they signaled that the government would not allow major financial institutions such as Fannie Mae to fail. They hoped that their assurances would be enough to maintain confidence in the assets that depended on these firms' continued solvency and prosperity. It would have worked if the story these symbolic measures invoked were not already broken. But it was. Specifically, what was broken was the story assigning value to mortgage-backed securities and other derivatives based on unrepayable loans. Unlike camels or bushels of grain, but like all modern currencies, these have value only because people believe they have value. Moreover, this is not an isolated belief, but is inextricably linked with millions of other beliefs, conventions, habits, agreements, and rituals.

The next step was to begin injecting massive amounts of cash into failing financial institutions, either in exchange for equity (effectively nationalizing them, as in the case of Fannie Mae, Freddie Mac, and AIG) or in exchange for essentially nothing whatsoever, as in the TARP program. In the latter, the Treasury Department guaranteed or bought banks' toxic assets in hopes of improving their balance sheets so that they would start lending again, thus keeping the credit bubble expanding. It didn't work. The banks just kept the money (except what they paid to their own executives as bonuses) as a hedge against their exposure to untold quantities of additional bad assets, or they used it to acquire smaller, healthier banks. They weren't about to lend more to consumers who were already maxed out, nor to overleveraged businesses in the teeth of a recession. Property values continued to fall, credit default rates continued to rise, and the whole edifice of derivative assets built upon them continued to crumble. Consumption and business activity plummeted, unemployment skyrocketed, and people in Europe began rioting in the streets. And why? Just because some numbers changed in some computers. It is truly amazing. It only makes sense when you see these numbers as talismans embodying agreements. A supplier digs minerals out of the ground and sends them to a factory, in exchange for what? For a few slips of paper, or more likely, in exchange for some bits flipping in a computer, which can only happen with the permission of a bank (that "provides credit").

Before we become too alarmed about the giveaways of trillions upon trillions of dollars to the wealthy, let us touch back again on the reality of money. What actually happens when this money is given away? Almost nothing happens. What happens is that bits change in computers, and the few people who understand the interpretations of those bits declare that money has been transferred. Those bits are the symbolic representation of an agreement about a story. This story includes who is rich and who is poor, who owns and who owes. It is said that our children and grandchildren will be paying these bailout and stimulus debts, but they could also simply be declared into nonexistence. They are only as real as the story we agree on that contains them. Our grandchildren will pay them only if the story, the system of meanings, that defines those debts still exists. But I think more and more people sense that the federal debt, the U.S. foreign debt, and a lot of our private mortgage and credit card debts will never be repaid.

We think that those Wall Street tycoons absconded with billions, but what are these billions? They too are numbers in computers, and could theoretically be erased by fiat. The same with the money that America owes China or that Third World nations owe the banks. It could be gone with a simple declaration. We can thus understand the massive giveaways of money in the various financial rescue programs as yet another exercise in perception management, though this time it is an unconscious exercise. These giveaways are ritual acts that attempt to perpetuate a story, a matrix of agreements, and the human activities that surround it. They are an attempt to uphold the magical power of the voodoo chits that keep the college grad on a career path and the middle-aged man enslaved to his mortgage—that give the power to a few to move literal mountains while keeping the many in chains.

Speaking of China, it is instructive to look at the physical reality underlying the trade imbalance. Basically what is happening is that China is shipping us vast quantities of stuff—clothes, toys, electronics, nearly everything in Wal-Mart—and in return we rearrange some bits in some computers. Meanwhile, Chinese laborers work just as hard as we do, yet their day's wages buy much less. In the old days of explicit empires, China would have been called a "vassal state" and the stuff it sends us would have been called "tribute."[3] Yet China too will do everything it can to sustain the present Story of Money, for essentially the same reason we do: its elites benefit from it. It is just as in Ancient Rome. The elites of the imperial capital and the provinces prosper at the expense of the misery of the people, which increases over time. To mollify them and keep them docile and stupid, the masses are provided with bread and circuses: cheap food, cheap thrills, celebrity news, and the Super Bowl.

---

3. Sometimes the power shifts to the vassal as the hegemonic power becomes decadent and reliant on imported wealth to the point that it loses its own ability to create wealth. It looks like this is happening with China today. Perhaps China is only temporarily playing a vassal role in pursuit of another end.

Whether we declare it to end, or whether it ends of its own accord, the story of money will bring down a lot with it. That is why the United States won't simply default on its debt. If it did, then the story under which the Middle East ships us its oil, Japan its electronics, India its textiles, and China its plastic would come to an end. Unfortunately, or rather fortunately, that story cannot be saved forever. The fundamental reason is that it depends on the maintenance of exponentially growing debt in a finite world.

When money evaporates as it is doing in the current cycle of debt deflation, little changes right away in the physical world. Stacks of currency do not go up in flames; factories do not blow up; engines do not grind to a halt; oil wells do not run dry; people's economic skills do not disappear. All of the materials and skills that are exchanged in human economy, upon which we rely for food, shelter, transportation, entertainment, and so on, still exist as before. What has disappeared is our capacity to coordinate our activities and focus our common efforts. We can still envision a new airport, but we can no longer build it. The magic talisman by which the pronouncement "An airport shall be built here" crystallizes into material reality has lost its power. Human hands, minds, and machinery retain all their capacities, yet we can no longer do what we once could do. The only thing that has changed is our perceptions.

We can therefore see the bailouts, quantitative easing, and the other financial measures to save the economy as further exercises in perception management, but on a deeper, less conscious level. Because what is money, anyway? Money is merely a social agreement, a story that assigns meaning and roles. The classical definition of money—a medium of exchange, a store of value, a unit of account—describes what money does, but not what it *is*. Physically, it is now next to nothing. Socially, it is next to everything:

the primary agent for the coordination of human activity and the focusing of collective human intention.

The government's deployment of trillions of dollars in money is little different from its earlier deployment of empty words. Both are nothing but the manipulation of various types of symbols, and both have failed for an identical reason: the story they are trying to perpetuate has run its course. The normalcy we took as normal was unsustainable.

It was unsustainable on two levels. The first level of "normal" is the debt pyramid, the exponential growth of money that inevitably outstrips the real economy. The solution at this level is what liberal economists (usually identifying themselves as Keynesians) propose: wealth redistribution, fiscal stimulus, debt write-downs, and so forth. Through these they hope to reignite economic growth—the second "normal" that is coming to an end.

HUMANITY'S COMING-OF-AGE ORDEAL

The story that is ending in our time, then, goes much deeper than the story of money. I call this story the Ascent of Humanity. It is a story of endless growth, and the money system we have today is an embodiment of that story, enabling and propelling the conversion of the natural realm into the human realm. It began millennia ago, when humans first tamed fire and made tools; it accelerated when we applied these tools to the domestication of animals and plants and began to conquer the wild, to make the world ours. It reached its glorious zenith in the age of the Machine, when we created a wholly artificial world, harnessing all the forces of nature and imagining ourselves to be its lords and possessors. And now, that story is drawing to a close as the inexorable realization dawns that the story is not true. Despite our pretenses, the world is not really ours; despite our illusions, we are not in control of it. As the unintended consequences of technology proliferate, as our communities, our health, and the ecological basis of civilization deteriorate, as we explore new depths of misery, violence, and alienation, we enter the story's final stages: crisis, climax, and denouement. The rituals of our storytellers are to no avail. No story can persist beyond its ending.

Just as life does not end with adolescence, neither does civilization's evolution stop with the end of growth. We are in the midst of a transition parallel to an adolescent's transition into adulthood. Physical growth ceases, and vital resources turn inward to foster growth in other realms.

Two key developments mark the transition from childhood to adulthood, whether on the individual or the species level. The first is that we fall in love, and this love relationship is different from that of the child to the mother. In childhood, the primary aspect of the love relationship is that of receiving. I am happy to give all I can to my children, and I want them to receive it without restraint. It is right for a child to do what is necessary to grow, both physically and mentally. A good parent provides the resources for this growth, as our Mother Earth has done for us.

So far, we humans have been children in relationship to earth. We began in the womb of hunter-gatherer existence, in which we made no distinction between human and nature, but were enwombed within it. An infant does not have a strong self-other distinction, but takes time to form an identity and an ego and to learn that the world is not an extension of the self. So it has been for humanity collectively. Whereas the hunter-gatherer had no concept of a separate "nature" distinct from "human," the agriculturist, whose livelihood depended on the objectification and manipulation of nature, came to think of nature as a separate category. In the childhood of agricultural civilization, humanity developed a separate identity and grew large. We had our adolescent growth spurt with industry, and on the mental plane entered through Cartesian science the extreme of separation, the fully developed ego and hyperrationality of the young teenager who, like humanity in the Age of Science, completes the stage of cognitive development known as "formal operations," consisting of the manipulation of abstractions. But as the extreme of yang contains the birth of yin, so does the extreme of separation contain the seed of what comes next: reunion.

In adolescence, we fall in love, and our world of perfect reason and perfect selfishness falls apart as the self expands to include the beloved within its bounds. A new kind of love relationship emerges: not just one of receiving, but of giving too, and of cocreating. Fully individuated from the Other, we can fall in love with it and experience a reunion greater than the original union, for it contains within it the entire journey of separation.

The first mass awakening of the new love consciousness happened in the 1960s with the birth of the environmental movement. At the pinnacle of our separation, triumphantly surveying our apparent conquest of nature, we began to notice how much she had given; we became aware of her hurts, her wounds, and we began to desire not only to take from earth, but to give to earth too, to protect and cherish her. This desire was not based on a fear of extinction—that came later—but on love. We were falling in love with the earth. In that decade, the first photographs of this planet were beamed down from orbiting satellites, and we were transformed by the planet's beauty. To view earth from the outside was the penultimate step of separation from nature; the ultimate step was the ascension of the astronauts, physically leaving nature behind. And they fell in love with earth too. Here are the words of astronaut Rusty Schweickart:

> From the moon, the Earth is so small and so fragile, and such a precious little spot in that Universe, that you can block it out with your thumb. Then you realize that on that spot, that little blue and white thing, is everything that means anything to you—all of history and music and poetry and art and death and birth and love, tears, joy, games, all of it right there on that little spot that you can cover with your thumb. And you realize from that perspective that you've changed forever, that there is something new there, that the relationship is no longer what it was.

The second hallmark of the transition to adulthood is an ordeal. Ancient tribal cultures had various coming-of-age ceremonies and ordeals that purposely shattered the smaller identity through isolation, pain, fasting, psychedelic plants, or other means, and then rebuilt and reincorporated it into a larger, transpersonal identity. Though we intuitively seek them out in the form of drinking, drugs, fraternity and military hazing, and so on, modern men and women usually have only a partial experience of this process, leaving us in a kind of perpetual adolescence that ends only when fate intervenes to tear our world apart. Then we can enter a wider self, in which giving comes just as naturally as receiving. Having completed the passage to adulthood, a man or woman takes full possession of his or her gifts and seeks to contribute to the good of all as a full member of the tribe.

Humanity is undergoing an analogous ordeal today. The multiple crises converging upon us are an ordeal that challenges our very identity, an ordeal that we have no assurance of even surviving. It calls forth unrealized capacities and compels us to relate to the world in a new way. The despair that sensitive people feel in the face of the crisis is part of the ordeal.[4] Like a tribal initiate, when we as a species emerge from it, we too will join the community of all being as a full member of the "tribe" of life. Our unique capacities of technology and culture, we will turn to contribute to the good of all.

In humanity's childhood, a money system that embodied and demanded growth, the taking of more and more from earth, was perhaps appropriate. It was an integral part of the story of Ascent. Today it is rapidly becoming obsolete. It is incompatible with adult love, with cocreative partnership, and with the graduation into the estate of a Giver that comes with adulthood. That is the deep reason why no financial or economic reform can possibly work that does not include a new kind of money. The new money must embody a new story, one that treats nature not only as a mother, but as a lover too. We will still have a need for money for a long time to come because we need magical symbols to reify our Story of the People, to apply it to the physical world as a creative template. The essential character of money will not change: it will consist of magical talismans, whether physical or electronic, through which we assign roles, focus intention, and coordinate human activity.

The next part of this book will discuss such a money system, as well as the economy and psychology that will accompany it. There is a personal—some might say spiritual—dimension to the meta-

---

4. Actually, all is well: the crisis is exercising its evolutionary function. But don't let that assuage your panic. All is well, but only because of our perception that all is horribly wrong.

morphosis of stories that we are entering. Today's usury-money is part of a story of separation, in which "more for me is less for you." That is the essence of interest: I will only "share" money with you if I end up with even more of it in return. On the systemic level as well, interest on money creates competition, anxiety, and the polarization of wealth. Meanwhile, the phrase "more for me is less for you" is also the motto of the ego, and a truism given the discrete and separate self of modern economics, biology, and philosophy.

Only when our sense of self expands to include others, through love, is that truism replaced by its opposite: "More for you is also more for me." This is the essential truth embodied in the world's authentic spiritual teachings, from Jesus's Golden Rule, which has been misconstrued and should read, "As you do unto others, so also you do unto yourself," to the Buddhist doctrine of karma. However, to merely understand and agree with these teachings is not enough; many of us bear a divide between what we believe and what we live. An actual transformation in the way we experience *being* is necessary, and such a transformation usually comes about in much the same way as our collective transformation is happening now: through a collapse of the old Story of Self and Story of the World, and the birth of a new one. For the self, too, is ultimately a story, with a beginning and an end. Have you ever gone through an experience that leaves you, afterward, hardly knowing who you are?

The mature, connected self, the self of interbeingness, comes into a balance between giving and receiving. In that state, whether you are a person or an entire species, you give according to your abilities and, linked with others of like spirit, you receive according to your needs.

Not coincidentally, I have just paraphrased a fundamental tenet of socialism: "From each according to his abilities, to each according to his needs." This is a good description of any gift network, whether a human body, an ecosystem, or a tribal gift culture. As I will describe, it is also a good description of a sacred economy. Its currency contributes to a very different Story of the People, of the Self, and of the World than usury-money. It is cyclical rather than exponential, always returning to its source; it encourages the protection and enrichment of nature, not its depletion; it redefines wealth as a function of one's generosity and not one's accumulation; it is the manifestation of abundance, not scarcity. It has the potential to recreate the gift dynamics of primitive societies on a global scale, bringing forth human gifts and directing them toward planetary needs.

I remember as a teenager reading Ayn Rand's *Atlas Shrugged*, whose black-and-white characters, hyperrationality, and moral absolutism appealed strongly to my adolescent mind. The book is a manifesto of the discrete and separate self, the mercenary ego, and it appeals to adolescent minds to this day. The book devoted its most vitriolic ridicule to the phrase "From each according to his abilities, to each according to his needs," painting a picture of people outdoing each other in their postures of neediness so as to be allotted a greater share of resources, while producers had no motivation to produce. This scenario, which was in certain respects played out in the Communist block, echoes a primal fear of the scarcity-conditioned modern self—what if I give and receive nothing in return? This desire of an assurance of return, a compensation for the risk of generosity, is the fundamental mind-set of interest, an adolescent mind-set to be superseded by a more expansive adult self that has matured into full membership in the community of being. We are here to express our gifts; it is among our deepest desires, and we cannot be fully alive otherwise.

Most needs have been monetized, while the amount of labor needed to meet those monetized needs is falling. Therefore, in order for human gifts to receive their full expression, all this excess human creativity must therefore turn elsewhere, toward needs or purposes that are inimical to the money of Separation. For without a doubt the regime of money has destroyed, and continues to destroy, much that is beautiful—indeed, every public good that cannot be made private. Here are a few examples: a starry night sky free of light pollution; a countryside free of road noise; a vibrant multicultural local urban economy; unpolluted lakes, rivers, and seas; the ecological basis of human civilization. Many of us have gifts that would contribute to all of these things, yet no one will pay us to give them. That's because money as we know it ultimately rests on converting the public into the private. The new money will encourage the opposite, and the conflict between our ideals and practical financial reality will end.

Usury-money is the money of growth, and it was perfect for humanity's growth stage on earth and for the story of Ascent, of dominance and mastery. The next stage is one of cocreative partnership with earth. The Story of the People for this new stage is coming together right now. Its weavers are the visionaries of fields like permaculture, holistic medicine, renewable energy, mycoremediation, local currencies, restorative justice, attachment parenting, and a million more. To undo the damage that the Age of Usury has wrought on nature, culture, health, and spirit will require all the gifts that make us human, and indeed is so impossibly demanding that it will take those gifts to a new level of development.

This might seem hopelessly naive, vague, and idealistic. I have drawn out some of the logic in *The Ascent of Humanity* and will flesh it out in greater detail in the second half of this book. For now, weigh the competing voices of your idealism and your cynicism, and ask yourself, "Can I bear to settle for anything less?" Can you bear to accept a world of great and growing ugliness? Can you stand to believe that it is inevitable? You cannot. Such a belief will slowly but surely kill your soul. The mind likes cynicism, its comfort and safety, and hesitates to believe anything extraordinary, but the heart urges otherwise; it urges us to beauty, and only by heeding its call can we dare create a new Story of the People.

We are here to create something beautiful; I call it "the more beautiful world our hearts tell us is possible." As the truth of that sinks in, deeper and deeper, and as the convergence of crises pushes us out of the old world, inevitably more and more people will live from that truth: the truth that more for you is not less for me; the truth that what I do unto you, so I do unto myself; the truth of living to give what you can and take what you need. We can start doing it right now. We are afraid, but when we do it for real, the world meets our needs and more. We then find that the story of Separation, embodied in the money we have known, is not true and never was. Yet the last ten millennia were not in vain. Sometimes it is necessary to live a lie to its fullest before we are ready to take the next step into the truth. The lie of separation in the age of usury is now complete. We have explored its fullness, its farthest extremes, and seen all it has wrought, the deserts and the prisons, the concentration camps and the wars, the wastage of the good, the true, and the beautiful. Now, the capacities we have developed through this long journey of ascent will serve us well in the imminent Age of Reunion.

PART II

THE ECONOMICS OF REUNION

As our sojourn of separation comes to an end and we reunite with nature, our attitude of human exceptionalism from the laws of nature is ending as well. For decades, the environmental movement has been telling us, "We are not exempt from nature's laws." Increasingly, painfully, we are experiencing the truth of that. A child takes from his mother, blissfully heedless of her sacrifices and her pain; and so we have taken from earth during the long infancy of the human species. Our money system, our economic ideology, has for better or worse been an agent of that taking. Now, as our relationship to earth shifts toward that of a lover, we become acutely aware of the harm we are doing. In a romantic partnership, what you do to your partner bounces back to you; her pain is your pain.

And so, as humanity faces the coming-of-age ordeal of the present crises and transitions into adulthood, a new economic system is emerging that embodies the new human identity of the connected self living in cocreative partnership with Earth. Our economic system and money system will no longer be agents of taking, of exploitation, of the aggrandizement of the separate self. They will instead be agents of giving, of creation, of service, and of abundance. The following chapters describe the elements of this sacred economy. All of them are apparent already, latent within the old institutions, and even being born from them. For this is not a revolution in the classic sense, a purge, a sweeping away of the old; it is rather a metamorphosis. The Age of Reunion has long gestated within the institutions of Separation. Today, it is beginning to come forth.

CHAPTER 9

THE STORY OF VALUE

It was an old story that was no longer true ... Truth can go out of stories, you know. What was true becomes meaningless, even a lie, because the truth has gone into another story. The water of the spring rises in another place.

—Ursula K. Le Guin

Money is inextricably woven into our civilization's defining stories: of self, and of humanity collectively. It is part and parcel of the ideology and mechanics of growth, the "ascent of humanity" to overlordship of the planet; it has also played a central role in the dissolution of our bonds to nature and community. As these stories crumble, and as their monetary dimension crumbles apace, we have the chance to consciously imbue money with the attributes of the new stories that will replace them: the connected self, living in cocreative partnership with Earth. But how to imbue money with a story?

In its several-thousand-year history, money has gone through an ever-accelerating evolution in its form. The first stage was commodity money—grain, oil, cattle, metal, and many other things—that functioned as media of exchange without possessing any fiduciary value. This stage lasted several millennia. The next step was coinage, which added fiduciarity to the intrinsic metallic value of silver and gold. Money consisted then of two components: a material and a symbolic.

It was quite natural that eventually the symbol would become detached from the metal, which is what happened with the advent of credit money in the Middle Ages and even before. In China, the first paper money (which was actually a kind of bank draft) was in use by the ninth century and circulated as far as Persia.[1] In the Arab world, a form of check was in wide use around that time as well. Italian traders used bills of exchange as early as the twelfth century, a practice that spread rapidly and was followed in the sixteenth and seventeenth century by fractional-reserve banking.[2] This was a major innovation, since it freed the money supply from the metal supply and allowed it to grow organically in response to economic activity. The detachment of money from metal was gradual. During the fractional-reserve banking era, which lasted several centuries, bank notes were still, at least in theory, backed by metal.

Today the era of fractional-reserve banking is over, and money has become pure credit. This is not widely recognized. Many authorities, including most economics textbooks and the Federal Reserve itself,[3] still maintain the pretense that reserves are a limiting factor in money creation, but in practice they almost never are.[4]

---

1. Temple, *The Genius of China*, 117, 119.

2. Vallely, "How Islamic Inventors Changed the World."

3. See, for example, the Chicago Federal Reserve's publication "Modern Money Mechanics," which is widely available on the internet.

4. If a bank's margin reserves are insufficient to meet requirements, it simply borrows the necessary cash from the Fed or the money markets. If there is a system-wide insufficiency of reserves, then the Fed expands the monetary base through open-market operations. That is why M0 growth typically lags behind M1 and M2 by many months—the opposite of what one would expect from the multiplier effect if we lived in a fractional reserve system (see Keen, "The Roving Cavaliers of Credit"). That is also why recent "quantitative easing" by the Fed and other central banks has done little to increase the money supply.

Banks' real constraints on money creation are their total capital and their ability to find willing, creditworthy borrowers—that is, those with either uncommitted earning potential or assets to use as collateral. In other words, social agreements govern the creation of money, primary among them the dictum, encoded in interest, that money should go to those who will make even more of it in the future. Today's money, as I shall explain, is backed by growth; when, as is happening now, growth slows, the entire financial edifice begins to crumble.

Money, which developed in parallel with technology, suffers similar flaws. Each bears a relentless compulsion to grow: technology because of the ideology of the technological fix, using yet more technology to remedy the problems caused by existing technology; money because of the dynamics of interest I have described, issuing more debt to pay the interest on existing debt. The parallel is quite exact. Another similarity is that each has usurped domains properly belonging to other modes of relationship. But in neither case do I advocate rolling back history. Both technology and money have developed to their present forms, I believe, for a purpose; credit money is the natural terminus of the evolution of money toward pure fiduciarity, pure agreement. Having arrived there, we are free to make that agreement purposeful. We are like an adolescent who, having developed her physical and mental capacities through childhood play, is now ready to turn those capacities toward their true purpose.

Some observers, seeing the disastrous consequences of today's credit-based currencies, advocate a return to the good old days of currencies backed by something tangible, such as gold. They reason that commodity-backed currency would be noninflationary or would eliminate the compulsion for endless growth. I think some of these "hard currency" or "real money" advocates are tapping in to an atavistic desire to return to simpler days, when things were what they were. Dividing the world into two categories, the objectively real and the conventional, they believe that credit-money is an illusion, a lie, that must inevitably collapse with every bust cycle. Actually, this dichotomy is itself an illusion, a construct that reflects deeper mythologies—such as the doctrine of objectivity in physics—that are also breaking down in our time.

The difference between an unbacked and backed currency is not as great as one might suppose. On the face of it, they seem very different: a backed currency derives its value from something real, while an unbacked currency has value only because people agree it does. This is a false distinction: in either case, ultimately what gives money value is the story that surrounds it, a set of social, cultural, and legal conventions.

At this point the "real money" or backed-currency advocate might object, "No, that's just the point: a backed currency gets its value from the underlying commodity, not from agreements."

Wrong!

First let us consider the standard example of what advocates call "real money": pure gold and silver coinage. These are valuable, they say, because the commodity they are made from is valuable. That is the source of their value, and the markings on them are there as a guarantee, to bestow confidence in their weight and purity. But despite nostalgia for the real money of yore, historically much gold and silver coinage did not fit this description, but had a value that exceeded its commodity value (see Chapter 3). It differs from paper money by degree, not in essence. Paper and electronic money are not a departure from metallic currency, but an extension of it.

To further complicate matters, what is this "commodity value"? Like money, property is a social construct. What is it to own something? Physical possession is only ownership if that possession is socially legitimate; with legitimacy, physical possession isn't even necessary. After all, in today's commodity markets, most investors never touch the things they buy. Their transactions are a set of rituals, symbolic manipulations invested with power through shared beliefs. The fictive nature of ownership is not a recent phenomenon. The famous money of the Yap islanders, huge stone rings that are too heavy to move, can nonetheless change owners quite easily when everyone agrees that so-and-so is the new owner. Gold never needs to leave the vault to be a currency backing. *In fact, it never needs to leave the ground.* Even if we did adopt a gold standard, most transactions would still use paper or digital symbols. Only the story conferring value upon those symbols would differ.

Moreover, the value of commodities depends on social agreements as well. This is especially true of gold, which, unlike other forms of genuine commodity money such as cattle or camels, has very little utilitarian value. You can make pretty ornaments from it, but it has very little industrial utility compared to other precious metals such as silver or platinum. That means that the value of gold depends on convention. That makes it an odd choice indeed for those who want money whose value is independent of convention, money that has "real" value.

What is true for gold is true for other commodities as well. In a society with a high degree of division of labor like our own, the utility of most commodities depends, like money's, on a web of social agreements. How useful to you is an iron ingot? A barrel of crude oil? A ton of industrial-grade sodium hydroxide? A bushel of soybeans? To varying degrees, they are valuable only in the context of vast numbers of people performing the specific, interrelated roles that put such things to use. In other words, commodities, like money, also have a fiduciary value in addition to their intrinsic value—indeed, upon close examination the distinction breaks down almost entirely.

Let us think more deeply about what it means for money to be backed. Superficially it is straightforward. To take the example of the U.S. dollar before 1972, it meant, "You can take a dollar to the Federal Reserve and redeem it for one-thirtieth (or whatever it was) of an ounce of gold." But this simple picture is fraught with complications. For most users of dollars, even if it were permitted, it was not practically feasible to go to the nearest Federal Reserve vault. As far as I know, the gold was hardly ever physically transported even for balance of payment settlements among banks. The banks' gold was kept in the Federal Reserve banks; their ownership of it was a matter of entries in record-books, and not of physical possession. The system would have worked even if no gold were physically present. No one except foreign banks ever actually exchanged dollars for gold. Why would anyone when it was dollars, and not gold, that were used as money? We think that dollars (in the gold standard era) were valuable because they could be exchanged for gold, but is the opposite perhaps not truer, that gold was valuable because it could be converted into dollars?

We tend to assume that in a backed paper or electronic money system, the backing is the real money and the paper only its representation. In fact, it is the paper that is the real money. Its association with gold was a projection of meaning, almost a magical formula, that gave us permission to believe in the story of value. The story creates value. In fact, it was never possible for everyone to redeem their paper money for gold. If too many people tried, the central bank could (and often did) simply declare that it would no longer redeem it.[5] The supposed hard fact of the paper's convertibility to X amount of gold is a construct, a convenient fiction, that depends on a web of social agreements and shared perceptions.

Similarly, before the United States abrogated the Bretton-Woods agreement in the early 1970s, world currencies were pegged to the U.S. dollar, which was in turn pegged to gold. If a country accumulated reserves of U.S. dollars, it could redeem them by having the Federal Reserve ship it a few tons of gold. This was not such a big problem right after World War II, but by the late 1960s nearly all the U.S. gold reserve had been shipped overseas, threatening the Fed with bankruptcy. So, the United States simply announced it would no longer redeem dollars for gold within the international banking system, just as it had ceased to do so domestically some four decades earlier, revealing the gold standard as a convenient fiction.

The proclamation that money is backed is little different from any other ritual incantation in that it derives its power from collective human belief. However true this was of gold, it is truer still of more recent, more sophisticated backed-currency proposals, such as Bernard Lietaer's terra currency, and recent proposals for revised IMF Special Drawing Rights, to be backed by a commodity basket reflecting overall economic activity. There is merit in this approach; indeed it is a step in the direction I envision in this book. But this backing is obviously a fiction: no one is ever going to exchange their terras for actual, physical delivery—on their doorstep—of

---

5. This in fact happened many times; during the Great Depression it happened in nearly every country. Holders of currency demanded gold from banks and ultimately central banks, which eventually said no. In the United States in the 1930s it actually became illegal under Roosevelt's Executive Order 6102 to hold more than a small amount of gold. Yet the dollars whose value supposedly depended on gold did not become worthless.

the prescribed combination of oil, grain, carbon credits, pork bellies, iron ingots, and whatever else is on the list. No single person ever needs any of these things in his personal possession. Their value is collective, existing only within a vast web of economic relationships. But this is OK! Actual, practical redeemability is not necessary to qualify something as a backed currency. Yes, the redeemability is a fiction, a story, but stories have power. All money is a story. We have no alternative to creating money within a matrix of stories. Nothing I have written disqualifies backed currencies. But if we are to choose a backed currency, let us be clear about the reasons. It is not to make the money "real" in a way that unbacked currencies are not. It is to imbue money with the story of value that we want to create.

The story of backing can be used to limit and guide the creation of money. Today, we limit that right to banks and guide it by the profit motive—money goes to those who will make more of it. Properly and historically speaking, though, the issue of money is a special, sacred function, not to be relinquished lightly. Money bears the magical power of the sign and embodies the agreement of an entire society. Part of a society's soul lives within it, and the power to create it should be guarded as jealously as a shaman guards his medicine pouch. In the wrong hands, its power can be used to enslave. Can we deny that that has happened today? Can we deny that people and whole nations have become thralls of the moneylenders?

Not only do we naturally associate money with the sacred, but whatever we use for money tends to *become* sacred: "Where your treasure is, there will be your heart also" (Matthew 6:21). Thus it was that people came to worship gold. Of course, they did not profess to worship it, but actions speak louder than words. It was gold they coveted, gold they sacrificed for, gold they revered, gold that they invested with a supernatural power and a special holy status. The same happens to cattle in cattle-trading cultures and to wheat or olive oil in cultures where these were used as commodity-money. They took on a sacred status, set apart from other commodities.

The last hundred years have increasingly been an era of unbacked currency, and also an era where nothing is sacred. As I said in the introduction, if anything is sacred today it is money itself. For it is money that has the properties we associate with the disembodied divinity of dualism: ubiquity, abstraction, nonmateriality, yet the ability to intercede in material affairs to create or to destroy. To remove divinity completely from materiality is, again, to hold nothing sacred—nothing real, nothing tangible. Yet the absence of the sacred is an illusion: as many have pointed out, science has become the new religion, complete with its story of cosmogenesis, its mysterious explanations of the workings of the world couched in arcane language, its priests and their interpreters, its hierarchy, its initiation rituals (the PhD defense, for example), its system of values, and much more. Similarly, the apparent absence of backing is an illusion too. Credit-money is (via a different kind of social agreement than explicitly backed currencies, but an agreement nonetheless) backed by the entirety of an economy's goods and services and, more deeply, by growth.[6] Created as interest-bearing debt, its sustained value depends on the endless expansion of the realm of goods and services. Whatever backs money

---

6. Look at it this way: bank-issued credit is backed by the collateral on the loan or, in the case of unsecured loans, by the future earnings of the borrower. Economy-wide then, the sum total of all credit-money issued is backed by the sum total of all existing and future goods and services in the economy and, therefore, by the promise of growth. Another way to see it is that without growth, the default rate will rise, and the money supply will shrink.

becomes sacred: accordingly, growth has occupied a sacred status for many centuries. In various guises of the story of Ascent—progress, harnessing natural forces, conquering final frontiers, mastering nature—we have carried out a holy crusade to be fruitful and multiply. But growth is sacred to us no longer.

This book will describe a concrete way to back money with the things that are becoming sacred to us today. And what are those? We can see what they are through people's altruistic efforts to create and preserve them. The money of the future will be backed by the things we want to nurture, create, and preserve: by undeveloped land, clean water and air, great works of art and architecture, biodiversity and the genetic commons, unused development rights, unused carbon credits, uncollected patent royalties, relationships not converted into services, and natural resources not converted into goods. Even, indeed, by gold still in the ground.

Not only does association with money (and therefore with abstract "value") elevate a thing to a sacred status, it also impels us to create more and more of it. Gold's association with money encourages the continued (and very environmentally destructive) effort to mine more gold. To dig holes in the ground and fill them back up again is the epitome of wasted work, yet that is essentially what gold mining does. At huge effort, we dig gold ore out of the ground, transport it, refine it, and eventually put it into other holes in the ground called vaults. This effort, and the scarcity of gold, is one (very haphazard) way to regulate the money supply, but why not regulate it through purposeful social and political agreements, or through some more organic process, and save all that hole digging?

The above-mentioned problem with gold extends to other commodities. In places where cattle serve as money, they take on a value beyond the utility of their milk and meat, with the result that people maintain herds larger than they really need. As with gold mining, this wastes human labor and burdens the environment. I am afraid that any commodity-based money will have the same effect. If it is oil, then an incentive will be created to pump more oil—the amount needed for fuel, plus an additional amount for money. Generalized, the principle is, "The use of any thing for money will increase the supply of that thing."

Chapter 11 draws on this principle to create a money system to increase the supply of things we agree are positive goods for humanity and the planet. What if money were "backed" by clean water, unpolluted air, healthy ecosystems, and the cultural commons? Is there a way to encourage the creation of more and more of these in the same way that the social agreement of gold's value drives us to mine more and more of it? Just as the monetization of gold causes us to covet it and seek to produce more of it, and to relinquish it only to meet a real, pressing need, so also might the use of these things for money cause us to create more of them, to create a more beautiful planet, and to sacrifice them only for a well-considered reason, only in response to a real need, only to create something as valuable as what has been destroyed. We destroy many things today for the sake of money, but we do not willingly destroy money itself. And so it shall be.

The question of currency backing leads us to broader and more essential questions: Who gets to create money, and by what process? What limits should govern the amount of its creation? What are the agreements that money embodies? More generally, what is the story of value that we impart to money?

Since the days of ancient Greece, money has always embodied an agreement. Usually, though, the agreement has been an unintentional one. People believed gold was valuable, rarely stopping

to think that this value was conventional. Later, fiat paper currencies were obviously conventional, yet as far as I know no one ever
designed their issue with a specific social purpose in mind beyond
providing a medium of exchange. Never has it been asked, "What
story of the world are we creating, and what kind of money will
embody and reinforce that story?" No one decided to create a
fractional-reserve banking system with the conscious purpose of
impelling the expansion of the human realm. Today, for the first
time, we have the opportunity to infuse some consciousness into
our choice of money. It is time to ask ourselves what collective story
we wish to enact upon this earth, and to choose a money system
aligned with that story.

In the rest of this book I will draw the broad outlines of a
money system embodying humanity's emerging new relationship
to ourselves and to the earth, a money system that reflects and
nourishes the things that are becoming sacred to us. I will also
offer ideas on how to get there from here, on both a collective
and a personal level. This sacred economy will bear the following
characteristics:

It will restore the mentality of the gift to our vocations and
economic life.
It will reverse the money-induced homogenization and deper-
sonalization of society.
It will be an extension of the ecosystem, not a violation of it.
It will promote local economies and revive community.
It will encourage initiative and reward entrepreneurship.
It will be consistent with zero growth, yet foster the continued
development of our uniquely human gifts.
It will promote an equitable distribution of wealth.

It will promote a new materialism that treats the world as sacred.

It will be aligned with political egalitarianism and people power and will not induce more centralized control.

It will restore lost realms of natural, social, cultural, and spiritual capital.

And, most importantly, it is something that we can start creating right now!

The next few chapters will present and synthesize various themes of the new Story of Value that will define a future money system. Weaving them together, a picture will emerge of an economy that is very different from what we know today.

CHAPTER 10

THE LAW OF RETURN

Socialism failed because it couldn't tell the economic truth;
capitalism may fail because it couldn't tell the ecological truth.

—Lester Brown

Here is a certainty: the linear conversion of resources into waste is unsustainable on a finite planet. More unsustainable still is exponential growth, whether of resource use, money, or population.

Not only is it unsustainable; it is also unnatural. In an ecology, no species creates waste that other species cannot use—hence the maxim, "Waste is food." No other species creates growing amounts of substances that are toxic to the rest of life, such as dioxin, PCBs, and radioactive waste. Our linear/exponential growth economy manifestly violates nature's law of return, the cycling of resources.

A sacred economy is an extension of the ecology and obeys all of its rules, among them the law of return. Specifically, that means that every substance produced through industrial processes or other human activities is either used in some other human activity or, ultimately, returned to the ecology in a form, and at a rate, that other beings can process.[1] It means there is no such thing as industrial waste. Everything cycles back to its source. As in the rest of nature, our waste becomes another's food.

---

1. That means that certain substances, even if they are biodegradable, violate the law if we produce them in excessive quantities.

Why do I call such an economy "sacred" rather than natural or ecological? It is because of the sacredness of gifts. To obey the law of return is to honor the spirit of the Gift because we receive what has been given us, and from that gift, we give in turn. Gifts are meant to be passed on. Either we hold onto them for a while and then give them forward, or we use them, digest them, integrate them, and pass them on in altered form. That this is a sacred responsibility is apparent from both a theistic and an atheistic perspective.

From the theistic perspective, consider the source of this world we have been given. It would be a grave error to say, as some evangelicals have told me, that it is fine to use nature destructively, because after all God gave it to us. To squander a gift, to use it poorly, is to devalue the gift and insult the giver. If you give someone a present and he trashes it right in front of your face, you might feel insulted or disappointed; certainly you'll stop giving gifts to that person. I think that anyone who truly believes in God wouldn't dare treat Creation that way but would instead make the most beautiful use possible of life, earth, and everything on it. That means we treat it as the divine gift that it is. In gratitude, we use it well and give in turn. That is the theistic reason why I call a zero-waste economy sacred.

From an atheistic perspective, a zero-waste economy is the economic realization of the interconnectedness of all beings. It embodies the truth that as I do unto the other, so I do unto myself. To the extent that we realize oneness, we desire to pass our gifts forward, to do no harm, and to love others as we love our selves.

On a very practical level, this vision of sacred economy requires eliminating what economists refer to as "externalities." Externalized costs are costs of production that someone else pays. For example, one reason vegetables from California's Central Valley are cheaper to buy in Pennsylvania than local produce is that they don't reflect their full cost. Since producers are not liable to pay the current and future costs of aquifer depletion, pesticide poisoning, soil salinization, and other effects of their farming methods, these costs do not contribute to the price of a head of lettuce. Moreover, the cost of trucking produce across the continent is also highly subsidized. The price of a tank of fuel doesn't include the cost of the pollution it generates, nor the cost of the wars fought to secure it, nor the cost of oil spills. Transport costs don't reflect the construction and maintenance of highways. If all these costs were embodied in a head of lettuce, California lettuce would be prohibitively expensive in Pennsylvania. We would buy only very special things from faraway places.

Many industries today can only operate because their costs are externalized. For example, statutory caps on liability for oil spills and nuclear meltdowns make offshore drilling and nuclear power profitable for their operators, even as the net effect on society is negative. Even if BP goes bankrupt trying, there is no way the company will, or can, pay the full costs of the spill in the Gulf of Mexico. Society will pay the costs, in effect transferring wealth from the public to the company's investors.[2] Any industry with the potential for catastrophic losses is essentially enacting a transfer of wealth from public to private hands, from the many to the few. Those industries operate with free insurance. They get the profits, we assume the risks. It is also so in the financial industry, where the largest operators can take huge risks knowing that they will be

---

2. Even if the company goes bankrupt and wipes out current stock- and bondholders, past investors have already profited.

bailed out if those risks fail. Externalized costs render economical things that are actually uneconomical, such as deep-sea oil drilling and nuclear power.

The elimination of externalities thwarts the business plan of the ages: "I keep the income and someone else pays the costs." I fertilize my field with nitrogen fertilizer, and the shrimp fishermen pay the cost of eutrophication downriver. I burn coal to make electricity, and society pays the medical costs of mercury emissions and the environmental costs of acid rain. All of these strategies are variations on a theme I've already described: the monetization of the commons. The capacity of the earth to absorb various kinds of waste is a form of commonwealth, as is the richness of the soil, the seas, and the aquifers. The collective leisure time of society might be considered a commons as well, which is depleted when polluters make messes for everyone else to clean up.

"I keep the income, and someone else pays the costs" reflects the mind-set of the separate self, in which your well-being is fundamentally disconnected from mine. What does it matter what happens to you? If you are poor, or sick, or in prison, what does that matter to me, as long as I sufficiently insulate myself from the social and environmental toxicity out there? What does it matter to me if the Gulf of Mexico is dying under an oil slick? I'll just live somewhere else. What does it matter to me that there is a thousand-mile-wide gyre of plastic in the Pacific Ocean? From the perspective of separation, it doesn't matter—in principle we can insulate ourselves from the effects of our actions. Profiting by externalizing costs is part and parcel of that perspective. But from the perspective of the connected self, connected to other people and to the earth, your well-being is inseparable from my own because you and I are not fundamentally separate. The internalization of all costs is simply the economic embodiment of that principle of interbeingness: "As I do unto others, so I do unto myself."

Internalizing costs also reflects the perceptions of a gift culture. In the circle of the gift, your good fortune is my good fortune, and your loss is my loss, because you will have correspondingly more or less to give. From that worldview, it is a matter of common sense to include damage to society or nature on the balance sheet. If I depend on you for the gifts you give me, then it is illogical to enrich myself by impoverishing you. In such a world, the best business decision is the one that enriches everybody: society and the planet. A sacred economy must embody this principle, aligning profit with the common weal.

Understanding this principle, some visionary businesspeople have attempted to realize it voluntarily through concepts like the "triple bottom line" and "full-cost accounting." The idea is that their company will act to maximize not just its own profits, but the aggregate of people, planet, and profit—the three bottom lines. The problem is that these companies must compete with others who do the opposite: export their costs onto people and the planet. The triple bottom line and full-cost accounting are useful as a way to evaluate public policy (because they include more than just economic benefits) but when it comes to private enterprise, the first two Ps often run counter to the third. If I am a fisherman trying to fish sustainably, competing with industrial trawlers with hundred-mile-long nets, my higher costs will render me unable to compete. That is why some means is needed to force the internalization of costs and integrate the triple bottom line into a single bottom line that includes all three. We cannot merely hope that people "get it." We must create a system that aligns self-interest with the good of all.

One way to bring externalized costs (and externalized benefits) onto the balance sheet is through cap-and-trade systems and other tradable emissions allowances.[3] Although such systems have borne mixed results in practice (sulfur dioxide ceilings have been relatively successful, while the EU's carbon credits have been a disaster), in principle they allow us to implement a collective agreement on how much is enough. "Enough" depends on the capacity of the planet or the bioregion to assimilate the substance in question. For sulfur dioxide, Europe and America might have separate ceilings to control acid rain; Los Angeles might have its own ozone or nitrous oxide ceiling; the planet might have a single CO_2 and CFC ceiling. Enforcing aggregate ceilings circumvents Jevon's paradox, which says that improvements in efficiency don't necessarily lead to less consumption but can even lead to greater consumption by reducing prices and freeing capital for yet more production.[4]

Considerable controversy surrounds present-day cap-and-trade proposals, and by and large, I agree with their critics. A truly effective emissions allowance program would be an auction system with no offsets, no free credits, no grandfather clauses, and strict sanctions on noncomplying countries. Even so, problems remain: price volatility, speculative derivatives trading, and corruption. Enforcement is an especially critical problem because cap-and-trade gives a big advantage to manufacturers in places with lax enforcement, which could result in more total pollution than the present regula-

---

3. In such systems, a total emissions ceiling is set, and the right to emit allocated among countries or enterprises. Pollution rights may be bought and sold, so that if a factory reduces its emissions, it can sell its unused quota to someone else.

4. For example, when the cost of lighting drops due to the introduction of CFC bulbs, some facilities respond by increasing their use of outdoor lighting. When computer memory gets cheaper, developers write software that requires more memory. When any resource is used more efficiently, the demand for it goes down and lowers the price, thereby increasing demand.

tory regime.[5] Another problem is that in a cap-and-trade system, individual restraint frees up resources or allowances to be used by someone else, leading to a feeling of personal powerlessness.

The problems with cap-and-trade suggest a different approach: direct taxes on pollution, such as Paul Hawken's carbon tax. Fossil fuels could be taxed on import, and the proceeds rebated to the public. This is another way to force the internalization of costs, and would be especially appropriate in situations where the social and environmental costs are easy to quantify and remedy. As with cap-and-trade, international enforcement is a big problem, as manufacturing would become more profitable in countries that refused to levy the tax or collected it inefficiently. It might also require frequent rate adjustment in order to attain the desired ceiling.

For those readers who recoil at the suggestion of another tax, consider that the two mechanisms I have described, cap-and-trade systems and green taxes, are not actually new levies upon society. Someone is going to be paying the costs of environmental destruction regardless. In the present system, this "someone" is either innocent bystanders or future generations. These proposals merely shift these costs onto those who create them and profit from them.

However it is accomplished, when the costs of pollution are internalized, the best business decision comes into alignment with the best environmental decision. Suppose you are an inventor and you come up with a great idea for a factory to cut pollution by 90 percent with no loss of productivity. Today, that factory has no incentive to implement your idea because it doesn't pay the costs of that pollution. If, however, the cost of pollution were internalized,

---

5. Polluters in lax-enforcement countries could sell allowances to polluters in countries with good enforcement, allowing the latter to pollute at low cost and the former to pollute beyond the total emissions ceiling.

your invention would be a hot item. A whole new set of economic incentives emerges from the internalization of costs. The goodness of our hearts, which want to cut pollution even if it isn't economic, would no longer have to do battle with the pressures of money.

While both cap-and-trade programs and pollution taxes have a role to play in the internalization of social and ecological costs, we could also integrate them into the structure of money itself, an intentional kind of money that embodies our reverence for the planet and our emerging sense of the role and purpose of humanity on earth. It unites the internalization of costs with the rectification of the great injustice of property described in Chapter 4, returning the commons to the people while nonetheless giving free rein to the spirit of entrepreneurship. It implements the principle of Chapter 9: to make money sacred by backing it with the things that have become sacred to us. Among them are precisely the same things that green taxes and the like aim to preserve. While the details of cap-and-trade, currency issue, and so forth may have a technocratic feel to them, the underlying impulse, which the next chapter will flesh out, is to align money with the things we hold sacred.

Whether it is accomplished through traditional taxation or cap-and-trade, or by integrating it into money itself, we are embarking on a profoundly different relationship to Earth. In the days of the Ascent, the story of the growth of the human realm and the conquest of the wild, in the time of humanity's childhood, when the world seemed to have infinite room to accommodate our growth, there was no need for collective agreements on how many fish to catch, how many trees to cut, how much ore to dig, or how much of the atmosphere's capacity to absorb waste to use. Today, our relationship to the rest of nature is changing on a fundamental level, as it is impossible to ignore the limits of the environment. The fisheries, the forests, the clean water, and the clean air are all obviously close to depletion. We have the power to destroy the earth, or at least to cause her grievous harm. She is vulnerable to us, as a lover is to a lover. In that sense, it is no longer appropriate to think of her only as Mother Earth. A child, in his wanting, does not take his mother's limits into account. Between lovers it is different. That is why I foresee a future in which we maintain local, regional, and global ceilings on the use of various resources. Fishery catches, groundwater use, carbon emissions, timber harvests, topsoil depletion, and many more will be carefully monitored and held to sustainable levels. These resources—clean water, clean air, minerals, biota, and more—will be sacred to us, so sacred that I doubt we will refer to them as "resources," any more than we refer to our own vital organs as resources, or dream of depleting them.

Actually, we *do* deplete our own vital organs, for purposes analogous to those for which we deplete the vital organs of the earth. As one would expect from an understanding of the connected self, what we do to the earth, we do to ourselves. The parallels run deep, so for brevity's sake I'll limit myself to just one: the parallel between our drawdown of the earth's stored fossil fuel and the depletion of the adrenal glands through chemical and psychological stimulants. In traditional Chinese medical thought, the adrenal glands are part of the kidney organ system, which is understood to be the reservoir of the original qi, the life force, as well as the gateway to an ongoing supply of acquired qi. When we are in harmony with our life purpose, these gateways to the life force open wide and give us a constant supply of energy. But when we lose this alignment, we must use increasingly violent methods (coffee, motivational techniques, threats) to jerk the life force through the adrenals. Similarly, the technologies we use to access fossil fuels have become more and more violent—

hydraulic fracturing (or fracking), mountaintop removal, tar sand exploitation, and so on—and we are using these fuels for frivolous or destructive purposes that are evidently out of alignment with the purpose of the human species on earth. The personal and planetary mirror each other. The connection is more than mere analogy: the kind of work that we use coffee and external motivation (e.g., money) to force ourselves to do is precisely the kind of work that contributes to the despoliation of the planet. We don't really want to do it to our bodies; we don't really want to do it to the world.

We want to become givers and not just takers in our relationship to Earth. With that in mind, I will touch upon one more aspect of the law of return and the cosmic unity of giving and receiving. It would seem that there is a flagrant exception to the law of return in nature, something that ecosystems do not recycle, something that enters constantly anew and exits always as waste. That something is energy. Radiating out from the sun, it is captured by plants and converted along the food chain from one form to another, moving irreversibly toward its final destination: waste heat. Sooner or later, all the low-entropy electromagnetic radiation from the sun is radiated back out from the earth as high-entropy heat.[6]

I am not surprised that ancient people worshiped the sun, the only thing we know that gives without expectation or even possibility of return. The sun is generosity manifest. It powers the entire kingdom of life, and, in the form of fossil fuels, solar, wind, and hydroelectric power, can power the technosphere as well. Marveling at this virtually limitless source of free energy, I can touch upon the utter, almost infantile, gratitude that ancient sun-worshipers must have felt.

---

6. "Later" could be hundreds of millions of years, for example when we burn coal.

But there is more to the story. A vein runs through spiritual tradition that says that we, too, give back to the sun; indeed that the sun only continues to shine through our gratitude.[7] Ancient sun rituals weren't only to thank the sun—they were to keep it shining. Solar energy is the light of earthly love reflected back at us. Here, too, the circle of the gift operates. We are not separate from even the sun, which is why, perhaps, we can sometimes feel an inner sun shining from within us, irradiating all others with the warmth and light of generosity.

---

7. Interestingly, as the age of ingratitude has reached its peak over the past thirty years, the sun's radiation has apparently changed, and the strength of the helio-sphere has decreased significantly. It might be my imagination, but I remember the sun being more yellow when I was a child. And from 2008 to 2010, sunspot activity diminished to unprecedented levels (see, e.g., Clark, "Absence of Sunspots"). Could it be that the sun, the epitome of generosity, is entering a turbulent phase mirroring the financial crisis on earth, which is after all a crisis of giving and receiving?

CHAPTER 11

CURRENCIES OF THE COMMONS

All money is a matter of belief.

—Adam Smith

We live on a naturally abundant planet, the source of life-sustaining gifts for us all. As observed in Chapter 4, the planet's riches—soil, water, air, minerals, the genome—were created by no man and should therefore be the property of none, but held in common stewardship for all beings. The same holds for the accumulation of human technology and culture, which is the bequest of our collective forebears, a source of wealth that no living person deserves less than any other.

But what to do with this realization? These truths are closely aligned with the Marxist and anarchist critique of property, but the Marxist solution—collective ownership of the means of production, administered by the state—does not reach deeply enough; nor does it address the real problem.[1] The real problem is that in both the communist and corporate-capitalist systems, a power elite makes and benefits from the decision of how to deploy society's wealth.

---

1. I should acknowledge here that pure Marxist theory does not see state ownership as the final stage of communism, but says that the state will eventually wither away, and, presumably, the concept of property along with it.

The convention of property—common or private—is used in both cases to justify and facilitate the allocation of wealth and power.

The metamorphosis of human economy that is underway in our time will go more deeply than the Marxist revolution because the Story of the People that it weaves won't be just a new fiction of ownership, but a recognition of its fictive, conventional nature. What is property but a social agreement that a certain person has certain rights to use something in certain prescribed ways? Property is not an objective feature of reality, and to reify it and make it into something elemental, as both capitalistic and communistic theory do, is to unconsciously enslave ourselves to the story that contains it. I do not think that a sacred economics can start with ownership as an elemental property because that conception buys into a worldview, a story of self and world, that is not true, or that is true no longer— the discrete and separate self in an objective universe. So instead of saying, as a Marxist might, that the bequest of nature and culture should be collectively owned, let us cease applying the concept of property to these things altogether and think instead of how to justly, creatively, and beautifully embody their value in an economic system.

Today, access to money, via credit, goes to those who are likely to expand the realm of goods and services. In a sacred economy, it will go to those who contribute to a more beautiful world. While we may not all agree on what that world looks like, many important common values are emerging in our time. I have been gratified to discover, in my interaction with people from all parts of the political spectrum, a near-universal reverence for community, for nature, and for the beautiful products of human culture. Around these common values, which political language tends to obfuscate by superimposing divisions atop our common humanity, the currency of sacred economy will emerge.

In this chapter I will refer to "government" in the context of currency issue, but keep in mind that like all of our institutions, government is going to change dramatically in coming years. Ultimately, I envision decentralized, self-organizing, emergent, peer-to-peer, ecologically integrated expressions of political will. Parallel to this, I envision an ecology of money as well, an economic system with many complementary modes of circulation and exchange. Among them will be new extensions of the gift, freeing work from compulsion and guaranteeing the necessities of life to all.

Whatever form it takes, an essential purpose of government— maybe *the* essential purpose of government—is to serve as the trustee of the commons. The commons includes the surface of the earth, the minerals under the earth, the water on and under the ground, the richness of the soil, the electromagnetic spectrum, the planetary genome, the biota of local and global ecosystems, the atmosphere, the centuries-long accumulation of human knowledge and technology, and the artistic, musical, and literary treasures of our ancestors. As social reformers have observed for over two thousand years, no single person can make rightful claim to any of these things.

In the past, I might have said that the purpose of government is to administer these treasures for the benefit of all people. That's a good start, but today, as we step into the relationship of Lover Earth, I say instead that government embodies our collective stewardship of these treasures on behalf of earth itself, which includes humanity as its newest organ. We can no longer look upon humanity as just another life-form on the planet because we have the power to alter or even destroy the planet as no other species ever has before.

What could be a better basis for a money system—the story of value—than these things that are so precious, so sacred, so *valuable?*

Accordingly, part of a sacred money supply will be "backed" by those things of which we are collective stewards. Here is one way it could work: first, we reach a collective, politically mediated agreement on the right amount of nature to turn toward human purposes: how much of the produce of the sea, how much of the soil, the water; how much of the capacity of the atmosphere to absorb and transform waste; how much of the land's ability to recover from the scars of mineral extraction; how much of the gift of fossil fuels, metal ores, and other wealth; how much of nature's quiet to give over to machine noises; how much of the dark night sky to give to city lights. These decisions often require scientific understanding, but just as often they embody value judgments. Both contribute to our collective agreement on how much natural capital to consume.

Such a decision is something new on the face of the earth. To be sure, governments today use regulations and taxes to halt or slow the consumption of certain parts of the commons, but never yet have we gotten together to ask, "How much is enough?" Ancient villages protected their commons through tradition, custom, and social pressure (the "tragedy of the commons" is largely a myth[2]), but on the scale of society today, we need to engage a political process to reach and implement a consensus. This process would consider the scientific consensus about what use of the commons is sustainable, as well as the social consensus about the relative importance of, say, the labor-saving convenience of internal combustion engines versus the pleasures of a quiet autumn day.

---

2. The tragedy of the commons is a pseudo-historical story meant to illustrate the free-rider problem. In it, the meadow in a village commons was stripped bare of vegetation, because it was to each villager's advantage to graze as many sheep there as possible. When everyone pursued their own advantage, the result was overgrazing and losses for all.

Once we have decided how much of each commons should be made available for use, we can issue money "backed" by it. For example, we might decide that the atmosphere can sustain total sulfur dioxide emissions of two million tons a year. We can then use the emissions rights as a currency backing. The same goes for the rest of the commons. The result would be a long list comprising all the elements of the commons we agree to use for economic purposes. Conceptually, it might look something like this:

> Our money derives its value from the right to harvest 300,000 tons of cod from the Newfoundland cod fishery, the right to draw 30 million gallons of water monthly from the Ogallala Aquifer, the right to emit 10 billion tons of CO_2, the right to pump 2 billion barrels of oil from the ground, the use of the X-microhertz band of the electromagnetic spectrum ...

How to implement this in practice? One way would be for the government to simply create money and spend it into the economy in the way governments spend tax revenues today. The money would circulate through the economy and eventually back to the government when producers redeem it for the backing items. This could happen through auction, or relative prices for the backing items could be set in advance and then adjusted each year according to actual prices on the secondary market. Either way, the redemption of money for backing items would function just like a tax on resources and pollution.

Let's look at a concrete example of how it might work. A local government issues salaries to police, firefighters, and the local ecological cleanup crew. One of them spends her salary on food, electricity, and a new transmission for her car. The food comes from a local farm, which spends part of the money for the right to pump

300,000 gallons of water a year from the local aquifer. This payment goes to the local government, which is the steward of that part of the commons.

Meanwhile, part of the money for the transmission goes to a factory somewhere, which pays part of that for pollution credits needed to operate. That cost is embodied in the price of the transmission, which also reflects the pollution credits for the gasoline used to transport it, the mineral rights for the iron ore used to make the steel, and so forth. These payments go to various stewards of the commons, some local, some regional, some national or global. Any factory that figures out a way to use less of the commons—for example, to make less pollution, or to use recycled metal from old junkyards—will be able to reduce its costs and earn a higher profit. The profit motive thereby becomes the ally, not the enemy, of our desire to heal the earth.

Remember the principle that whatever commodity we use as money becomes valuable, so that we seek more of it. When gold is money, we mine more gold, beyond any practical need for it. In societies where cattle are money, people keep herds beyond what they need. If we use oil or energy as a currency backing, as some propose, then we will try to produce and hoard more oil. But what if we use oil still in the ground, gold still under the mountain, and forests still in their pristine state as currency backing? Won't we then elevate their value, too, and seek to create more and more of them? The mechanism is not at all mysterious. If you have to pay the full environmental costs of oil extraction, you will diligently find ways to keep it in the ground. If you have to pay for each unit of pollution, you will strive to pollute less.

An alternative means to the same end would be for the government to create credit-money by borrowing from the central bank at zero interest and repaying the loans with money from the sale of the items of the commons it holds in trust. The government could also issue bonds to investors and the central bank exercise monetary policy as it does today by purchasing or selling varying amounts of these bonds on the open market. It is crucial that these bonds bear zero (or negative) interest, a possibility I will explain in the next two chapters. Otherwise, a need for perpetual growth in the use of the commons would be created.

Either way, producers would have a financial incentive to minimize their use of the commons. No such incentive exists today, or if it does, it exists only haphazardly. This system would fully internalize social and ecological costs. Today, when a mining company drains an aquifer or a trawling fleet depletes a fishery, the costs to society and the planet are external to the producer's own balance sheet. With this system, that is no longer true. Since these costs would be passed onto downstream industries and eventually to consumers, consumers would no longer face today's dilemma that the cheapest products are those that cause the most social and environmental damage, while the fair-trade and eco-friendly products are way more expensive. Instead, products that avoided pollution in their manufacture would be cheaper because pollution quotas would cost a lot of money. Products would be more expensive in proportion to the amount of the natural commons consumed in their production.

Some might object that this system would necessitate a lot of bureaucracy and paperwork, since it requires keeping track of every pollutant and social cost generated in the process of production. My answer to that is twofold. First, this system embodies the new attitude of environmental responsibility that *wants* to know and take responsibility for the effects of our actions on other beings.

Look what happens to the earth, when we are oblivious to the risk of oil spills and nuclear disasters. Increasingly, we want to know what we are doing, we want to know all the effects of our actions, and we want to take responsibility for them. This attitude is quite natural for the connected self that knows, "As I do unto the other, so I do unto myself."

Secondly, what I have described is actually much less complicated than today's byzantine and uneconomic system of regulation, which puts environmental responsibility and financial profit in opposition. From the user's perspective, it is nothing more than a shift of taxation away from sales and income and toward raw materials and pollution. Private producers would have to pay for things that are now "free"—free to them at least. You might see this as a form of indirect taxation, but another way to look at it is that producers are simply paying for the things they take from the commons, the things they take from us all. It is only fair. We might say that such taxation is simply the enactment of the principle that "those who benefit from the larger community of life must also contribute to the larger community of life." Those who take from the commonwealth must contribute to the common good in equal measure.

The kind of taxes, the means of levying contributions to the common good, that we have today are nearly the opposite of what we want to create in our world. We can take from the commons—that which no one should own—without paying for it, yet the one thing we can be said to own—our own productive labor—is subject to taxation in the form of income tax. Meanwhile, we are forced to pay a tax on the circulation of goods—a sales tax—while there is no tax on the accumulation of wealth not used for exchange. We have it backward. The money system I am describing in this chapter reverses income tax, shifting taxes away from what you earn and onto what you take. The next chapter describes a similar reversal of sales tax, shifting costs away from spending and onto hoarding.

Despite my upbringing in a politically liberal household that justifies income taxes on the grounds that they put more of the tax burden on those most able to pay, I always felt a kind of primal indignation about income tax. It seems unfair. Why should the most productive or hardworking people pay more? It makes much more sense to make people pay for what they are actually taking.

For the reader unfamiliar with unorthodox economic thought, I want to emphasize that this proposal fits into a respectable historical context. It is a synthesis of several elements. The idea of shifting taxes onto polluters and resource consumption was developed by A. C. Pigou in the early twentieth century and carried forward by such people as Herman Daly, Paul Hawken, and numerous environmentalists. The idea of eliminating profit from the ownership of the commons goes back to the tradition of Henry George that I discussed in Chapter 4.[3] Numerous recent thinkers have suggested backing currency with such things as energy and other resources (though as far as I know they haven't considered backing it with energy and resources still in the ground). What I am describing in this chapter is the natural extension of the ideas of Henry George and Silvio Gesell into the ecological age, firmly grounded in two or three converging traditions of thought.

The most important item of the commonwealth is undoubtedly the land itself, the subject of the original criticisms of the institution of property. The proposals of George and Gesell that arise from this criticism fit seamlessly into the monetary system I

3. The unfairness and economic inefficiency of economic rents were recognized by classical economists as well and come under criticism in the writings of Adam Smith, David Ricardo, and John Stuart Mill. See Hudson, "Deficit Commission Follies."

have described. For what is George's "single tax" but a fee paid for the right to use the commons (of land)? This tax, which applies to the underlying value of land independent of any improvements upon it,[4] could also take the form of a lease or a right-to-use payment. Obviously, since improvements to land are immobile and often require years or decades to build, lessees would have to enjoy the first right to renew. Many gradual and gentle ways have been proposed to realize the reclamation of the land commons for the public; there is no need to confiscate existing real estate holdings, but only to enact the principle that the earth belongs to everyone.[5] That means that no one should be allowed to benefit financially from owning the land.

The same goes for the electromagnetic spectrum, the minerals under the earth, the genome, and the accumulated fund of human knowledge. These should be available for rent, not ownership, and the rents should go to the public. Presumably, those who can put these assets to best use would be the most eager to rent them. There would still be room for entrepreneurship—even more so than today since access to resources would be based not on prior ownership but on most effective use. There would be no more profiting from "I own and you don't."

---

4. This distinction is actually somewhat problematic. The value of the land and the value of "improvements" on the land cannot always be separated. For one, human activity can alter the land permanently and change its "underlying value." Secondly, improvements can attract other people to the area, raising land prices generally regardless of improvements. Thus, paradoxically, improving land can raise the value of the underlying unimproved land, creating a disincentive to make improvements. I think these difficulties, which apply to some degree to other kinds of natural capital, are resolvable, but a detailed discussion is beyond the scope of this book.

5. For example, land could gradually be bought out from private ownership by instituting a 3-percent land-value tax initially paid for by existing equity so that owners would only have to start paying the tax thirty-three years later.

The foregoing account of currency issue may have left the impression that it is the federal government that will create most of the money. This is not what I envision. Many of the commons on which money will be based are best administered bioregionally. Many pollutants, for instance, wreak their most devastating effects on local ecosystems, and only indirectly on the planet as a whole. It does little good to restrict global emissions of ozone when the damage to people and trees comes from regional concentrations of it. Thus it might be the state of California, or perhaps smaller political divisions of it, that issue currency backed by ozone emissions allowances. In some cases, where there is an overlap of local and global effects, polluters might have to pay for two different allowances for the same pollutant.

The most important commons, the land, is also inherently a local commons—in fact, land provides the very definition of "local." Overall, basing money on the commons entails a general devolution of financial and ultimately political authority to the local level. Of course, there are some kinds of commonwealth, and some human endeavors, that involve the entire planet; inescapably, then, there must be political power on a global level with the ability to coordinate human activity, probably using money. But global or national governments should not administer any form of the commons that is inherently regional or local. Since so much of the commons— land, watersheds, minerals, some fisheries, and the capacity of the ecosystem to handle many types of pollution—is local, the money system I describe corresponds to a shift in political power away from centralized governments. Local governments will have the power to issue money backed by real wealth.

So far I have described how national and local governments could issue money based on the natural wealth they administer in trust for communities, humanity, and the earth. Yet not every source of wealth is something from the collective commons. Critics of property going back to the early Christian fathers recognized that a person at least owns his or her own time, labor, and life. After all, we are born with nothing else, and shall return to the grave with not even that. If anything, our lives are our own. Shouldn't individuals, then, be able to issue money or obtain credit "backed" by the their own productive resources?

Well, we already do this today, when private enterprises and individuals create money through bank credit. Whether or not we can say we "own" our lives, surely we are the stewards of our time, our energy, and the creative power that dwells within us. If a government can issue currency based on the productive wealth it holds in trust, why can't a private entity do the same?

I ask this question because some monetary reformers think this is a bad idea and have built entire economic philosophies around gold or fiat money systems in which fractional-reserve banking and private creation of credit-money would be prohibited. I will address this issue in some depth because it represents an important line of thinking in the New Economics. Recent proposals by monetary historian Stephen Zarlenga have even found sympathy in the fringes of American politics, notably with Congressman Ron Paul. The abolition of fractional-reserve banking also is part of the philosophies of certain followers of the social credit movement, the Austrian School of economics, and many others. Their logic seemed compelling to me at first, and they provide a very thorough account of the disastrous effects of debt growth in the mid- and late-twentieth century, when money became decoupled from gold. A 100-percent reserve system, it is claimed, would prevent debt from outstripping money—but how, then, to prevent concentration of wealth in the presence of interest?

Except for the Austrian School, most proponents of 100-percent reserves also support some kind of economic redistribution or monetary expansion, such as direct spending of government fiat money into the economy so that debtors can obtain enough money to repay principle and interest on loans. Frederick Soddy, among the first modern economists to recognize the impossibility of unlimited exponential growth and to distinguish between money and wealth, proposed a 100-percent reserve requirement for banks, excluding them from the business of money creation, but also provided that the government would spend money into existence at levels sufficient to prevent deflation. Irving Fisher, a founder of mathematical economics and arguably America's greatest economist, put forth a very similar proposal that he called "100-percent money." Major Douglas went even farther by advocating a social dividend to be paid to all citizens.

I spent quite a while trying to resolve the question of whether fractional-reserve banking or full-reserve banking is consistent with sacred economics. After wrestling with the formidable complexities of the issue and reading papers going back to the 1930s, one day I gave up and lay down on the couch where, predictably and somewhat to my chagrin, it dawned on me that the two systems are not as fundamentally different as most people think. The confusion, which is rife on the internet, comes on one level from a simplistic and incorrect view of how fractional-reserve banking actually works, and on a deeper level from an artificial and irrelevant distinction between what is conventional and what is real. I present an alternative view in the appendix.

Here, suffice it to say that the proposals of this book can fit into either system. Overall I am more sympathetic to a system that includes private credit, first because it allows organic, endogenous money creation independent of a central authority; second because it more easily incorporates exciting new modes of economic cooperation such as commercial barter rings and mutual-credit systems; third because it allows for much more flexibility in financial intermediation and capital formation; and fourth because it simplifies interbank credit clearing. Moreover, as some of Irving Fisher's associates began realizing in the mid-1930s, it is nearly impossible to prevent fractional-reserve deposits from appearing in covert forms.[6] I draw this point out in the appendix, but consider: even if you issue an IOU to a friend, and your friend gives it to another friend in lieu of cash, you are increasing the money supply.

Whatever the advantages and shortcomings of private money creation via credit, and whether the government issues fiat money or creates credit money in partnership with a central bank, a vastly greater proportion of money will originate outside the private banking system than it does today. The reason is quite simple: much of the natural commonwealth that is used as the basis for private credit creation today would become public. No longer, for example, would a company be able to take out a business loan based on projected future revenues from depleting an aquifer. The future costs of that depletion will have been internalized and returned to the

---

6. Economist Henry Simons wrote to Fisher in 1934, "Savings-deposits, treasury certificates, and even commercial paper are almost as close to demand deposits as are demand deposits to legal-tender currency. The whole problem which we now associate with commercial banking might easily reappear in other forms of financial arrangements. . . . Little would be gained by putting demand deposit banking on a 100% basis if that change were accompanied by increasing disposition to hold, and increasing facilities for holding, liquid 'cash' reserves in the form of time-deposits. The fact that such deposits cannot serve as circulating medium is not decisively important; for they are an effective substitute medium for purposes of cash balances. The expansion of time deposits, releasing circulating medium from 'hoards,' might be just as inflationary as expansion of demand deposits—and their contraction just as deflationary." Cited in Allen, "Irving Fisher," 708–9.

public via use-rights payments. There might still be opportunity to profit, however—for example, if someone finds a more efficient or productive use of the same amount of water. Such things are a legitimate basis for private credit creation; what is illegitimate is to create money by taking something that should belong to all.

Because of today's concentrated private ownership of the commonwealth, the profits that come through mere ownership are also highly concentrated. When producers (and ultimately consumers) pay the full cost of embedded energy and raw materials and the fair rental price for the land and other commons, then much of the wealth that concentrates in few hands today will accrue instead to the stewards of the commons. The situation will be analogous to what happens when a nation such as Venezuela or Bolivia nationalizes its oil fields. Foreign producers can still operate the fields, but they profit only from the service of extracting the oil and not from ownership of the oil itself. That part of the profit goes to the nation. What happens to that money depends on politics—it could go to a coterie of corrupt officials, or it could go to public works projects, or it could be paid directly to the people as a kind of royalty (as in Alaska, where each resident gets an annual payment of several thousand dollars). Extended beyond oil to the entire commons, this makes enormous amounts of money available to various levels of government, especially at the local and bioregional level, replacing current forms of taxation.

Another consequence of commons-based currency is that we would pay a lot more for many things that are cheap today because their prices would embody costs that we now pass on to other people or future generations. Goods would become more expensive in comparison to services, providing an economic incentive for repairing, reusing, and recycling. Gone would be the skewed economics that makes it cheaper to buy a new television set than repair an old one. Gone would be the present financial incentive for planned obsolescence. A new business model (emerging already in some industries) would blossom: extremely durable, easily repairable machines that are leased rather than sold to consumers.

It was only two generations ago that appliances as humble as a toaster would be taken to repair shops. Even shoes and clothes were mended. Not only are such services inherently local, thus helping to invigorate local economies, but they also contribute to an attitude of caring toward our material things, and by extension toward materiality in general. A life full of throwaway stuff is not a rich life. How can we have a sacred economy if we don't treat its subjects—the things that people create and exchange—with reverence? I find it very satisfying that a money system based on a protective reverence for nature induces, on the individual level, the same reverent attitude toward the things we make from natural raw materials.

On the collective level, this reverence will take the form of a much different emphasis on government spending. The huge resources made available through reclaiming the commons for the public good can go toward healing the damage of past centuries of despoliation of that commons. Ecological disasters will relentlessly direct our attention to the urgent need to heal the forests, wetlands, oceans, atmosphere, and every other ecosystem from the devastation wrought in the industrial era. The urgency of this need will shift our energy away from consumption and war.

War is an unavoidable accompaniment to an economic system that demands growth. Whether through the colonization of lands or the subjugation of peoples, we have a constant need to access new sources of social and natural capital to feed the money machine. Wars also increase consumption, alleviating the crisis of overcapacity described earlier. Competition for resources and markets was thus a primary driver of the wars of the twentieth century, both among the great powers, and against anyone who resisted colonization and imperialism. Limiting resource consumption is one of the pillars of a steady-state or degrowth economy, which short-circuits this primary driving force for war and frees up vast resources to turn toward the goal of healing the planet.

The money system I have described goes a long way in reversing the age-old injustice of property, as well as the predation of the few against the many and against the future inherent in the exploitation of the commons. There is a big piece missing, though: as established in Chapter 5, the same injustice that inheres in property inheres in money as well. I have described a new story of value and how to embody it in money but so far left untouched its compulsion, which is independent of the story of value, to drive either growth or concentration of wealth (or both). Is it possible to treat money as a commons in the same way as the land or the atmosphere? Is it possible to reverse the mechanism of interest, which, like the expropriation of the commons, allows those who own it to profit by its mere ownership? It is to this crucial matter we turn next.

CHAPTER 12

NEGATIVE-INTEREST ECONOMICS

Debt can endure forever; wealth cannot, because its physical dimension is subject to the destructive force of entropy.

—Frederick Soddy

Suppose I have twelve loaves of bread, and you are hungry. I cannot eat so much bread before it goes stale, so I am happy to lend some of it to you. "Here, take these six loaves," I say, "and when you have bread in the future, you can give me six loaves back again." I give you six fresh loaves now, and you give me six fresh loaves sometime in the future.

In a world where the things we need and use go bad, sharing comes naturally. The hoarder ends up sitting alone atop a pile of stale bread, rusty tools, and spoiled fruit, and no one wants to help him, for he has helped no one. Money today, however, is not like bread, fruit, or indeed any natural object. It is the lone exception to nature's law of return, the law of life, death, and rebirth, which says that all things ultimately return to their source. Money does not decay over time, but in its abstraction from physicality, it remains changeless or even grows with time, exponentially, thanks to the power of interest.

We associate money very closely with self. As the word "mine" implies, we see our money almost as an extension of our selves, which is why we feel "ripped off" when it is taken from us. Money, then, violates not only the natural law of return, but the spiritual law of impermanence. Associating something that persists and grows over time with a self that ages, dies, and returns to the soil perpetuates an illusion. Though we all know better, we imagine somehow that by adding wealth we add to ourselves and can gain the imperishability of money. We store it up for old age, as if we could thereby forestall our own decay. What would be the effect of money that, like all other things, decays and returns to its source?

We have attached an exponentially growing money to a self and world that are neither exponential nor even linear, but cyclic. The result, as I have described, is competition, scarcity, and the concentration of wealth. The answer to the question I posed earlier, "What has gone wrong with this beautiful idea called money, which can connect human gifts and human needs?" comes down in large part to interest, to usury. But usury itself is not some isolated phenomenon that could have been different if only we'd made a wiser choice somewhere down the line. It is irrefrangibly bound to our sense of self, the separate self in an objective universe, whose evolution parallels the evolution of money. It is no accident that the first highly monetized society, ancient Greece, was also the birthplace of the modern concept of the individual.

This deep link between money and being is good news because human identity today is undergoing a profound metamorphosis. What kind of money will be consistent with the new self, the connected self, and a world in which we increasingly realize the truth of interconnectedness: that more for you is more for me? Given the determining role of interest, the first alternative currency system to consider is one that structurally eliminates it, or even that bears interest's opposite. After all, if interest causes competition, scarcity, and polarization, then might not its opposite create cooperation, abundance, and community? And if interest represents the proceeds from the ancient and ongoing robbery of the commons, might not its opposite replenish it?

What would that opposite look like? It would be a money that, like bread, becomes less valuable over time. It would be money, in other words, that decays—money that is subject to a negative interest rate, also known as a demurrage charge.[1] Decaying currency is one of the central ideas of this book, but before I lay out its history, application, economic theory, and consequences, I would like to say a bit about the term "decay," which I have been advised to avoid due to its negative connotations.

Why does "decay" seem negative, and "preservation" a virtue? This attitude arises again from the story of Ascent, in which humanity's destiny is to transcend nature; to triumph over entropy, chaos, and decay; and to establish an ordered realm: scientific, rational, clean, controlled. Complementary to it is a spirituality of separation, in which a nonmaterial, eternal, deathless, divine soul

---

1. Demurrage originally referred to a storage cost for goods, for example in addition to freight shipping costs. This term naturally applies to decaying currency because it applies to the use of money as a "store" of value. The goods for which it could be exchanged have upkeep costs, carry costs, and storage costs; therefore so should the money. The disadvantage of this term is that it is unfamiliar to most people and awkward.

Depreciating currency captures the idea that the value of the money declines with time. Unfortunately, the term is easily misunderstood to mean a depreciation in the purchasing power of the currency itself, rather than in the value of each token unit of it. Usually, depreciation refers to the value of a currency in relation to other currencies.

"Negative interest" conveys the basic idea very effectively, especially in describing the system as a whole. It can create confusion, however, since interest usually applies to lending money and not to money itself. I will use these various terms interchangeably in this book, along with Silvio Gesell's term, "free-money."

inhabits an impermanent, mortal, profane body. So we have sought to conquer the body, conquer the world, and arrest the processes of decay. Unfortunately, by so doing we also arrest the larger process of which decay is part: renewal, rebirth, recycling, and the spiraling evolution toward more vastly integrated complexity. Thankfully, the stories of Separation and Ascent are drawing to a close. It is time to reclaim the beauty and necessity of decay, both in our thinking and in our economics.

HISTORY AND BACKGROUND

Early forms of commodity-money, such as grain, cattle, and the like were certainly subject to decay: grain spoils, cattle age and die, and even farmland reverts to wilderness if left untended. There have also been metallic money systems that approximated the phenomenon of decay by incorporating a kind of built-in negative interest rate. A crude example of such a system was in wide use in the Middle Ages in Europe's *Brakteaten* system, in which coins were periodically recalled and then reminted at a discount rate.[2] In England, Saxon kings recoined silver pennies every six years, issuing three for every four taken in, for a depreciation rate of about 4 percent per year.[3] This effectively imposed a penalty on the hoarding of money, encouraging instead its circulation and investment in productive capital. If you had more money than you could use, you would be happy to lend it, even at zero interest, because your coins would decrease in value if you held them too long. Note that the money supply didn't necessarily shrink as a result of this system,

---

2. Kennedy, *Interest and Inflation-Free Money*, 40.
3. Zarlenga, *Lost Science of Money*, 253.

since the lord would presumably inject the difference back into the economy to cover his own expenses. This negative interest on money was thus a kind of a tax.

The pioneering theoretician of negative-interest money was the German-Argentinean businessman Silvio Gesell, who called it "free-money" (*Freigeld*), a name that I will adopt in his honor. The system he proposed in his 1906 masterwork, *The Natural Economic Order*, was to use paper currency to which a stamp costing a small fraction of the note's value had to be affixed periodically. This effectively attached a maintenance cost to monetary wealth. Like any physical commodity, such money "goes bad" (at a rate determined by the value of the stamps required to keep the currency valid). For example, if a dollar bill required a one-cent stamp every month to stay valid, it would depreciate at an annual rate of 12 percent.[4]

Gesell arrived at the idea of demurrage-charged currency from a different direction than I have. He was writing in an era when almost no one questioned the desirability of economic growth, and visionary though he was, Gesell never doubted (as far as I know) the capacity of the earth or technology to accommodate it forever.[5] His primary concern was to remedy the inequitable and unjust distribution of wealth in his time, the unprecedented poverty amidst unprecedented abundance. This he attributed to a huge unfair advantage held by the possessors of money: they possess a "hoardable commodity that is at the same time the money medium." Other commodities (except possibly land) are not hoardable in the same way that gold or other currency is: they rot, rust,

---

4. Without the stamps, it would effectively be worth 88 cents.

5. Only a few of Gesell's writings have been translated into English. I would be interested to know whether he touches upon any ecological themes in his voluminous German writings.

or decay; are subject to theft or obsolescence; incur storage and transport costs; and so on. He wrote,

> Gold does not harmonize with the character of our goods. Gold and straw, gold and petrol, gold and guano, gold and bricks, gold and iron, gold and hides! Only a wild fancy, a monstrous hallucination, only the doctrine of "value" can bridge the gulf. Commodities in general, straw, petrol, guano and the rest can be safely exchanged only when everyone is indifferent as to whether he possesses money or goods, and that is possible only if money is afflicted with all the defects inherent in our products. That is obvious. Our goods rot, decay, break, rust, so only if money has equally disagreeable, loss-involving properties can it effect exchange rapidly, securely and cheaply. For such money can never, on any account, be preferred by anyone to goods.
>
> Only money that goes out of date like a newspaper, rots like potatoes, rusts like iron, evaporates like ether, is capable of standing the test as an instrument for the exchange of potatoes, newspapers, iron, and ether. For such money is not preferred to goods either by the purchaser or the seller. We then part with our goods for money only because we need the money as a means of exchange, not because we expect an advantage from possession of the money.[6]

But today, as in Gesell's time, money *is* preferred to goods. The ability to withhold the medium of exchange allows money holders to charge interest; they occupy a privileged position compared to holders of real capital (and even more so to those who sell their time, 100 percent of which disappears each day it goes unsold).

---

6. Gesell, *The Natural Economic Order*, chapter 4.1.

The result is an increasing polarization of wealth because everyone essentially pays a tribute to the owners of money.

A corollary to Gesell's point is that it is unfair for us to pay simply for the means to make exchanges. Gesell believed that the simple desire to make an exchange should be enough. If I have something to offer that you need, why should we have to pay for the means to give and receive it? Why should you have to pay for the privilege of receiving a gift? This is one of the ways in which Gesell's money deserves the moniker "free." As we shall see, a credit system based on depreciating currency allows zero-interest loans. While we must still repay loans, no longer must we pay for them. In that sense, money becomes free.

Gesell advocated currency decay as a device for decoupling money as a store-of-value from money as a medium of exchange. Money would no longer be preferred to physical capital. The result, he foresaw, would be an end to the artificial scarcity and economic depression that happens when there are plenty of goods to be exchanged but a lack of money by which to exchange them. His proposal would force money to circulate. No longer would the owners of money have an incentive to withhold it from the economy, waiting for scarcity to build up to the point where returns on real capital exceed the rate of interest. This is the second reason for calling it "free-money": *freed* from the control of the wealthy, money would circulate freely instead of coagulating in vast, stagnant pools as it does today.

Gesell saw the interest-bearing property of money as a brake on prosperity. As soon as goods become so abundant that returns on capital investment go lower than the minimum rate of interest, the owners of money withhold it from investment. The money to perform transactions disappears from circulation, and the familiar crisis of overcapacity looms, with its paradoxical accompaniment of scarcity of goods for the vast majority of people.

The money system in 1906 was quite different from that of today. Most currencies were still, at least in theory, backed by precious metals, and there was nothing like the vast expansion of credit over the monetary base that we have today. Indeed, Gesell viewed credit as a substitute for money, a way for businesses to conduct transactions in the absence of currency. But today credit and money are nearly identical. Current economic theory sees the use of credit as money as a positive development, in part because it allows the money supply to expand or contract organically in response to the demand for a medium of exchange. However, as we have seen, interest-bearing credit not only responds to, but also compels, the growth of the money economy. Moreover, in its present form it is no less subject to scarcity than was money in Gesell's time.

Although virtually unknown through the second half of the twentieth century, Gesell's ideas enjoyed a wide following in the 1920s and 1930s and came to influence prominent economists such as Irving Fisher and John Maynard Keynes. Fisher promoted Gesell's ideas vigorously in the United States, and Keynes offered uncharacteristic praise, calling him an "unduly neglected prophet" and his work "profoundly original."[7] In the turmoil following World War I, Gesell was even appointed Minister of Finance of the ill-fated Bavarian Republic, which lasted less than a year. In the 1920s,

---

7. Keynes discusses Gesell in Chapter 23 of his classic *General Theory of Money, Employment, and Interest.* He finds his reasoning sound but incomplete, saying that it "just failed to reach down to the essence of the matter." I will deal with his main criticism, that Gesell neglects to consider the liquidity premium of other forms of money, in a later section.

a stamp scrip currency—the *wara*—issued by a friend of Gesell's, circulated in Germany, but there as elsewhere it took an economic depression to launch it in earnest. Whether in collective life or personal, real change rarely comes in the absence of crisis.

In 1931, a German coal mine operator decided to open his closed mine by paying his workers in *wara*. Because he also agreed to redeem the scrip for coal, which everyone could use, local merchants and wholesalers were persuaded to accept it. The mining town flourished, and within the year at least a thousand stores across Germany were accepting *wara*, and banks began accepting wara-denominated deposits.[8] This put the currency on the radar screen. Feeling threatened, the German government tried to have the *wara* declared illegal by the courts; when that failed, it simply banned it by emergency decree.[9]

The following year, the depressed town of Wörgl, Austria, issued its own stamp scrip inspired by Gesell and the success of the *wara*. The Wörgl currency was by all accounts a huge success.[10] Roads were paved, bridges built, and back taxes were paid. The unemployment rate plummeted and the economy thrived, attracting the attention of nearby towns. Mayors and officials from all over the world began to visit Wörgl until, as in Germany, the central government abolished the Wörgl currency and the town slipped back into depression.

---

8. This is according to contemporary news accounts (e.g., Cohrssen, "Wara").

9. Fisher, *Stamp Scrip*, chapter 4.

10. Thomas Greco cites three contemporary accounts that appear in the 1934 journal *Annals of Collective Economy:* Alexander von Muralt, "The Wörgl Experiment with Depreciating Money"; M. Claude Bourdet, "A French View of the Wörgl Experiment: A New Economic Mecca"; and Michael Unterguggenberger, "The End Results of the Wörgl Experiment." Greco disputes the contention that the currency's success is attributable to demurrage.

Both the wara and the Wörgl currency bore a demurrage rate of 1 percent per month. Contemporary accounts attributed to this the very rapid velocity of the currencies' circulation. Instead of generating interest and growing, accumulation of wealth became a burden, much like possessions are a burden to the nomadic hunter-gatherer. As theorized by Gesell, money afflicted with loss-inducing properties ceased to be preferred over any other commodity as a store of value. It is impossible to prove, however, that the rejuvenating effects of these currencies came from demurrage and not from the increase in the money supply, or from the economically localizing effect of a local currency such as the Wörgl.

Another currency that emerged around this time, and that is still in use today, was the WIR in Switzerland. The currency is issued by a cooperative bank and is backed only by the mutual agreement of its members to accept it for payment. Founded by adherents of Gesell's theories, the currency originally bore a demurrage charge that was eliminated during the high-growth period after World War II.[11] As I shall explain, negative interest is unnecessary in a very high-growth environment; today, as we approach a steady-state economy and enter a new phase of development, it may be attractive once more.

In the United States many "emergency currencies," as they were called, were issued in the early 1930s. With the national currency evaporating through an epidemic of bank failures, citizens and local governments created their own. The results were mixed, and very few of them incorporated Gesell's design, but rather imposed a fee per transaction rather than per week or per month.[12] This

---

11. Wüthrich, "Alternatives to Globalization."
12. Champ, "Stamp Scrip."

has the opposite effect of demurrage because it penalizes circulation rather than hoarding. However, in 1933 at least a hundred cities were preparing to launch stamped currencies of their own, many of the correct, Gesellian, type.[13] Moreover, with the backing of Irving Fisher, a bill was introduced in both the House of Representatives and the Senate that would have issued one billion dollars of stamp scrip nationally. This and many of the proposed state and local currencies would have had a much, much higher demurrage rate—2 percent per week—that essentially would have made the currency self-liquidating in one year. This is an entirely different animal from the Wörgl currency and most modern proposals, but it shows that the basic concept was being seriously considered. Here is an excerpt from the Bankhead-Pettengill amendment to the Costigan-LaFollette unemployment relief bill (S. 5125) of 1933:

> The Secretary of the Treasury shall cause to be engraved and printed currency of the United States in the form of stamped money certificates. Said certificates shall be in the denomination of $1 each, and the issue shall be limited to $1,000,000,000. Said certificates shall be of a suitable size to provide space on the backs thereof for affixing postage stamps. . . . The face of said certificates shall set forth substantially the following: "This certificate is legal tender for $1 for payment of all debts and dues, public and private, customs, duties, and taxes: Provided, That on the date of its transfer there shall be affixed 2-cent postage stamps for all dates prior to such date of transfer, as set forth in the schedule on the back hereof."

---

13. Fisher, *Stamp Scrip*, chapter 5.

Senate Bill 5125 never came to a vote, and a month later Roosevelt banned all "emergency currencies" by executive decree when he launched the New Deal. According to Bernard Lietaer, the reason he did this was not because the local and state currencies wouldn't be effective in ending the Depression, but because it would mean a loss of central government power.[14]

Today we are at the brink of a similar crisis and face a similar choice between temporarily shoring up the old world through an intensification of centralized control or letting go of control and stepping into the new. Make no mistake: the consequences of a free-money system would be profound, encompassing economic, social, psychological, and spiritual dimensions. Money is so fundamental, so defining of our civilization, that it would be naive to hope for any authentic civilizational shift that did not involve a fundamental shift in money as well.

MODERN APPLICATION AND THEORY

The idea behind free-money, so popular in the early twentieth century, has lain dormant for sixty years. It is resurgent now, as the economic crisis demolishes the sureties of the past half-century and calls forth the thinking that came out of the Great Depression. Part of this is a Keynesian revival, since the monetarist prescription of lowering interest rates and purchasing government securities to stimulate the economy has hit a limit—the "zero bound" beyond which central banks cannot lower interest rates. The standard Keynesian response (based, however, on a partial reading of Keynes) is fiscal stimulus—the replacement of flagging consumer

---

14. Lietaer, *The Future of Money,* 156–160.

spending with government spending. President Barack Obama's first economic stimulus was a Keynesian measure, although probably insufficiently vigorous even within that paradigm.

The zero bound problem has gotten some mainstream people thinking about negative interest rates: my research for this chapter uncovered a paper by a Federal Reserve economist,[15] a *New York Times* article by a Harvard economics professor,[16] and an article in *The Economist* magazine.[17] When Keynesian stimulus fails (ultimately, for the reason of the depletion of the commons, as I've discussed), the far more radical solution of decaying currency may be on the radar screen. Presently, the economy is in mild recovery, and the delusional hope of a return to normal still possible to maintain. But because of the near-depletion of the various forms of common capital, the recovery will probably be anemic, and "normal" will recede into the distance.

The first obvious failure of Keynesian stimulus came in Japan, where massive infrastructure spending starting in the 1990s failed to reignite economic growth there. There is little room in any highly developed economy for further domestic growth. The solution for at least twenty years has been, in effect, to *import growth* from developing countries by using the monetization of their social and natural commons to prop up our own debt pyramid. This can take several forms: debt slavery, where a nation is forced to convert from subsistence production and self-sufficiency to commodity production to make payments on foreign loans; or dollar hegemony, in which highly productive countries like China have

---

15. Champ, "Stamp Scrip."
16. Mankiw, "It May Be Time."
17. "The Money-Go-Round," *Economist*, January 22, 2009.

no alternative but to finance U.S. private and public debt (because what else are they going to do with those trade surplus dollars?). Eventually, though, the solution of importing growth must fail too, as developing countries, and the planet as a whole, reach the same limits that developed countries have.

Official economic statistics have hidden the probability that the Western economies have been in a zero-growth phase for at least twenty years. Whatever growth there has been has come largely from such things as real estate bubbles, the prison industry, health care costs, insurance and financial services, educational costs, the weapons industry, and so forth. The more expensive these are, the more the economy is assumed to have grown. In areas where there has been growth, such as the internet, much of this is actually a covert form of importing growth. Internet-based revenue comes mostly from sales and advertising, not from new production. We are more efficiently greasing the wheels of the conveyor belt of goods from China to the West. In any event, developing countries cannot keep the growth machine running forever. The more it slows, the more it will be necessary to get around the zero bound.

While the idea of fixing stamps onto currency seems quaint, recently several prominent economists have proposed modern alternatives. Since most money is electronic anyway, the key measure is some kind of liquidity tax (as proposed by Irving Fisher as early as 1935) or, equivalently, a negative interest rate on deposits in the Federal Reserve. The latter measure was proposed by Willem Buiter, then a professor of economics and now chief economist at Citibank, in a 2003 paper in the *Economic Journal* and then in the *Financial Times* in 2009 (see the bibliography). It has also been broached by Harvard economics professor Greg Mankiw and

American Economics Association president Robert Hall,[18] and even discussed by Federal Reserve economists.[19] I hope these names make it clear that this is not a crackpot proposal.

Of course, physical currency would need to be subject to the same depreciation rate as reserves, which could be accomplished either through Gesell's method, by having expiry dates on currency, by replacing it with (or redefining it as) bearer bonds with a negative interest rate, by using cash currency that is distinct from the official unit of account, or by letting the exchange rate between bank reserves and currency fluctuate.[20] Another option would be to ban official physical currency altogether, which could vastly increase the power of government since every electronic transaction could be recorded. Frightening as that is to those (including myself) who are wary of the surveillance state, my response to that concern is, "Too late." Already today nearly all important transactions are done electronically anyway, with the notable exception of those involving illegal drugs. Cash is also used extensively in the informal economy to help people avoid taxes, a motive that would disappear if taxation were shifted away from incomes and onto resources as I propose.

Moreover, there is no reason why unofficial currencies shouldn't thrive alongside the official, negative-interest electronic currency. Whether these are electronic or paper depends on the application: probably commercial barter rings and credit-clearing cooperatives would use electronic money while local, community-based currencies might prefer paper. Either way, transactions using these currencies would be outside the purview of the central government. Their com-

---

18. Hall and Woodward, "The Fed Needs to Make a Policy Statement."
19. Koenig and Dolmas, "Monetary Policy in a Zero-Interest Economy."
20. The latter two options are discussed by Buiter, "Negative Interest Rates."

munity of use would decide what level of record-keeping to exercise over the currency. People who operate completely in a local economy, such as hippies, back-to-the-landers, and other people I love, would lead economic lives invisible to the central authorities. There are, however, other reasons to make all transactions and financial records open, not only to the government, but to everyone. This, indeed, has been proposed more generally as an antidote to the surveillance state— make surveillance technology public and ubiquitous—and it is happening already with the proliferation of video cameras in cell phones, hand-held gaming consoles, and other devices. When the activities of government are just as transparent to the people as the activities of the people are to the government, we will have a truly open society.

I want to emphasize the practicability of the modern negative-interest proposals. While Gesellian stamp-scrip currency seems like an anachronistic pipe dream that would involve massive economic disruption, levying a charge on reserves would require almost no new financial infrastructure. Indeed, it is an extension of where monetary policy has already been headed. The same Federal Reserve, the same central banks, the same basic banking system could remain intact. Of course, profound changes would follow, but they would be evolutionary changes that would spare society the disruption of scrapping the financial system and starting anew. As I wrote in Chapter 5, "Sacred economics is part of a different kind of revolution entirely, a transformation and not a purge."

Some central banks have already flirted with negative interest. In July 2009 the Riksbank (Sweden's central bank) went negative, levying a 0.25 percent charge on reserve deposits, a level at which it remained as of February 2010.[21] This is negligibly different from

---

21. Data from the Riksbank's official website, www.riksbank.com/swedishstat/.

zero, but the justification for lowering the rate that far also applies to lowering it still farther. The Riksbank, Buiter, Mankiw, and other mainstream advocates of negative interest rates see them as a temporary measure to force the banks to restart lending and make cheap credit available until the economy starts growing again, at which point, presumably, interest rates would rise back into positive territory. If, however, we are entering a permanent zero-growth or degrowth economy, negative interest rates could become permanent too.

The proper rate of interest, positive or negative, depends on whether the economy is to grow or shrink. In the old thinking, monetary policy was intended to spur economic growth or to restrain it to a sustainable level. In the new thinking, monetary policy strives to match the base interest rate to the economic growth (or degrowth) rate. Keynes estimated that it should be "roughly equal to the excess of the money-rate of interest over the marginal efficiency of capital corresponding to a rate of new investment compatible with full employment." This formula would need to be modified if, as I suggest in Chapter 14, we should no longer and can no longer seek full paid employment as a positive social good (this is a necessary consequence of steady-state economics and not so scary in the presence of a social dividend). Essentially, though, what Keynes is suggesting is that the liquidity tax be set at a level to compensate for the excess of interest over the average return on investment in productive capital. In other words, it must be set at a level so that there is no advantage to holding wealth versus using wealth.

Buiter and Mankiw are no liberals, which is significant because their proposals are contrary to the interests of the creditor class that conservatives typically represent. Liberal economists sometimes advocate a near equivalent to demurrage: inflation. Inflation is mathematically very similar in its effects to a depreciating currency in that it encourages the circulation of money, discourages hoarding, and makes it easier to repay debts. Free-money has several important advantages, however. In addition to eliminating classic costs of inflation (menu costs, shoe-leather costs, etc.), it does not impoverish people on a fixed income. Here is a typical pro-inflation argument by Dean Baker of the Center for Economic and Policy Research:

> If it is politically impossible to increase the deficit, then monetary policy provides a second potential tool for boosting demand. The Federal Reserve Board can go beyond its quantitative easing program to a policy of explicitly targeting a moderate rate of inflation (e.g., 3–4 percent) thereby making the real rate of interest negative. This would also have the benefit of reducing the huge burden of mortgage debt facing tens of millions of homeowners as a result of the collapse of the housing bubble.[22]

The problem is, in a deflationary environment when banks aren't lending, how can the Fed create inflation? This is the biggest problem with the inflation solution in a situation of overleveraging and overcapacity. Quantitative easing exchanges a highly liquid asset (base money, reserves) for less liquid assets (e.g., various financial derivatives), but that won't cause price or wage inflation if the new money doesn't reach people who will spend it.[23] Even if the Fed monetized all debt, public and private, the essential prob-

---

22. Baker, "No Way Out."
23. Actually, it can cause price inflation due to a speculative bid-up of commodity prices in the absence of productive investment opportunities.

lem would remain. Owing to the zero lower bound, the Fed was powerless to inflate its way out of the debt trap in 2008 and 2009. Here we return to the original motivation for free-money: to get money circulating.

In a negative-interest reserve system, banks would be anxious not to keep reserves. If the negative rate were on the order of 5 to 8 percent (which is what Gesell, Fisher, and other economists thought it should be), then it would even be in banks' interest to make zero-interest loans, possibly even negative-interest loans. How would they make money, you ask? They would do it essentially the same way they do it today.[24] Deposits would be subject to a negative interest rate, too, only smaller than the reserve interest rate. Banks would take demand deposits at, say, −7 percent interest, or time deposits at perhaps −5 percent or −3 percent, and make loans at −1 percent or 0 percent. (You can see now why cash would need to depreciate as well; otherwise who would deposit it at negative interest?)

Negative interest on reserves is compatible with existing financial infrastructure: the same commercial paper markets, the same interbank money markets, even, if we desire it, the same securitization and derivatives apparatus. All that has changed is the interest rate. Each of these institutions has a higher purpose that lurks within it like a recessive gene, awaiting the time of its expression. This is

---

24. Some of my more knowledgeable readers will no doubt protest that it is a misconception that banks make money off interest rate spreads. When banks make a loan, they say, they do not lend out depositors' money but rather create new money—credit—by a simple accounting entry. Unfortunately, this too is a distortion of the ontogeny of money. I explain this further in the Appendix: Quantum Money and the Reserve Question. The upshot for present purposes is that negative-interest banking would be fundamentally similar in many important respects to banking today (at least before the "casino economy" took over).

equally true of that most maligned of institutions, the "heart" of the financial system: the Federal Reserve (and other central banks).

Contrary to orthodox belief, the heart does not pump blood through the system, but rather receives it, listens to it, and sends it back out again.[25] It is an organ of perception. According to what it senses about the blood, the heart produces a vast array of hormones, many of them only recently discovered, that communicate with other parts of the body, just as its own cells are affected by exogenous hormones. This listening, modulating role of the heart offers a very different perspective on the role of a central monetary authority: an organ to listen and respond to the needs of the system, rather than to pump money through it. The Fed is supposed to listen to the pulse of the economy to regulate the money supply in order to maintain interest rates at the appropriate level.[26] The injection of new money into the economy could be done the same way it is today—open market operations—or through government spending of fiat money, depending on which version of commons-use rents are employed. Generally speaking, money lost to demur-

---

25. Most physiologic descriptions of the heart liken it to a pump, but the heart does not provide the propulsive force for blood circulation at all. It would be impossible for a 300-gram organ to pump a viscous fluid through thousands of miles of small blood vessels. In fact, embryonic circulation begins before a functioning heart is even present, possessing its own endogenous momentum sustained by its relationship to the entire circulatory system and indeed the entire body. The heart temporarily halts the flow, which expands the atrium before being released into the ventricle. It is more similar to a hydraulic ram than a pump, with the addition of a twisting function to maintain the blood's spiraling motion.

26. As a matter of fact, the Fed already attempts to exercise this listening, modulating function. Meredith Walker, a former Fed economist, describes how much of her work to prepare for Open Market Committee meetings involved communicating with myriad businesses and financial institutions, in effect listening to the pulse of the economy. Monetary policy was a natural response to this listening, except when political interference stymied the natural response and tilted the Fed toward more of a controlling role, similar to a pump.

rage must be injected back into the economy; otherwise the level of reserves would shrink every year, regardless of the need for money to facilitate economic activity. The result would be the same pattern of defaults, scarcity, and concentration of wealth that threatens us today. Therefore, we still need a financial heart that listens to the blood and signals for the creation of more (or less) of it.

The alert reader might object that if currency and bank deposits were subject to negative interest, people would switch to some other medium of exchange that served as a better store of value: gold, for instance, or commercial paper. If you have raised this objection, you are in good company. Writing in praise of Gesell's ideas, John Maynard Keynes issued the following caveat: "Thus if currency notes were to be deprived of their liquidity-premium by the stamping system, a long series of substitutes would step into their shoes—bank-money, debts at call, foreign money, jewelry and the precious metals generally, and so forth."[27] This objection can be met on several fronts (nor did Keynes see it as an insuperable obstacle, but merely a "difficulty" that Gesell "did not face"). Bank money would, as described above, be subject to the same depreciation as physical currency. Debts at call require a risk premium that offsets the liquidity premium.[28] Commodities, jewelry, and so forth suffer high carry costs. Most important, however, is that money is ultimately a social agreement that, through legal tender laws, customs, and other forms of consensus, can be consciously chosen and applied. Ultimately, Keynes judged, "The idea behind stamped money is sound."

As a practical matter, everything in the material and social world

---

27. Keynes, *The General Theory of Employment, Interest, and Money*, book 4, chapter 23, section 4.

28. Besides, in this system, interest rates on highly liquid debts-at-call would tend toward the demurrage rate.

has carry costs, as Gesell pointed out with his examples of newspapers, potatoes, and so on. Machinery and equipment break down, require maintenance, and become obsolete. Even the very few substances that don't suffer oxidation, such as gold and platinum, must be transported, guarded, and insured against theft; precious metal coinage can also be scraped or clipped. That money is an exception to this universal law, the law of return, is part of the broader ideology of human exceptionalism relative to nature. Decaying currency is therefore no mere gimmick: it is an acknowledgment of reality. The ancient Greeks, unconsciously drawing on the qualities of this new thing called money, created a conception of spirit that was similarly above nature's laws—eternal, abstract, nonmaterial. This division of the world into spirit and matter, and the consequent treatment of the world as if it were not sacred, is coming to an end. Ending along with it is the kind of money that suggested this division in the first place. No longer will money be an exception to the universal law of impermanence.

Keynes' "difficulty" highlights the importance of not creating artificial stores of wealth that, like money today, violate nature's laws. One example is property rights on land, which historically were the vehicle for the same concentration of wealth that money has brought us today. Negative interest on currency must accompany Georgist or Gesellian levies on land as well, and indeed on any other source of "economic rents." The physical commons of land, the genome, the ecosystem, and the electromagnetic spectrum, as well as the cultural commons of ideas, inventions, music, and stories, must be subject to the same carry costs as money, or Keynes's concern will come true. Thankfully, we have a serendipitous convergence of rightness and logic, that the social obligation entailed by use of the commons doubles as a liquidity tax on any substitute store of value. Fundamentally, whether applied to money or to the commons, the same principle is at stake: we only get to keep it if we use it in a socially productive way. If we merely hold it, we shall lose it.

Not everyone would benefit from free-money, at least in the short run. Like inflation, depreciating currency benefits debtors and harms creditors. Writing about inflation, this commentator sums it up neatly:

> The root cause of this desire for very low inflation is a desire on the part of the bond-holding classes to see a real return on risk-free investment and deposits.... It is scandalous that people should be paid a real return for lending cash back to the central bank that prints it.... The need for rich people, lightly taxed, is that they can afford to take risk, and so drive investment and growth in the real economy. If they want part of their portfolio in risk-free deposits, they should not expect it to maintain its relative wealth.[29]

This argument taps into the long tradition of George and Gesell I have drawn upon, which recognizes that people should not be able to profit from the mere fact of ownership. Holders of wealth are its caretakers, its stewards, and if they do not put it to socially beneficial use, then eventually that wealth should flow away to others who will.

Revolutionaries past, recognizing that illegitimacy of most accumulations of wealth, sought to sweep the slate clean through confiscation and redistribution. I advocate a gentler, more gradual approach. One way to look at it is as a tax on holdings of money,

---

29. Anonymous comment on http://blogs.ft.com/maverecon/2009/05/negative-interest-rates-when-are-they-coming-to-a-central-bank-near-you/.

ensuring that the only way to maintain wealth is to invest it at risk or, shall we say, to make wise decisions on how to direct the magical flow of human creativity. Certainly, this is an ability that deserves reward, and herein lies an essential missing piece of Marxist theories of value that ignore the entrepreneurial dimension to the allocation of capital.

While the bold yet still mainstream economists I've mentioned see negative interest as a temporary measure to promote lending and escape a deflationary liquidity trap, its true significance runs much deeper. A liquidity trap is not a temporary aberration caused by a bubble collapse; it is an ever-present default state originating in the declining marginal efficiency of capital,[30] itself a result of technological improvement and competition. As Keynes pointed out,

> As the stock of the assets, which begin by having a marginal efficiency at least equal to the rate of interest, is increased, their marginal efficiency (for reasons, sufficiently obvious, already given) tends to fall. Thus a point will come at which it no longer pays to produce them, *unless the rate of interest falls pari passu.* When there is no asset of which the marginal efficiency reaches the rate of interest, the further production of capital-assets will come to a standstill.[31]

As I have argued already, this eventuality has been delayed for a long time as technology and imperialism have transferred goods and services from the commons into the money economy. As the commons is exhausted, however, the need to remove the interest rate

---

30. The marginal efficiency of capital refers to the expected return on each dollar of new investment.

31. Keynes, *The General Theory of Employment, Interest, and Money,* chapter 17, section 2.

barrier intensifies. Presciently, Keynes opines, "Thus those reformers, who look for a remedy by creating artificial carrying-costs for money through the device of requiring legal-tender currency to be periodically stamped at a prescribed cost in order to retain its quality as money, or in analogous ways, have been on the right track; and the practical value of their proposals deserves consideration."[32] Such a measure (and the modern equivalent I've discussed) would allow capital investment with a *negative marginal efficiency*—in other words, banks would willingly lend money to enterprises that make a zero or slightly less than zero return on investment.

Given that the root cause of our economic crisis is the inevitable slowing of growth, and given that we are transitioning to an ecological, steady-state economy, decaying currency proposals offer more than a temporary fix for a stagnant economy; they promise a sustainable, long-term foundation for a permanently nongrowing economy. Historically, economic contraction or stagnant growth has meant human misery: economic polarization, a sharpening of the divide between the haves and the have-nots. Free-money prevents this from happening by providing a way for money to circulate without needing to be driven by growth-dependent lending.

Combined with the other changes in this book, free-money will have profound effects on human economy and psychology. We have gotten so used to the world of usury-money that we mistake many of its effects for basic laws of economics or human nature. As I shall describe, a money system embodying a new sense of self and a new story of the people—the connected self living in cocreative partnership with Earth—will have very different effects. The intuitions developed over centuries will be true no longer. No

---

32. Ibid., sec. 3.

longer will greed, scarcity, the quantification and commoditization of all things, the "time preference" for immediate consumption, the discounting of the future for the sake of the present, the fundamental opposition between financial interest and the common good, or the equation of security with accumulation be axiomatic.

THE DEBT CRISIS: OPPORTUNITY FOR TRANSITION

A golden opportunity to transition to negative-interest money may be nigh in the form of the "debt bomb" that nearly brought down the global economy in 2008. Consisting of high levels of sovereign debt, mortgage debt, credit card debt, student loans, and other debts that can never be repaid, the debt bomb was never defused but just delayed. New loans were issued to enable borrowers to repay old ones, but of course unless the borrowers increase their income, which will only happen with economic growth, this only pushes the problem into the future and makes it worse. At some point, default is inevitable. Is there a way out?

There is. The answer lies in a modern-day version of the Solonic economic reform 2,600 years ago: debt forgiveness and reform of the conventions of money and property. At some point, it will be necessary to face reality: the debts will never be repaid. Either they can be kept in place anyway, and debtor individuals and nations kept in perpetual servitude, or they can be released and the slate wiped clean. The problem with the latter choice is that because savings and debt are two aspects of a whole, innocent savers and investors would be instantly wiped out, and the entire financial system would collapse. A sudden collapse would result in widespread social unrest, war, revolution, starvation, and so forth.

In order to prevent this, an intermediate alternative is to reduce the debt gradually.

The 2008 financial crisis offered a clue as to how this might happen as part of the transition to a negative-interest economy. When crisis threatened major financial institutions with insolvency, the response by the Federal Reserve was to monetize bad debts, which means that it bought them—exchanging toxic financial instruments for cash. It continues to monetize government debt (which is also unlikely ever to be repaid) through the quantitative easing program. At some point, to avoid total collapse, similar measures will be required in the future on an even broader scale.

The problem is that all this money goes to creditors, not debtors. Debtors do not become any more able to pay; nor do the creditors become any more willing to lend. The Fed's action drew intense criticism because it in effect gave predatory financial institutions cold hard cash in exchange for the junk investments they had irresponsibly created and traded, whose market value was probably only pennies on the dollar. They received face value for them, and then, adding insult to injury, invested the cash in risk-free bonds, paid it as executive bonuses, or bought up smaller institutions. Meanwhile, none of the underlying debt was forgiven the debtors. The program therefore did nothing to ameliorate the polarization of wealth.

What would happen if debt were monetized into free-money? Then, although creditors would not lose their money overnight as they do with defaults or systemic financial collapse, the bailout wouldn't further enrich them either, because they would receive a depreciating asset. As for the debtors, the monetary authority could reduce or annul their debts by any amount it thought appropriate (which would likely be determined through a political process). This might involve reducing the interest rate to zero or even reducing

229

the principal. So, for example, interest on student loans could be reduced to zero, mortgage principal cut to prebubble levels, and third-world sovereign debt forgiven entirely.

While it is true that this monetization of debt could vastly increase the monetary base, because the money would be subject to demurrage, it would naturally shrink back again over time. The monetary authority could also shrink it more quickly by selling the restructured debt on the open market.

Without negative interest or debt forgiveness described herein, Fed bailouts amount to "free money" (and not free-money) for the people who already have the most of it. If the big banks and financiers are permitted to keep their lucre, at least in exchange they should accept a system tilted against further accumulation. Yes, the financial interests stand to lose, albeit gradually, from this proposal, but what is the alternative? The increasing polarization of wealth is not sustainable.

The opportunity we had in 2008 will repeat itself, because the debt crisis won't go away (without miraculously high economic growth). Each time, the solution has been yet more debt, which is shifted from individuals and corporations to nations, and back again, always growing. For example, when Ireland's banks were on the verge of failure in 2010, the government bailed them out, transferring the problem onto its own balance sheet and engendering a sovereign debt crisis. To avert catastrophe, the IMF and ECB gave Ireland new loans at 6 percent interest to pay the old. Unless the Irish economy grows by more than 6 percent a year (impossible given the harsh austerity measures upon which the loans were conditioned), the problem will reappear in a few years and be even worse. We are merely kicking the problem into the future.

The bondholders don't want to take a loss. They want more

and more for themselves.[33] In the long run, it is mathematically impossible to redeem that wish. It can be sustained only as long as the rest of society is willing to accept worsening conditions: more austerity, more poverty, and more income devoted to servicing debt.

At some point, we as a society will say, "Enough!" A bailout will still be necessary, for the consequences of a sudden system-wide default would be catastrophic. But when it happens—and it could happen simultaneously in many debt categories—let us face the truth. The concentration of wealth, and the usury behind it, must end. We may have no choice but to rescue the wealthy, for each part of the global economy is connected to all the others, but let that rescue come at a price: the gradual freeing of society from debt.

THINKING FOR THE FUTURE

Amid all the technical details of money and finance, let us not lose sight of the heart of this endeavor: to restore money to its true purpose as a connector of gifts and needs and as a magical talis-man that coordinates human creativity toward a common end. It feels strange to say that money is a key part of the more beautiful world my heart tells me is possible, because money has long been repellant to me as an obvious cause of so much ruin and evil.

However, our repugnance toward money is based on what money has been, not on what it could be. Negative-interest money, backed by things that are sacred, in an ecological economy, turns the intuitions of the Age of Usury on their head. It is utterly

---

33. When interest exceeds economic growth, they are indeed claiming a larger and larger proportion of society's wealth for themselves—and at no risk, thanks to the bailouts.

revolutionary, fundamentally altering the human experience. This transformation reverberates across all levels, from outer to inner, from the economic to the spiritual.

In Chapter 9, "The Story of Value," I explained how the current social agreement on money creation is, "Thou shalt issue money only to those who will earn even more of it," which ultimately comes down to participating in the expansion of the realm of goods and services. Society's energy is directed toward that which will expand the realm of money and property, the human realm, the owned realm. It is part of the Ascent of Humanity to dominion over nature.

Lowering interest rates below the zero lower bound makes investments possible that have a zero or negative return on capital. Does this idea sound counterintuitive to you? Does it seem to contradict the whole concept of an "investment"? It *is* counterintuitive, but only because our intuitions have been so conditioned by a centuries-long culture of growth that we can barely conceive the possibility of another function of money, or of a business model not dependent on profit. (Of course we have nonprofit organizations, but these are fundamentally distinct from for-profit businesses. This is a distinction that will fade.)

Here is an example to bring home how weirdly counterintuitive this is. Imagine you go to a bank and say, "I'd like to borrow money for my business. Here is my business plan. See, if you lend me $1,000,000, I will earn $900,000 in four years' time. So I'd like you to lend me $1,000,000 at negative interest, and I'll pay you back $900,000 in installments over four years."

"We love your business plan," says the bank. "Here is your money." Why do they agree? Because that $1,000,000 dollars, if left as cash, would depreciate at an even higher rate, say 7 percent, so that after four years only about $740,000 would be left. It is to the bank's benefit to make the loan described above.

Another way to understand the dynamics of decaying currency is that, like inflation, it reverses the discounting of future cash flows. In *The Ascent of Humanity* I offer the following example:

> Whereas interest promotes the discounting of future cash flows, demurrage encourages long-term thinking. In present-day accounting, a forest generating $1 million dollars a year sustainably forever is more valuable if clear-cut for an immediate profit of $50 million. (The "net present value" of the sustainable forest calculated at a discount rate of 5 percent is only $20 million.) This discounting of the future results in the infamously short-sighted behavior of corporations that sacrifice (even their own) long-term well-being for the short-term results of the fiscal quarter. Such behavior is perfectly rational in an interest-based economy, but in a demurrage system, pure self-interest would dictate that the forest be preserved. No longer would greed motivate the robbing of the future for the benefit of the present. As the exponential discounting of future cash flows implies the "cashing in" of the entire earth, this feature of demurrage is highly attractive.

Imagine you are the President of the World and receive the following offer from aliens: "Supreme Leader, a sustainable gross world product (GWP) is $10 trillion a year. We would like to make you an offer: $600 trillion for the entire earth. True, we plan to extract all of its resources, destroy the topsoil, poison the oceans, turn the forests into deserts, and use it as a radioactive waste dump. But think of it—$600 trillion! You'll all be rich!" Of course you would say no, but collectively today we are essentially saying yes to this offer. We are carrying out the aliens' plan to a tee, making over the next ten years perhaps $600 trillion (current GWP is $60 trillion a year). Through a million little choices every day, we are cashing in the earth.

And this is all quite economic. At prevailing rates, $600 trillion generates annual income of at least $20 trillion. In *Ascent* I quoted several prominent economists who argue that since agriculture amounts to only 3 percent of GDP, global warming or a 50-percent drop in agricultural output wouldn't matter much. At most, GDP (the total "goodness" level, remember) would drop by only 1.5 percent. It seems absurd, but within the logical construct of usury it is quite rational. In a 1997 article in *Nature* ecological economist Robert Costanza valued the global ecosystem at $33 trillion, only 20 percent higher than GWP that year. He meant well, hoping to provide an economic reason (and not just a moral reason) to preserve the planet, but according to the same logic, the logic of "value," it would be in our interest *not* to preserve it if we received a better offer.

Furthermore, don't you find it dispiriting to resort to the argument that we should preserve the ecosystem because of all the money we'll save? This argument buys into the basic assumption that causes so much trouble to begin with: that money is an appropriate standard of value; that all things can and should be measured and quantified; that we can best make choices by adding up numbers.

"Sustainability" has been a buzzword for so long now that it has almost become a cliché. Yet despite the fact that everyone approves of it, sustainability has been fighting a losing battle against profit. Forests are dying, lakes are drying up, deserts are spreading, and rain forests continue to fall to clear-cutting—the pace has hardly slowed despite four decades of environmentalists' best efforts. At every turn they must fight the money power, which helplessly seeks short-term profit even at the expense of its own long-term survival. As Lenin wrote in a somewhat different context, "The capitalists will sell us the rope with which we will hang them." The myopia of capital stems, at a deep level, from interest, which necessitates the discounting of future cash flows.

With interest rates below zero, the opposite thinking prevails. Imagine again that you are President of the World. Now the aliens' offer isn't looking so attractive. At negative interest, in fact, no amount of money would be enough to cash in the earth, because money in the future is actually more valuable than the same quantity of money in the present, and its future value increases exponentially with time. You would say to the aliens, "We're not selling the earth at any price."

Isn't that what we should be saying today, when the economy insists on putting a price on the ecological basis of civilization and life itself? Isn't that what we should be saying today as well to any exchange of the infinitely precious for a finite sum of money? It is time, I think, to stop "cashing in" beauty, life, health, and our children's future.

I realize my example of cashing in the earth is far-fetched and that one could construct an economic argument challenging it. My point is that negative interest fundamentally alters what kind of behavior is "economic." Activities that bring benefits thirty, fifty, or a hundred years hence—indeed, that bring benefits to the seventh generation—acquire an economic motivation as opposed to today, when only an idealistic person would do such a thing. With negative interest and depreciating currency, no longer will our ideals do battle against our economic self-interest.

Consider a practical example. Suppose you are considering

whether to install solar panels to power your business. The initial cost is, say, $100,000, and it will bring you savings of $1,000 a year. Currently, it would be uneconomic to install them, as the net present value of $1,000 a year is much less than $100,000 (even at very low interest). But if interest is zero or negative, the decision becomes economic. Today people are already making such decisions even though they are uneconomic, because the truth in our hearts contradicts economic logic. In our hearts we know that the ideology that equates money with the good is wrong. We need to bring money and goodness back into their promised alignment.

One more example: suppose you own a forest. Either you can obliterate it by selling it for clear-cutting and quarrying, for an immediate profit of $1 million, or you can log it sustainably for $10,000 a year in perpetuity. Well, interest on $1 million is at least double that sustainable logging income—you might as well cash it in. But if interest rates are negative, that logic no longer holds.

The internalization of external costs works synergistically with decaying currency to make money a force for good. The former aligns private interest with public interest; the latter promotes long-term thinking over short-term thinking. Although both are improvements on the current system, neither by itself will guarantee a sustainable world. Together, they align economic decisions with the long-term interests of society and the planet.

Of course, there are times when long-term thinking isn't appropriate. We have many needs that we prefer to fulfill now rather than in the future. If we are starving, we would rather have one meal today than a hundred a year from now. The Austrian School of economics especially, but more generally neoclassical economics as well, extrapolates from such examples to claim that it is human nature to want to consume as much as possible right now. In their view, interest is a kind of compensation for deferring consumption, a reward for delayed gratification. In other words, you, dear reader, would love to maximize your utility by spending all your money right now, but are induced not to because you know that you'll be able to have even more later, thanks to interest. This is known in economics as the *time preference postulate*. Time preference—our supposed preference for immediate consumption—is crucial to the discounted utility model developed by Paul Samuelson in the 1930s that lies at the foundation of most mainstream economic theory today. It is also crucial to many modern "refutations" of Keynes. Moreover, in the lone mathematical economics paper I discovered addressing demurrage-based currencies, the time preference postulate was the key variable in constructing a (specious) demonstration that such currency harms the public welfare.[34]

The Keynesian logic I have deployed minimizes time preference. Keynes did not dismiss it altogether but said that human beings naturally tend to spend a smaller proportion of their income as their income rises. It seems quite obvious that if you are starving, you will spend all your income immediately on food; if you have enough money to meet all your urgent needs, you may spend some of the surplus on books, perhaps, or entertainment; when those desires have been fulfilled, maybe you'll buy a Rolls-Royce. But the greater your income, the less urgency there is to spend it. Keynes believed therefore that people have a propensity to save without needing an incentive (interest) to defer consumption. Indeed, he thought that this propensity to save can be destructive when it leads to concentration of wealth. That is why he was sympathetic to low or even negative interest rates.

---

34. Rösl (2006).

In reading some of the literature from the late 1930s and 1940s, I was struck by the intensity and thinly disguised emotionality of the criticism directed at Keynes by establishment economists.[35] This sort of contumely is typical of any debate when the orthodox establishment intuits that a new theory challenges the core defining precepts of its field. Keynes's theory presents at least two very deep challenges. First, his idea of a natural tendency to save essentially claims that money itself is subject to diminishing marginal utility—the more I have of it, the less useful each additional dollar is to me.[36] This seems obvious to me, but it is apparently not so obvious to classical economists, who make a linear equation between money and the utility of the individual and society. In fact, they define it that way and state the base assumption that human beings seek to maximize self-interest by maximizing money.

If we reject the linear equation of money and utility (i.e., "the good"), we also reject the dearly held ideology that we can maximize the common good by maximizing economic growth. We deny as well the utilitarian argument for wealth-maximizing capitalism, opening the door to ideas that emphasize equitable distribution of wealth instead. Mathematically, if money is subject to diminishing marginal utility, the optimal distribution of money is: as equitably as possible. Offering a justification for the redistribution of wealth away from the rich, Keynesian thought is, quite naturally, anathema for the ideologues of the rich.

---

35. See, for example, Holden, "Mr. Keynes' Consumption Function and the Time Preference Postulate." This paper illustrates the ideological principles that are at stake, phrased therein as "psychological laws."

36. Diminishing marginal utility is often illustrated by fertilizer application. The first ton doubles yield; the next ton increases yield by 10 percent; the next by only 1 percent, and so on. This is a very general principle. Why shouldn't it apply to money too?

But Keynes's view of liquidity preference implies an even deeper challenge than that. Consider again the opposite view, exemplified by the classical economists and Austrian School advocates, that people are by nature profligate. As the nineteenth-century economist N. W. Senior put it, "to abstain from the enjoyment which is in our power, or to seek distant rather than immediate results, are among the most painful exertions of the human will."[37] Here is a more recent example, by a follower of von Mises:

> No supply of loanable funds could exist without previous savings, that is, without *abstention from some possible consumption* of present goods (an excess of current production over current consumption). . . . There would be no interest or time-preference rate. Or rather, the interest rate would be infinitely high, which, anywhere outside of the Garden of Eden, would be tantamount to leading a *merely animal existence*, that is, of eking out a primitive subsistence by facing reality with nothing but one's bare hands and only a *desire for instant gratification*.[38]

Interest, then, is a reward for thrift, for self-restraint. In this view we find an echo of some of the deep, hidden ideologies underlying our civilization; for example, that human progress both spiritual and material comes through winning a war against nature: natural forces on the outside, and desire, pleasure, and the animal drives on the inside. Abstemiousness becomes a high virtue; without it, this ideology goes, we would be no better than animals. We would not

---

37. Senior, *Outline of the Science of Political Economy,* quoted in Handon and Yosifon, "The Situational Character," 76. One cannot help notice the implication that a painful exertion of the will is an admirable virtue.

38. Hoppe, "The Misesian Case against Keynes"; emphasis added.

have ascended into a separate and better human realm, removed from nature. Karl Marx put it thus:

> The cult of money has its asceticism, its self-denial, its self-sacrifice—economy and frugality, contempt for mundane, temporal, and fleeting pleasures; the chase after the *eternal* treasure. Hence the connection between English Puritanism, or also Dutch Protestantism, and money-making.[39]

This mentality pervades our culture. You must delay gratification. You must restrain your desires with the thought of future rewards. Pain now is gain later. Do your homework for the grade. Go to work for the salary. Do the workout to be healthy. Go on a diet to be thin. Devote your life to something that pays well, even if it isn't your passion, so that you can have an enjoyable retirement. In all of these things we apply a regime of threat and incentive designed to overcome our laziness, our selfishness. Interest becomes a motivator in the war against the self, the overcoming of our wanton improvidence.

But is this really human nature? Is it really our nature to consume and overconsume without thought for other people, other beings, or our own future? No. The ancient Greeks, not given to overly charitable views of human nature, had it right. As Aristophanes said, in all things—bread, wine, sex, and so on—there is satiety. Our needs are limited, and when we have fulfilled them, we turn to other things and are moved to generosity. "But of money, there is no satiety." It is not the propensity to consume that bears no limit; to the contrary, limitless desire *arises with* money. After

---

39. Marx, *Grundrisse*, 230.

attaining a surfeit of consumables, people covet money itself, not what it can buy, and this desire has no limit. Neoclassical economics (and the Austrian School) has it backwards, and Gesell and Keynes were right to seek to strip money of at least some of its unique features that make desire for it limitless. Keynes was aware—indeed he explicitly stated—that the dominance of liquidity preference over time preference was a foundational assumption of his theory: a "psychological law," as he called it.

Of course, for some people—food addicts, sex addicts, alcohol addicts—there is indeed no satiety in those things Aristophanes listed. Does this prove that human beings are greedy after all? Actually, the example of addiction illuminates what is wrong with money. Addiction happens when we use something as a substitute for what we really want or need—food, for example, as a substitute for connection; sex as a substitute for emotional intimacy; and so on. Money as universal end becomes a substitute for many other things, including those very things that the money economy has destroyed: community, connection to place, connection to nature, leisure, and more.

When we speak of the "liquidity" of money, we mean simply that we can readily exchange it for anything else we want. Now in a money economy, we can actually exchange *any* commodity for any other commodity, just not so readily, via the medium of exchange (money). Why then, should we prefer money to other commodities? Excepting cases in which we have a need that must be met swiftly, which indeed justify keeping on hand modest amounts of the medium of exchange, the only reason to prefer money is that it does not suffer loss in storage. The imperishability of money makes it not only a universal means, but a universal end as well. By making money impermanent, we preserve it as means but not as end and in so doing inspire a conception of wealth radically different from anything we have known.

MORE FOR ME IS MORE FOR YOU

With the introduction of free-money, money has been reduced to the rank of umbrellas; friends and acquaintances assist each other mutually as a matter of course with loans of money. No one keeps, or can keep, reserves of money, since money is under compulsion to circulate. But just because no one can form reserves of money, no reserves are needed. For the circulation of money is regular and uninterrupted.

—Silvio Gesell

The equivalent in modern economics of "universal means" and "universal end" are "medium of exchange" and "store of value." One way to understand the effect of negative interest is that it splits these two functions. This is a profound shift. Most economists consider medium of exchange and store of value to be defining functions of money. But combining these two functions into a single object begs trouble because a medium of exchange needs to circulate to be useful, while a store of value is kept (stored) away from circulation. This contradiction has, for centuries or more, created a tension between the wealth of the individual and the wealth of society.

The tension between the wealth of the individual and the wealth of society reflects the atomistic conception of the self that has risen to dominance in our time. A money system that resolves this tension therefore promises profound consequences for human consciousness. In Chapter 1 I wrote, "Whereas money today embodies the principle, 'More for me is less for you,' in a gift economy, more for you is also more for me, because those who have give to those who need. Gifts cement the mystical realization of participation in something greater than oneself, which is yet not separate from oneself. The axioms of rational self-interest change because the self has expanded to include something of the other." Can we imbue money with the same property as the gift?

In an economy based on free-money, wealth means something quite different from what it means today and in fact takes on much the same character that it had in primitive, gift-based societies. In hunter-gatherer societies, which were generally nomadic, possessions were a literal burden. The "carry cost" that everything except money bears today was quite real. In sedentary agricultural societies as well, possessions such as cattle and stores of grain, while sought after, did not give the same degree of security as being embedded in a rich web of social relationships of giving and receiving. Grain can rot and cattle can die, but if you have been generous with your wealth to the community, you have little to fear.

Free-money reintroduces the economic mind-set of a hunter-gatherer. In today's system, it is much better to have a thousand dollars than it is for ten people to owe you a hundred dollars. In a negative-interest system, unless you need to spend the money right now, the opposite is true. Since money decays with time, if I have money I'm not using, I am happy to lend it to you, just as if I had more bread than I could eat. If I need some in the future, I can call in my obligations or create new ones with anyone within my network who has more money than he or she immediately needs. Similarly, when a primitive hunter killed a large animal, he or she would give away most of the meat according to kinship status, personal affection, and need. As with decaying money, it was much better to have lots of people "owe you one" than it was to have a big pile of rotting meat, or even of dried jerky that had to be transported or secured. Why would you even want to, when your community is as generous to you as you are to it? Security came from sharing. The good luck of your neighbor was your own good luck as well. If you came across an unexpected large source of wealth, you threw a huge party. As a member of the Pirahã tribe explained it when questioned about food storage, "I store meat in the belly of my brother."[40] Or consider the !Kung concept of wealth explored in this exchange between anthropologist Richard Lee and a !Kung man, !Xoma:

> I asked !Xoma, "What makes a man a //kaiha [rich man]—if he has many bags of //kai [beads and other valuables] in his hut?"
>
> "Holding //kai does not make you a //kaiha," replied !Xoma. "It is when someone makes many goods travel around that we might call him //kaiha."
>
> What !Xoma seemed to be saying was that it wasn't the number of your goods that constituted your wealth; it was the number of your friends. The wealthy person was measured by the frequency of his or her transactions and not by the inventory of goods on hand.[41]

Wealth in a free-money system evolves into something akin to the model of the Pacific Northwest or Melanesia, in which a leader "acts as a shunting station for goods flowing reciprocally between his own and other like groups of society."[42] Status was not associ-

---

40. Everett, "Cultural Constraints on Grammar and Cognition in Pirahã."
41. Lee, *The Dobe !Kung*, 101.
42. Sahlins, *Stone Age Economics*, 209.

ated with the accumulation of money or possessions, but rather with a huge responsibility for generosity. Can you imagine a society where the greatest prestige, power, and leadership accord to those with the greatest inclination and capacity to give?

Such was the situation in archaic societies. Status came through generosity, and generosity created gratitude and obligation. To be a lord or king, you had to hold sumptuous feasts and give lavish gifts to peers and underlings. We have an especially clear example of this in the *Nibelungen,* the great German saga of the high middle ages that draws on source material from much earlier. When Kriemhild, widow of the great hero Siegfried, starts lavishly giving away the hoard she inherited from him, the king feels so threatened that he has her murdered and the treasure dumped into the Rhine (where it remains to this day!). The king's authority was sustained by gifts, and that authority was undermined when someone else started giving greater gifts than he.

The zero-interest loans in a free-money economy are analogous to the gifts of yore. While such loans may appear to violate the gift principle that the reciprocal gift not be specified in advance, they *are* gifts: gifts not of money but of the *use* of money. In ancient times, the obligations and expectations generated by gifts were socially determined. The same is true here: the social determination takes the form of contracts, agreements, laws, and so forth. Underlying these specific forms, the dynamic is equivalent: those who have more than they need give it to others. It is just that simple, an expression of the innate generosity of the human being I described in Chapter 1. All that is needed is a money system that encourages, rather than deters, that generosity. No miraculous change in human nature is necessary. As I describe it in *The Ascent of Humanity,*

Whereas security in an interest-based system comes from accumulating money, in a demurrage system it comes from having productive channels through which to direct it—that is, to become a nexus of the flow of wealth and not a point for its accumulation. In other words, it puts the focus on relationships, not on "having." It accords with a different sense of self, affirmed not by enclosing more and more of the world within the confines of me and mine, but by developing and deepening relationships with others. It encourages reciprocation, sharing, and the rapid circulation of wealth.

Sometimes people ask whether negative-interest currency, like inflation, wouldn't stimulate even greater consumption. In economics terms, this would happen only if the demurrage rate were too high, leading to a preference of goods over money as a store of value.[43] The two should be equal. But let's investigate this issue a bit more deeply. When I describe a currency of abundance, people protest, "But we *do* live in a world of scarcity. Natural resources are finite, and we have used them nearly all up. The problem is that we have treated them as if they were unlimited." Accordingly, one might think that an attitude and currency of abundance is the last thing we need.

---

43. If the demurrage rate were too high, speculative capital investments could also happen, resulting in overcapacity, inflation, and a boom-bust cycle. The Fed or central bank would need to exercise the same functions it (supposedly) does today, quelling economic overheating by raising interest rates (bringing the demurrage rate closer to zero). There may even be times in the future when it is appropriate for interest rates to climb back into positive territory. Such a time would be a high rate of economic growth. That way the risk-free interest rate would be less than the economic growth rate, obviating the concentration of wealth that interest usually causes. However, I think that such a scenario is unlikely when growth is no longer subsidized by the unsustainable drawdown of natural resources, and when the reclamation of social capital has shrunk the realm of paid services.

In answer to this concern, consider first whether our currency of scarcity has actually limited our consumption of scarce resources. It has not. The scarcity of money has aggravated their conversion into money. It is an attitude of scarcity, not of abundance, that has led to the depletion of our natural commons. Competition and the accumulation of *more than one needs* are the natural response to a perceived scarcity of resources. The obscene overconsumption and waste of our society arise from our poverty: the deficit of being that afflicts the discrete and separate self, the scarcity of money in an interest-based system, the poverty of relationship that comes from the severance of our ties to community and to nature, the relentless pressure to do anything, anything at all, to make a living. In contrast, the natural response to an atmosphere of abundance is generosity and sharing. This includes sharing within the human realm and beyond it as well. Whence our frenetic race to convert nature into commodities that don't even meet real needs, if not from insecurity?

Think about it. Is it from an attitude of scarcity or abundance that someone buys fifty pairs of shoes? Is it the secure person or the insecure person who buys a third sports car and a 10,000-square-foot house? Whence this urge to own, to dominate, to control? It comes from a lonely, destitute self in a hostile, ungiving world.

Free-money embodies the spiritual teachings of abundance, interconnectedness, and impermanence. These teachings, however, present a truth that is in conflict with the world we have created through our beliefs, in particular that set of beliefs that composes the story of money. It is time to get used to a new world, in which we no longer try to get rich by keeping, by hoarding, by *having*. It is a world in which we are rich by giving. The New Age "prosperity programming" teachers I criticized in Chapter 6 are actually announcing an important truth. We do indeed need to take on an attitude of abundance and to create a world that embodies it.

My dear reader, think about it: is it really who you are to say, "I will lend you money—but only if you give me even more in return"? When we need money to live, is that not a formula for slavery? Significantly, the forgiveness of debts for which Solon was famous was prompted in part by the indebted servitude of a growing proportion of the population. Today, young people feel enslaved to their college loans, householders to their mortgages, and entire Third World nations to their foreign debt. Interest is slavery. And since the condition of slavery demeans the slaveholder as much as the slave, in our hearts we want none of it.

If you lend money to someone, is it really who you are to hold that obligation over her head, forever and ever? Interest on a loan amounts to that: it is a pressure to pay it back. It is the threat, "If you don't pay me back, this is going to grow and grow." A zero-interest or negative-interest loan bears with it a certain freedom. It lacks that threat of life-long debt slavery.[44] I find negative interest to be quite natural. If I loan money to a friend, and she doesn't pay me back, eventually I want to say, "Forget about it—I don't want to hold this over your head forever." I don't want to hold on to old things, old debts. A negative-interest money system reinforces this salutary tendency, native to all of us, to let go, release the past, and move on.

---

44. This doesn't mean that creditors couldn't seize collateral or have courts enforce collection judgments against debtors for failure to make payments by the due date. It would mean, however, that the longer they waited, the less they could collect.

CHAPTER 13
STEADY-STATE AND DEGROWTH ECONOMICS

Infinite growth of material consumption in a finite world is an impossibility.

—E. F. Schumacher

SUSTAINABILITY RECONSIDERED

The last two chapters have outlined an economy that is sustainable: it incorporates the ecological limits of the planet, and it thrives without a structural need for endless growth in consumption. But is sustainability to be our highest aspiration?

I have long been impatient with "sustainability," as if that were an end in itself. Isn't it more important to think about what we want to sustain, and therefore what we want to create? Many beautiful, necessary things are not sustainable: pregnancy, for example. I am heartened by the recent shift of thinking away from sustainability and toward transition. What we are transitioning to will be far more sustainable than our current way of life, but that is not the ultimate goal, just as the ultimate goal of life is not merely to stay alive.

A core concept of sacred economics is that it is an extension of ecology rather than an exception to it. So we have to ask, is nature fundamentally stable, sustainable, or harmonious? Does it have the characteristics that we want in a society? Some people dismiss the idea that nature is harmonious or balanced, emphasizing instead its cruel, competitive, and wasteful aspects. This position has deep ideological implications, for it justifies the program of Ascent: to dominate and master nature through science and technology. Usually, people sympathetic to this view also carry a Hobbesian view of primitive society and human nature and see civilization with its various methods of social control to be a great improvement over brutal, primitive times. This is part of the story of Ascent—to rise above our animal nature into an exclusively human realm.

The view of nature as a vast competitive arena, a Darwinian struggle for survival among discrete competing organisms, reverberates throughout economic theory. In biology this paradigm has come under increasing challenge, but its economic translation still reigns supreme among most professional economists and policymakers. Just as Darwinian "selfish genes" are supposed to maximize their reproductive self-interest, so does Adam Smith's "economic man" seek to maximize economic self-interest. This is a core assumption of economics instrumental in formulating the laws of supply and demand.

In the last two decades, a momentous paradigm shift has emerged in biology that emphasizes cooperation, symbiosis, and homeostatic maintenance of wholes larger than the individual organism. Furthermore, the very notion of genetic integrity has come under question as new discoveries demonstrate the importance of gene sharing across organism and species boundaries. The downfall of the paradigm of competing separate selves in biology corresponds to similar developments in psychology, sociology, and—yes—economics. Competition and the "survival of the fittest" can no longer be axiomatic in any field.

That is not to say that competition is unimportant, or that nature is unchanging. Unsustainable processes do happen in nature, and they are not aberrations. They too serve a purpose: to propel systems from one phase to another.

At a recent conference, someone objected to my view of the law of return by observing that natural systems sometimes *do* produce large amounts of waste products that no other organism can utilize and that poison the environment for all. He was perhaps thinking of the Precambrian oxygen catastrophe, when photosynthesizing organisms emerged and "poisoned" the atmosphere with their waste product, oxygen. In the classic view, this malfunction of nature would have meant the end of life on earth if it weren't for the extremely fortunate emergence of aerobic organisms that could remove oxygen from the atmosphere. This wasn't nature's harmony—it was a highly unlikely chance mutation. The conclusion is that we cannot rely on nature's harmony, that we are always on the verge of catastrophe and therefore must exercise technological control over nature, over the body, and over human nature. This is the ideology of Ascent, which is congruent to the economic ideology of growth and inimical to the ideal of a steady-state economy. My questioner didn't go this far; his point was basically, "Don't appeal to natural law to justify a zero-growth economy."

I would like to embed the catastrophe phenomenon in a larger context. It is true that positive-feedback loops such as the Precambrian oxygen catastrophe exist in nature. They come at special moments, though—moments of transformation. It is, for example, a positive feedback cascade of self-reinforcing, self-augmenting hormones that triggers the childbirth process. Childbirth labor is unsustainable—it would kill the mother if it continued too long—but once its goal is accomplished, the mother returns to homeostasis.

Positive feedback phases take an organism or ecosystem from an old steady-state phase to a new one.

We can look at money in exactly this way. Money, along with technology, is one of the key "hormones" of the human metaorganism that is propelling us on an unsustainable course toward a new estate. Technology builds on past technology and creates problems that necessitate yet more technology. Capital builds on past capital and is created through interest-bearing debt that requires exponentially more capital to be created in the future. Unsustainable, yes, but only unnatural if we try to sustain it past its time. Positive feedback processes always hit limits. Earth's contractions intensify only up to a point—then a baby is born. What we see with alarm as an exponential growth curve is actually part of a phase transition curve.

TRANSITION TO STEADY-STATE: BUMP OR CRASH?

Figures 2 through 5 illustrate this point. The solid line represents the growth of money, population, energy consumption, resource use, CO_2 emissions, and lots of other things up until the present time. It is an exponential curve. The dotted lines represent four possible futures. Figure 2 represents the techno-topian myth of Ascent, which says that exponential growth can and will continue forever as we conquer the galaxy and the universe. It says that when we grow past the limits of the earth, we will colonize the stars and terraform new planets; that the infinitude of the universe will contain our infinite exponential growth.

Current economic policy still embodies the curve in Figure 2. Although many people today recognize that continued exponential growth threatens the basis of life on earth, this realization hasn't yet

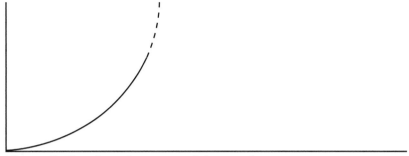

Figure 2. Continued exponential growth

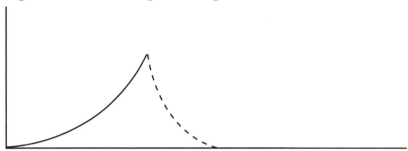

Figure 3. Peak and collapse

infiltrated into mainstream economic discourse, which still focuses on growth.

The fear of the pessimists is that the continuation of the heretofore exponential curve can be no other than Figure 3—a catastrophic crash back to the baseline. This is essentially the prediction of "collapsist" thinkers in the anticivilization and Peak Oil movements, who compare our present condition to the demographics of animals like locusts, who have a massive population explosion that pushes their numbers far above the land's carrying capacity, followed by a population crash. We too, they say, are living far above the earth's carrying capacity, and so a population implosion is inevitable.

Doom-and-gloom, collapsist scenarios such as Armageddon, popularizations of 2012 prophecies, or other cataclysmic end-of-the-world events have a certain emotional appeal, an appeal I must confess to have felt at times myself. Part of me wants out. I am not alone in this. Many of us are tired of the modern world, with its violence, alienation, poverty, and deadness, and we despair of ever changing it. A world-changing event that does it for us is appealing, whether it is some miracle technology come to save us, or Jesus come to save us, or UFOs, or even some geological, social, or economic cataclysm. Many collapsist thinkers are also drawn to what might follow collapse: a lower-tech, communal society connected to nature, spirit, and the old ways. Furthermore, the prospect of economic or environmental collapse gratifies that vindictive part of us that wants to say, "I told you so!"—the part that wants to see the wicked punished.

Unfortunately, collapse scenarios involve immense suffering: hundreds of millions or billions of casualties. Moreover, they involve the erasure of the entire edifice of civilization, the good along with the bad. That would be OK if indeed technology and culture were a mistake, but I think that like those of all beings, our gifts have a purpose, a purpose we have yet to discover. We are emerging now from childhood, and the crises we have created offer the first opportunity to apply our gifts to their true purpose. In a subtle way, to reject our gifts wholesale is just as much a mind-set of Separation as to exalt them above the rest of nature. Both are a kind of anthropocentric exceptionalism. Can we not reunite with nature as a mature species?

With that in mind, I offer two more curves that equally fit the data points we have up until now. Figure 4 shows a curve that is quite common in nature: a time of rapid growth that eventually slows and approaches a steady state. This curve could map the growth of an adolescent human, the total biomass of vegetation regrowing on barren land, or the population of bacteria newly

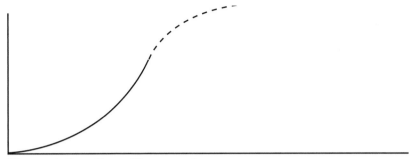

Figure 4. Leveling off to steady-state

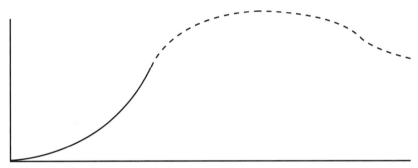

Figure 5. Peak, then steady-state

introduced into a petri dish with a constant food supply. Figure 5 represents another common pattern: a peak above long-term sustainable levels followed by a gradual decline toward a steady-state.

Phases of rapid growth driven by competition, followed by a phase transition into a steady state, are quite common in nature. Think of an immature ecosystem with weeds and saplings racing for sunlight. This is but a phase of a larger process that culminates in a symbiotic, complex, nonlinear, and stable forest. Immersed in an economy and ideology corresponding to the immature ecosystem, we have seen its headlong competition as nature's way. Perhaps humanity too is maturing, self-organizing into mutualistic wholes in which competition and growth are no longer primary.

As a matter of fact, recent demographic statistics seem to show not a population crash, but a rapid deceleration of growth. We

255

could see either a leveling off of population as it approaches an asymptote at about 8 or 9 billion people (Figure 4), or a peak at about that level followed by a decline toward a steady state of a couple billion (Figure 5). Interpreting these curves in economic terms, either the monetization of life will slow down and stop (i.e., economic growth will gradually slow until we reach a steady-state, zero-growth economy), or it will contract a bit first before stabilizing at a lower level (lower per-capita GDP) than today. Figure 4 shows the first scenario, Figure 5 the second. In both cases, population and economy, I foresee the latter.

Demographic statistics support this conjecture. As a country approaches full industrialization, its birthrate slows—in most cases to below the replacement rate. This implies a gentle, natural decline in population, not a catastrophic mass die-off. I think that on a healing planet, both GDP and population will peak within the next three decades, level off, and then contract by a few percent per decade until they reach a sustainable level.[1] The trend has started already: according to 2006 U.N. projections, the world's fertility rate has dropped in the last decade from 2.65 to 2.55 live births per woman. Over the past half-century, fertility rates in the most highly industrialized countries have dropped dramatically, in most cases to well under the replacement level of 2.1. Interestingly, the inverse correlation between a nation's human development index (HDI, a measure of well-being that avoids many of the flaws of GDP) and its fertility rate has, in the last few years, reversed at the upper extreme of HDI. In other words, the fertility rate is show-

---

1. GDP is likely to contract more quickly and less smoothly than population, perhaps by 1 to 2 percent per year, or about one-half per generation. This is on a global scale. In some countries growth will persist longer than in others.

ing signs of recovery to near replacement levels when economic development nears completion.[2]

I don't intend these statistics to be anything more than suggestive of a possibility. I'm not going to attempt to predict the future, but I think that the ravages of Separation such as the conversion of health capital into money, will result in drastically reduced fertility and increase mortality over the next half-century. The world population circa 2100 may be moderately smaller than it is today. In economy, we will reclaim much of the monetized, privatized realm for the commons and the gift. Much that is commodity today will no longer be commodity as new, cooperative economic forms spring up to meet local needs.

The severity of the "bump" in Figure 5 depends on how far we overshoot the sustainable baseline. I believe that we missed our chance for an effortless (Figure 4) transition in the 1960s, which really represented the natural zenith of the Age of Separation. And we caught a glimpse of it, too! We caught a glimpse of a more beautiful world, so close. The hippies saw it and lived it for a few shining moments, but the old stories were too strong. Instead of the hippies pulling us all into a new world, we dragged them back into ours.

The longer the Age of Separation persists, the more traumatic the transition will be, and the farther and more abrupt the drop to a sustainable baseline. In the limit case, it approaches the calamity of Figure 3. That is why it is so important to protect whatever we can of the remainder of the commons, to limit growth and preserve real wealth to sustain life after the bump—"to hasten the crash and mitigate its severity." Even today, forty squandered years

---

2. Yong, "Fertility Rates Climb Back Up."

after the Great Awakening of the 1960s, it is still not too late for a soft landing.

SHRINKING MONEY, GROWING WEALTH

Today, economic recession is the bogeyman of policy makers, who quite understandably associate it with unemployment, poverty, and social unrest. I have explained already how a negative-interest system allows credit to circulate even in a shrinking economy, thereby avoiding polarization of wealth and a deflationary spiral. Even so, many people would be aghast at a call for negative economic growth: wouldn't that, by definition, mean that society were made poorer? Wouldn't that, by definition, mean a decline in the volume of goods and services available for the public benefit?

No, it would not. Negative economic growth doesn't entail a decline in wealth at all, nor a decline in the availability of what we call "goods and services." Remember, goods and services at present are defined as *things that are exchanged for money.* If they are provided through some other, nonmonetary, mechanism, then the statistical "economy" can shrink even as the real economy—what people make and do for each other—grows richer.

I will not mince words: in this book I am calling for economic degrowth, a shrinking of the economy, a recession that will last decades or centuries. Obviously, the word "recession" has negative connotations today, though it really just means a time of receding. I am most emphatically *not* saying that we must make some sacrifices to our quality of life for the good of the planet. Rather, we need but reduce the role of money. If our future includes a diversification in the modes of human sharing, then economic growth no longer has the same meaning it has today. We don't need to become more altruistic and self-sacrificing, forgoing our own benefit for the good of others. How tightly we hold to the equation of money and self-interest! But it shall be so no longer. Let me illustrate by way of some examples how we can all become richer through the shrinkage of the money realm.

Today already there is a vast software industry that operates using very little money. I wrote this book on OpenOffice, a software package available for a voluntary donation that was written mostly by a community of unpaid programmers. One might say that those programmers are "paid" not in money, but in the esteem of their fellows, a kind of social currency. I prefer to see their productivity as a gift economy, which naturally generates respect and gratitude among community members. Either way, this mode of production does not show up in GDP statistics. We could easily have a shrinking "economy" that offers more and more, better and better, products like these. And the more there are, the less we need money; the less we need money, the more leisure time we have; the more leisure time we have, the more we can afford to make our own offerings to the gift economy.

For many categories of goods, marginal costs of production are now practically zero. This is true of nearly all digital products, such as software, music, movies, and so forth. Considerable costs may be involved in the production of the first unit, but after that, the cost per unit is essentially zero. The industry has tried therefore to create an artificial scarcity through copyright protection, digital rights management schemes, and so forth. It is quite irrational that the only way we have of rewarding the creators of digital content is to give it to fewer people than could benefit from it. Every person could have access to every movie, song, and software program in existence, and it would cost the producers no more than it does today. Nonscarce goods should not be subject to payment in scarce currency. Indeed, many producers of nonscarce goods have given up trying to maintain their artificial scarcity and try to make money instead by asking for voluntary payments, selling advertising, or charging for technical support, training, or in the case of music, live concerts. Time, attention, space in a concert venue, and so on are all scarce resources, and they fit much more easily into the money realm. Nonetheless, the net result is economic degrowth: as one writer puts it,

> Their basic idea, which is great as far as it goes, is to use free content to piggyback monetized auxiliary services: Linux distros [distributions] offering tech support and customization, music companies selling certified authentic copies available at a convenient location, Phish selling concert tickets, etc. One thing they fail to adequately address, though, is that the total amount of cash available from such auxiliary services is less than what proprietary content brought in.... Encarta sales didn't bring in money equivalent to the exchange value it destroyed for Britannica et al. And Wikipedia destroyed billions in net monetized value for both hard-copy encyclopedias and Encarta.[3]

If this trend continues (and it appears to be spreading as more and more traditional media move online), we will indeed see a perfect example of greater wealth accompanied by a smaller (money) economy.

Digital goods are an extreme example of a more general phenomenon. Many other products are trending toward near-zero marginal costs. The actual marginal production cost of most pharmaceutical medicines is but pennies per pill. Even bulk industrial

---

3. Caron, "Abundance Creates Utility but Destroys Exchange Value."

commodities such as screws cost much less than in the past, not only in terms of money and human labor but even, sometimes, in terms of energy input. This is because of the accumulation of decades or centuries of innovation. It is another aspect of our divine bequest—in this case of culture rather than nature—from which all human beings equally deserve to benefit.

The evolution toward sacred economy is of a whole with a more general civilizational transformation. Parallel changes are happening in medicine, education, agriculture, government, science, and every other institution of our culture. Changes in each realm reinforce changes in the rest. So it is with the economic effects of the shift toward natural medicine. A mere century or two ago, only a very few people paid for medical care, which was provided through an informal network of folk healers, herbal doctors, and, for most common maladies, grandmothers and neighbors. Herbal knowledge was widely dispersed and usually applied without payment. Even if it were fully professionalized, the profit potential of herbal medicine (and most other forms of natural medicine) is far lower than that of high-tech medicine. Compared to the complex, high-tech processes that go into pharmaceutical medicine, herbal medicine is cheap to produce. Many of the best medicinal plants are near-ubiquitous weeds. A shift toward herbal medicine, homeopathic medicine, and the myriad mind-body modalities blossoming today promises economic degrowth, yet it entails no reduction in our quality of life.[4]

---

4. To be sure, there are things at which technological medicine excels. It is inferior to herbal medicine at treating most of the chronic conditions that afflict people today, but it is unsurpassed in most emergency situations. I am not advocating its termination, only its recession back into its proper realm. The same goes for many of the other bloated institutions that dominate our society.

Another area for economic degrowth is architecture and urban design. In addition to disconnecting us from community, nature, and place, the expansive, alienating suburbs of the last two generations demand enormous consumption of resources. Now, though, planners and builders are rediscovering the virtues of high-density urban design, smaller dwellings, mass-transit-friendly layouts, and multiuse developments that don't require so much driving. All of these changes cause economic shrinkage: fewer "goods" such as roads, gasoline, lumber, and so on are needed. With more vibrant public spaces, people also have less need to live in huge private spaces. People living in community depend less on externally produced entertainment and have more occasion to share and assist each other. All of that means a decrease in money-mediated activity.

DISINTERMEDIATION AND THE P2P REVOLUTION

Another source of economic shrinkage is the disintermediation that the internet has made possible. *Disintermediation* refers to the elimination of intermediaries: agents, brokers, middlemen, and so forth. Consider the example of Craigslist, which according to one estimate has destroyed $10 billion of annual revenue from classified ads, replacing it with only $100 million of its own revenues.[5] Google has also made advertising more efficient (cheaper), not only seizing ad revenue from existing media but also reducing total industry-wide advertising expenditures. (Total "adspend" across all media fell by 9 percent in 2009.) Of course, as advertising has become cheaper, it has also become more ubiquitous; even so, the total size

---

5. Jarvis, "When Innovation Yields Efficiency."

of the ad industry has peaked. Yes, we are passing through the time of "peak advertising" as the commons of the public attention has been saturated. I hope you aren't too sad about the end of growth in advertising, which has been a major contributor to GDP growth. Meanwhile, many of the traditional functions of advertising and marketing which were once paid services are now being met for free through social networking. Similarly, the blogosphere has taken over many of the functions of traditional news distribution, but again at much less cost. The same is true of travel agency, stock brokerage, and many other industries where brokers and agents are no longer necessary. All of these factors contribute to economic deflation.

Disintermediation and open source software are both part of a more general phenomenon: the peer-to-peer (P2P) revolution. The older hierarchical and centralized structures of distribution, circulation, and production required a lot of money and human effort to administer. Moreover, their very nature isolated people from each other within narrow specialties, making gift exchange impossible.

Disintermediation is even affecting the credit system and subverting banks' traditional role as financial intermediaries connecting investors and borrowers. Corporations bypass banks by obtaining financing directly from money markets, while new P2P lending websites such as LendingClub and Prosper.com now allow individuals to borrow directly from each other. Commercial credit-clearing rings, mutual factoring systems, and commercial barter networks, which I will discuss later, are other ways that information technology is reducing the role of centralized intermediary institutions. All of these developments will reduce GDP by lowering spending on "financial services."

Because these ever-cheaper "information economy" services are a factor of production in nearly every other sector, degrowth here is contagious. This is true even in industries that we think of as growth industries. In 2000, for example, $371 billion was spent on PC hardware, including printers, servicing, and data storage. By 2009, this had shrunk to $326 billion. Obviously, this drop is not because we are buying fewer computers; it is because costs have fallen dramatically.

The commonest profit model on the internet is to run ads, essentially limiting the size of the entire digital economy to what level of advertising the physical economy can support. But the internet cannibalizes even itself: websites that offer free product reviews and price comparison searches render the very advertising that supports them obsolete.

What is happening is that the business model that has worked for all human history (find something people do for themselves or each other in a gift economy, take it away from them, and then sell it back) is being reversed. The internet is allowing people once again to do things for themselves and each other without paying for it. Eric Reasons comments,

> Maybe the reason we're having such a hard time finding out ways to monetize various internet services like Twitter, Facebook, and YouTube, is that they can't be monetized ... or at least not at replacement rates to the industries and services that they're supplanting. This is exactly what the print media is finding out the hard way as it tries to shift to an online model.[6]

The internet is a participatory gift economy, a P2P network in which there is no consistent distinction between a producer and a consumer. When we share news, product recommendations, songs,

---

6. Reasons, "Innovative Deflation."

and so forth with our online networks, we do not charge anyone for our "information services." It is a gift economy. The content of most websites is free as well. Reasons concludes,

> We're told to believe in our future in a knowledge-based economy, but nobody has really figured out how to make real money of it. Of those who are making money off of it (Craigslist, Google), they are making pennies per dollar in the old markets that they've upset or practically eliminated with their innovation. This isn't because we haven't found the right monetization scheme yet. It is because innovation is leading to efficiency and not growth, and that is exerting deflationary pressure on bloated industries. Moreover, it is largely being done by us, the end user, in our free time, because we want to create and share, not just consume.

While a redirection toward a participatory gift economy is new, the threat of overcapacity and underemployment has bedeviled capitalism for centuries, indicating that we don't need to work as hard as we do to support human life. Indeed, the imminent advent of an age of leisure has been before us ever since the first industrial machines came into use, machines that could "do the work of a thousand men." Yet the implied promise, that soon we would all have to work only one-thousandth as hard, shows no signs of manifesting. And here I am promising it again. Will this vision likewise prove to be a mirage? No. The key difference is that we won't rely on technological improvements in efficiency alone to enable greater leisure. The key is degrowth, not efficiency. It seems very counterintuitive: that degrowth—economic recession—will be what ushers in true affluence for the many.

In a growth economy, the labor that could be freed up through technological progress is devoted instead to producing more and more stuff. If in 1870 it took ten labor-hours to produce the necessities of life for a household, and today it takes one labor-hour to produce the same quantity of things, then our system conspires to make us consume as much as ten households did in 1870. We hear talk about the American consumer, the engine of global economic growth. Implicit is a vision of wealth identified with endlessly accelerating consumption. A new computer every month, a new car every year, a bigger house every five years—new, more, bigger, better. It seems insane, but it is economically necessary in our present system because deflation dynamics lurk close at hand, awaiting the day when consumption lags behind productivity growth.

I do not foresee an abrupt transition to the economy I describe. Let us indulge our gentle disposition and allow that the habits of slavery are of long standing and may need some time to unwind. I foresee a degrowth rate of around 2 percent, so that our use of raw materials, our pollution of the air and water, and our time spent working for money not love falls by about half with each generation, until eventually the pace of degrowth slows as the economy approaches an equilibrium relationship with the planet a couple hundred years from now.

The system I have described offers an alternative to this future of bigger, better, and more followed by catastrophic collapse. Negative interest allows productive investment to continue, and money to circulate, even when the marginal return on capital is zero or less, while a commons-backed currency frees work to go toward nonconsumptive purposes. Next I will describe a third thread in the tapestry: the social dividend, which frees the purchasing power of workers from the need for full employment in the money economy.

CHAPTER 14

THE SOCIAL DIVIDEND

Most men would feel insulted if it were proposed to employ them in throwing stones over a wall, and then in throwing them back, merely that they might earn their wages. But many are no more worthily employed now.

—Henry David Thoreau

Clearly the most unfortunate people are those who must do the same thing over and over again, every minute, or perhaps twenty to the minute. They deserve the shortest hours and the highest pay.

—John Kenneth Galbraith

THE PARADOX OF LEISURE

In large part, the history of technology is the history of labor-saving devices. A diesel backhoe can do the work of five hundred men with shovels. A bulldozer can do the work of five hundred lumberjacks with axes. A computer can do the work of five hundred old-time accountants with pens and paper. After centuries of technological advances, why do we find ourselves working just as much as ever? Why do most people on earth still live in a daily experience of scarcity? For centuries, futurists have predicted an imminent age of leisure. Why has it never happened?

The reason is that, at every opportunity, we have chosen to produce more rather than to work less. We have been helpless to choose otherwise.

Under the current system, growth in leisure is impossible without some kind of wealth redistribution. Imagine what would happen if, all of a sudden, a magical technology were found that could double the productivity of every worker. Now the same amount of goods is available with half the labor. If (as in a steady-state or degrowth economy) demand does not increase, then half the workers are now superfluous. To stay competitive, firms must fire half their workers, make them part-time, or pay them less. Aggregate wages will fall by half since no one will pay workers more than the revenues they are generating for the employer. The laid-off workers no longer have the money to buy the products, even though they are about 50 percent cheaper. In the end, despite more goods being available with less effort, the money to buy those goods doesn't get to the people who could use them. Leisure has increased all right; it is called "unemployment"—and the results are catastrophic: a rapid concentration of wealth, deflation, bankruptcies, and so on as described in Chapter 6.

The ensuing socioeconomic calamity can be averted in two ways: wealth redistribution or growth. To accomplish the former, we could simply take money away from the employed and give it to the unemployed, subsidize firms in keeping superfluous employees, or pay everyone a social wage regardless of whether they work or not. These redistributive policies diminish the relative wealth and power of the holders of money. The other solution, in the above scenario, would be to double demand so as to keep everyone employed.

Since, generally speaking, the rich are in control of things and don't want their wealth to be redistributed, the traditional solution to the problem of overproduction and underemployment is to somehow generate economic growth, which means increasing demand for new goods and services. One way to do that is through exports; obviously, this solution cannot work for the planet as a whole. Another way to increase demand is, as I have abundantly described, to colonize the nonmonetary realm—to make people buy what was once free. Finally, we can simply destroy excess production through war and waste. All of these measures keep everyone hard at work when natural demand has been sated.

The ideology of growth, the story of Ascent, says that natural demand can never be sated, that it is infinitely (upwardly) elastic. It assumes an endless supply of new markets, new needs, and new desires. But as I have observed, the only object of desire that knows no satiety is money. The assumption of limitless needs and therefore limitless demand drives the insanity we see today—and the economic logic that justifies it.[1]

---

1. Infinitely elastic demand, for example, justifies eternal deferment of a leisure economy based on the so-called lump-of-labor fallacy. I shall rename this the "lump-of-labor-fallacy fallacy," because this specious "fallacy" says that the amount of labor needed by the economy can always grow; therefore, improvements in technology won't allow us a shorter workweek or less time devoted to production.

A similar argument, Jevon's paradox, rests upon the same foundational assumption. Jevon's paradox says that improvements in efficiency don't lead to less resource use (including labor), but rather to more. For example, if lighting becomes cheaper, we will use more of it. If we switch to compact fluorescent bulbs that use one-fifth the electricity, we'll install five times more of them. Since they are so cheap, maybe I'll install some new ones in my backyard in case we have a party next summer. Applied to the degrowth factors I described above, Jevon's paradox says that cheaper advertising will mean even more of it. But this, again, assumes an infinite upward elasticity of demand. It assumes that our capacity to use lighting, advertising, and so on is infinite. A more sophisticated version of this argument would say that even if demand is fully saturated in one area, any improvements in efficiency will free up money that will be applied toward some other area. So the assumption is that overall needs are infinite. Accompanying that assumption is another: that there is no limit to the amount of nature, culture, and so on that we can bring into the money realm. In earlier times, it indeed seemed as though nature's resources were unlimited, but today the limits are obvious.

The economically educated reader can apply a parallel logic to other concepts of classical economics, such as Say's law, the broken window fallacy, and so on. All partake of the story of Ascent: that our rise to dominion over nature will continue forever.

In the past we always had a choice of what to do with gains in efficiency: work less or consume more. Compelled by a growth-dependent money system, we consistently chose the latter. Instead of working less hard to meet existing needs more easily, we have constantly created new needs to meet or, more often, transferred needs from the gift into the money realm or sought to fulfill infinite needs with finite things. Such has driven our ascent, the development of our gifts of hand and mind. Though the cost to nature, culture, spirit, and humanity has been high, this development is not without its rightful purpose. Today, as the natural and cultural commonwealth is exhausted, the context of our choice—work less or consume more—is changing. The age of ascent is winding to a close, and we seek to apply the gifts we have developed toward their true purpose in a new relationship to Earth. The age of growth is over. John Maynard Keynes expressed a premonition of this epochal shift in *Economic Consequences of the Peace:*

> On the one hand the laboring classes accepted ... a situation in which they could call their own very little of the cake that they and Nature and the capitalists were co-operating to produce. And on the other hand the capitalist classes were allowed to call the best part of the cake theirs and were theoretically free to consume it, on the tacit underlying condition that they consumed very little of it in practice. The duty of "saving" became nine-tenths of virtue and the growth of the cake the object of true religion. There grew round the nonconsumption of the cake all those instincts of puritanism which in other ages has withdrawn itself from the world and has neglected the arts of production as well as those of enjoyment. *And so the cake increased; but to what end was not clearly contemplated.* Individuals would be

exhorted not so much to abstain as to defer, and to cultivate the pleasures of security and anticipation. Saving was for old age or for your children; but this was only in theory—the virtue of the cake was that it was never to be consumed, neither by you nor by your children after you.[2]

On the collective level, not consuming the cake means choosing growth over leisure. More efficient production technology allows us either to work less or to work just as hard and produce more stuff. Our economic system requires and embodies the latter choice. But despite today's association of "Keynesian" economics with fiscal stimulus, Keynes himself never saw stimulus as a permanent solution. As a society, we have been artificially stimulating demand now for seventy years, through military spending, highway construction, and subsidies for accelerating extraction, construction, consumption, and imperialism. Attempting to uphold economic growth and keep the marginal efficiency of capital ahead of interest, we have trapped ourselves in a pattern of more and more production, whether we need it or not. Adapting to this trap, economic theory, with its assumption of infinite wants, says we will always "need it," always need to produce more and more, if not in one industry then in another. I have described this process differently: as a depletion of first one realm and then another of natural, social, cultural, and spiritual capital. Keynes did not state it so explicitly, living as he did in the ideological context of Ascent, but he clearly intuited it. His use of the past tense in the above passage suggests, at least to me, that one day it would be time to eat the cake: to choose less work over more stuff.

---

2. Keynes, *Economic Consequences of the Peace*, 20; emphasis mine. I was alerted to this passage by www.lump-of-labor.org.

A positive risk-free interest rate is the economic aspect of the "exhortation" Keynes described to "cultivate the pleasures of security and anticipation" or, in my language, to mortgage the present moment to the future, to choose security, or a semblance thereof, over freedom. You see, the economic logic I have described has a personal dimension as well. For the past age, we have had an incentive to choose work over leisure, even when we didn't need the money, because interest promises that our money will be able to buy even more leisure in the future. By abstaining from pleasure and leisure—and indeed, all too often, from our best impulses—we might even attain the economic version of heaven: early retirement. But as often with religion, the promise of heaven only serves to keep us in chains. The time of our servitude, though, is over. The condition of the planet now urgently demands that we turn our attention away from "growing the cake."

THE OBSOLESCENCE OF "JOBS"

Ever since the dawn of the industrial era, we have borne an ever-present anxiety that we will be replaced by machines. And indeed this has come to pass for many, as machines take over functions once performed by humans. The only way to maintain full employment has been through growth, and yet here I am calling for an end to growth and an end to full employment (for money) as well. So, given that our age-old anxiety is upon us, let us examine what, exactly, it means for our labor to be replaced by a machine.

To be taken over by a machine, the job one is doing must have been mechanical to begin with. As society as a whole became more mechanized, more and more jobs took on the machine's characteristics of uniformity, routine, and standardization. This was unavoidable when these jobs were to operate machines or otherwise plug into machine-dominated processes. Herein lies a much deeper source of our anxiety: not that we will be replaced by machines, but that we will *become* machines, that we will live and work like machines.

The most famous antimachine movement, the Luddites of the early nineteenth century, were aware of this. According to researcher Kirkpatrick Sale, theirs was not a blind, superstitious hatred of machinery; they thought machinery had its proper place. They were outraged not only by their loss of livelihood but by the shoddy products, numbing tedium, constant danger, and dehumanizing conditions of the factories. They were resisting the mechanization of labor. The replacement of highly skilled, autonomous production with degrading, dangerous factory work is an affront to the human spirit.

The goal of a compassionate economy, therefore, is not to provide "jobs," as most liberal politicians seem to think. Once work has become mechanical, it is in a sense too late—inhuman work might as well be done by machines. I cannot help but remark on the inanity of economic programs that seek to make more "jobs," as if we needed more goods and more services. Why do we want to create more jobs? It is so people have money to live. For that purpose, they might as well dig holes in the ground and fill them up again, as Keynes famously quipped. Present economic policies attempt just that: witness the current efforts to reignite housing construction at a time when there are 19 million vacant housing units in the United States![3] Wouldn't it be better to pay people to

---

3. Moreover, millions more houses are far larger than necessary. In some countries, thirty people live quite happily in the space that an upper-middle-class American family inhabits. Interestingly, the economic depression is beginning to reverse this trend toward isolation and the atomization of family as grown children are forced to move back in with their parents or vice versa.

do nothing at all, and free up their creative energy to meet the urgent needs of the world?

Clearly, we possess the means and face the necessity to grow less, to work less, and to turn our energies toward other things. It is time to redeem the age-old promise of industry: that technology will allow a dramatic reduction in the workweek and usher in an "age of leisure." Unfortunately, the term *leisure* carries connotations of frivolity and dissipation that are inconsistent with the urgent needs of the planet and its people as the age turns. There is a vast amount of important work to be done, work that is consistent with degrowth because it won't necessarily produce salable product. There are forests to replant, sick people to care for, an entire planet to be healed. I think we are going to be very busy. We are going to work hard doing deeply meaningful things that no longer must fight upstream against the flow of money, the imperative of growth. Yet I also believe we will have more true leisure—the experience of the abundance of time—than we do today. The scarcity of time is one reason we overconsume, attempting to compensate for the loss of this most primal of all wealth. Time is life. To be truly rich is to have sovereignty over our own time.

So far I have described a system that shifts financial incentives toward the preservation and expansion of the ecosystem and the rest of the commons, allowing money to flow to those who need it in the absence of growth. But there is an even more radical way to end the principle of "money shall go to those who will generate even more of it" upon which modern banking is based. Why not just give people money? Everyone?[4] This is the idea of a "social

---

4. This would not entail permanent inflation unless the total money supply increased. However, in the system outlined herein, there are many ways to reduce the monetary base to allow a money-supply-neutral social dividend. Besides traditional

dividend" or "social wage," advocated in the 1920s by Major Douglas, founder of the social credit movement.

The idea has both an economic and a moral rationale. Douglas, a British engineer, observed the same thing Marx did—that workers receive a shrinking share of revenues as industry becomes less labor-intensive and more capital-intensive—eventually leading to poverty, polarization of wealth, and economic depression due to falling demand. As a remedy, he proposed issuing fiat money in an amount sufficient for all citizens to purchase the products of their own labor, both as a direct per-capita payment and as a rebate on purchases—a negative sales tax. This proposal is not as far outside the economic mainstream as you may think—the stimulus checks sent out to all U.S. households in 2008 were a dilute form of a social dividend and were intended to have precisely the effect Douglas envisioned: to bring money to those who will spend it and counter economic depression.[5] These were not welfare checks given only to the poor. They were stimulus checks given to everyone.

The leisure-and-redistribution alternative to growth is gaining credibility as the economic downturn persists. In Germany, the *Kurzarbeit*, or "short work," program subsidizes shorter workweeks in order to forestall unemployment, in flagrant denial of the so-

---

methods such as taxation and central bank open market operations, the redemption of resource-backed currency could also be employed to control the money supply. Finally, decaying currency and negative interest on bank reserves reduce the money supply by the demurrage rate. Give the current money stock and a demurrage (negative interest) rate of 5 percent, this would allow a money-supply-neutral annual payment of $1,000 per household. If large amounts of other debt instruments are monetized in bailouts, as may become necessary to rescue the financial infrastructure, the revenue from demurrage could easily be ten times that.

5. Of course, at the same time much larger amounts of public money were being lavished on the very financial institutions that were complicit in the crisis to begin with.

called lump-of-labor fallacy (see note 1). Instead of laying off 20 percent of its workforce, a firm shortens everyone's workweek by 20 percent. Most of each employee's pay cut is reimbursed to the employee by the government. Employees can keep their jobs, working 20 percent less with only a 4- or 8-percent pay cut.[6] The results have been impressive: German unemployment stayed lower than expected through the recession, and the auto industry, where the policy was implemented most vigorously, did not lose a single full-time manufacturing job in the first half of 2009.[7] The *Kurzarbeit* program is akin to a social dividend on a limited scale, and bears a similar economic and humanitarian motivation.

There is also a philosophical or moral rationale for a social dividend that I became aware of as a teenager when I read a story by Philip Jose Farmer titled, "Riders of the Purple Wage." Echoing Douglas, Farmer reasoned that industrial technology has given humanity access to such vast, nearly effortless wealth that it shouldn't be necessary for anyone to work very hard to receive the necessities of life. The easy affluence made possible by technology, and by the natural wealth of the earth, is the collective treasure of the entire human race; merely by being born, each person is entitled to a share of it. Certainly no person has more right than any other to benefit from, say, the inventions of Robert Boyle or Thomas Edison, much less the vast cultural context that made their work possible. You or I have no more right to this cultural endowment than we have to the land or the genome. It comes to us as the gift of humanity as a whole; it is the gift of our ancestors, just as the land is the gift of Earth, Nature, or the Creator.

---

6. Hassett, "U.S. Should Try Germany's Unemployment Medicine."
7. James, "Cure for U.S. Unemployment Could Lie in German-Style Job Sharing."

Let us not be quick to accept the glib phrase I passed off above: "the easy affluence made possible by technology." This phrase buys into the ideology of Ascent, which as I have described is bound up with the ideology of endless economic growth. Somehow, despite centuries of labor-saving technologies, we have no more leisure than did hunter-gatherers, Neolithic villagers, or Medieval peasants. The reason is the overproduction and overconsumption of those things that technology can produce and the underproduction and underconsumption of those things it cannot. Usually, those latter things are precisely those that defy the homogenizing, depersonalizing rule of money: all that is unique, intimate, and personal. I will return to this theme later; for now, simply observe that in the realm of those needs that do admit to quantification, our needs are easily met. We should not need to work very much to procure the physical necessities of life: food, clothing, and shelter. Certainly we should have to work no more than the average twenty hours that the Kalahari aborigines spent on subsistence, in a harsh desert with Stone Age tools, in 1970. Certainly, we should feel no less secure, and no more anxious about "making a living," than the high Medieval peasants with their 150 saint's days off.

THE WILL TO WORK

What insanity would rather have us build more unnecessary houses than, say, save sea turtle eggs from oil spills? It ultimately comes down to the depletion of the commons being profitable, and its restoration a matter of altruism. The proposals in this book reverse this dynamic. Internalization of costs redirects the flow of money, and the flow of human activity, away from consumption and toward the sacred. Negative interest money allows investment to go to uses that don't generate even more money than went in and ends the discounting of the future. However, these measures alone may not be enough because some of the work necessary for the healing of the world is fundamentally uneconomic.[8]

The question, then, is how to create conditions that allow people to do important work that does not generate an economic return. As with redistribution of wealth, there are essentially two ways. One is the social dividend I have described, which exists today in dilute form as stimulus checks, tax credits, welfare payments, and so forth. This gives people the economic freedom to pursue activities that no one will hire them to do (because they won't generate income for an employer) and that produce nothing salable.

The second way to foster noneconomic work is for the government (or other entity) to pay people to do the beautiful and necessary things that we have come to value. We saw a harbinger of this during the New Deal, when we hired millions of the unemployed not only to build infrastructure that would one day generate a positive economic return but also to do such things as compile and preserve folk music and create recreational areas. Extended further, this is essentially the vision of state socialism. However, central planning often misses important needs, invites totalitarian abuse of power, and fails to engage the creativity of individuals and grass-roots organizations. With the social dividend, we are trusting that, unconstrained by economic necessity, people will naturally choose good and necessary work. These free, uncon-

---

8. By *uneconomic* I mean that it generates a negative financial return on investment, less even than the demurrage rate. One could make an economic argument that if *all* costs were internalized, and all effects on society and the ecosystem quantified, then all beneficial activity would become economic. However, the quantification of everything is part of the problem. It is better to leave some of the world unquantified and in the realm of the gift.

strained choices—the outgrowth of unfettered desire—will help identify what work is sacred.

At stake are two competing visions of human nature, and therefore two visions of how to run society. One says, "Free people from economic exigency, and they will do beautiful work." The other says, "Provide beautiful work, and use economic exigency to induce people to do it." The first trusts people's natural desire to create and their capacity to self-organize; the second puts the decision of how to allocate human labor into the hands of policy makers. I think that both will have a place for a long time to come, and that eventually, as political processes become more inclusive, grass-roots, and self-organizing, the two will merge into one.

One objection to a social dividend or equivalent entitlements is that people would have no motivation to work. We think, "If people weren't under some sort of pressure to work, they would do nothing at all. They need some sort of incentive." Why work if your basic needs are met without working? In this view, scarcity, even artificial scarcity, is a positive good because it counteracts the inborn laziness of the human being. This logic taps in once again to the logic of control, domination, and the war against the self. But is it really human nature to want to do nothing productive? Do we really need rewards to cajole us into labor and penalties to punish indolence?

Or, put in another way, is it human nature to desire never to give, but only to take?

I think not. Perhaps you can identify with my own experience, that some of the most painful times of my life were when I was unfulfilled in my work, when I was not applying my gifts toward a purpose I believed in. I remember quite well a meeting with a software company in Taiwan, where I worked as a translator and business consultant in my twenties. We were discussing some new technology, 3D sound or something like that, and everyone in the room seemed avidly concerned about its implications for their product. I had a moment of incredulity: "Wait a minute, you mean you people actually care about this? Because I don't care at all whether this or any other product has 3D sound." The next feeling was bleak despair because I realized I only cared because I was paid to care, and I couldn't imagine a realistic alternative to that. "Do I ever get to do something that I care about for real?" I thought. "When do I get to live *my* life, not the one I'm paid to live?"

A fundamental premise of this book is that human beings naturally desire to give. We are born into gratitude: the knowledge we have received and the desire to give in turn. Far from nudging reluctant people to give unto others against their lazy impulses, today's economy pressures us to deny our innate generosity and channel our gifts instead toward the perpetuation of a system that serves almost no one. A sacred economy is one that liberates our desire to work, our desire to give. Everybody I know has so much to give, and most of them feel they cannot because there is no money in it. Yet that is not because their gifts are unwanted. There is much beautiful work to be done. Money as we know it fails to connect gifts and needs. Why does everyone have to work so hard just to survive when (whether thanks to technology or not) such needs could easily be met with a tiny fraction of human labor? It is because of the scarcity-inducing nature of money.

The assumption that people do *not* want to work runs very deep in economics and taps into a yet deeper source: the story of the separate self. If more for you is less for me, if your well-being is irrelevant or inimical to my own, why should I desire to give anything to anyone? The "selfish gene" of biology, seeking to maximize its reproductive self-interest, is congruent to the "rational actor" of economics, seeking to maximize its financial self-interest. We supposedly don't want to do any work that contributes to the benefit of others unless there is something in it for us. We don't really desire to give; we must be forced to, paid to.

Economics textbooks speak of the "disutility" of work, assuming that if not "compensated" with wages, people will naturally prefer to . . . prefer to do what? Prefer to consume? Prefer to do nothing? To be entertained? The justification for a scarcity-based economic system is built into its premises, which include deep prejudices about human nature. This book assumes a different human nature: that we are fundamentally divine, creative, generous beings; that to give and to create are among our deepest desires. To embody this understanding in the money system, we must find ways to richly reward gifts to society, without those rewards becoming a form of pressure or slavery.

Not only is the experience of scarcity an artifact of our money system, but the laziness we view as human nature is a valid response to the kind of work that system engenders. If you find yourself being lazy, procrastinating, doing slipshod work, showing up late, not concentrating, and so on, then perhaps the problem isn't your character after all: perhaps it is a soul's rebellion against work that you don't really want to do. It is a message that says, "It is time to find your true work: that through which you can apply your gifts toward something meaningful." Ignore that message, and your unconscious will enforce it through depression, self-sabotage, illness, or accident, disabling you from living any more a life not aligned with your generosity.

In a sacred economy, people will still work hard—not because they have to, but because they *want* to. Have you ever wanted to give your time or labor to a good cause but refrained from doing so because you couldn't "afford to"? A social dividend frees gifts to flow toward needs and aligns our labor with our passion, our generosity, and our art.

Many people will work at paying jobs anyway, either to supplement the social dividend (which would probably be at bare subsistence level) or because they like those jobs on their own merits. But it would be a choice, not a necessity. In the absence of the coercive mechanism of "making a living," there would be little market for degrading or tedious jobs. To attract workers, employers will have to provide jobs that are meaningful and work conditions that respect human dignity. Many such jobs will exist because so much of the work financed by a commons-based money system will be by nature meaningful (because of financial incentives to conserve and restore).

Tellingly, even without a social dividend, people do enormous amounts of uncompensated work anyway. The entire internet is built mostly by volunteer labor, from open-source server software to free content. Entire organizations are staffed by hard-working volunteers. We do not need financial incentives to work, and in fact we do our best work when money is not an issue.[9] What would the world be like if people were supported in doing the beautiful things they must struggle against economic necessity to do today?

Sacred Economics envisions a world where people do things for love, not money. What would you be doing in such an economy? Would you be reclaiming a toxic waste dump? Being a "big sister"

---

9. According to a number of studies by social psychologists and economists, money is only an effective motivator in routine, mindless tasks. For anything requiring creativity and conceptual thinking, the introduction of monetary incentives can actually impede performance. This seems quite obvious, since they would distract from the task at hand. See the work of Dan Pink for more information on this topic.

to troubled adolescents? Creating sanctuaries for victims of human trafficking? Reintroducing threatened species into the wild? Installing gardens in inner-city neighborhoods? Putting on public performances? Helping decommissioned veterans adjust to civilian life? What would you do, freed from slavery to money? What does your own life, your true life, look like? Underneath the substitute lives we are paid to live, there is a real life, *your* life.

To be fully alive is to accept the guidance of the question, "What am I here for?" Most jobs today deny that feeling, since we are evidently not here to work on an assembly line or to push product or to do anything complicit in human impoverishment or ecological destruction. No one really wants to do such work, and someday, no one shall.

WHO SHALL REMOVE THE GARBAGE?

Is that a realistic pronouncement? Let me share with you a little rumination I wrote last spring.

A Slave World

I am writing at this moment in a large airport. Thousands of people work at jobs associated with this airport, and few of the jobs actually befit a human being.

I traveled to the airport in a hotel shuttle. On the way I told the driver, a Peruvian immigrant, about the talk I had given this weekend and about my vision of a more beautiful world, and at one point, by way of illustration, I said, "Here you are driving back and forth to the airport all day—surely you must have moments when you think, 'I was not put here on earth to do this.'"

"Yeah, that's for sure," he said.

I can't help but think the same as I watch the cashier at the airport kiosk, typing in purchase items and handing out change and saying, "Thank you sir, have a nice day," and the man going from trash can to trash can, emptying them into his cart and changing the plastic bag, silent and sullen, wooden-faced. What kind of world have we created, that a human being spends all day doing such tasks? What have we become, that we are not outraged by it?

The men and women at the ticket counters and gate counters have slightly more stimulating work, work that might take a few days or weeks to master, rather than a few hours, but still, their work falls far short of engaging the ability and creativity of a human being (although it might be satisfying for other reasons, like service to others, making people happy, meeting people, etc.). The same goes for the flight attendants. Only the pilots, air traffic controllers, and mechanics do work that might reasonably occupy the learning capacities of the human mind for more than a few months.

Strange it is to me, that the very worst, most brutal of all these jobs also receive the lowest pay. I understand the economics of it, but something in me rebels against that logic and wants the baggage handlers, drivers, and cashiers to be paid more, not less, than the pilots.

Without these menial workers, this airport and this society would not run in its current form. My travel depends on their labor, labor for which they are paid barely enough to survive.

And why do they consent to such work? Certainly not because of any aspiration to spend their lives doing it. If you can ask one of them why they do it, they will tell you, if they are not too insulted to speak, "I have to do it. I have to make a living, and this is the best work I could find."

So my trip today is only happening because people are doing jobs they don't want to do, for the sake of their survival. That's what "making a living" means. A threat to survival is, essentially, a gun to the head. If I force you to labor for me under threat of death, then you are my slave. To the extent we live in a world that runs on the labor of many people doing jobs that are beneath human dignity, not just in airports of course, but in factories, sweatshops, plantations, and nearly everywhere else, we live in a slave world. Anything we obtain from the labor of slaves comes at an insupportable spiritual cost: a painful void or disintegrity deep within that makes us ashamed to look people in the eye.

Can we bear to shrug this away and resign ourselves to living in a slave world? I want to be able to look every man and woman in the eye, knowing that I do not benefit from their indignity.

* * * *

I have a more selfish motive, too, for not wanting to live in a slave world: the products of slave labor embody the spirit that goes into them. Who but a conscript would produce the crappy, dispirited, toxic, ugly, cheap objects and buildings that surround us today? Who but a slave would be so resentful and unpleasant in providing services?[10] The vast majority of our "goods and services" are made by people who only do so for the money, who only do their work because they "have to." I want to live in a world of beautiful things created by people who love what they do.

Anyone indoctrinated with the prejudice that work is something objectionable will think me naive to propose a system where no one is forced to work. Who would grow the food? Remove the garbage? Sweep the streets? Work in the factories? I do not suggest that unpleasant work will be eliminated any time soon; just that there will be less and less of it. Already, despite our politicians' best efforts to create *more* of it in the form of jobs, and despite our best efforts to keep consumption growing, there are fewer "jobs" available.

---

10. The fact that people are often friendly and pleasant even in such jobs is testament to the unquenchable nobility of the human spirit.

But who will remove the garbage? Must we resign ourselves to a society where the worst jobs are left to the least fortunate? Must we resign ourselves to a society in which some people must do work that is beneath them, coerced into it by money-based survival pressure? When we agree that some degrading jobs are necessary, and when we agree that we must have an economy that forces some people to do those jobs (or go homeless and hungry), then we are essentially agreeing to slavery: "Do it or die." So, is it possible to have a modern economy, with its fine division of labor, that doesn't necessitate careers as toilet scrubbers and garbage collectors? Let us consider the matter in some detail, applied to that epitome of degrading labor, garbage collection.[11]

Why do we need garbage collectors in the first place? Why is there so much garbage to collect? It is because we consume so much throwaway junk, because we don't compost food scraps, and because we use so much packaging that is not reused or recycled. Throwaway products and packaging are possible because they are artificially cheap. Most of the costs of resource extraction and industrial processing to make the packaging are externalized, as is the cost of disposal in landfills and incinerators. When, as proposed in Chapter 12, these costs are internalized, throwaway production will become much less economical, and such things as refillable containers will gain an economic logic to reinforce their environmental logic. Similar considerations apply to composting food scraps, as home gardening will gain an economic motivation with the removal of hidden subsidies (transport, water, chemicals,

---

11. Degrading, that is, in our perception. Any work that isn't violent to others can be performed with dignity, playfulness, or love.

etc.) for distant mega-agriculture. There is really no reason why we should produce so much trash.[12]

The evolution of trash collection will be different in its details from the evolution of factory work, janitorial services, supermarket cashier work, or any of the often unpleasant and degrading occupations that make the world go 'round today. Each will be reduced or eliminated in a different way. Small, multicrop farms eliminate much of the drudgery of stoop labor. Small inns, bread-and-breakfasts, and couch-surfing reduce the need for professional hotel maids. Technology, mechanization, and robotics will continue to obviate assembly-line labor. Incentives to produce fewer but more durable goods reduce manufacturing and increase maintenance and repair work, which is far less routine and more fulfilling. Industrial design will gain a new incentive to minimize tedium rather than cost since jobs will be filled by desire rather than necessity.

Few people will willingly work on an assembly line for eight hours, pick endless rows of tomatoes, or clean toilets all day unless they feel they have no alternative. We will give everyone an alternative; therefore, the economy will have to evolve to eliminate such roles. We won't need to eliminate them completely. Dishwashing, toilet cleaning, and stoop labor are tedious and degrading only if we do them too long. I have worked on my brother's small organic farm and with a small construction outfit. None of that work was oppressive because we worked on a small scale doing a variety of

---

12. The very phenomenon of trash is relatively recent. My ex-wife, growing up in rural Taiwan in the early 1970s, remembers that there was no such thing as a garbage truck in her village. Everything was reused, recycled, composted, or burned. Even today, in Harrisburg, Pennsylvania, without much infrastructure to support recycling and reuse, my household garbage production is about one-fourth that of my neighbors. So I think it is perfectly reasonable to expect that in a generation, we will need perhaps one-tenth the trash collection that we have today.

tasks. Sure, there are tedious chores, such as digging three rows of potatoes or cutting slots into two hundred struts, but these weren't multiday ordeals, and were usually accompanied with banter or afforded an opportunity for reflection. A season or two collecting garbage a few hours a day, or washing dishes, flipping burgers, or cleaning hotel rooms, isn't so oppressive. Indeed, there are times in life when we want to rest into some routine labor. I have had such times myself, when routine physical labor was a balm to the spirit.

The vast reduction in what goes by the name of "work" today is not going to leave us idle, to dissipate our time in vapid pleasures. I stated above that human needs are finite, but we do have certain needs that are in a sense infinite. The need for connection to nature, the need to love, play, and create, the need to know and be known—none can be satisfied by buying more things. We are attempting to satisfy our need for the infinite through an accumulation of more and more of the finite. It is like trying to build a tower to heaven.

The nonmonetary realm properly includes all that cannot be quantified. Today we live in an overabundance of the quantifiable and a paucity of the unquantifiable: huge but ugly buildings, copious but empty calories, ubiquitous but trashy entertainment. Do you not agree that a shrinking of the money realm would be a refreshing change?

A finite need—calories, shelter, clothing, and so on—is a quantifiable need and thus fits naturally into the realm of commodity and therefore of money. We meet them easily, and indeed, thanks to technology, more and more easily.[13] It stands to reason that we

---

13. The fact that billions of people today are in want of the bare necessities of life isn't because we can't meet their needs; it is because we don't meet their needs (see Chapter 2). The reason is an economic system that induces artificial scarcity and misdirects the flow of labor and resources.

should have to work less and less hard to meet our finite needs and that a greater and greater proportion of human time and energy could be spent on the infinite: art, love, knowledge, science, beauty. Accordingly, it also stands to reason that a smaller and smaller proportion of human activity be in the money realm, the job realm.

Up until now, we have instead sought to make the infinite finite, and thereby debased art, love, knowledge, science, and beauty all. We have sold them out. When commercial application guides science, we end up not with science but with its counterfeit: pseudoscience in service of profit. When art bows to money, we get "art" instead of *art*, a self-conscious self-caricature. Similar perversions result when knowledge is subordinated to power, when beauty is used to sell product, and when wealth tries to buy love or love is turned toward gaining wealth. But the age of the sellout is over.

The long ascent of the monetized realm is drawing to a close, and its role in our work and our lives is changing so as to upend long-held intuitions, fears, and limitations. Since the time of the ancient Greeks, money has been, increasingly, both a universal means and a universal end, the object of limitless desire. No longer. Its retreat has begun, and we will devote more and more of our energy to those areas that money cannot reach. The growth of leisure, or, more accurately, the growth of labor done for love, goes hand in hand with the degrowth of the money economy. Humanity is entering its adulthood, a time when physical growth ends and we turn our attention to that which we want to give.

CHAPTER 15

LOCAL AND COMPLEMENTARY CURRENCY

A proper community, we should remember also, is a commonwealth: a place, a resource, an economy. It answers the needs, practical as well as social and spiritual, of its members—among them the need to need one another. The answer to the present alignment of political power with wealth is the restoration of the identity of community and economy.

—Wendell Berry

A sacred way of life connects us to the people and places around us. That means that a sacred economy must be in large part a local economy, in which we have multidimensional, personal relationships with the land and people who meet our needs, and whose needs we meet in turn. Otherwise we suffer a divide between the social and the material, in which our social relationships lack substance, and in which our economic relationships are impersonal. It is inevitable, when we purchase generic services from distant strangers and standardized products from distant lands, that we feel a loss of connection, an alienation, and a sense that we, like the things we buy, are replaceable. To the extent that what we provide is standard and impersonal, we *are* replaceable.

One of the effects of a homogeneous national or global currency is the homogenization of culture. As the money realm expands to include more and more of material and social life, our materials and relationships become standardized commodities, the same everywhere that money can reach. Nowhere is this more evident than in the United States, the "landscape of the exit ramp," where the same stores, same restaurants, and same architecture dominate every locale. And everywhere we are the same employees and consumers, living in thrall to distant economic powers. Local distinctiveness, autonomy, and economic opportunity disappear. Business profits are sucked away to distant corporate headquarters and ultimately to Wall Street. Instead of vibrant, economically diverse communities with their own local character, we have a monoculture where every place is the same.

The money system described so far in this book removes many of the barriers to local economic sovereignty and weakens the pressure toward globalization. Here are three ways:

1. Much global trade is only economic because of hidden social and ecological subsidies, which would be eliminated by the internalization of costs.

2. Commons-backed currency relocalizes economic power since many of the commons are local or bioregional in nature.

3. Negative-interest money removes the pressure to maintain growth through the conversion of the unique, local relationships and natural wealth of other lands into commodities. Ultimately, local difference stands in the way of commoditization and therefore of growth.

However, because the habits and infrastructure of local economy have largely disappeared, additional measures are necessary to rebuild community-based, place-based economies. This chapter discusses one of these measures: the localization of money itself.

I am not advocating the abandonment of global trade. While many things that should be local, such as food, have become global, there are many realms of collective human creativity that by their nature require a global coordination of labor. Moreover, economists' doctrines of efficiency of scale and comparative advantage (that some places and cultures are better suited to certain kinds of production) are not entirely without basis.[1] In general, though, sacred economics will induce the local sourcing of many commodities that are shipped across oceans and continents today.

While the changes described thus far make globalization less economic, my affinity for local economy is not primarily motivated by economic logic: the maximization of some measurable quantum of well-being. It comes rather from a longing for community. The threads of community are of two types: gift and story, warp and woof. In short, a strong community weaves together social and economic ties. The people we depend on, and who depend on us, are the same people whom we know and who know us. It is just that simple. The same goes for the broader community of all beings:

---

1. They are, however, exaggerated. Comparative advantage is often a cover for hidden subsidies, and efficiency of scale is often a cover for market leverage and bargaining power. An example of the former is the U.S. sugar industry, beneficiary of both direct government subsidies and indirect subsidies in the form of soil and water depletion, which allow it to undercut producers in other countries. The indirect subsidies are especially pernicious, because in essence they represent the competitive advantage of more efficient drawdown of natural capital. If one producer grows crops sustainably and another depletes aquifers and topsoil at no cost to himself to undercut the first, he is in effect gaining a public subsidy. The measures described in this book negate such subsidies. Internalizing the costs of depletion of the natural commons negates subsidies from the natural commons, and ending future cash-flow discounting deters producers from using the future to subsidize the present. Both of these measures will make local production more economically viable.

the land and its ecosystems. Lacking community, we suffer a painful deficit of being, for it is these multidimensional ties that define who we are and expand us beyond the miserable, lonely, separate ego, the "bubble of psychology in a prison of flesh." We yearn to restore our lost connections, our lost being.

Local economy reverses the millennia-long trend toward the homogenization of culture and connects us to the people and places we see every day. More than fulfilling the longing for community, it also benefits society and the environment. Not only does it entail less energy consumption, it also makes the social and ecological consequences of economic decisions harder to ignore. Today, indeed, it is quite easy to pretend that our economic decisions have no consequences. The things we use with little thought are part and parcel of birth defects in Chinese cities, strip-mining of West Virginia mountains, and the desertification of previously lush regions. But these effects are distant, reaching us only as pixels on a TV screen. Quite naturally, we live as if they weren't happening. If the people who grow your food and make your stuff live in Haiti or China or Pakistan, then their well-being or suffering is invisible. If they live nearby, you can still exploit them perhaps, but you can't easily avoid knowing it. Local economy faces us with the consequences of our actions, tightening the circle of karma and fostering a sense of self that includes others. Local economy is therefore aligned with the deep spiritual shift of our time.

THE CATCH-22 OF LOCAL CURRENCY

Local currency is often proposed as a way to revitalize local economies, insulate them from global market forces, and re-create community. There are at present thousands of them around the world, unofficial currencies issued by groups of ordinary citizens. In theory, local currency offers several economic benefits:

1. It encourages people to shop at local businesses since only they are willing to accept and use local currency.
2. It increases the local money supply, which increases demand and stimulates local production and employment.
3. It keeps money within the community since it cannot be extracted to distant corporations.
4. It allows individuals and businesses to bypass conventional credit channels and thus offers an alternative source of capital for which the interest (if any) will circulate back to the community.
5. It facilitates the circulation of goods and services among people who may not have sufficient access to national currency but who may have time and skills to offer.

Say you want to buy a hamburger and have local currency. You might buy it at a locally owned restaurant rather than McDonald's, even if the price is higher, because McDonald's won't accept the local currency. What does the hamburger joint do with the local currency then? Well, it can't buy beef from the national distribution chain with it, but maybe it could buy beef from a local farmer, or pay part of employees' wages with it. And what would the farmer or the employees do with it? Buy things from other local suppliers, including people who eat at the hamburger joint. This is how local currencies strengthen local economies.

Unfortunately, the practical results of local currency initiatives have been disappointing. A common pattern is that the currency is launched with much enthusiasm and continues to circulate as long as the founders promote it. But eventually they get burned out, the novelty factor wears off, and people stop using it. According to one study, as of 2005 some 80 percent of all local currencies launched since 1991 were defunct.[2] Another common pattern is that local money accumulates in the hands of the few local retailers that are willing to accept it and who cannot find ways to spend it. Finally, even where local currencies have been relatively successful, they comprise an insignificant portion of total economic activity.[3] If we are to realize the theoretical advantages of local currencies, it is imperative that we acknowledge that they aren't working today and figure out why. After all, they *did* work quite well in the nineteenth and early twentieth century. In the nineteenth, paper money consisted of "bank notes" issued by local banks and accepted only in the economic region where the banks were located. As recently as the 1930s, local currencies were so successful that central governments actively suppressed them. What has happened since then to make them (with a few notable exceptions) the plaything of social idealists?[4]

Several factors are at work. The first is that the economy has become so delocalized that it is hard to keep local currency circulating. In the words of one shopkeeper in Germany, speaking of one of the more successful local currencies, the Chiemgauer, "We do accept it, but we don't know what to do with it." His acceptance was reluctant—understandable when few of his suppliers are local. Local

---

2. Collom, "Community Currency in the United States," 1576.

3. For example, according to one study (Jacob, "The Social and Cultural Capital of Community Currency"), users of one of the most successful local currencies, Ithaca Hours, reported spending an average of only $350 per year worth of local currency—and these users comprise a very small part of Ithaca's population.

4. The same study (Jacob, "The Social and Cultural Capital of Community Currency") reports that users tend to be well-educated, progressive, countercultural activists. Time banks and some LETS systems are exceptions to this generalization; the former in particular are well-suited to hospitals, elder care, and other underserved populations. Another significant exception is commercial credit currencies such as the WIR, discussed later in this chapter.

currencies are viable only to the extent that producers are making goods and services that are consumed locally by people who themselves produce locally consumed goods and services. In the 1930s, economies were still highly local. People had goods and services to exchange but no money to use as a medium due to bank failures and hoarding. Today, the situation is quite different. Most people provide services that only make sense in a vast, often global, coordination of labor. Local currency cannot facilitate a supply and production chain that involves millions of people in thousands of places.

However, while some products, such as electronics, are inherently global in the nature of their manufacture, many products could be produced locally but are nonetheless part of global production systems. This implies a considerable untapped potential for local currencies. Unfortunately, much of the infrastructure of local production and distribution has disappeared. Local currencies can be part of the rebuilding of that infrastructure, but by themselves they are not enough. If nothing else changes, they are consigned to a very marginal, usually subcritical role. As things stand, local money is not very useful to us because we import nearly everything we use from outside our region.

Why would anyone be willing to accept local currency to begin with? One reason is idealism, but if we are to rely on idealism, then why not just apply that idealism to the existing currency and use it to "buy local"? Why bother with a complementary currency? What we want is to align our ideals with what is practical, not to bear them in opposition. Besides, the recent history of complementary currencies suggests that idealism is not enough, that they stagnate and disappear when that initial idealistic enthusiasm wears off. The question, then, is how local currencies might be aligned with economic self-interest.

We have to see local currency within a larger economic context. If a region has its own currency, yet is so integrated into the global commodity economy that nearly all its production is sold abroad and most of its consumption is purchased from abroad, then it might as well not even bother with its own currency. Under such conditions, the currency must be freely convertible (since economic circulation goes to and from the global market), making it into little more than a proxy currency for the dominant global unit of account (presently the U.S. dollar). Such a place is little more than a colony, and indeed that is what most places have become, especially in the United States, where towns have lost their local character and serve only as production and consumption centers for the global economy. For a region, city, or country to have a robust currency of its own, it must have a robust economy of its own as well. Key to building one is what economist Jane Jacobs called "import replacement"—the sourcing of components and services locally, and the development of the associated skills and infrastructure. Otherwise, a place is subject to the whims of global finance and dependent on commodity prices over which it has no control.

In "developing" countries that still have strong local economic infrastructure, local currencies help to preserve that infrastructure and insulate them from global financial predation. But in highly developed economies dominated by a national or supranational currency, anyone seeking to establish a local currency faces something of a catch-22. Local currencies only work if there is a local system of locally circulating production for which it can mediate exchange. Yet for such a system to grow and withstand the pressures of the global commodity economy, it needs a protected local currency. Import replacement cannot happen if local producers must compete with unrestricted, cheap imports. That is why such an economy can only manifest as an intentional choice motivated by a new Story of the People that generates shared vision, values, and goals. In other words, it will happen only through some form of democracy, popular action, and a government that responds to the will of its people rather than the will of international banks, investors, and the bond market. These forces are always ready to offer again the old story of the people: competition, growth, separation, conquest, and ascent.

Several historical examples bear this point out. Compare the disastrous results in countries that have "opened their markets" to "free trade" in recent years with the earlier success of Taiwan, South Korea, and Japan, who intentionally fostered local industries with import replacement, tariffs, and industrial planning, while limiting the convertibility of their currencies. I am most familiar with the case of Taiwan, having translated in the 1990s a multivolume history of the development of its small and medium enterprises.[5] In the 1950s and 60s, Taiwan placed stringent conditions on foreign investment. Foreign-invested factories were required to purchase a high percentage of components locally, encouraging the development of domestic industry. In Japan, South Korea, and Singapore as well, formal and informal mechanisms gave domestic enterprises a privileged status.[6] At the same time, they imposed currency controls and restrictions on the repatriation of profits. Foreign investors could freely convert their currencies into won, Taiwan dollars, and

---

5. C. J. Lee et al., *The Development of Small and Medium-Sized Enterprises in the Republic of China.*

6. The informal mechanisms include business culture taboos against foreign firms, interlocking boards of directors and family ties giving preference to local firms, and unofficial government favoritism in awarding contracts. From the outside, many of these mechanisms look like nepotism and corruption, but they acted to preserve these countries' economic sovereignty. Next time you read about corrupt foreign governments, take it with a grain of salt.

so on, but they couldn't convert it back again as freely. Today, these countries have a large middle class, world-class industrial plants, and tremendous overall wealth, despite starting in great poverty after World War II.

Compare their policies with those of Mexico, which allowed foreign manufacturers to set up factories in the Maquiladora zone, with no taxes, no limits on the expatriation of profits, and no requirement to source components in Mexico. Mexico and the many other countries offering such "free-trade zones" merely provided low-cost labor and freedom from environmental restrictions, essentially selling off their natural and social capital without gaining much know-how or infrastructure in return. Instead of enriching their economies, they bled them. Then the factories moved to take advantage of even cheaper labor elsewhere. First GATT, then NAFTA and the WTO and EMU destroyed in one country after another the protections that kept local economies from becoming helpless colonies of commodity export and consumption. The only beneficiaries were the elites, who are relatively independent of the local economy. Unlike the masses, they can import what they need and move away if conditions become too terrible.

Monetary autonomy is a crucial part of political sovereignty. Ultimately, political sovereignty means very little if outside corporations can strip-mine that society's natural and social capital—its resources, skills, and labor—and export them to global markets. At the present writing, Brazil, Thailand, and other countries are taking measures to protect their economies from the flood of cheap U.S. dollars that has resulted from the Fed's quantitative easing program. Left unchecked, these dollars would allow foreigners to buy up domestic equities, mines, factories, utilities, and so on. These countries recognize that meaningful sovereignty is economic sovereignty.

What is true for nations is also true for smaller regions. However, compared to tweaking interest rates to below the zero lower bound, the proposal that local and regional governments issue their own currency may seem naively impractical. Actually, it is a very accessible solution that is constantly being suppressed. Although it is illegal for states to issue currency in the United States and many other countries, people find ways around laws when the necessity arises.

The case of Argentina's financial crisis of 2001–2002 is most illuminating. When provincial governments completely ran out of money to pay employees and contractors, they paid them in low-denomination bearer bonds instead (one-peso bonds, five-peso bonds . . .). Local businesses and citizens readily accepted these bonds, even though nobody really expected they would ever be redeemable for hard currency, because they could be used to pay provincial taxes and fees. Acceptance for payment of taxes enhanced the social perception of value, and as with all money, value and the perception of value are identical. The currencies, which were all denominated in a common unit of account, circulated far beyond their region of issue. They revived economic activity, which had ground to a halt since, after all, people still had the capacity to produce goods and services that other people needed, lacking only the means to make exchanges. This was only possible because Argentina is fundamentally a rich country that had not been completely converted into export commodity production. At the same time, Argentina's government repudiated its foreign debt, temporarily cutting it off from imports and increasing the need for local self-reliance. At that point the IMF stepped in with emergency loans to induce the country to keep its debts on the books.

As of 2011, we are still living, if no longer in normal times, at least in the inertia of the habits of those times. Accordingly, local currencies still face an uphill battle, languishing without government support. Even worse, governments present them with crippling handicaps through tax laws. Citizen-created currencies are unacceptable for payment of taxes, yet transactions made in these currencies are subject to income and sales taxes. That means that even if you used local currency exclusively, you would have to pay taxes in U.S. dollars—even though you earned none![7] Taxing people in a currency they don't use is tyrannical—it was a cause of the American Revolution and a key instrument of colonialism (see the discussion of the "hut tax" in Chapter 20).

In places where local currencies have been effective, either they have received government support, or they have emerged in war zones and other extreme circumstances. In Argentina in 2001–2002 and the United States and Europe during the Depression, local governments actually issued currency themselves. Moreover, in those places and times, there was still a lot of local production, subsistence farming, local distribution and supply networks, and local social capital in general. Local currencies had a real chance there and, unsurprisingly, provoked the hostility of the central authorities. In the case of Argentina, the IMF demanded their abolition as a prerequisite for aid.

Nonetheless, the efforts of local currency activists over the last twenty years have not been in vain. They have created a model—many models, in fact—to be applied when the next crisis erupts and the unthinkable becomes common sense. They are creating a new logic, a new template, working out the kinks, gaining experience

---

7. On the other hand, the IRS's position is understandable: without this requirement, people could use proxy currencies to avoid taxes. Nonetheless, the tax system puts local and complementary currencies at a distinct disadvantage.

that will become essential very soon. So let us examine some of the types of complementary currency being explored today that may have a role in the coming sacred economy.

EXPERIMENTS IN LOCAL MONEY
Proxy Currencies

The first kind of local currency I'll consider is the dollar (or euro) proxy currency such as the Chiemgauer or the BerkShare. You can buy a hundred BerkShares for $95 and buy merchandise at the usual dollar price; the merchant then redeems a hundred Berk-Shares for $95 at participating banks. Because of this easy convertibility, merchants readily accept them, as the 5-percent discount is well worth the extra business volume. However, the same easy convertibility limits the currency's effect on the local economy. In principle, merchants receiving BerkShares have a 5-percent incentive to source merchandise locally, but in the absence of local economic infrastructure, they usually won't bother.

Proxy currencies do little to revitalize local economies or to expand the local money supply. They provide a token of desire to buy local but a very small economic incentive to do so. Since Berk-Shares originate as dollars and are convertible into them, anyone with access to the former also has access to the latter. The international equivalent is found in countries that adopt a currency board. We call these *dollarized economies* because they have effectively surrendered any monetary independence. Proxy currencies like Berk-Shares are useful as a consciousness-raising tool to introduce people to the idea of complementary currencies, but by themselves they are ineffectual in promoting vibrant local economies.

Complementary Fiat Currencies

More promising are fiat currencies, such as Ithaca Hours, that actually increase the local money supply. Many Depression-era scrips also fall into this category. Essentially, someone simply prints up the money and declares it to have value (e.g., an Ithaca Hour is declared equal to ten U.S. dollars). For it to be money, there must be a community agreement that it has value. In the case of Hours, a group of businesses, inspired by the currency's founder Paul Glover, simply declared that they would accept the currency, in effect backing it with their goods and services. During the Depression, scrip was often issued by a mainstay local business that could redeem it for merchandise, coal, or some other commodity. In other cases, a city government issued its own currency, backed by acceptability for payment of local taxes and fees.

The effect of fiat currencies is much more potent than that of proxy currencies because fiat currencies have the potential of putting money in the hands of those who would otherwise not have it. It is only inflationary if those accessing the money offer no goods or services in return.[8] In extreme economic times, it is often the case that there are plenty of people willing to work and plenty of needs to met; only the money to mediate these transactions is missing. So it was during the Great Depression, and so it is becoming today. Municipalities all over the world are facing severe budget cuts due to lack of tax revenue, forcing important maintenance and repair tasks to languish and even laying off police and firefighters; meanwhile, many of their residents who could do those tasks sit unemployed and idle. Though legal hurdles presently stand in the way,

---

8. In that case, the money supply would increase without increasing the amount of goods and services (i.e., there would be more money chasing fewer goods).

cities can and probably will issue vouchers, acceptable in payment of city taxes, in lieu of U.S. dollars to hire people to do necessary work. Why not? Many of the taxes are in arrears anyway. When local government is the issuer, scrip much more easily takes on the "story of value" that makes it into money.

Such currencies are often called *complementary* because they are separate from, and complementary to, the standard medium of exchange. While they are usually denominated in dollar (or euro, pound, etc.) units, there is no currency board that keeps reserves of dollars to maintain the exchange rate. They are thus similar to a standard sovereign currency with a floating exchange rate.

In the absence of local government support, because complementary fiat currencies are not easily convertible into dollars, businesses are generally much less willing to accept them than they are proxy currencies. That is because in the current economic system, there is little infrastructure to source goods locally. Locally owned businesses are plugged into the same global supply chains as everyone else. Regrowing the infrastructure of local production and distribution will take time, as well as a change in macroeconomic conditions driven by the internalization of costs, the end of growth pressure, and a social and political decision to relocalize. Noneconomic factors can influence the social agreement of money. The idealism of a few that sustains local currency today will become the consensus of the many.

Time Banking

There is one resource that is always locally available and always needed to sustain and enrich life. That resource is human beings: their labor, energy, and time. Earlier I said that local currencies are viable only to the extent that producers are making goods and services that are consumed locally by people who, themselves, produce locally consumed goods and services. Well, we are always "producers" of our time (by the mere act of living), and there are many ways to give this time for the benefit of others. This is why I believe that time-based currencies (often called "time banks") offer great promise without needing huge changes in economic infrastructure.

When someone performs a service through a time bank, it credits his or her account by one time dollar for each hour spent and debits the recipient's account by the same. Usually, there is some kind of electronic bulletin board with postings of offerings and needs. People who could otherwise not afford the services of a handyman, massage therapist, babysitter, and so on gain access to help from a person who might otherwise be unemployed. Time banks tend to flourish in places where people have a lot of time and not much money. It is especially appealing in realms requiring little specialization, in which the time of any person is in fact equally valuable. A prime example is the famous *fureai kippu* currency in Japan, which credits people for time spent caring for the elderly. Time banking is also used extensively by service organizations in America and Britain. It can also apply to physical goods, typically by way of a dollar cost for materials and a time dollar cost for time.

In our atomized society, the traditional ways of knowing who has what to offer have broken down, and commercial means of disseminating this information (such as advertising) are accessible only with money. Time banks connect individuals who would otherwise be oblivious to the needs and gifts each can offer. As one time bank user puts it,

Everyone has a skill—some might surprise you. An elderly shut-in who doesn't drive can make beautiful wedding cakes. A woman in a wheelchair who needs her house painted used to train police dogs and now provides puppy training. The retired school-teacher who needs her leaves raked has a kiln and is teaching ceramics. A common question when we meet each other is, "What do you do?" "What do you need?" or "What can I do for you?"[9]

Beyond the meeting of immediate needs, you can see from this description the power of time banks to restore community. They generate the kind of economic and social resiliency that sustains life in times of turmoil. As money unravels, it is important to have alternative structures for the meeting of human needs.

The fundamental idea behind time banks is deeply egalitarian, both because everyone's time is valued equally and because every-one starts out with the same amount of it. If there is one thing that we can be said to truly own, it is our time. Unlike any other possession, as long as we are alive, our time is inseparable from our selves. Our choice of how to spend time is our choice of how to live life. And no matter how wealthy one is in terms of money, it is impossible to buy more time. Money might buy you life-saving surgery or otherwise enhance longevity, but it won't guarantee long life; nor can it purchase more than twenty-four hours of experience in each day. In this we are all equal; a money system that recognizes this equality is intuitively appealing.

When time-based currency replaces monetary transactions, it is a great equalizing force in society. The danger is that time currency

---

9. From "An Introduction to Time Banking" (anonymous post on www.getrichslowly. org/blog/2008/03/13/an-introduction-to-time-banking/).

can also end up transferring formerly gift-based activity into the realm of the quantified. The future, perhaps, belongs to nonmonetary, nonquantified ways of connecting gifts and needs. Still, at least for a long time to come, time banks have an important role to play in healing our fragmented local communities.

RECLAIMING THE CREDIT COMMONS

Another way to foster local economic and monetary autonomy is through the credit system. When an economic community applies formal or informal mechanisms to limit the acquisition of credit and, consequently, the allocation of money, the local economy can maintain its independence just as if it had instituted currency controls. To illustrate this point, consider an innovation commonly mentioned in discussions of complementary currency: mutual-credit systems, including commercial barter rings, credit-clearing cooperatives, and local exchange trading systems (LETS). When a transaction takes place in a mutual-credit system, the account of the buyer is debited and the account of the seller is credited by the agreed-upon sales price—whether or not the buyer has a positive account balance. For example, say I mow your lawn for an agreed price of twenty credits. If we both started at zero, now I have a balance of +20 and you have a balance of −20. Next, I buy bread from Thelma for ten credits. Now my account is down to +10 and hers is also +10.

This kind of system has many applications. The above scenario exemplifies a small-scale, locally based credit system often called LETS. Since its inception in 1983 by Michael Linton, hundreds of LETS systems have taken root around the world. Mutual credit is equally useful on the commercial level. Any network of businesses that fulfill the basic requirement that each produce something that one of the others needs can form a commercial barter exchange or credit-clearing cooperative. Rather than issue commercial paper or seek short-term loans from banks, participating businesses create their own credit.

In commercial barter exchanges, firms sell excess inventory and unused capacity for which there is no immediate cash market to others in the exchange for trade credits. The buyer conserves cash, and the seller builds up credits to use in future transactions. No idealist commitment to complementary currencies is necessary to motivate businesses to join; in fact, most exchanges levy a hefty fee for membership. Some six hundred commercial barter exchanges operate around the world today, involving some half a million firms.[10]

A more recent innovation is mutual factoring, conceived by Martin "Hasan" Bramwell. Typically, businesses receive orders far in advance of receiving payment for those orders. To obtain the cash necessary to fulfill the order, they would ordinarily have to sell the account receivable at a discount to a third party (called a "factor"), such as a bank. Mutual factoring bypasses the banks and allows accounts receivable to be used as a liquid medium of exchange among participating businesses.

The most famous commercial mutual-credit system is undoubtedly the Swiss WIR, in operation since 1934, which boasts tens of thousands of members and trade volume of over a billion Swiss francs. As of 2005, its volume dwarfed that of all the rest of the world's commercial barter rings combined.[11] According to economist James Stodder, both the WIR and other commercial barter

---

10. Statistics from the International Reciprocal Trade Association.
11. Stodder, "Reciprocal Exchange Networks," 14.

exchanges exert a contracyclical effect, showing greater exchange activity during economic downturns, a fact he attributes to their ability to create credit.[12] This demonstrates the ability of complementary currency and credit systems to shield participants from macroeconomic fluctuations and sustain local economies.

In any mutual-credit system, members have access to credit without the involvement of a bank. Instead of paying money to use money, as in an interest-based credit system, credit is a free social good available to all who have earned the trust of the community. Essentially, today's credit system is an example of the privatization of the commons I discussed earlier in the book, in this case the "credit commons"—a community's general judgment of the creditworthiness of each of its members. Mutual-credit systems reclaim this commons by issuing credit cooperatively rather than for private profit.

Mutual credit is not so much a type of currency as a means of issuing that currency. In the dominant system, it is primarily banks that grant access to money by extending credit. In a mutual-credit system, this power goes to the users themselves.

The development of mutual-credit systems is extremely significant, for credit essentially represents a society's choice of who gets access to money and how much of it. Mutual credit replaces the traditional functions of banks. People with a negative credit balance are under social pressure, and the pressure of their own conscience, to offer goods and services that will bring their account back into positive territory. But I'm sure you can see a potential problem with this system when applied on a large scale. What is to prevent one of the participants from running up a higher and

---

12. Ibid.

higher negative balance, in essence receiving goods for nothing? The system needs a way to prevent this and eliminate participants who abuse it.

Without negative-balance limits, a mutual-credit currency can be created in unlimited amounts simply by the will to make a transaction. This might seem like a good thing, but it won't work if that currency is used to exchange scarce goods.[13] Ultimately, money represents a social agreement on how to allocate labor and materials. Not everyone can have access to enough credit, say, to construct a multibillion-dollar semiconductor plant or buy the world's largest diamond.

More sophisticated mutual-credit systems have flexible credit limits based on responsible participation. Global Exchange Trading System (GETS; a proprietary credit-clearing system) and Community Exchange System (CES) use complicated formulas in which credit limits rise with time according to how much or how well one has participated in the system. Those who have fulfilled their negative-balance obligations in the past get a larger credit limit. This formula functions just like a conventional credit rating.

The real world, however, does not always conform to a formula. Different kinds of businesses have different credit needs, and sometimes exceptional circumstances arise that merit a temporary increase in credit. Some mechanism is needed to set these limits and to grant or reject requests for credit. This might require research, familiarity with industries and markets, and knowledge of the borrower's reputation and circumstances. It could also encompass the social and ecological effects of the investment.

---

13. It might work quite well for nonscarce goods, such as digital content. User ratings for YouTube videos and other online creations are a kind of nonscarce currency.

Whatever entity performs this function, be it a traditional bank, cooperative, or P2P community, must have a good general understanding of business and must be willing to assume responsibility for its evaluations.

New forms of P2P banking run up against the same general problem of determining creditworthiness over the anonymous gulf of cyberspace. One could imagine a system in which a database connects you, who have $5,000 you want to lend for six months, to a distant person who wants to borrow it for six months. You don't know her. How do you know she is creditworthy? Perhaps some user rating system à la eBay could provide a partial solution, but such systems are easily gamed. What you really need is a trustworthy institution that knows her better than you do to assure you of her creditworthiness. You lend your money to that institution, and that institution lends it to her. Sound familiar? It's called a bank.

Banking, like money, has a sacred dimension: a banker is someone who finds beautiful uses for money. If I have more money than I can use, I can say, "Here, Ms. Banker, please find someone who can use this money well until I need it back." Decaying currency, described in Chapter 12, aligns this conception of banking with self-interest. It will continue to be a necessary function even when "better" no longer means "to increase my personal wealth."

Whether it is through social consensus, formulas, or the decisions of specialists, there must be some way to allocate credit. Banking functions, whether implicit or explicit, will always exist. Today, a banking cartel has monopolized these functions, profiting not only from its expertise in allocating credit toward its most remunerative use but also from its monopoly control over the former credit commons. Ultimately, a new banking system might arise from the ground up, starting with small mutual-credit cooperatives that form exchange agreements with each other. Convertibility among different mutual-credit systems is a hot topic in the field, with prototypes being developed by CES and the Metacurrency Initiative.[14] The challenge is to strike a balance between convertibility, in order to allow long-distance trade, and insulation of the members' internal economy from outside predation or financial shocks. These are essentially the same issues that face small sovereign currencies today.

Mutual-credit systems reclaim the functions of banking for a local community, a business community, or a cooperative entity. They foster and protect the internal economy of their members, insulating it from external shocks and financial predation in the same way that local currencies do. Indeed, local currencies will never be able to expand beyond marginal status unless they have a credit mechanism that protects them from the speculative runs that numerous national currencies have suffered in the last twenty years. Local and regional credit-clearing organizations can exercise capital control functions similar to those that wiser nations imposed when developing their economies through import substitution. The most famous mutual-credit system, Switzerland's WIR, provides a rather extreme model for this principle: once you buy into it, you are not permitted to cash out. On a local level, this would force foreign investors to source components locally. Less extreme but similar measures were applied by Taiwan, Japan, Singapore, and South Korea in the 1950s and 1960s, when they restricted foreign companies' repatriation of profits.

One of the "imports" that local and regional governments can replace is credit itself. The above-mentioned Asian countries did this

---

14. See *Community Currency Magazine* for cutting-edge discussions of this and related issues in local currency and credit.

too, keeping the banking industry off-limits to foreign banks through government policy and informal cultural barriers. On a regional or local level, and even without a local currency, governments can replace exogenous credit by operating their own public banks.[15] If we are to pay for credit, then shouldn't that payment stay in the local economy? Today, state and local governments deposit tax proceeds with multinational banks that lend it wherever they can profit the most; indeed, in an era of banking consolidation they have little choice, as local banks have merged into larger ones. State-owned banks, exemplified by the Bank of North Dakota, can lend locally, finance local projects without having to issue high-interest debt on the bond market, exercise a contracyclical effect by lending during credit crunches, and keep banking profits local instead of exporting them to Wall Street. Publicly owned banks needn't be driven by profit, and any profits they do make can be returned to their owners, the people, thus restoring the credit commons. These advantages pertain even in the present monetary system.

On the national level, public banking is little different from the power to issue currency, a power that the United States (and most other countries) has abdicated and given to a private institution, the Federal Reserve. But in theory, it could set up its own bank and lend money to itself, essentially printing money at zero or negative interest. Or it could bypass the banking system and create money directly, as authorized by the Constitution and enacted during the Civil War.[16] The currency proposals outlined in Chapter 11 would

---

15. See the writings of Ellen Brown, author of *Web of Debt*, for a thorough argument in favor of public banking. An article that observes the similarity between public banks and mutual credit currencies is Brown's "Time for a New Theory of Money," available at www.commondreams.org/view/2010/10/29-3.

16. Dennis Kucinich has recently revived the idea in H.R. 6550: National Emergency Employment Defense Act of 2010.

enable local governments to do the same, issuing money "backed" by the bioregional commons under their stewardship. Ultimately, political divisions may shift into greater conformity with biological and cultural regions. Regional governments will have more autonomy than they do today when they have the power to issue their own money.

The decision of how to allocate capital on a large scale is more than an economic decision; it is a social and political decision. Even in today's capitalist society, the largest investment decisions are not always made on considerations of business profits.[17] Putting a man on the moon, building a highway system, and maintaining armed forces are all public investments that do not seek a positive return on capital. In the private sector, though, bank profit determines the allocation of capital, which is the allocation of human labor, creativity, and the riches of the earth. What shall we, humanity, do on earth? This collective choice is a commons that has been privatized and shall be restored to us all in a sacred economy. That does not mean removing investment decisions from the private sector, but rather changing the nature of credit so that money goes to those who serve the social and ecological good.

The reclamation of the credit commons will take many forms: P2P lending (described in the previous chapter), mutual-credit systems, credit unions and other cooperative banks, publicly owned banks, and innovative new kinds of banks such as Sweden's J.A.K. Bank. In different ways, these systems return the power of money and credit to the people, whether mediated through grass-roots P2P structures as in mutual-credit systems, or through politically constituted institutions such as public banks. And since political

---

17. More and more, these political decisions are made in the interests of business.

sovereignty is worth little in the absence of monetary sovereignty, reasserting local, regional, and (in the case of small countries) national control over credit is an important path toward the relocalization of economy, culture, and life.

CHAPTER 16

TRANSITION TO GIFT ECONOMY

Under capitalism, man exploits man.
Under communism, it's just the opposite.

—John Kenneth Galbraith

The new exchange systems we are exploring blur the boundary between the monetary and nonmonetary realms and therefore the standard definition of the "economy." Really, what is the economy? Underneath the ephemera of money—slips of paper, bits in computers—what changes when the economy grows or shrinks? How would we measure it in the absence of a common unit of account? Ultimately, what economics attempts to measure, underneath money, is the totality of all that human beings make and do for each other.

That we should even attempt to measure this at all is quite odd. I have already leveled judicious criticism at the fat target of economics' equation of money with the good. However, alternative measures of economic progress, such as the genuine progress indicator or national happiness index, suffer similar problems on a subtler level. Certainly they are improvements over GDP, for they no longer count such things as prisons and armaments as positive contributors to the good, and they add to economic wellness such things as leisure time. Nonetheless, they still assume that we can and should quantify the good, and that in order to do so, we must convert everything into a standard unit of measure.

Money and measure are indeed closely intertwined. Money originated, in fact, as measure: standardized quantities of commodities and then metals. The age of money has coincided with the program of reductionism and objectivity, which sought through science to attain mastery over the world. What can be measured can be mastered, as we imply when we claim to have taken the measure of a man. The immeasurable was excluded from science—"consign it to the flames," Hume said—and from economics as well. Thus it has come to pass that standard of living has diverged from quality of life. The former is a quantifiable standard; the latter is not.

Of all the things that human beings make and do for each other, it is the unquantifiable ones that contribute most to human happiness. You might, for instance, quantify leisure time and assign it a dollar value to calculate a society's well-being, but how is that leisure time spent? It could be spent mired in an addiction, in mindless entertainment, in intimacy with another person, or in telling stories to children. And even if we somehow accounted for these distinctions, could we quantify how present someone is when they are telling those stories? Can we quantify how anxious someone is when at work? If public policy is guided by the maximization of a quantity—be it GDP or some other measure—the most important things will surely be left out.

Quantifiable needs are also finite—another reason to question a money system predicated on the infinite growth of finite demand for finite resources. Qualitative needs are different: they are neither quantifiable nor finite. It is in this realm that the ideology of Ascent finds its true spiritual motivation. Growth, on one level, might end—the growth of the monetized realm, the growth of our appropriation of nature—but another kind of development will continue: the growth of the human spirit, with its infinite need for beauty, love, connection, and knowledge. A zero-growth future is not a stagnant future, no more than a human life stagnates when a teenager grows her last inch at age sixteen.

Money, which facilitates the meeting of our quantifiable needs, will have a place in human life for many centuries to come. It will occupy a diminished role, however, as I described in the chapter on degrowth. Instead of obsessively fulfilling and overfulfilling our finite needs to the present degree of obscene hypertrophy, we will turn our energy to the unmet qualitative needs that so impoverish us today.

To meet our unquantifiable needs, we need nonmonetary circulation. When the qualitative is matched with the quantitative, the infinite to the finite, then the former is debased. The exchange of beauty for money, intimacy for money, attention for money—all smell of prostitution. The distaste of the artist for the world of commerce is not just an egotism that says he is above it all. When money tries to buy beauty, love, knowledge, connection, and so forth, either the buyer receives a counterfeit, or the seller, having sold the infinitely precious for a finite sum, is exploited. It is really quite simple; as the Beatles put it, "Money can't buy you love."

That is why we need other ways for our gifts to circulate. The matter is complicated, though, by the fact that the quantifiable is often a vehicle for the unquantifiable. I am not advocating two separate realms, the monetary and the gift, but rather a mixed system in which money takes on more of the properties of gift and mediatory structures of gifting arise to take over the role of money.

Whether or not money is involved, the fundamental issues of economy—what people make and do for each other—are these:

(1) how to connect the provider of a gift with the person who needs that gift; (2) how to acknowledge and honor those who give generously of their gifts; and (3) how to coordinate the gifts of many people across space and time in order to create things transcending the needs or gifts of any individual. Though it may not be obvious, these goals correspond roughly to the three cardinal functions of money: medium of exchange, unit of account, and store of value.

Many quasi-monetary and nonmonetary ways to achieve these three goals are emerging today. In the open-source software world, for example, P2P technologies allow a community of programmers to envision projects, coordinate talents, and recognize the contributions of its members, all without using money. In a way, the esteem of peers, based on the quality and quantity of previous contributions, is a form of "currency" that allows some members to exercise greater influence over group decisions than others. It is not quantified though; nor is it quantifiable without losing something of its essence. We can reduce esteem and prestige to a number, but let us recognize that this is in fact a reduction. Just as when analog recordings are rendered into digital formats, something of the warmth, humanity, and infinity of the original is lost.

Many online systems do indeed convert reputation and contribution to a number. The user rating systems of websites like Amazon and eBay are one such quasi-currency. Not only can users rate and review products, they can also rate each others' ratings, creating a self-policing system. What is essentially a gift economy (no one receives any direct reward for writing reviews) is evolving structures that parallel the mediatory functions of money.

Timothy Wilken, a medical doctor, philosopher, and gift-economy activist, has taken this idea a step further in his GIFTegrity system, currently in beta. It asks each member to provide a profile listing what he or she wishes to give and to receive. The recipient of a gift rates the transaction, and these ratings determine the order in which potential recipients of one's gifts will be listed. If you have given a lot, your name will be near the top when someone is searching for a recipient of the gift he wants to offer. If you then receive a gift, your rating will drop a bit to reflect that your giving and receiving have moved closer into balance. These ratings points act very much like money.

In a traditional community, no such rating system would be necessary, as the giving and the needs of each member would be common knowledge. Systems like GIFTegrity seem to offer the possibility of bringing gift relationships into a broader realm. But rather than obviating the need for money, they are recreating it, albeit as something much closer to its original essence as a token of gratitude. The ratings in GIFTegrity and similar systems *are* money. You receive points for giving; you expend them in receiving. Such systems bear a fundamental limitation of money as well, in that the qualitative resists quantification on a linear scale. Of course, they are superior to today's usury-based money; but this kind of technocratic alternative, however brilliant, doesn't speak to what has been lost in our quantification of the world. We want to recover the infinite. Ratings and points don't meet our deep need for the personal ties, gratitude, and multidimensional stories that circulate in gift culture.

Am I contradicting myself, saying that money originated as a token of gratitude and that money originated as measure? Money was inhabited, as it were, by two spirits from the very beginning. It was both an extension of gift economics (which was once nearly all there was) into the realm of mass society and an incursion of measuring, counting, keeping, and controlling into the original openness of gift mentality. Yet in speaking of money as a token of gratitude I am also using the word "originate" in a nonnormal sense, referring to an origin not in time but in, for lack of a better phrase, the mind of God. I am referring to money's teleological origin, the purpose for which it came into being in this world.

The measure function of money has a counterpart in gift economics, for even though gifts do not come with a specific expectation of return, nonetheless they ordinarily happen within view of the community. The anonymous giving that we elevate today to the highest category of generosity had a minor role in gift cultures past and present. Communities were generally aware of the needs, gifts, and degree of generosity of their members. Money substitutes for this awareness: in theory, at least, it confers the benefits of social recognition onto the people who contribute. In practice, the scope of recognized contribution has been limited to contribution to the "ascent" of humanity, the growing of the human realm. But even with a degrowth currency, the deeper problem remains that money by nature can operate only in the realm of the quantifiable. We face the question of how to facilitate the flow of the nonquantifiable across the vast social distances of mass society. In hundreds of thousands of years of human existence, this is a new problem.

Perhaps we can begin reconstructing gift economy from the ground up. Today, money has taken over even on small scales, where informal consensus and the social witnessing of generosity could facilitate the three above-mentioned functions of connecting, honoring, and coordinating gifts. As more and more people recognize the social impoverishment of the conversion of relationship into money, and as the money system itself unravels, people are finding ways to reclaim these functions. One of my favorites is the Gift Circle, developed by Alpha Lo and now replicating itself around the country. In this weekly gathering, participants state one or more things they would like to give and one or more things they would like to receive. Often, it seems, a magical synchronicity of wants and needs unfolds. "You need a potato masher? We have three." Or, "You need a ride to the airport on Friday? My husband is flying out then, too." Witnessing the generosity of others, over time participants feel more and more comfortable asking of and giving to others in the circle. Help is always a phone call away. If, during the week, someone helps another fix her car, then she can tell of this gift in the next circle so that the gift may be witnessed. A sense of community grows along with the knowledge that if you give, you will be known as a giver, and people will desire to give to you in turn.

Another way to accomplish something similar is to use a website to offer gifts, make requests, and record what has been given. When this is done on a large scale, the means of fulfilling these functions looks more and more like money. Without personal familiarity with what is being given and received, some means of standardization becomes necessary. On a small scale, though, merely witnessing the flow of gifts, whether directly or via the medium of stories, suffices. Without that witnessing, gifts are less potent in creating community. This is the flaw in such systems as Freecycling and Craigslist (although the fact that people use these at all testifies to our innate generosity). Newer systems such as Giftflow, Neighborgoods, Shareable, GIFTegrity, and many others recognize and remedy this flaw.

Notice that all I have described so far accelerates the degrowth of the economy. When we give each other rides to the airport instead of hiring a taxi, when we share power tools instead of buying new ones, or when we give away our spare potato masher, we reduce consumer demand and cut into economic growth. The shrinkage of the monetary realm hastens the demise of the old regime and the transition into steady-state economics. It also makes that transition much less frightening. When we are ensconced in gift communities that honor and reciprocate generosity, then we depend less on money and associate it less with survival.

Could the Gift Circle concept scale up beyond the community level in which people know each other first- or secondhand? In the very long term, we might be able to envision a moneyless gift society based on the model of "circles of circles." It would seem that money is necessary in the global coordination of labor, but if we look at this global coordination more closely, the actual number of people that any given person interacts with is not that great. When more than a few hundred people must cooperate to produce something, the entire community of production naturally resolves into subcommunities and sub-subcommunities, down to the level at which gift economics works. People within each circle could give to each other, and each circle as an integrated entity could give to other circles in its larger circle, and then each of those to other circles of circles. This vision involves a fundamental reorganization of society: bottom-up, peer-to-peer, autopoietic, self-organizing.

In the metahuman body we call society, money is like a signaling molecule that directs resources to where they are needed. It mediates economic relationships among our collective body's far-flung parts. It is one of many symbolic systems that defines and coordinates our "organs": governments, institutions, and organizations of all types. Unfortunately, money conveys only certain kinds of information (mostly about quantifiable gifts, needs, and desires). To achieve health, we therefore need other ways of "organ"-izing and coordinating human activity.

There is today an explosion of innovation in creating decentralized, nonhierarchical modes of collaboration and ownership. These are a kind of substructure for a circles-of-circles gift economy of the future. At the more conservative end of the spectrum are employee-owned companies with traditional management structures, of which there are several hundred of medium to large size in the United States. More radical are enterprises that use democratic or collaborative methods to manage the company: various collectives and co-ops. Perhaps the most notable of these is the Mondragon Cooperative in Spain, comprising over 250 companies and some 90,000 employee/owners, making it one of Spain's largest companies. Founded during the reign of the Fascist dictator Franco, it somehow managed to explicitly espouse and embody the principle of the "sovereignty of labor" and other values of participatory democracy. I leave it to the reader to learn more about this fascinating enterprise, a pioneer in participatory management and cooperative ownership.

In creating new modes of organization that can accommodate the unquantifiable, we are just entering an age of experimentation. Many of these experiments have failed and will fail, for example the Communist block's forced collectivization with central management by bureaucrats. Doubtless many new forms of collaboration will arise as we digest the lessons of past and current attempts.[1]

---

1. One noteworthy model is Better Means (www.bettermeans.com), which describes its work as the "open enterprise model." Strategic decisions, work items, compensation, and equity are all determined through self-correcting rating and voting processes. Those who contribute the most value—as determined by themselves, by those who work with them on projects, and by those who voted the project into existence in the first place—receive credits that can be redeemed for money. Credits also give the contributor temporary equity in the company, lasting for a time equal to the time elapsed between when the credits were earned and when they were redeemed. Ownership therefore accords to those who contribute and gradually fades away when one stops contributing. The Better Means open enterprise model is in use today by businesses and nonprofits. Still undergoing refinement, it incorporates some key concepts from the open source and P2P movements, such as "lazy consensus," "agile project management," "peer evaluation," "reputation feedback," and many more.

The monetary proposals I have laid forth in this book will encourage nontraditional structures of ownership and management. Just as they will eliminate the profiting from passive ownership of money, land, and the commons generally, so will they discourage profiting from passive ownership in corporations, which today are a vehicle of the control of said assets.

The advent of collaborative gift structures will fundamentally alter the experience of employment. Today, the interests of workers and owners are fundamentally at odds. It is in the owners' interest for the workers to do maximum work for as little pay as possible. It is in each individual worker's interest to do as little work as possible for maximum pay. Good management can mitigate this fundamental opposition by tying pay to "performance" and by appealing to professional pride, loyalty, or team spirit, but the underlying contradiction remains. Employees commonly receive rewards for their success in office politics rather than authentic contributions, while recognizing "team spirit" as the internal PR that it often is. "If we are really all in it together," they wonder, "how is it that I can be fired at any time but the owners cannot? Any lasting value I create is theirs." In this world, any employee who truly identifies with his employer is a dupe. This becomes obvious whenever a company downsizes or streamlines. "I've given you twenty years of loyal service; how can you let me go?" As one insurance executive explained to an employee, "If you want loyalty, get a dog." Of course, most employers aren't so hard-hearted, but market discipline hardens a soft heart.

Well, market discipline is going to change. As money aligns with social and ecological good, and as new structures arise that reward contribution to the commonwealth, the relationships around work will lose their spirit of mutual exploitation. The raison d'être of business organizations will shift. Quantifiable contributions to the good of society and the planet will receive monetary reward, and unquantifiable contributions will accrue rewards of status, gratitude, and goodwill mediated through the new social and symbolic structures emerging today.

Such innovations are the wave of the future. In all realms, the model of wealth from owning will give way to that of wealth by giving. The desire to own, to control, is the desire of the self of separation, the self that seeks to manipulate others to its own advantage, to extract wealth from nature and people and all that is other. The connected self grows rich by giving, by playing its role to the fullest in the nourishment of that which extends beyond itself. As we step into the connected self, organizational structures are emerging that are in tune with it. They align the self-interest of the individual with that of the organization and the interest of the organization with that of society and the planet. Unlike classic collectivist models, they allow the exuberant expression of the extraordinary gifts of the individual, yet turn those gifts toward the benefit of all.

The open collaborative structures of an extended gift economy transcend the old opposition between the individual and the group. When I say that extraordinary individual gifts will turn toward the benefit of all, some readers might protest, "But shouldn't individual excellence be rewarded?" Conservative friends in particular are immediately suspicious of my ideas, supposing that they entail the subsumption of the individual. They think that in a system that discourages accumulation and turns excellence toward the benefit of all, there would be no incentive or reward for greatness. Meanwhile, the traditional Left accepts the same basic premises, differing only in the conviction that the subsumption of the individual is good and necessary. In this view, a virtuous person labors in noble self-sacrifice for the common good, spurning any reciprocation or reward.

Both of these views come from the paradigm of separation that holds that "more for you is less for me." More for the group is less for the individual. But in gift culture, that is simply untrue. A great giver of precious gifts can ascend to the highest pinnacle of honor and enjoy all that is within the power of human beings to bestow. Such is the nature and the power of gratitude. Unfortunately, the intuitions of gift culture are alien to us now, for though they live deeply in our hearts, they are absent from the economic and ideological structures of our society. The next part of this book describes how to restore the intuitions and practices of gift culture, starting on the personal level.

The bankruptcy of the economics of the separate self is now plain to see. In the capitalist world in which individual accumulation has been permitted, we have experienced not the exuberant expression of our gifts, but their suppression, their enslavement, and their perversion toward the purpose of taking and controlling, for these activities are what the present money system compels and rewards. Worse, these ostensible rewards have been a delusion: money, its purchases, and its accumulation substituting for connection, love, beauty, play, meaning, and purpose. The noncapitalist world fared us no better. Whether it comes from communist ideology or religious teaching, self-abnegation is life-denying; invariably, the life denied expresses itself in shadow forms that wreak the same consequences, or worse, as the outright aggrandizement of the separate self.

The Age of Separation, however, is winding to a close, and we are beginning to relearn how to live the truth of our connectedness. All that I have laid out so far in this book assumes (and fosters) a shift in our consciousness, without which nothing of sacred economics would be practicable. I am not *calling* for such a shift though—I am observing it, bearing witness to it, and, I like to think, contributing to it. It is happening as you read these words, and it will happen all the swifter as the multiple crises borne of Separation converge upon us. The world is changing, and ourselves with it. We not only must create the economic structures of the connected self living in cocreative partnership with earth; we can also, right now, learn how to think and live in them.

CHAPTER 17

SUMMARY AND ROADMAP

First they ignore you, then they laugh at you,
then they fight you, then you win.

—Mohandas Gandhi

Before I explore more deeply the shift in personal economic thinking and practice that is part of sacred economy, I will summarize its key macroeconomic elements. Some are coming into place already; others are still outside the purview of acceptable political discourse and await a deepening of the crisis for the unthinkable to become common sense.

The transition I map out is evolutionary. It does not involve confiscation of property or the wholesale destruction of present institutions, but their transformation. As the following summaries describe, this transformation is under way already, or incipient in existing institutions.

The reader may notice that, except where they are off the map entirely, most of these developments fall on the left side of the political spectrum. That is because they gradually redistribute wealth from the rich to everybody else. Whereas the moneyed classes have always desired higher interest rates, and labor lower interest rates, this book foresees them going negative. Whereas liberals are fond of social welfare programs, this book foresees their universalization in a social dividend. Whereas corporate interests advocate the gutting of environmental and social protections, this book foresees the reclamation of the commons. The single major exception to the foregoing is the elimination of the income tax, which will actually benefit that small subset of the wealthy whose wealth comes from entrepreneurial productivity rather than control of money and property generating economic rents.

1. NEGATIVE-INTEREST CURRENCY

Motivation: Negative interest on reserves, and a physical currency that loses value with time, reverses the effects of interest. It enables prosperity without growth, systemically encourages the equitable distribution of wealth, and ends the discounting of future cash flows so that we no longer are pressed to mortgage our future for short-term returns. Moreover, it embodies the truth about the world, in which all things decay and return to their source. No longer is money an illusory exception to nature's law. Finally, since money in some sense represents the accumulated power of millennia of technological development, which is the common inheritance of all human beings, it is unjust for someone to profit merely by owning it, as happens in the current system of risk-free positive interest.

Transition and policy: We were on the brink of a transition to decaying currency in 2009, as central banks pushed interbank interest rates to near zero and flirted with breaching the zero lower bound. Today the economy is in an anemic recovery, but the underlying problems of stagnation and debt still remain. Each new crisis, each new bailout, offers the opportunity to buy out unrepayable debts with decaying currency, thereby rescuing the financial infrastructure without further intensifying the concentration of wealth. Moreover, when traditional monetary stimulus and Keynesian fiscal stimulus fail beyond doubt, as has happened in Japan, then central banks can hardly ignore the obvious next step of pushing interest rates below zero. To prevent currency wars, this should happen as a coordinated policy of all sovereign powers, or it should be built into a global currency.

The Federal Reserve does not at present have the authority to levy negative interest on reserves or to issue depreciating bank notes. In any country such authority resides, as it should, in legislative bodies. The time is ripe for this idea to enter the economic and political discourse, as central bankers fret about the impotence of their monetary tools. The current stagnation of the velocity of money demonstrates that lowering interest rates to zero stimulates lending only if there is the prospect of significant economic growth. The new round of quantitative easing will only underscore this point as excess reserves increase. In the absence of growth, banks would rather hold money at zero interest than lend it into the economy. But would they be willing to hold it at −2 percent? Or −5 percent?

Effect on economic life: For everyone but the investing class, the everyday experience of using money will be the same. Hard as it may be for the wealthy to imagine, most people today live paycheck to paycheck and rarely accumulate more than a couple months' worth of savings. For the more affluent, savings would still be possible, but the value of savings would gradually decrease over time unless invested at risk. There will be no way to grow money risk-free, to make "money work for you." Even government bonds will pay zero interest or less. For large purchases, whether on the personal or corporate level, low-interest or zero-interest loans rather than savings will be the primary financing vehicle. (This is happening already anyway.) Businesses will have access to investment capital that does not require them to devote a high proportion of their future cash flow to servicing debt, removing the "grow or die" imperative that governs economic life today.

2. ELIMINATION OF ECONOMIC RENTS, AND COMPENSATION FOR DEPLETION OF THE COMMONS

Motivation: Polarization of wealth is inevitable when people are allowed to profit from merely owning a thing, without producing anything or contributing to society. These profits, known as economic rents, accrue to the holders of land, the electromagnetic spectrum, mineral rights, oil reserves, patents, and many other forms of property. Because these forms of property either were prior to any human being or are the collective product of human culture, they should not belong to any private individual who does not use them for the benefit of the public and the planet.

In addition, today it is possible to profit by depleting aspects of the commonwealth such as biodiversity, aquifers, soil, ocean fisheries, and so on. These properly belong to all of us, and their depletion should only happen by common agreement and for the common good.

Transition and policy: Some states and nations already levy land-value taxes, and others have nationalized oil and minerals. The country of Bolivia and the state of Alaska, for example, assert public ownership over oil rights, so that oil companies earn money only for their services in extracting the oil, and not from owning the oil. Shifting the tax burden away from labor and toward property will become more and more attractive as wage earners' situations become desperate. Finally, as intractable regulatory battles over water rights show, building resource conservation directly into the money system is an idea whose time is coming.

Measures such as Georgist land-value taxes, leasing of mineral rights, and the use of the subjects of economic rent as a currency backing as described in this book are ways to return economic rents to the people, so that private interests can only profit by using property well, not by merely owning it. Anything that comes from the commons should be subject to fees or taxes. Intellectual property can be returned to the commons by shortening the terms of copyrights and patents, thereby acknowledging the cultural matrix from which ideas arise. We must also keep new sources of wealth, such as the genome, the electromagnetic spectrum, and the new "commons" of the internet, in the public domain, allocating their use only to those who use it to benefit society and the planet.

Effect on economic life: With a shift of taxation onto property and resources, sales and income taxes will be reduced or eliminated, and a strong economic incentive for conservation created. Since economic rents enrich those who already own, eliminating them will foster a more equitable distribution of wealth. In the realm of intellectual property, the widening of the public domain will encourage cultural creations that are not geared toward profit, as the "raw materials" of artistic and intellectual creation will be less subject to royalties and the limitations of private property.

3. INTERNALIZATION OF SOCIAL AND ENVIRONMENTAL COSTS

Motivation: Just as it is possible today to deplete aquifers without paying society for it, it is also possible to deplete the earth's capacity to absorb and process waste, the geosphere's capacity to recycle carbon, and the human body's capacity to deal with toxic pollutants. Today, pollution and other forms of environmental degradation generate costs that are usually borne by society and future generations, not the polluters. Not only is this patently unfair, but it also encourages continued pollution and environmental degradation.

Transition and policy: Regulation with financial penalties for infractions is at present the primary means to reverse the economic incentive to pollute, but it suffers many flaws, both in practice and in underlying theory. Primarily, it provides an incentive to meet standards but no incentive to exceed them. Nor does it allow us to implement an overall ceiling on total emissions of a given pollutant or total drawdown of a natural resource. Current proposals to remedy these shortcomings include cap-and-trade schemes and green taxes. Many such schemes have been proposed and, in some places, implemented. Cap-and-trade (for sulfur dioxide) has worked quite well in reducing acid rain but poorly for decreasing CO_2 emissions. These are steps in the right direction, but ultimately every form of pollution and depletion should be subject to payment.

For each type of pollutant and each natural resource, we must determine how much emission or drawdown the planet and its bioregions can sustain. Rights to emit these pollutants or use these resources can then be allocated in various ways. In some cases we might want to specify through central planning who gets to do and use what: farmer A gets to draw 100,000 gallons from the aquifer; farmer B 120,000; factory C 200,000; and so on. But because this generates economic inefficiency, in most cases we will want to use taxes on pollution and resources, or cap-and-trade auction systems, to provide economic rewards for conservation and pollution reduction. Better yet would be to base the money system itself on the gifts of the earth by backing currency with Earth's resources and its capacity to absorb and transform waste.

Effect on economic life: These measures end the opposition between ecology and economy. They align the best business decision with the best environmental decision, turning the power of entrepreneurial innovation toward the service of the planet. Huge new industries will arise devoted to conservation, pollution control, and toxic waste remediation. Zero-waste manufacturing will become the norm. The high expense of raw materials will encourage continued progress toward miniaturization and efficiency.

With economic disincentives for cheap, throwaway goods, manufactured items will become more expensive, more durable, and more repairable. We will care about our things more, maintain them and keep them. Large, resource-intensive goods such as cars, machines, and certain tools and appliances will be shared within a neighborhood or other community. Residential areas will become more compact; houses will become smaller; and larger homes will house extended families and other structures beyond the nuclear family.

As with the elimination of economic rents, these measures shift taxes away from income and onto resources so that we are taxed not on what we contribute but on what we take. Ultimately, income will not be taxed at all, freeing us from onerous record-keeping responsibilities and intrusive government monitoring.

4. ECONOMIC AND MONETARY LOCALIZATION

Motivation: As community has disintegrated around the world, people yearn for a return to local economies where we know personally the people we depend on. We want to be connected to people and places, not adrift in an anonymous global monoculture. Moreover, global commodity production puts localities into competition with each other, fomenting a "race to the bottom" in wages and environmental regulations. Moreover, when production and economic exchange are local, the social and environmental effects of our actions are much more obvious, reinforcing our innate compassion.

Transition and policy: The trend toward local economy has already started. Spiking energy costs and ecological awareness prompt businesses to source more supplies locally, and millions of consumers are awakening to the health benefits of locally grown, fresh food. People everywhere show a strong desire to reconnect with community, and some city and regional governments have initiated "buy local" campaigns. Thousands of communities around the globe have launched local currencies, and although these occupy a tiny niche today, they get people used to the idea and provide a template for future local currencies backed by local governments.

The other elements of sacred economics synergize with localization. Internalization of costs will remove many illusory economies of scale that favor long-distance transport, while the elimination of economic rents will ameliorate the obscene wage differentials that now exist between rich and poor countries.[1] Both these factors will

---

1. That is because low wages are in effect subsidized by the nonmonetized commons. When much is still available for free from the land and the community, the cost of living and therefore wages can be very low.

encourage a reversal of some of the economic globalization that has happened in the last two hundred years. Meanwhile, as much of the natural, social, and cultural commons is local or bioregional in character, a money system backed by the commons will naturally strengthen local political and economic sovereignty.

Recent financial crises have shown that as soon as national currency stops working, local governments are quick to step in by creating their own money. It happened in Argentina in 2002; it almost happened in California in 2009; and with the likely breakup of the Economic and Monetary Union (EMU), a significant devolution of monetary sovereignty back to smaller nations may be happening in Europe. As the present crisis deepens, regional governments and smaller nations will have a chance to reclaim economic sovereignty by issuing currency and protecting it from global financial markets through capital controls, foreign-exchange transaction taxes, and so forth. Governments can also give preferential treatment to local businesses in allocating contracts. Finally, local and regional governments can reclaim their credit sovereignty from international finance by establishing public banks and other credit-generating institutions.

Economic life: While many high-tech products and services are by their nature global, hidden subsidies and decades of policy have thrust many things that can and should be local into the global commodity economy. In the future these will revert to local production. Most of the food that we eat will be grown in the bioregions in which we live. Houses and many manufactured products will use local materials, often recycled, and be produced on a smaller scale. Small towns will experience an economic revival, and "Main Street" will be repopulated by authentic local businesses.

5. THE SOCIAL DIVIDEND

Motivation: Thousands of years of technological advances have made production of the quantifiable necessities of life extremely easy. These advances, the gift of our ancestors, should be the common property of all humanity. All deserve a share of the wealth they have made possible. The same is true of the natural wealth of the earth, which was made by no man. The current economic system essentially forces us to work for what is already ours. It is more just to pay out the proceeds of the economic rent compensation, pollution taxes, and so on (see 2 and 3 above) to all citizens as a social dividend. This also serves to mitigate concentration of wealth and prevent deflationary crises. The social dividend would ideally provide the bare amount to cover life's necessities; beyond that, people could still choose to earn their own money. It frees work from the pressure of necessity; people would work because they want to, not because they have to.

Transition and policy: A social dividend already exists in the state of Alaska, where each citizen shares in the state's oil revenues and receives an annual check for several thousand dollars. Recent stimulus checks are another harbinger of the social dividend that is to come. A further existing model is the welfare system, which is derided with the term "entitlements." But perhaps we should embrace that epithet and extend it to every citizen—after all, are we not all entitled to the vast abundant wealth that Earth and our ancestors have bequeathed us?

Entitlements already in place, such as food stamps, public health insurance, tax credits to low- and middle-income families with children, social welfare programs, unemployment compensation, and stimulus checks can be expanded and universalized. Such measures run counter to the current political trend of "austerity," but the rapidly intensifying misery those policies engender may lead to social unrest and political upheaval. At that time the political will shall emerge to redistribute wealth. When that happens, let us not think punitively, in terms of taxing the rich; let us rather take the attitude of giving all citizens their due. A social dividend is a covert redistribution of wealth because while all receive equally, the wealthy pay proportionally more taxes to fund it.[2] In the vision of this book, it will be funded by demurrage charges, pollution fees, and payments for the use of the commons (see 1, 2, and 3 above).

Economic life: While there will still be poor people and wealthy people, poverty will no longer entail extreme anxiety. Those who are oriented toward creating things that other people want and need will earn more money; those who are focused on simplicity, living in nature, or artistic self-expression may have to get by on the bare necessities. The point of economic life, however, will no longer be to "make a living." Freed of that pressure, we will turn our gifts toward that which inspires us—for more and more of us, that is the healing of society and the planet from the ravages of Separation. (If you still think that freedom from survival pressure will lead to dissipation and indolence, please go back and reread "The Will to Work" in Chapter 14.)

---

2. Another way to fund it is with fiat money created by the government and paid to all citizens. This also is a covert form of wealth redistribution, since unless an equivalent amount of money is removed from the economy through taxation, inflation will result, diminishing the relative wealth of the creditor class.

6. ECONOMIC DEGROWTH

Motivation: Over hundreds of years of inventing labor-saving devices, from the spinning jenny to the digital computer, we have at every turn chosen to consume more rather than to work less. This choice, driven by the money system, accompanied an accelerating drawdown of social and natural capital. Today, the option of accelerating consumption is no longer available to us. Absent the driving force of positive risk-free interest, economic growth will no longer be necessary to promote the flow of capital, and a degrowth economy will become feasible. Technology will continue to advance, and we will be left with the second option: to work less or, more accurately, to work less for money.

Transition and policy: This is already happening. Persistently high unemployment rates (near 20 percent, counting discouraged workers) in industrialized countries, together with overcapacity of production, imply that there is simply not enough paid work to employ everyone to produce all we need. To be sure, there is much necessary and beautiful work to be done—but much of it fundamentally does not generate an economic return. Unemployment is considered an evil today, but it would not be if it were supported by a social dividend and spread out over the economy. What if everyone worked 20 percent less, instead of 20 percent of the people working not at all? This economic circumstance coincides with a shift in consciousness as more and more of us reject the conventional notion of work—the division of life into two exclusive zones, work and leisure.

Decaying currency, resource-based economics (2 and 3 above), and the social dividend all support a degrowth economy. We must also deprogram ourselves from the growth-is-good mantra that guides public policy today. In the 2009 stimulus program, the rationale for the roads, bridges, and other projects was to stimulate growth—it was not a conscious decision that we actually need more roads and bridges. Similarly, housing starts are welcome as a sign of growth, and not as an expression of a belief that we need more subdivisions and sprawl. Policies such as monetary and Keynesian fiscal stimulus, which in their new incarnation will be negative-interest money and the social dividend, must be reframed: they are not to get the economy growing again; they are to circulate money to those who need to spend it. Generally speaking, this will not trigger growth if the commons is protected from monetization; instead it will shift the allocation of resources and the focus of economic activity.

Economic life: The poor and middle classes will experience greater affluence, as if the economy were growing, because the benefits of higher wages and easier employment that ordinarily only happen in a context of growth-driven business investment will be able to happen in a steady-state or degrowth economy. People will spend more and more of their time in noneconomic activities as the money realm shrinks and the realm of gifts, voluntarism, leisure, and the unquantifiable grows. Digital content—images, music, video, news, books, etc.—will continue its trend toward zero-cost availability. While resource-based production will be far more expensive, human input will continue to benefit from the ongoing accumulation of technology so that in many high-tech realms, we will do more with less. People will also share more and consume less, borrow more and rent less, give more and sell less—all reflecting and engendering economic degrowth.

7. GIFT CULTURE AND P2P ECONOMICS

Motivation: The expansion of the money realm has come at the expense of other forms of economic circulation, in particular gifts. When every economic relationship becomes a paid service, we are left independent of everyone we know and dependent, via money, on anonymous, distant service providers. That is a primary reason for the decline of community in modern societies, with its attendant alienation, loneliness, and psychological misery. Moreover, money is unsuited to facilitate the circulation and development of the unquantifiable things that truly make life rich.

Transition and policy: Thankfully, the money realm is already beginning to shrink, and that degrowth allows new space for gift economics. The internet is in important respects a gift network, and it has made it easy to give away information that was once very costly to produce. In various ways, this has pushed services like advertising (think Craigslist), travel agency, journalism, publishing, music, and many more toward the gift realm. It has also facilitated gift-based modes of open-source production. What once required paid intermediaries and centralized administrative structures now happens directly. People and businesses are even creating credit, via mutual-credit systems, without the intermediation of banks. Meanwhile, on the local level the ideals of the connected self, the yearning for community, and sheer economic exigency are leading people to restore gift-based community structures.

Governments can liberalize tax and banking regulations to give free rein to the new systems of economic circulation emerging today. The commons in which these systems reside, in particular the internet, must be kept public. Governments can also establish and promote mutual-credit systems for business and industry, shielding the domestic or local economy from predation by international capital.

Economic life: People will meet their needs, whether for goods, services, or money itself, in a great variety of ways. Face-to-face gift circles and online coordination of gifts and needs will allow many needs to be met without money. People will have much more of a sense of being a part of a community they rely on. Complementary, user-created credit systems, along with internet-based P2P lending, will obviate some of the traditional need for banks. On a local level as well as mediated through global networks, new nonquantified "currencies" of recognition and gratitude will emerge that connect and reward qualitative contributions to society and the planet.

* * * *

As you can see, all of the seven elements I have described are tightly synergistic. Indeed, none can stand on its own. Negative-interest currency, for instance, won't work if other sources of economic rent are still available to invest in. Localization depends in large part on the removal of hidden subsidies that make global trade economic. Gift economies allow the quality of life to improve even as the economy shrinks.

Together, the various strands of sacred economy I have described in Part II of this book weave a tapestry, an organic matrix that we can see emerging today. The new economy will not come from a new beginning, a sweeping away of the old and a starting afresh; it is rather a phase transition, a metamorphosis.

Just as no piece of sacred economy can stand alone, so also does each piece naturally induce the others. But if there is a linchpin, it is the end of growth, the transition of the human species to a new relationship with Earth, a new Story of the People. Ultimately, it is our emerging desire to be Earth's partner, and our newfound spiritual realization of the uniqueness and connectedness of all beings, that underlies what I have called sacred economics.

PART III

LIVING THE NEW ECONOMY

The transition to sacred economy is part of a larger shift in our ways of thinking, relating, and being. Economic logic alone is not enough to sustain it. Many economic visionaries have devised mathematically persuasive revolutions in money and property, but of the handful that ever came to fruition, none survived the test of time. The final third of this book, therefore, is devoted to the shift of consciousness and practice that goes along with the new money systems I have described. As we heal the spirit-matter rupture, we discover that economics and spirituality are inseparable. On the personal level, economics is about how to give our gifts and meet our needs. It is about who we are in relation to the world. By changing our everyday economic thinking and practices, we not only prepare ourselves for the great changes ahead; we also set the stage for their emergence. By living the concepts of sacred economics, we ease its acceptance by all and welcome it into the world.

CHAPTER 18

RELEARNING GIFT CULTURE

Lovers must not, like usurers, live for themselves alone.
They must finally turn from their gaze at one another
back toward the community.

—Wendell Berry

We have in our age created a distinction between money exchanges and gifts. The former is in the realm of rational self-interest; the latter is at least partially altruistic or selfless. This division of economics into two separate realms mirrors other defining dichotomies of our civilization: man and nature, spirit and matter, good and evil, sacred and profane, mind and body. None of these withstand deep scrutiny; all of them are crumbling as the Age of Separation draws to a close. And so, just as we erase the matter-spirit distinction and resacralize all of matter, just as we give up on the effort to transcend nature and realize that we are part of it, so also shall we return the spirit of the gift to all aspects of human economy, whether or not money is involved.

Each aspect of the monetary evolution described in this book imbues money with the properties of gift:

1. Over time, giving and receiving must be in balance. The internalization of ecological costs ensures that we will take no more from earth than we can give.

2. The source of a gift is to be acknowledged. The restoration

of the commons means that any use of what belongs to all is acknowledged by a payment that goes to all.

3. Gifts circulate rather than accumulate. Decaying currency ensures that wealth remains a function of flow rather than of owning.

4. Gifts flow toward the greatest need. A social dividend ensures that the basic survival needs of every person are met.

The foundation of a sacred economy, then, is gift consciousness. The remainder of this book explores the ways in which we can restore the mentality of the gift in our own lives to foster and prepare for the coming world.

I am not suggesting that you become a saint and abandon selfishness. Gift culture is not so simple. As we imbue matter with the qualities we once ascribed to spirit, we are also imbuing spirit with the messy qualities of matter. No longer is the spiritual realm of our conceptions a place of perfect order, harmony, goodness, and justice. Similarly, as we imbue money with some of the characteristics of gift culture, we must recognize that the gift realm never was, and may never be, a realm of pure disinterested selflessness.

Consider the ideal of the free gift, which Jacques Derrida characterizes as follows: "For there to be a gift, there must be no reciprocity, return, exchange, countergift, or debt." This would preclude any benefit accruing to the giver, such as social status, praise, expressions of gratitude, and even, perhaps, the feeling that one has done something virtuous. The closest example of this in real life would be anonymous charity, or perhaps the alms given to Jain ascetics, who make sure to offer neither thanks nor praise for the food.[1] Jain religious beliefs are quite relevant to this association of

---

1. Laidlaw, "A Free Gift Makes No Friends," 46–7.

the free gift with purity, spirituality, and nonworldliness. The Jain seek through asceticism to burn away karma and purify themselves while creating no new ties with the world. Thus they take care never to visit the same house twice and never to respond to an invitation, striving toward the ideal of an unexpected guest receiving pure charity untainted by any worldly bond.

The Jain are an extreme case, but similar ideals inhabit the other world religions. Christians, for instance, are enjoined to fast, pray, and give charity in secret. Buddhists following the Bodhisattva path are supposed to dedicate their lives to the liberation of all beings, putting others ahead of themselves. In Judaism, the principle of *chesed shel emet*, the highest form of kindness, is to give with no hope of repayment or gratitude, while the highest level of charity is when neither donor nor receiver knows who is giving or receiving. Anonymous charity is one of the five pillars of Islam, and huge Islamic charities are funded anonymously. I don't think I need cite too many examples to persuade the reader of the association of altruism and anonymous charity with religion.

The religious ideal of the free gift that doesn't create any social bonds is, ironically enough, very similar to monetary transactions! These also generate no obligation, no tie: once the money is paid and the goods delivered, neither party owes the other anything. But with the exception of the idealized true gifts described above, gifts are very different. If you give me something, I will feel grateful and desire to give in turn, either to you or to someone else that social custom prescribes. Either way, an obligation has been created, an assurance of continued economic circulation within the gifting community. Anonymous gifts don't create such ties and don't strengthen communities. The recipient might be grateful, but that gratitude has no object save the universal or abstract.

351

Gratitude, moreover, arises not just from the receiving of gifts, but also from their witnessing. The generosity of others moves us toward generosity ourselves. We desire to give to those who are generous. We are moved by their openness, by their vulnerability, by their trust. We want to take care of them. With the possible exception of anonymous charity, gifts don't happen in a social vacuum. They expand the circle of self, linking our self-interest with that of anyone who, when he has more than he needs, will give us what we need. The religious ideal of the unattached gift, which diffuses the resultant gratitude to the universal level, has a place insofar as we wish to identify with the community of all being. But I do not think that the resolution of the Age of Separation is a state of universal oneness. Rather, we will step into a multidimensional self that identifies with all being, yes, but also with humanity, its own culture, its bioregion, its community, its family, and its ego-self. Accordingly, the anonymous, unencumbered gift has an important but limited role to play in the coming economy.

This was certainly the case in primitive gift cultures. While there did exist the equivalent of the universal, unrequitable gift in the form of sacrifices to the gods, most gifts were social in nature. In his classic 1924 monograph *The Gift*, Marcel Mauss establishes a strong case against the existence in primitive societies of a free gift. Generally speaking, Mauss said, appropriate gifts and return gifts were quite precisely determined and were enforced through social approbation and obloquy, status and ostracism, and other forms of social pressure. This is a desirable state of affairs: the obligations and commitments that arise from gifts and their expected requital are a glue that holds the society together.

We can feel the absence of that social glue today. In the logic of me and mine, any obligation, any dependency, is a threat. Gifts naturally create obligations, so, in the Age of Separation, people have become afraid to give and even more afraid to receive. We don't want to receive gifts because we don't want to be obligated to anyone. We don't want to owe anybody anything. We don't want to depend on anyone's gifts or charity—"I can pay for it myself, thank you. I don't need you." Accordingly, we elevate anonymous acts of charity to a lofty moral status. It is supposed to be a great virtue to give without strings attached, to expect nothing in return.

Part of living in the gift is to recognize and abide by the obligation to receive as well as to give. Mauss gives the example of the Dayaks, who "have even developed a whole system of law and morality based upon the duty one has not to fail to share in the meal at which one is present or that one has seen in preparation."[2] I personally experienced something of this during my years in Taiwan, where vestiges of the old gift-based culture of agrarian times still persisted in the older generation. There, not only was it a serious faux pas to fail to offer food to a visitor to your home, but it was also quite rude to refuse it. If dinner was in preparation, it would not necessarily be polite to attempt a gracious exit before mealtime (without a really convincing excuse). To refuse a gift is to spurn relationship. If gifts create bonds and widen the circle of self, then to refuse to give or receive a gift says, "I refuse to be connected to you. You are an *other* in my constellation of being." As Mauss puts it, "To refuse to give, to fail to invite, just as to refuse to accept, is tantamount to declaring war; it is to reject the bond of alliance and commonality."[3]

---

2. Mauss, *The Gift*, 13.
3. Ibid.

To reject this bond is a serious matter. Author Mark Dowie speaks of an Alaskan tribe he lived with that convened a meeting of elders to discuss the grave transgression of a certain tribesman on the sharing ethic. The person in question was hoarding the fruits of his hunting for himself, flouting the tribe's gift customs. How seriously did the elders view his behavior (which was of long standing)? The purpose of their meeting was to decide whether or not to kill him.[4]

In many situations, a kind of implicit negotiation takes place in which the two parties trade excuses and rebuttals of them until they agree on a gift that appropriately reflects the degree of bond to be created.[5] "Oh, I couldn't; I just ate (lie). Maybe just a cup of tea." The tea comes, accompanied by a sumptuous platter of mung bean pastries, dried plums, and watermelon seeds. I partake sparingly of some of the seeds. The host gives me some pastries to take with me. And so on. This subtle dance of giving and receiving is absent from a commodity economy such as ours.

But even in America, alienated as we are from gift culture, we still feel its logic. You may have had the experience of receiving a favor from someone and then offering to pay for it, and feeling the letdown and distancing that ensue. To pay for a gift renders it no longer a gift, and the bond that was being established is broken.

The aversion to obligation enhances the attractiveness of money transactions. As Richard Seaford says, "What is surrendered in a commercial transaction is completely and permanently separated

---

4. Interview on radio station KWMR, "A Conversation with Charles Eisenstein and Mark Dowie," April 4, 2009.

5. In Taiwan, sensing intuitively the local etiquette, I was sometimes led into uncomfortable situations. I remember once visiting an elderly man to practice my Taiwanese; that morning lesson was accompanied by a platter of sliced beef and a newly opened bottle of whiskey. It was an offer that could not be refused.

from the person who surrendered it."[6] When we pay for everything we receive, we remain independent, disconnected, free from obligation, and free from ties. No one can call in favors; no one has any leverage over us. In a gift economy, if someone asks for help, you can't really say no: that person and the whole society says, explicitly or not, "Hey, remember all the things we have done for you? Remember when we babysat your children? When we rescued your cow? When we rebuilt your barn after the fire? You owe us!" Today we want to be able to say, "I paid you for that babysitting. I paid you for shoveling my sidewalk. I've paid for everything you've done for me. I don't owe you anything!"

Because it creates gratitude or obligation, to willingly receive a gift is itself a form of generosity. It says, "I am willing to owe you one." Or, in a more sophisticated gift culture, it says, "I am willing to be in the debt of the community." Extending the principle further, to fully receive the gifts bestowed upon us says, "I am willing to be in the debt of God and the universe." By the same token, in refusing gifts we seem to excuse ourselves from the obligations that arise naturally with gratitude. The taxicab driver Stewart Millard observes,

> The first conclusion I reached is that money makes us exquisitely inept at real human relationship. If I have just gotten a new set of tires from my friend Greg at his tire shop (I, indeed, was sitting in his parking lot thinking about this!) and no money was exchanged, then how would I repay Greg? And, a bit more subtle question arose: What if I didn't accept this offer (gift) of tires from Greg?

6. Seaford, *Money and the Early Greek Mind*, 203.

By accepting the gift of tires without money, then an automatic set of behaviors and consideration arise. What can I offer in return? I could wait for him to ask, or I can do the more arduous task of actually getting to know Greg, and thus allowing a more organic exchange to take place. Money means I can pay, and then pay no more attention to my fellow human across the counter. No getting to know him, no exchange of life to accommodate a natural mingling of flows in dependence and appreciation. A reason we are so intolerant of each other is simply because we have money. If that person is displeasing, we just take our money elsewhere—and the original is just left blowing in the wind.

One of the most important gifts you can give is to fully receive the gift of another. Today we have many ways of rejecting, or partially receiving, a gift. Anything we do to lessen the obligation implied by receiving is a form of rejection—for example, reminding the giver of what you gave her last year; implying that you deserve or are entitled to the gift; pretending that, whatever you received, you didn't want it that much; or offering or insisting on paying for something. When someone pays me a compliment, I sometimes reject it by denying its truth, projecting false humility, or devaluing it with words like, "Oh, everybody does it; it's not so special." When someone says, "Thank you," sometimes I find myself rejecting it with words like, "It was nothing." Someone might say, "Your writing has changed my life," and I might respond, "The change was within you already, and my writing was merely its agent. Others read the same words with no effect." While there is truth in this response, nonetheless I have sometimes used it to deflect gifts of praise or thanks that I was afraid to fully receive, to fully take in.

Another way to reject the gift of a compliment is to pay a return compliment with excessive alacrity, distracting from the first compliment before it has a chance to sink in. When gratitude inspires a return gift, we must not give it too quickly, or it becomes a mere transaction, not so different from a purchase. Then it cancels out obligation rather than tying giver and receiver more closely.

To fully receive is to willingly put yourself in a position of obligation, either to the giver or to society at large. Gratitude and obligation go hand in hand; they are two sides of the same coin. Obligation is obligation to do what? It is to give without "compensation." Gratitude is what? It is the desire to give, again without compensation, borne of the realization of having received. In the age of the separate self, we have split the two, but originally they are one: obligation is a desire that comes from within and is only secondarily enforced from without.[7] Clearly then, reluctance to receive is actually reluctance to give. We think that we are being noble, self-sacrificing, or unselfish if we prefer to give rather than to receive. We are being nothing of the sort. The generous person gives and receives with an equally open hand. Do not be afraid to be under obligation, to be in gratitude. We are afraid of obligation because, quite rightly, we are wary of "have to"; we are wary of forceful compulsion, wary of the coercion that underlies so many

---

7. Gift societies combine obligation and gratitude inseparably. In the potlatches of Melanesia and the Pacific Northwest, giving could be an act of social dominance, nearly of aggression. But even outside this extreme, it is generally true that, as anthropologist Mary Douglas says, "right across the globe and as far back as we can go in the history of human civilization, the major transfer of goods has been by cycles of obligatory returns of gifts" (emphasis mine). So when we opine as to what does and does not constitute a true gift, let us keep in mind the function that gifts have played in the psychology and society of countless gift cultures up through the present day. Who are we, who live almost wholly in a commodity culture, to presume to know what a gift is?

of our society's institutions. But when we convert "have to" into "want to," we are free. When we realize that life itself is a gift, and that we are here to give ourselves, then we are free. After all, what you have taken in this life dies with you. Only your gifts live on.

You can see how pervasive gift refusal is in our culture and how much relearning there is to do. Much of what goes by the name of modesty or humility is actually a refusal of ties, a distancing from others, a refusal to receive. We are as afraid to receive as we are to give; indeed, we are incapable of doing one without the other. We may imagine ourselves as selfless and virtuous for being more willing to give than to receive, but this state is just as miserly as its reverse, for without receiving, the wellspring of our own gifts dries up. Not only is it miserly, it is arrogant: What do we imagine to be the source of what we give? Ourselves? No. Life itself is a gift, life and all that nurtures it, from mother and father to the entire ecosystem. None were created through our own efforts. The same goes for our creative abilities, physical and mental, which some, intuiting this truth, might call God-given.

Of course, sometimes it is perfectly appropriate to refuse a gift, specifically when you don't want to create the kind of tie the gift implies. All gifts have "strings attached." But often our reluctance to receive comes not from aversion to a specific tie, but to ties in general.

New Age spiritual clichés about "opening up to abundance" make me queasy, yet as with most clichés there is truth beneath them. Fear of receiving, though, isn't just a matter of low self-worth or feeling undeserving, as some self-help gurus would have us believe: it is also, ultimately, a fear of giving. The two go hand in hand—always! Together, they are a fear of life, of connection; they are a kind of reticence. To give and to receive, to owe and be owed, to depend on others and be depended on—this is being fully alive. To neither give nor receive, but to pay for everything; to never depend on anyone, but to be financially independent; to not be bound to a community or place, but to be mobile ... such is the illusory paradise of the discrete and separate self. Corresponding to the spiritual conceit of nonattachment, to the religious delusion of nonworldliness, and to the scientific ambition to master and transcend nature, it is proving to be not a paradise but a hell.

As we awaken from our delusions of nonattachment, independence, and transcendence, we seek to reunite with our true, expansive selves. We yearn for community. Independence and nonattachment were never anything but delusions anyway. The truth is, has always been, and always will be that we are utterly and hopelessly dependent on each other and on nature. Nor will it ever change that the only alternative to depending, receiving, loving, and losing is to not be alive at all.

To be sure, there is truth in nonattachment too, a truth that gift culture reflects when we hold on less tightly to our things. This nonattachment exists within a context of attachment and connection, not independence or dissociation. Indeed, gifts aid in the release of ego attachments because they expand the self beyond the ego, aligning self-interest with the welfare of a larger, interconnected being. Gifts both serve and result from the expansion of self beyond ego; they are both cause and consequence. Feeling a connection to the other, we desire to give. The more we give, the more we feel our connections. The gift is the sociophysical manifestation of an underlying unity of being.

Detached from the world, one can do little good or harm in it. Immersed in the world, we are challenged to use our wealth wisely.[8] It is generous to plunge fully into the social realm of ties and obligations. By giving of one's gifts in a way that *is* public, in a way that, contrary to religious ideals, might generate return, we increase the throughput of gifts through ourselves, magnifying our capacity and need to give. The idea is not to force a return gift or contrive to receive one—that is not a gift at all—but to meet a need and create a tie.

Gifts, along with stories, are the threads of relationship, of community. The two are intimately related. Stories can be a kind of gift, and stories accompany gifts as well, enhancing their unique, personal dimension. The compulsion to tell the story of the gift is almost irresistible. I remember my grandmother: "Well, first I looked in Macy's, but they didn't have it there, so then I went to J. C. Penney's..." In any event, stories of who gave what to whom are part of the social witnessing that inspires generosity and the feeling of community.

The attitude of the giver—"I give to you freely and trust that I will receive what is appropriate, whether from you or from another in our gift circle"—strikes a deep chord. There is something eternal and true about the spirit of gratitude and generosity that expects no reward and contrives no obligation.[9] So here is a paradox: on

---

8. The path of the ascetic is, according to this idea, only right if it comes from the honest realization that "I am not ready to use wealth (in all its forms) well, so I will abstain from it until I am prepared." Indeed, I have met very few people who use wealth well, which is not surprising since wealth is a gift, just as our talents, energy, and time are gifts; and to use it well, we must be oriented toward the spirit of giving.

9. Therefore, I think that Mauss is missing something important, seeing the dynamics of gift societies through a polarizing lens. Despite Mauss's philosophical opposition to the utilitarian downplaying of humans as social beings and emphasis on individualism, he still buys into some of the doctrine's deep assumptions, in particular that people are primarily motivated by self-interest. He asks at the beginning of *The Gift*, "What rule of legality and self-interest, in societies of a backward or archaic type, compels the gift that has been received to be obligatorily reciprocated?" (3). The very question excludes mechanisms outside self-interest and obligation that could explain the second part of his query: "What power resides in the object given that causes its recipient to pay it back?"

the one hand, the obligation-generating function of gifts creates social solidarity and community. On the other hand, our hearts respond to gifts that seek to create no obligation, that demand no reciprocation, and we are touched by the generosity of those who give without expectation of return. Is there a way to resolve this paradox? Yes—because the source of obligation needn't be social pressure levering the self-interest of a discrete and separate self. It can instead arise naturally, unforced; the result of gratitude. This obligation is an autochthonous desire, a natural corollary to the felt-state of connection that arises, spontaneously, upon receiving a gift or witnessing an act of generosity.

The logic of the discrete and separate self says that human beings are fundamentally selfish. Whether for the selfish gene of biology or the economic man of Adam Smith, more for you is less for me. Accordingly, society must apply various threats and incen-

---

9. *(continued)* If Mauss's account of gift dynamics is complete, then we might well ask how the present money-mediated system is any different. Through the medium of money, we too exert social pressure, leveraging self-interest, to make sure that gifts are reciprocated. Monetary debt directly parallels the gift-generated obligations in Mauss's "archaic societies." Moreover, in those societies that Mauss cites in which, for status reasons, the reciprocated gift must be greater than the one received, usury has a counterpart as well. One conclusion that we might draw from these parallels is that nothing has changed: that today's money economy is but an extension, into the machine age, of archaic gift economies. But another conclusion that equally fits the facts is that Mauss has projected present-day mind-sets and motivations onto the people of the past. The latter conclusion has its own buttressing evidence—for example, numerous travelers' accounts of the open, childlike generosity of the natives they encountered. Even Christopher Columbus was moved (though not moved enough to refrain from murdering and enslaving them): "[The Arawak] are so ingenuous and free with all they have, that no one would believe it who has not seen it.... Of anything they possess, if it be asked of them, they never say no; on the contrary, they invite you to share it and show as much love as if their hearts went with it." His descriptive terms point to something significant. Their ingenuousness suggests something childlike and primal about their generosity; their lovingness suggests a motivation very different from Mauss's socially enforced self-interest.

tives to align the selfish behavior of the individual with the interests of society. Today, new paradigms in biology are replacing the neo-Darwinian orthodoxy while movements in spirituality, economics, and psychology challenge the atomistic Cartesian conception of the self. The new self is interdependent and, even more, partakes for its very existence in the existence of all other beings to which it is connected. This is the connected self, the larger self, which extends to include, by degrees, everyone and everything in its gift circle. Within that circle, it is not true that more for you is less for me. Gifts circulate so that the good fortune of another is also your good fortune. Immersed in this expansive sense of self, one needs no coercive mechanisms to enforce sharing. The social structures of the gift still serve a purpose: to remind its members of the truth of their connectedness, to rein in anyone who may have forgotten, and to provide gift structures that work to meet the society's needs. Who gives what to whom? The right answer is specific to each culture and depends on its environment, its kinship system, its religious beliefs, and much else. A gift structure evolves over time and guides a culturally appropriate distribution of resources.

This, in essence, is also what we want the money economy to do: to connect human (and nonhuman) needs with the gifts of man, woman, and nature that can meet them. Each of the economic and monetary proposals in this book seeks, in one way or another, to accomplish this goal. The old economic regime is inimical to it, with its concentration of wealth, its exclusion of those who cannot pay (such as poor people, other species, and the earth) from the circulation of gifts, its anonymity and depersonalization, its shattering of community and connection, its denial of cyclicity and the law of return, and its orientation toward the accumulation of money and property. Sacred economy bears the opposite of all these conditions: it is egalitarian, inclusive, personal, bond-creating, sustainable, and nonaccumulative. Such an economy is coming! The old one cannot last. It is time to prepare for it by living from its principles today.

CHAPTER 19

NONACCUMULATION

When the accumulation of wealth is no longer of high social importance, there will be great changes in the code of morals. We shall be able to rid ourselves of many of the pseudo-moral principles which have hag-ridden us for two hundred years, by which we have exalted some of the most distasteful of human qualities into the position of the highest virtues.

—John Maynard Keynes

Be charitable before wealth makes thee covetous.

—Sir Thomas Browne

I have in this book articulated a conception of wealth as flow rather than accumulation. This is not a new idea: wealth only became an accumulation with the rise of agricultural civilization. Because hunter-gatherers are, with very few exceptions, nomadic, possessions are a literal burden to them. But the farmer is sedentary; moreover, the farmer's livelihood depends on the storage of food, especially in the case of grain-based agriculture. Hunter-gatherers stayed at populations beneath the carrying capacity of the unmodified ecosystem; in times of drought or flooding, they could easily move and adapt. Not so the farmer. For the farmer, seven lean years could easily follow seven fat ones, which meant that the best security was to keep large stores of food. To accumulate and store was the best form of security; from it flowed wealth, status, and many of the habits we identify today as virtues: thrift, sacrifice, saving for a rainy day, good work habits, industriousness, and diligence.

Living without food storage, hunter-gatherers worked no harder than necessary to meet immediate needs and enjoyed long periods of leisure. The farmer's leisure comes with a bit of guilt—he could be working a little harder, storing up a little more just in case. On the farm, there is always something that needs to be done. We have today inherited and taken to an extreme the attitudes of the farmer, including the agricultural definition of wealth.[1] After agriculture, these attitudes (work ethic, sacrifice of present for future, accumulation, and control) reached their next level of expression in the Age of the Machine,[2] which led to accumulations of wealth undreamed of by the richest pharaoh.

And today we are in the so-called Information Age, which is yet another intensification of the same attitudes, and which has seen an accumulation of wealth, a contrasting poverty, and an alienation from the natural world far exceeding any precedent. Many observers have pointed out that each such "age" is succeeding (actually overlaying) the last at an exponentially accelerating pace.

---

1. Please note that this dichotomy between the forager and the farmer is somewhat artificial. One merged gradually into the other, and the original attitudes of the forager were slow to die; indeed, some of them linger on to this day. The swidden farmer, the high Medieval peasant, and the Bantu herdsman enjoyed a pace of life nearly as leisurely as that of the hunter-gatherer.
2. Associated with the Industrial Revolution, the Age of the Machine is not distinct from the agricultural age but rather is an overlay onto it. Its beginnings go back to the builder societies of the ancient world, whose pyramids and monuments demanded the same division of labor and the same standardization of products, processes, and human functions that characterize the modern factory system. They also resulted in the same human misery, toil, and poverty.

Very roughly speaking, the age of agriculture lasted three millennia, the age of industry three centuries, the information age three decades.[3] Now, many sense, we are on the verge of a singularity: perhaps a flurry of new ages telescoped into years, months, days, and then a transition into a wholly new era, something unknowable and qualitatively different from anything before. We may not know much about it yet, but one thing that is certain about the coming Age of Reunion is that humanity will no longer pretend exemption from nature's laws.

Certainly, accumulation is one of the violations of natural law that is inconsistent with the new human being and her relationship to nature. Hoarding resources beyond an individual's capacity to consume them is not unknown in nature, but it is rare, and many types of food storage (e.g., squirrels sequestering nuts) have other explanations.[4] Generally speaking, natural systems are characterized by resource flow, not accumulation. In an animal, cells do not store more than a few seconds' worth of sugar but trust in the ongoing supply of their universe, the body.

Evolutionary biologists offer two explanations of resource hoarding in humans from the perspective of genetic determinism. The first is that it offers security, a survival advantage. Hunter-gatherers and other species would do it too, the argument goes, but they generally lack the means. The second explanation is that the

---

3. I would precede these with a 30,000-year age of symbolic culture (that's about how old the earliest representational art is—and, in one view, symbolic language as well), a 300,000-year age of fire, and a 3,000,000-year age of stone.

4. For example, the squirrels are actually planting trees, thus acting as an agent of the trees' propagation. The tree feeds the squirrel, and the squirrel helps the tree reproduce, just like the relationship between wasps and fig trees and between countless other species. Observing such relationships, it is easy to understand why early humans saw nature in terms of the Gift.

ostentatious accumulation and consumption of resources are a kind of mating display. As biologist Walter K. Dodds puts it,

> Display of control over, and consumption of, resources by men and women escalates (contributes to luxury fever) because the excess appropriation of resources is a sexually selected characteristic. In a society in which standard of living is high, it is not enough simply to display control of sufficient resources to ensure the survival of you, your mate, and your offspring. You must control more resources than are controlled by your potential competitors for mates to make an attractive display.[5]

Granted the premises of conventional genetic theory (a critique of which is beyond the scope of this book), the logic seems airtight. Quite subtly, though, the argument is based on circular reasoning that projects our present environment of scarcity, anxiety, and competition onto nature. The ability to accumulate and overconsume resources is a reproductive advantage only in a society where resources are not equitably shared. In a gift-based sharing culture, the welfare of your children does not depend so much on whether your mate is a great hunter or prolific gatherer. Moreover, anthropological evidence contradicts Dodds's thesis. Consistently, hunter-gatherers and primitive agriculturalists underproduced, preferring leisure over accumulation and control of resources.[6] There was no gene-driven competition for ostentatious display of wealth; to the contrary, hoarding resulted not in high status but in opprobrium. Moreover, the widespread sharing of resources rendered productive capacity moot. If anything was genetically selected, it would be

5. Dodds, *Humanity's Footprint,* 123.
6. See Marshall Sahlins's *Stone Age Economics* for numerous demonstrations of underproduction.

the inclination to share and to contribute to the well-being of the tribe. With small exaggeration, we can say that in a gift community, rational self-interest is identical to altruism.

The mistaken intuitions of the discrete and separate self infect us so deeply that we often assume them, in disguised form, as axiomatic truth. In asking, "What is human nature?" we project back to an imaginary time when it was "every man for himself," or perhaps rather, every family for itself, and assume that communities were a later development, an improvement on the raw state of nature. Significantly, two of the seminal philosophers in this area, Hobbes and Rousseau, who had opposite views on life in a state of nature, agreed on this point. For Hobbes, life was "*solitary*, poor, nasty, brutish, and short" (emphasis mine), and it was solitary for Rousseau too:

> Whereas, in this primitive state, men had neither houses, nor huts, nor any kind of property whatever; every one lived where he could, seldom for more than a single night; the sexes united without design, as accident, opportunity or inclination brought them together, nor had they any great need of words to communicate their designs to each other; and they parted with the same indifference. The mother gave suck to her children at first for her own sake; and afterwards, when habit had made them dear, for theirs: but as soon as they were strong enough to go in search of their own food, they forsook her of their own accord; and, as they had hardly any other method of not losing one another than that of remaining continually within sight, they soon became quite incapable of recognizing one another when they happened to meet again.[7]

---

7. Rousseau, *A Dissertation on the Origin of Inequality among Men,* part 1.

Whether or not it was true then, it is certainly true now that accumulation adds at least some measure to our security, and even to our sexual attractiveness. But not for long. The mentality of accumulation is coincident with the ascent of separation, and it is ending in tandem with the Age of Separation as well. Accumulation makes no sense for the expanded self of the gift economy.

An important theme in all my work is the integration of hunter-gatherer attitudes into technological society—a completion and not a transcendence of the past. I have already laid out in this book the monetary equivalent of nonaccumulation (decaying currency), of nonownership (elimination of economic rents), and of underproduction (leisure and degrowth). Tellingly, many people feel a pull toward these values on a personal level too, such as in the movement toward "voluntary simplicity" and in questioning the nature of work. Ahead of their time, these people have pioneered a new and ancient way of being that will soon become the norm.

Bill Kauth, founder of the Sacred Warriors and other organizations, is an internationally known social inventor and a rich man, though not in any conventional sense. He owns very little: an old car, some personal possessions, as far as I know no financial assets. Many years ago, he tells me, he took a personal vow he calls "income topping," pledging never to earn more than $24,000 in a year. And yet, he says, "I have eaten in some of the world's best restaurants, traveled to many of the earth's beautiful places, had an incredibly rich life."

In the age of the separate self, we carry a grain of cynicism and suspicion that colors our perceptions of other people and organizations. When we hear an inspirational speaker or participate in a transformative seminar, we secretly (or not so secretly) wonder, "How is this guy profiting from this? What is the gambit?" We instantly recognize any hypocrisy, such as "donations" that are in fact mandatory. Our suspicions are often well justified. Too many religious cults, spiritual movements, and multilevel marketing organizations end up with the people at the top getting rich, and we wonder, "Is this what it was about all along?" Bill Kauth was trying to find a way to tap into the considerable dynamism of multilevel marketing while eliminating the "greed factor," and he says income topping was the only thing that showed any promise.

The suspicion of any good thing that "it's actually all about someone trying to profit from me" has an internal counterpart, when we question our own motives. Again, sometimes this self-suspicion is well-founded. I have had occasions where it seemed that everything I ever did was for some base motivation; that all my gifts had been calculated attempts to impress someone or curry favor, that all my generosity was a pathetic attempt to win approval, that my every relationship was motivated by a secret scheme of profit. It seemed that I had never once in my life done something authentically generous; always I'd harbored a secret agenda of self-aggrandizement. This state of self-disgust has archetypal reverberations articulated in myth and religion. Jonathan Edwards's sermon "Sinners in the Hands of an Angry God" comes to mind, as does John Calvin's doctrine of the total depravity of man. In Buddhism, it is the humiliating realization of how much of one's actions come from ego, even and especially the attempt to transcend ego!

I agree with Bill that income topping is a powerful way to eliminate the suspicion that poisons organizations and ideas that have the potential to transform lives. It operates similarly on the internal level and, by eliminating self-doubt over our motivations, lends power to our words. It affirms to ourselves and others the sincerity of our motives and frees people to accept our gifts. Bill's vow was a deeply personal vow, which he didn't share with others until, decades later, he gave me permission to write of it. I thought initially that it would have been more powerful for him to share it, but upon further reflection I changed my mind. The essential energy of that vow will radiate from him whether or not he articulates it to others. Moreover, by sharing it publicly one risks the suspicion (from oneself and others) that its true motive is vanity: to look good, to win approval. Bill indicated, however, that at some point he intended to turn the concept into a community commitment, to reinforce mutual trust and interdependency.

The salutary psychological and social effects of income topping led me to think about it in the context of sacred economics, past and future. Rather than income topping, my readings about premodern cultures suggest that something more akin to "asset topping," which I call *nonaccumulation,* was widely enforced. Recall the Alaskan tribe referenced in Chapter 18: the offense was not in being too successful a hunter; it was in not sharing the meat.

Nonaccumulation models hunter-gatherer societies, in which there was great abundance but no accumulation, and in which prestige went to those who gave the most. To give the most, one also had to receive the most, either from nature or from other people. The great hunter, the skilled artist or musician, the energetic, the healthy, and the lucky would have more to give. In any event, this kind of prestige is to the benefit of all. It is only when high income translates into accumulation, frivolous consumption, or socially destructive consumption that it makes sense to restrict it. In other words, the problem is not with high income; it is with the results of the income getting stuck at some point in its circulation, accumulating and stagnating.

Nonaccumulation is a conscious intention not to accumulate

more than a modest amount of assets. It is born not of the desire to be virtuous, but of the understanding that it feels much better to give than to keep, that the seeming security of accumulation is an illusion, and that excessive money and possessions burden our lives. It is deeply aligned with the spirit of the gift, of which a core principle is that the gift must circulate. Recall Mauss: "Generally, even what has been received and comes into one's possession in this way—in whatever manner—is not kept for oneself, unless one cannot do without it." In other words, if you need it, use it. If not, pass it on. This is such an obvious principle that even a child can understand it. Why keep something for yourself that you cannot use? It is only the "what if" that drives us to keep and hoard: What if in the future I don't have enough? In a gift culture, what would happen is that someone would give you what you need. In a hoarding culture, the "what if" fear is self-fulfilling, creating the very conditions of vulnerability and scarcity that it assumes.

You might be thinking that since we indeed live in a hoarding culture and scarcity-inducing money system, nonaccumulation is impractical today. You might think wistfully that it would be nice if everyone else did it, but they don't, so you'd better protect yourself. This is all very logical. I cannot offer a rational argument to refute it. All I can do is to suggest, as you read this chapter, that you notice whether something besides reason tugs at your heart. Look where reason, practicality, and playing it safe have brought us. Maybe it is time to listen to that other something.

I usually do not advocate heroic, abrupt transitions. If you are wealthy, perhaps a good way to gently adopt nonaccumulation is to apply demurrage to your own accumulated wealth right now, shrinking it by about 5 percent per year. It is going to happen anyway in a sacred economy—why not start living it now?

Poor people, of course, have always lived in nonaccumulation. The economy is now forcing it upon the middle class as well, as most people buy things on credit instead of saving up for them. While interest-bearing debts will no longer dominate economic life in the future, the obsolescence of savings, already well underway for the vast majority of Americans, is a forerunner of a nonaccumulative economy.

There is still a role for large aggregations of capital, and there are people who have a gift for using money as a medium of sacred creativity, as a ritual talisman for the coordination of human activity and the focusing of human intention. It is money that decides whether, tomorrow, five thousand people will build a skyscraper, clean up a toxic waste dump, or create a high-tech film. Of course, there are other rituals through which we coordinate human activity, some of which invoke stories and powers prior even to money, but it is a potent tool nonetheless. This is the essence of "sacred investing," the subject of the next chapter. To the holders of wealth, I invite you to think in terms of what you will create through collective human agency. Or, how can you use money in the most beautiful way?

Each organism in nature, each cell in the body, can handle only a certain volume of energy throughput. We are the same. Too much flow through a channel can burst the channel. Too big an accumulation is a tumor. Frivolous purchases such as a castle you never go to, or a fifteenth Rolls-Royce, are symptoms of excessive income. The organism is desperately trying to dissipate the energy flow, letting go and holding on at the same time. What the profligate rich man really wants to do is to give it away so as to balance giving and receiving, yet instead he just buys stuff and keeps it. What is the fear that impels him to hold on even as he lets go? It is the fear that rules the separate self, alone in the universe. Accumulation is a way to enlarge the tiny separate self. Yet ultimately this enlargement is a blatant lie. We leave this world as we entered it: naked.

Most of the baubles of the rich are substitutions for what they truly need—sports cars substituting for freedom, mansions compensating for the lost connections of a shrunken self, status symbols in place of genuine respect from self and others. A sad game it is, the charade of wealth. Even the security it supposedly brings is a deceit, as life's travails have a way of infiltrating the fortress of wealth, afflicting its inhabitants with distorted forms of the same social ills that affect everyone else. Of course, you can imagine various medical emergencies and such in which wealth can be a lifesaver, but so what? We are all going to die anyway, and no matter how long you live, the moment will come when you look back upon your years and they seem short, a flash of lightning in the dark of night, and you realize that the purpose of life is not after all to survive in maximum security and comfort, but that we are here to give, to create that which is beautiful to us.

Lest you think I am doing some noble thing in practicing nonaccumulation, let me assure you that when I began to live in this way, I had no sense of self-sacrifice, but rather of lightness and freedom. I am a person of quite average generosity, and far from saintly. This is not a noble idea I am offering you; it is a practical one. First, because it keeps my heart light and free. Second, because I know that as I give, so shall I receive. Third, because I will live in an ongoing wealth of connectedness, the expansion of the circle of self that happens through the Gift. Fourth, because I believe that I will live beautifully even in material terms. For example, I love the sea, and for years I dreamed of one day living in a house by the shore. It is a dream so vivid I can hear the gulls and smell the salty air. I once thought that to have it, I would have to make an awful lot of money. Now I believe that though I may never "own" a house by the sea, I will be invited to stay in one "any time," and when the owner says, "Make yourself at home," he will mean it from the bottom of his heart.

If the world receives my work enthusiastically, then I expect to receive a great many gifts, far more than I can use for myself. What a waste it would be to accumulate great assets, stocks and bonds, investments and portfolios, basements and attics full of possessions! Why accumulate when there is so much excess in this world to share? Whether or not a decaying currency and gift economy appear in this lifetime, we can live in it right now. We can, to use Gesell's phrase, reduce money to the rank of umbrellas, freely lending it or giving it to friends who are in need. There is, of course, no guarantee that I will always receive the money or other gifts I need when I need them. I expect sometimes to have no money at all, but for this to be a matter of little anxiety. On the other hand, I might starve and regret not having accumulated and protected a nest egg. But I doubt it, and for me the freedom from worry and anxiety— the open, flowing, light experience of letting it go—far outweighs the risk. If you want guarantees, then go ahead and accumulate, until you discover that the promised security is a mirage, that life's vicissitudes have a way of invading the fortress of wealth.

At a deep level, the distinction between accumulation and non-accumulation is a false distinction that smuggles in assumptions of scarcity and separation. A gift mind-set experiences the abundance of the world as a personal abundance and lives an experience of life that conforms to that mind-set. The mind-set of separation sees gifts, loans, and savings as three very different things, but are they really? If I am in a phase of life where I receive more than I can use, I could give it away, thereby generating gratitude, or I could loan it to others, relying on obligation instead of gratitude, or I could just save the money, seemingly not relying on other people at all. But these three choices are not as different as they may seem. First, as discussed earlier, a very blurry line divides gratitude and obligation, and in gift cultures each reinforces the other. Whether it is gratitude that moves someone to give to those who have given or the social agreements that, ultimately, are based on the very same principle of gratitude (the rightness of giving to those who give), the result is the same. As for savings and investment, in a credit-based currency system like our own, these are no different from lending. A savings account is a loan-at-call to a bank. Like a loan, monetary savings says, "I have given to others in the past and can call upon others to give to me in the future." Even in the case of equities or physical commodities, accumulation depends on social conventions of ownership.

In a sense, then, it is impossible for the recipient of gifts *not* to accumulate. As long as I give within a social witnessing, I will build up a source of abundance for the future. (Even if there is no social witnessing, I believe the universe will return to us what we have given, perhaps in some other form, perhaps, indeed, multiplied a hundredfold.) Ultimately, then, the essence of nonaccumulation lies in the intention with which money is given, lent, invested, or saved. In the spirit of the gift, we focus on the purpose and let the return to ourselves be secondary, an afterthought. In the spirit of accumulation, we seek to ensure and maximize the return and let the destination of the gift, loan, or investment serve that end. The former is a state of freedom, abundance, and trust. The latter is a state of anxiety, scarcity, and control. Whoever lives in the former is rich. Whoever lives in the latter is poor, no matter how much wealth he or she possesses.

In the future, when social mechanisms are in place to eliminate economic rents (i.e., profits from merely owning land, money, etc.), the way of living I have described will accord with economic logic, not just spiritual logic. When money decays anyway, it is better to lend it to others at zero interest than it is to keep more than you need. Moreover, as the mentality of abundance becomes prevalent, the distinction between a loan, a gift, and an investment will blur. We will be secure in knowing that whether or not there is a formal agreement to repay a gift, an obligation has been created, if not with a particular person then with society or even the universe. This realization is a natural consequence of the new Story of Self—the connected self—that underlies the sacred economy we are transitioning into. More for you is more for me. From the spiritual perspective this has always been true, even at the height of the Age of Separation. From the economic perspective, it was true in the gift culture of yore, and it is becoming true again as we establish new economic institutions to recreate gift economics in a modern context.

These new, gift-aligned economic institutions are both a cause *and a result* of a change in general attitudes. When enough people begin to live in nonaccumulation, they will establish a psychic foundation upon which the new economic institutions can stand. Practically speaking, people will recognize the new kinds of money as something that reflects their values and spiritual intuitions. They will "get it"; they will adopt it enthusiastically. This is happening already: despite the huge structural disincentives for using complementary currencies, people still find them exciting and alluring. Even though there is as yet little economic reason to use them, people want to anyway, understanding intuitively that these currencies are in alignment with the new Story of Self they are stepping into. Already, our spiritual intuitions signal in advance the truth of coming times: that possessions are a burden, that true wealth comes from sharing, that as we do unto others, so we do unto ourselves.

CHAPTER 20

RIGHT LIVELIHOOD AND SACRED INVESTING

We have lived our lives by the assumption that what was good for us would be good for the world. We have been wrong. We must change our lives so that it will be possible to live by the contrary assumption, that what is good for the world will be good for us. And that requires that we make the effort to know the world and learn what is good for it.

—Wendell Berry

Surplus wealth is a sacred trust which its possessor is bound to administer in his lifetime for the good of the community.

—Andrew Carnegie

THE DHARMA OF WEALTH

Let us be clear: the purpose of nonaccumulation is not to exculpate oneself from the crimes of a money-based civilization. That is merely ego. You don't get virtue points for poverty; nonaccumulation is not a goal in and of itself. The goal is to enjoy true wealth, the wealth of connection and flow, rather than the counterfeit wealth of having. But what if you have wealth beyond what you can share in the ordinary flow of life?

To the conscientious person, such wealth might seem to be more a burden than a gift. We are bound, and we are pleased, to make right use of what we have been given. Wealth is no exception. Those who are blessed and cursed with a lot of it have no more reason to abdicate its duties than anyone has to spurn the gifts, responsibilities, and opportunities to serve that we are each born with.

Excess wealth, whether inherited from family or from an earlier time in one's own life, carries with it a desire to use it well. It is a dharma, a call to service. To squander it on baubles, to give it away senselessly, or to devote oneself to its increase are all ways of refusing that call. The challenge of excess wealth is to give of it in a way that is beautiful. This may take years or decades and involve long-term planning and the creation of entire organizations, or it may happen through a single generous act. Either way, this is the kind of investment that is aligned with a future economy in which status comes from giving, not having, and security comes not from accumulation, but from being a nexus of flow. It is an entirely different mentality from the traditional paradigm of investment, which we equate with the increase of wealth.

Originally I thought that we ought to do away with the word and concept of *investment* altogether. Then I considered its etymology: it means to clothe, as in to take naked money and put it into new vestments, something material, something real in the physical or social realm. Money is naked human potential—creative energy that has not yet been "clothed" with material or social constructions.

Right investment is to array money in sacred vestments: to use it to create, protect, and sustain the things that are becoming sacred to us today. These are the same things that will form the backbone of tomorrow's economy. Right investment is therefore practice for the coming world, both psychological practice and practical preparation. It accustoms one to the new mentality of wealth—finding channels for productive giving—and it creates and strengthens those channels, which might persist even when the present money system collapses. Money as we know it might disappear, but the relationships of gratitude and obligation will remain.

If you'll indulge a bit of poetic speculation, all I have said in the previous paragraph is also true of that other "coming world"— the world beyond the grave. You needn't believe in an afterlife to understand this. Imagine yourself on your deathbed, realizing that you will take nothing with you. Just as financial investments won't survive economic collapse, so also does the end of life mean the end of all our accumulations. At that moment, what will give you joy? The memory of all you have given. *Upon death, we take with us only what we have given.* As in a gift culture, that is what our wealth will be. By giving, we lay up treasures in heaven. When we merge with the All, we receive that which we gave to all.

For people with little money, the most beautiful way to use it probably starts with feeding oneself and one's children and meeting certain basic necessities of human life. Beyond oneself and one's loved ones, though, the beautiful use of money requires something we might call "investing." In a sacred economy, investment has a meaning nearly opposite of what it means today. Today, investing is what people do to preserve their wealth. In a sacred economy, it is what we do to share our wealth.

Like nonaccumulation, the concept is so simple that even a child can understand it. It says, "I have more money than I can use, so I will let someone else use it." That is an investment or a loan. And a bank or other investment intermediary is someone who is adept at finding someone else to use it. Banking, in its sacred dimension, says, "I will help you find someone who can use your money beautifully." I once shared this idea with an actual banker whom I met at a conference, and tears came to his eyes—tears of the recognition of the spiritual essence of his calling.

A thousand years from now, when money is so different from what we know today that we might not even recognize it as money, the basic idea of investment will remain. That is because, thanks to the fundamental abundance of the universe and the infinitude of human creativity, we will often have access to a flow of gifts far beyond our immediate needs. We will always have the wherewithal—increasing over time—to create marvels through collective human effort and in partnership with Lover Earth. At the most basic level, sacred investing is simply the intentional channeling of this superabundance toward a creative purpose. It begins with the meeting of needs and unfolds into the creation of beauty.

ROBBING PETER TO PAY PAUL

Right investing manifests the spirit of the gift. Unfortunately, present-day investing bears the opposite spirit: either it is motivated by the extraction not the bestowal of wealth, or the return gift is specified in advance or coerced thereafter, or both. It says, "I will give you the use of this money, but only if you give me even more in return." Whether it is an equity investment or a loan, I am profiting through my exclusive possession of a scarce resource, with the goal of controlling more and more of it. Another way to see it is that the impetus for the return gift is not gratitude. Despite what the chairman's message in the annual report says, the board of directors does not determine its dividend payment in a spirit of gratitude to its millions of faceless investors.

Even before an economy realizing the core principles of the gift crystallizes, we can begin living it. Right investing—investing according to the spirit and logic of the Gift—is possible right now. The ideas I am about to offer will become much more obvious after the transition to a new economy, and the overarching stories of that economy—the connected self and Lover Earth—will support them. Today, to apply these ideas requires faith, vision, and courage. You will not receive the affirmation of any person or institution still immersed in the old story. From their perspective, what I am about to offer you is insane.

What I am going to describe is far more radical than "socially conscious investing" or "ethical investing." While these ideas are steps in the right direction, they harbor an internal contradiction. By seeking a positive financial return, they perpetuate the conversion of the world into money.

Traditional investment, which is perfectly defensible in the context of Ascent, seeks to contribute to the growth of the money realm and gain a part of that contribution as a reward. The venture capitalist identifies high-growth opportunities and provides the money to bring them to fruition. In a steady-state or degrowth economy, this model is no longer appropriate, just as it *feels* no longer appropriate for more and more people in the investing class—hence the turn toward a different investment goal: the restoration, and not the more efficient exploitation, of the natural and social commons.

Let me restate: there is no money to be made for the investors in such restoration. Any "socially conscious investment" scheme that promises a normal rate of return harbors a lie, whether consciously or not. I will illustrate with two examples.

After a talk I gave, a very bright and compassionate woman active in socially conscious investing protested, "Surely not all profitable investments contribute to the liquidation of the commonwealth. What if I invest in a company that has a great new invention for, say, cheap, portable photovoltaic chargers? I help to capitalize that company; they sell lots of units; we all make money; and the planet benefits too." Fine, but if the company sold the units at a lower price (e.g., just high enough a profit margin to finance R&D and capital reinvestment), then wouldn't it do the planet even more good by making the device more accessible? The goal of paying interest or dividends to investors, to give them a positive rate of return, conflicts with the goal that makes the company socially or environmentally "conscious."

Let me be clear—I am not suggesting that entrepreneurs put themselves out of business by selling at breakeven. I am talking about investing, not earning. It is one thing to receive rewards for doing good work in the world; it is quite another to add money to money by virtue of having money. In the above example, it would be fine to charge enough to keep the business viable, to pay employees well, and to finance expansion, research, and so forth. But beyond that, corporations must earn an additional amount that goes out to investors in the form of interest payments or dividends. Where does this additional amount come from? From the same place all money today comes from: interest-bearing debt and the conversion of the world into money. So if you really want to contribute to the good of the world, don't ask for a return on your investment. Don't try to give and take at the same time. If you want to take (and you might have good reasons for doing so), then take, but don't pretend you are giving.

A second example will make this point clearer. Consider one of the most inspiring types of socially conscious investing: microloans to women in South Asia. These programs have apparently been a huge success, empowering women in India and Bangladesh with new livelihoods while bearing an extremely low rate of defaults. If there were ever an example of "doing well by doing good," this is it. You lend $500 to an Indian woman to buy a milch cow. She sells the milk to her fellow villagers and earns enough income to feed her family and pay off the interest and principal on the loan. Sounds great, but consider for a moment: where does the repayment money come from? It comes from the villagers. And where do they get that money? They get it through selling some other good or service—in other words, through the conversion of some part of their social or natural commons into money as described in Chapter 4. The effect is the same as that of the infamous "hut tax" that the British (and other colonial powers) used to destroy the self-sufficient local economies of Africa during the colonial era.[1] It was simply a small annual tax, payable only in national currency, that forced the indigenous people to sell their labor and their local commodities for that currency. Local economies quickly unraveled and turned into a market for British goods and a source of labor and raw materials.

With her cow, the woman has far more milk than her family can consume. To whom will she give the surplus? Because she must pay back a monetary loan, like it or not she will give it to those willing and able to pay for it. If the cow had been free, and she'd had no compulsion to earn money, she might have distributed the milk through the channels of a traditional gift network. With a financial obligation hanging over her head, she cannot do this even if she wants to. Following this thread farther, who are those willing and able to pay for milk? They are those who themselves earn a

---

1. See, e.g., Pakenham, *The Scramble for Africa*, 497–98.

cash income. People who need milk cannot get it if they are living mostly in a gift economy. The entry of a new "business" into the village nudges it away from traditional reciprocity networks and toward the world of money.

If it weren't for the interest on the loan, the infusion of $500 into the community might not be a bad thing. It is often the case in modern impoverished communities that people have goods and services to exchange but lack the means to exchange them because of the breakdown of gift culture. The original owner of the cow might use the money to pay villagers for things he needs, and when that money eventually circulates back to the woman who bought the cow, many needs have been met, and nothing has been lost. Even if all the money goes back to the investor, at least no money has left the village.

If the loan bears interest, it is a different story entirely. Making an interest-bearing loan to this woman is tantamount to extracting money from her village. Imagine thinking, "Ah, in this village there is wealth that has not yet been converted into money. I am going to take some of it! I am going to make them my debt slaves." Not a very charitable impulse.

One of the key attractions of local currencies is that they ensure that money stays in the community. An interest-bearing loan of internationally convertible currency does the opposite—it sucks money out of the community. The woman sells the milk to a local cheese maker, who sells cheese to a carpenter, who builds a cow shed for the woman, and so on. The money circulates and circulates, but it cannot stay in the community forever because the debt must be repaid. As for the interest, that can only be paid if local people sell something to the outside world. The pressure on the woman to pay interest is passed on to the community in the form of milk prices. This is the pressure that drives people in poor countries to work in factories and plantations. In a monetized economy, where the original gift networks have collapsed, you need money to live. You will sell whatever you can—your labor, your time, your environment—in order to get it.

Economists will tell you that as long as the local economy is growing faster than the interest rate on the milch cow loan (or actually, the totality of loans issued to the village), the village can pay off the principal and interest and still grow wealthier. In other words, if the whole village, like the woman with the cow, sells new goods and services at a higher rate than the interest rate, it will be able to make its payments and prosper. But now the same question repeats itself: where does the money come from? On a global level, interest-based investing compels competition and the endless depletion of the social, natural, cultural, and spiritual commons—the conversion of the gift economy into a money economy.[2]

How obvious it is that sacred investing has little to do with turning a profit. If you want to help the village, then give a woman a cow. Or if her dignity demands it, lend the money at zero interest (which is a gift of the use of money). If you care more about increasing your monetary wealth instead, then do that instead and forget the pretense. The saying is true: you cannot serve two masters. In both the examples I gave, at some point the conflicting agendas come to the surface, and one must choose: to serve God or Mammon. But this choice will no longer pertain in a sacred economy.

---

2. A slight caveat: in theory, if the interest rate is no higher than the default risk premium, then there will be no necessity for economic growth and the monetization of the commons. The relevant components of the real interest rate, however, are the liquidity premium and the market rate for money, determined by supply, demand, and government monetary policy. These represent profit from the mere ownership of money, which is indefensible based on the arguments of Chapters 4 and 5.

The two will be united—part of a more general reunion of opposites that motivates the phrase the Age of Reunion to describe the coming time.

Socially conscious investments that promise a good rate of return are "robbing Peter to pay Paul"—with a commission on the transaction for oneself. I hope the foregoing explanation was unnecessary to most of my readers. After all, basic common sense tells us that there is a problem with the idea of good works motivated by profit. Profit might sometimes happen incidentally, but a gift that comes with a coerced demand for a greater gift in return is not a gift at all, but a ruse or a plunder.

Is that really who you are, to enforce a coldhearted separation in your life between business and other human relationships? When you invest money at interest, you are indirectly participating in telling some poor chap, "I don't care what you have to do to get it—give me the money!" Your certificate of deposit is someone else's foreclosure threat. You may not be acting like Ebenezer Scrooge, but you are paying someone else to.

If interest-generating investments are fundamentally unethical, contributing to the despoliation of the natural and social commons, then obviously we should not invest money at interest. The same goes for any investment that drives the expansion of the realm of goods and services. As socially conscious investors, you don't want to contribute to the monetization of life and nature.

There is no escape from this principle. Occasionally I receive emails from people in the financial industry who read my work and describe their ideas on socially or environmentally conscious investment. I then propose my own idea: an investment fund that has, as an explicit goal, a zero return on investment. For some reason, none of the financial professionals to whom I suggested this has ever contacted me again! In a negative-interest economy, though, a zero return on investment would be considered quite good.

I am not advocating an age of altruism in which we forgo personal benefit for the common good. I foresee, rather, a fusion of personal benefit and common good. For example, when I give money to people in my community, I create feelings of gratitude that might motivate a return gift to me or an onward gift to someone else. Either way, I have strengthened the community that sustains me. When we are embedded in gift community, we naturally direct our gratitude not only toward the proximate giver but toward the community as a whole, and we take care of its neediest members (gifts seek needs). Our desire to give may very well express itself as a gift to someone in the community who has given us nothing herself. Therefore, we can see any gift, even one without expectation of direct return, as a form of "investment." We are still taking naked money and, if it is a good investment, clothing it in something fine. A poor investment clothes it in something ugly. It is just that simple.

The negative-interest currency of the future will align the spirit of the gift with economic self-interest, and zero-interest loans will no longer feel like a sacrifice. After all, holding on to the money brings a return of *less* than zero. In the time remaining to us before such a system takes over, it apparently goes against rational self-interest to lend money at no interest, or to give it away. That, however, is a very shortsighted self-interest because while the present money system may easily disintegrate in the next few years, the ties of gratitude that gifts create will persist through any social tumult. If you are someone who is concerned about Peak Oil or one of the other collapse scenarios, the best security you can have is to ensconce yourself in a gift network. Start being a giver now. Ten million dollars might be just so many slips of paper in a few years.

This is another way that what you give in "this world" might be your treasure in the next.

If you want to create a world of abundance, a world of gratitude, a world of the gift, you can start by using today's money, while it still exists, to create more gratitude in the world. If we have a large enough reservoir of gratitude, then our society can withstand practically anything. Again, we live in a world of fundamental abundance that we have, through our beliefs and habits, rendered artificially poor. So badly have we damaged planet and spirit that it will require a full outpouring of all our gifts to heal it. The outpouring of gifts comes from gratitude. Therefore, the best investment you can make with your money is to generate gratitude. It doesn't matter if the gratitude recognizes you as the giver. Ultimately, the proper object of gratitude is the Giver of all our own gifts, of our world, of our lives.

To get ready for that economy, and to live today in its spirit, instead of investing money with the purpose of making more of it, we shift the focus of investment toward using accumulated money as the gift that it is: a gift from the old world to the new, a gift from the ancestors to the future. It is analogous to the gifts of life, of mother's milk, of food and sensory stimulation and all the things that build us into adults, which we receive in order that we may enter adulthood and give onward of these gifts. The question, then, is how to use money in the consciousness of a gift. If you are not an investor, then the question becomes one of right livelihood.

OLD ACCUMULATIONS TO NEW PURPOSES

The question "What are wealthy individuals to do with their pile of money?" suggests a broader one: What are we as a society to do with the accumulated wealth of thousands of years? What is this wealth, anyway, if not actually or no longer "deferred consumption"?

Let us also revisit the essence of money. What exactly is it that accumulates in these vast accumulations of money? Money consists of ritual talismans by which we coordinate human intention and activity. Those who possess an accumulation of money have, at their disposal, the means to focus and organize society's labor. The increase of money can come only at the cost of the nonmonetized realm, but the expenditure of money can restore that realm as long as that expenditure is not an investment that seeks the further commodification of the social or natural commons. Money can be used to buy logging equipment to clear-cut a forest; equally it can be used to preserve and guard that forest. The first use is money creation; the second is money destruction (because it generates no further goods and services). Either way, accumulated money bestows the ability to coordinate human activity on a large scale.

The image of sitting atop the accumulated wealth of centuries of exploitation is of particular relevance to the baby boom generation, the last to have come of age during the zenith of our civilization. They have a foot in both worlds, the old and the new. They have access (many of them) to the pile of wealth from the old world, but they are young enough that their consciousness has shifted into alignment with the new. My generation, once called Generation X, is different. Many of us, even from educated backgrounds, never had a foot in the old world. By the time we came of age, it was so obviously bankrupt that we couldn't bring ourselves to make our fortunes there. For someone entering adulthood in the 1960s or 1970s, it was still possible to believe in the project of ascent; it was still possible to fully participate in the Story of the People: conquering space, conquering the atom, mastering the universe, onward and upward. I imagine that if I'd been born in 1957 rather than 1967 (or if my father hadn't given me *Silent Spring, 1984,* and *A People's History of the United States* to read as a teenager) I would have followed the Program and would be a math professor at a university somewhere today. But it was not to be. By the time I came of age in the eighties, our story of the people was no longer compelling. I, and millions like me, basically dropped out. Of course I am vastly overgeneralizing, but I think there is truth in saying that whereas the children of the fifties and sixties became millionaire programmers for Microsoft, the children of the seventies and eighties are playing with Linux. This is not to impute any moral failing onto the Microsoft millionaires! In their day, it was still possible for a dynamic, visionary twenty-something to be excited about what was going on in the commercial software industry. The same goes for the central institutions of politics, academia, the arts, science, medicine, and so on. Of course, even then the inevitable denouement of the story of Ascent was apparent to those with eyes to see, as it had been apparent to mystics for thousands of years. For most, though, the crises were too far off, and the ideology of human dominion too deeply ingrained, to divert them from full participation in the project of ascent.

The social dynamics of which I speak are in part an America-centric phenomenon, but I think they generalize to a world that is on the cusp of a new age. Like the American baby boomers, the world sits on top of a huge pile of wealth, the end product of ten thousand years of culture and technology. We have a mighty industrial infrastructure; we have roads and airplanes; we have a vast apparatus already in existence that, for centuries, has been devoted toward the expansion of the human realm and the conquest of the natural. The time has come to turn the tools of separation, dominance, and control toward the purpose of reunion, the healing of the world. Just as the wealthy baby boomer or heir of fortunes past can turn her wealth toward a beautiful purpose, and not worry that the wealth is somehow tainted by its origins, so also do we have the opportunity and the responsibility to use the accumulated fruits of our domination of the earth in a beautiful way. This is true even of the most heinous, exploitative technologies—such as genetic engineering and nuclear fission—that have taken the program of control to its pinnacle of hubris. In the age of interest, that is the age of growth, the primary motivating force behind any new technology was to open up new realms for the conversion of natural or social wealth into money. Genetic engineering enabled the genome to become an exploitable natural resource, just as the steam engine enabled the mining of deep-seam coal and the iron plow the breaking of heavy sod. What will technology look like when devoted to the opposite purpose—the restoration of the planet's health?

When humanity as a whole goes through the same shift of consciousness that so many individuals have gone through in the last few decades that expelled them from the Matrix, who knows to what purposes we will turn the technologies of profit? When humanity is no longer under compulsion to grow its realm, we will turn our collective ingenuity and the amassed knowledge, information, and technology of the ages toward purposes aligned with the consciousness of ecology, connectedness, and healing. This is not to say that technology won't change. Technologies that are dominant today will retreat to marginal applications, while marginal technologies, including those dismissed or ridiculed today, will come to the fore.

Whether it is the application of accumulated technology or accumulated money, we want to be sure that we are not using it in the old mode: as a tool to achieve more separation from nature or more financial wealth. That is why I suggest the concept of *using money to destroy money.* By this I mean to use money to restore and protect the natural, social, cultural, and spiritual commons from which it was originally created. This has the effect of hastening the collapse and mitigating its severity. Usury-money is subject to a grow-or-die imperative. Any item of social or natural capital that we make off-limits to commoditization hastens the demise of usury-money; it "starves the beast." The realm within which (monetized) goods and services can expand shrinks. Every forest we prevent from being turned into board feet, every piece of land we remove from development, every person we teach to heal herself and others, every indigenous culture we insulate from cultural imperialism is one less place for money to colonize. The efforts of liberals and reformers, though impotent to halt the onward progress of the Machine, have not been in vain. Pollution limits, for instance, have kept at least a portion of the skies from being converted into money. Labor standards have prevented at least a part of workers' well-being from being converted into money. The antiwar movement makes the war business less profitable. Right-wing criticisms of pro-environment, pro-labor, antiwar policies are correct—they *do* hurt economic growth. If I go to an indigenous culture, convince its people that subsistence farming is degrading and primitive, and induce them instead to work in a factory and join the market economy, then GDP rises (and I've created an "investment opportunity"). If, on the other hand, I inspire people to abandon their high-paying jobs and "go back to the land," then GDP falls. If I create a community where we no longer pay for child care but instead care for each others' children cooperatively, then GDP falls. And if we succeed in protecting the Alaskan Wildlife Refuge from oil drilling, that's tens of billions of dollars that will never materialize. That is why I say we are using money to destroy money. Sometimes, the master's tools *can* dismantle the master's house.

Another way to look at it is that these efforts to protect a portion of the commonwealth raise the "bottom" to which we must fall before a transformation to a new world can crystallize. My use of the language of addiction recovery is deliberate. The dynamics of usury-money are addiction dynamics, requiring an ever-greater dose (of the commons) to maintain normality, converting more and more of the basis of well-being into money for a fix. If you have an addict friend, it won't do any good to give her "help" of the usual kind, such as money, a car to replace the one she crashed, or a job to replace the one she lost. All of those resources will just go down the black hole of addiction. So too it is with our politicians' efforts to prolong the age of growth.

Thanks to the efforts of generations of do-gooders, we will still have a portion of our divine bequest. There is still goodness in the soil; there are still healthy forests here and there; there are still fish in some parts of the ocean; there are still people and cultures that haven't completely sold off their health and creativity. This remaining natural, social, and spiritual capital is what will carry us through the transition and form the basis to heal the world.

If you are an investor, it is time to shift your focus entirely to the creation of connections, the generation of gratitude, and the reclamation and protection of the commonwealth. The time for the mind-set of wealth preservation is over. Wealth preservation brings to mind a swarm of rats, each clambering over the others to reach the top mast of a sinking ship. Instead, they could cooperate to gather the pieces to build a raft that is seaworthy. We have a long voyage ahead of us.

RIGHT LIVELIHOOD

The same principles that apply to right investing apply also to right livelihood; indeed, right livelihood and right investment are two sides of the same coin. If right investing uses money as gift to support the creation of a more beautiful world, then right livelihood accepts that gift as it does that work.

Traditional employment receives money for helping expand the monetized realm. We find that in order to earn money, we must participate in the conversion of the good, the true, and the beautiful into money. That is because of the money system—credit ultimately goes to those who can most effectively create new goods and services (or take it from those who create them). An interest-based money system exerts a systemic pressure to convert the commonwealth into money, and the highest remuneration goes to those who do that most effectively. You want to get rich? Invent a way to chop down trees more efficiently. Create an advertising campaign that persuades other nations to drink Coke instead of indigenous beverages. Seeing the workings of the global economy, many idealistic young people decide they want no part of it. I get letters from them all the time. "I want no part of this. I want to do what I love in a way that hurts no one. But there is no money in that. How do I survive?" How do you survive, not to mention access the large amounts of money to do great things, in a world that rewards the destruction of the very things you want to create?

Fortunately, there are people today who will give you money to do things that won't create more of it. These are precisely the people (or organizations or governments) that follow the spirit of "right investing" described above. Of course, living off the charity of others is no solution if they have to work all the harder (at the business of destruction) in order to earn the money they give to you. However, as I have observed, humanity possesses vast stores of wealth in many forms, the accumulation of centuries of exploitation, that can now be turned to other purposes, for example to preserve and restore natural, social, cultural, and spiritual capital. Doing this won't create more money; therefore whoever is paying for it is ultimately giving a gift.

In other words, the key to "right livelihood" is to live off of gifts. These can come in subtle forms. For example, say you sell fair-trade products. When someone buys one, at several multiples the cost of a functionally equivalent sweatshop product, the cost difference is essentially a gift.[3] They didn't *have* to pay that much. The same is true if your work is to install solar water heaters or build shelters for the homeless. Many traditional social service jobs, like social work, teaching, and so on, partake in the energy of the gift as long as they don't contribute to the more efficient operation of the earth-devouring machine, for example by training children to be efficient producers and mindless consumers. The source of the money could be a buyer, a foundation, or even the government. What makes it a gift is the motive—that it does not aim to get the cheapest price or generate even more money in return. Traditional employment is the opposite: I pay you a wage and profit from your productivity (of salable goods and services), which exceeds your wage. Traditional employment assists in the conversion of the world into money.

In a subtle way, any endeavor that shrinks the money realm draws on gifts. If you offer reskilling courses, train holistic healers,

---

3. I am aware that "fair trade" has become in many instances a brand that covers up the usual exploitation of labor and commoditization of culture, but the principle still applies.

or teach permaculture, you are ultimately shrinking the realm of goods and services. Tracing the money you receive from such endeavors back to its origin, somewhere down the line someone has made a "bad investment," violating the principle that governs money creation today: "Money goes to those who will make even more of it." It is no accident that there is usually little money to be made in reversing the conversion of life and the world into money.

If you are partial to principles, you might say that right livelihood abides by two. It applies your time, energy, and other gifts toward something that enhances, preserves, or restores some aspect of the commonwealth, and the money (or other return gift) that comes in return does not require for its providence harm to nature and people. Or to put it simply, it benefits other beings and does not harm other beings. I, however, don't live by principles; nor do I recommend it. Shall I attempt to calculate the relative costs and benefits of printing this book? It uses wood pulp from trees on the one hand; it might inspire people to create earth-sustaining systems on the other. People are adept at construing their choices in a way that aligns them with their principles; if the disconnect is too great, they alter their principles and pretend they held them all along.

Therefore, when it comes to right livelihood, I trust what feels good and right. What, you might ask, if it feels good and right to market toothpaste or work for a hedge fund or design nuclear weapons? I would say, then do it. First, because as your awareness of the world grows, such work may no longer feel good and right. Second, because you will condition yourself to trusting that feeling, it will continue to guide you when it comes time to quit that job and do something courageous. Third, because denying our inner yearnings for the sake of principle is part of the story of Ascent, of overcoming nature. The idea that our desires are evil, that we must conquer them for the sake of something higher, is its interior reflection. It is the same mind-set that refrains from generosity, because what if I cannot afford it? The self-trust I advocate is inseparable from the basic premise of this book, laid out in Chapter 1: we are born into gratitude, born into the need and the desire to give.

In other words, trust that it is not your true desire to comply with the conversion of the world into money. Trust that you want to do beautiful things with your life.

In right livelihood, then, I suggest that we orient ourselves toward our need and desire to give. I suggest that we look at the world with eyes of, "What opportunity is there to give?" and "How may I best give of my gifts?" Hold that intention in mind, and unexpected opportunities arise. Quickly, any situation in which you are not giving your life gifts toward something that is good to you becomes intolerable.

It is OK if "what feels good and right" is merely feeding your family. The key is the attitude of service. If you attempt to guilt yourself into right livelihood, you will likely end up with its counterfeit. Some entire nongovernmental organizations (NGOs) are but enormous vanity projects, elaborate ways to allow people to approve of themselves. That's all ego. The purpose of right livelihood is not so you get to have a positive self-image. People who do it for that reason are quite obvious from their defensiveness, sanctimony, and self-righteousness. The purpose of right livelihood is to give your energies toward something you love. The concept should feel liberating, not like a moral burden, not another thing you are supposed to do right in order to be good.

To enter more deeply into right livelihood, bow into service each day. Trust your desire to give, remember how good it feels, and be open to opportunities to do so, especially when they are just at the edge of your courage. And if they are beyond the edge of your courage, don't torment yourself. The fears that block your givingness are not an enemy. They form a cocoon of safety. When we grow, the fears that were once protective become limiting; we become impatient with them and seek to break free. That impatience bears new courage. Today, this growth process is happening to humanity generally. The program of Ascent that once seemed good and right to us—pushing the frontiers of science, conquering the universe, triumphing over nature—seems right no longer, as the consequences of that ambition become painfully hard to ignore. Collectively we have entered a crisis moment, in which the old is intolerable and the new has not yet manifested (not as a common vision, though it has for many individuals).

So, when it comes to right livelihood or right investment, let us be gentle. For ourselves and others, let us trust the natural desire to give, and let us trust the natural growth process that propels us toward it. Instead of attempting to guilt ourselves and others into it (and generating resistance to our sanctimony), we can offer opportunities and encouragement to give, and we can be generous with our appreciation and celebration of the gifts of others. We can see others not as selfish, greedy, ignorant, or lazy people who just "don't get it," but rather as divine beings who desire to give to the world; we can see that and speak to that and know it so strongly that our knowing serves as an invitation to ourselves and others to step into that truth.

CHAPTER 21

WORKING IN THE GIFT

Strange is our situation here upon earth. Each of us comes for a short visit, not knowing why, yet sometimes seeming to a divine purpose. From the standpoint of daily life, however, there is one thing we do know: that we are here for the sake of others.

—Albert Einstein

TRUSTING GRATITUDE

The question comes up again and again: How can I share my gifts in today's money economy and still make a living? Some people who ask this question are artists, healers, or activists who despair of finding a way to "get paid for" what they do. Others have a successful business or profession but have begun to feel that something is amiss with the way they charge for their services.

Indeed, to charge a fee for service, or even for material goods, violates the spirit of the Gift. When we shift into gift mentality, we treat our creations as gifts to other people or to the world. It is contrary to the nature of a gift to specify, in advance, a return gift, for then it is no longer giving but rather bartering, selling. Furthermore, many people, particularly artists, healers, and musicians, see their work as sacred, inspired by a divine source and bearing infinite value. To assign it a price feels like a devaluation, a sacrilege. But surely the artist deserves to be compensated for his work, right?

The idea behind the word "compensation" is that you have, by working, made a sacrifice of your time. You have spent it doing work when you could have instead spent it on something you want to do. Another context in which we use the word is lawsuits, for example when someone seeks compensation for an injury, for pain and suffering.

In an economy that deserves the adjective "sacred," work will no longer be an injury to one's time or life; it will no longer be a matter of pain and suffering. A sacred economy recognizes that human beings desire to work: they desire to apply their life energy toward the expression of their gifts. There is no room in this conception for "compensation." Work is a joy, a cause for gratitude. At its best, it is beyond price. Doesn't it sound blasphemous to you to speak of, say, *compensating* Michelangelo for painting the Sistine Chapel or Mozart for composing his Requiem? No finite amount of money is sufficient in exchange for the divine. Of the most sublime works, the only appropriate means of offering them is to give them away. Even if, at the moment, few of us have access to the genius of a Mozart, we are all capable of sacred work. We are all capable of channeling, through our skills, something greater than ourselves. Something takes form through us, using us as the instrument for its manifestation on earth. Can you see how foreign the concept of "compensation" is to this kind of work? Can you feel the dishonor in selling a sacred creation? No matter what the price, you have sold yourself short, and you have sold short the source from whence the gift came. I like to put it this way: "Some things are too good to sell. We can only give them away."

Questions immediately arise in the reader. Despite the foregoing, you may have even caught yourself again thinking, "But doesn't an artist deserve to be compensated for his work?" The intuitions of separation run so deeply! So let us rephrase it: "Doesn't the giver of great gifts deserve to receive great gifts in return?" The answer, insofar as "deserves" means anything at all, is yes. In a sacred economy, this will happen through the mechanism of gratitude rather than compulsion. The attitude of the seller says, "I will give you this gift—but only if you pay me for it, only if you give me what I think it is worth." (Yet no matter what the price, the seller will always feel shortchanged.) The attitude of the giver, in contrast, says, "I will give you this gift—and I trust you to give me what you think is appropriate." If you give a great gift, and no gratitude results, then perhaps that is a sign that you have given it to the wrong person. The spirit of the Gift responds to needs. To generate gratitude is not the goal of giving; it is a sign, an indicator, that the gift was given well, that it met a need. That is another reason I disagree with certain spiritual teachings that say a person of true generosity will not desire to receive anything, even gratitude, in return.

Now let's make this practical. After wrestling with this issue for some time, I realized that while it feels wrong to charge money for my work, it feels fine to accept money from people who feel grateful for having received it. The degree of gratitude is unique to each person. I cannot know in advance how valuable this book will be to you; even you cannot know it in advance. That is why it is contrary to the spirit of the gift to pay for something unknown in advance. Lewis Hyde illustrates this point most insightfully:

> It may be clearer now why I said above that a fee for service tends to cut off the force of gratitude. The point is that a conversion, in the general sense, cannot be settled upon ahead of

time. We can't predict the fruits of our labor; we can't even know if we'll really go through with it. Gratitude requires an *unpaid* debt, and we will be motivated to proceed only so long as the debt is *felt*. If we stop feeling indebted we quit, and rightly so. To sell a transformative gift therefore falsifies the relationship; it implies that the return gift has been made when in fact it can't be made until the transformation is finished. A prepaid fee suspends the weight of the gift and depotentiates it as an agent of change. Therapies and spiritual systems delivered through the market will therefore tend to draw the energy required for conversion from an aversion to pain rather than from an attraction to a higher state.[1]

Accordingly, I have taken what steps I can to conduct my work in alignment with the spirit of the gift. For example, I make as much as possible of my writing, sound recordings, and videos available online for no charge and invite readers to give a gift in return that reflects their degree of gratitude. This gift need not go to me. If the gratitude is, for instance, toward the universe for making my work available, perhaps a more appropriate way of giving is to "pay it forward."

I use a similar model in my public speaking. When I am asked my speaker's fee, I say that I do not charge a fee. Usually I request that my travel expenses be covered; beyond that, I say something like, "It is up to you. Give me whatever amount, or none at all, that leaves you with a feeling of clearness, balance, and appropriateness, an amount that reflects your gratitude for my coming to be with you." This is not a formula, it is a spirit that adapts itself to each unique situation. If they have a standard speaker's honorarium, I

---

1. Hyde, *The Gift*, 66.

won't necessarily insist on an exception for myself. Moreover, sometimes an up-front offer communicates to me how much they desire what I have to offer. I want to give my gifts where they are wanted, and money is one of several ways to communicate that desire.

It is important not to make "living in the gift" into a fetish, or into a standard of virtue. Don't do it in order to be good. Do it in order to feel good. If you find yourself rejoicing (as I do) over a big fat check, that is OK! We humans are delighted to receive big gifts. Even if you find yourself (again, as I sometimes do) feeling miserly, resentful, and grasping, simply take note of that as well. The road back to the gift is a long one, so distanced from it we have become. I see myself as one of many explorers of a new (and ancient) territory, learning from the discoveries of others and from my own mistakes.

When I lead retreats, I charge only for room and board and other out-of-pocket expenses, and invite gifts.[2] It has taken some time for me to enter a state of consciousness where this model actually "works." If I resent those who give nothing, if I intend, through the enunciation of high-sounding principles, to coerce or manipulate people into giving beyond what genuine gratitude dictates, or if I subtly "guilt" people into giving by hinting at my hardship, sacrifice, or entitlement by virtue of poverty, then I am not living in the spirit of the gift at all. I am living instead in a subtle kind of scarcity mentality or beggary, and, as if to mirror that state, the flow of gifts dries up almost immediately. Not only do people refrain from giving, but my own wellspring of gifts dries up as well.

---

2. Why do I even charge to cover expenses? It is because I see the events as cocreations. We each contribute something to allow the event to happen. This is not in the realm of gratitude; it is in the realm of cocreation, a gathering of resources for the realization of an intention.

As long as my gift intention is authentic, I find that the inflow of gifts matches or exceeds the outflow. Sometimes the vehicle of the return gift is mysterious, indirectly traceable or not traceable at all to anything I have given, yet somehow, when it comes, it carries something of the spirit of the original offering. Sometimes only an exiguous trail of synchronicity and symbol connects the gift I have received with the gift I have given. The rational mind says the return gift has nothing at all to do with what I gave—"I would have received that anyway"—but the heart knows otherwise.

Because the return gift comes later, as we step into gift-based livelihood we live for a time in faith. With no assurance of return, we learn whether we really mean it. The ego struggles and thrashes, trying to find an assured benefit. If not money, maybe I can advertise my generosity to receive praise. Maybe I can secretly congratulate myself and feel superior to those who are less in the gift than I am. In my experience, each new step into the gift is scary. The letting go has to be real, or there will be no return.

BUSINESS IN THE GIFT

Now let us apply this model to other kinds of businesses. There are already a number of enterprises today that are implementing gift economics in creative ways. I don't uphold my own model as the best or only way of living in the gift. We are pioneering a new kind of economy, and it is going to take some trial and error to get it right. I'll offer a few examples of people doing business according to one or both of the key principles of the gift I have discussed: (1) The recipient, and not the giver, determines the "price" (the return gift); (2) The return gift is chosen after the initial gift has been received, not before.

In Berkeley, California, the Karma Clinic has been treating people with holistic medicine on a gift basis for two years. After the consultation or treatment, the client receives a "bill" that reads,

"Your consultation is a generous gift from someone that came before you. If you would like to gift-forward in that spirit, you can do so however you choose. Monetary or other gifts may be left in the gift box in the Karma Clinic office or mailed to ..." In Ashland, Oregon, another gift-based clinic called the Gifting Tree has formed. There are doubtless many more around the country, and they appear to be quite sustainable: the Victoria Attunement Center operated purely on a donation basis from 1982 to 1988 and, according to its founder Will Wilkinson, was completely self-supporting with over 300 client visits per month.

The gift model has also been applied to restaurants. The One World restaurant in Salt Lake City, in operation since 2003; the SAME (So All May Eat) Cafe in Denver, in operation since 2008; A Better World Cafe in New Jersey, which opened in 2009; the Karma Kitchen in Berkeley; and many more operate on a dona-tion-only basis—and many of them serve organic food to boot.

Recently the idea entered the mainstream when the national restaurant chain Panera Bread opened a pay-what-you-want store in St. Louis, Missouri. The menu is exactly the same as at its other stories, but the prices are guidelines only. Patrons are asked to pay whatever feels right: the sign at the counter says, "Take what you need, leave your fair share." If this experiment works, the company plans to expand the model to locations around the country. I won-der if they realize that they are pioneering not just a model of civic virtue, but also a model of business for the future.

On the internet, of course, an enormous gift economy thrives. Versions of all major types of productivity software are available at no charge. For example, the office suite OpenOffice, a collaborative effort by hundreds of volunteer programmers, is available at no charge. I am hesitant to use the phrase "for free" here, because those words imply almost a repudiation of any return gift. The OpenOffice organization does accept donations and encourages those who have downloaded the software to contribute in various ways.

Lots of bands offer their music "for free" online as well. The most notable pioneer of the gift business model for recorded music was Radiohead, which offered its 2007 *In Rainbows* album on a pay-what-you-will basis. Although nearly two-thirds of downloaders chose to pay nothing, hundreds of thousands did choose to pay a few dollars for it, and millions more copies were purchased on iTunes, as CDs, and through other channels. Critics dismissed this success as an anomaly made possible by Radiohead's iconic status, yet the basic model continues to proliferate, especially in the music industry as traditional distribution channels becomes increasingly impractical for most bands.

Astonishingly, there is even a law firm that has incorporated a pay-what-you-will element into its business. The Valorem Law Group, a trial law firm based in Chicago, has added a "value adjustment line" feature to its bills. At the bottom of the bill, above an empty "Total due" box, is a box labeled "Value adjustment." The client writes a positive or negative number there and adjusts the final fee accordingly. I am full of admiration for this firm, because from a legalistic point of view this feature is quite insane. Someone could "adjust" the bill by the full amount and pay nothing, and the firm would probably have no legal recourse.

Now let's generalize these examples into a broadly applicable business model. The fundamentals are quite simple. The first guideline is to charge money only to cover your own direct costs. This includes marginal costs and apportioned fixed costs, but not sunk costs. So, for example, if you install plumbing for someone, you would charge for materials (with zero markup), fuel to reach the site, and perhaps half a day's worth of your current payments on capital equipment (e.g., your truck loan, business loan, etc.). You would make it clear to the recipient that your time, labor, and expertise are a gift. The bill might have the total costs, and then a blank line labeled "gift," and then the line labeled "total" underneath it.

A variant of this model is to follow Valorem and display a normal fee that reflects the market price with a line under it labeled "value adjustment" or "gratitude adjustment." Most people will probably just pay the market price, but you can explain that they can adjust it if they are especially satisfied or dissatisfied with the work.

Another variant is not to charge anything at all but to delineate various line items such as "cost of materials," "apportioned cost of business expenses," "hours of labor," "market price for this service," and so on. That way the recipient can choose to pay nothing at all, not even for materials, but at least she has this information. This information, like the note in the Karma Clinic, is "the story of the gift" referenced earlier. Traditionally, gifts were often accompanied by stories that helped the receiver appreciate their value.

The gift business model is actually not as far from standard business practice as you might think. Today, a common negotiating tactic is to say, "Look, here are my costs; I can't go any lower than that."[3] It is not such a huge shift of perspective to say, "Here are my costs. You can pay me more according to the value you believe you have received." Often the customer will have a pretty good

---

3. Of course, actual costs are usually lower than anyone reveals, and other factors come into play such as the fixed costs of idle equipment and employees if no agreement is reached.

idea of the market price of the goods or services you are offering and, if there is any genuine humanity at all in the business relationship, will probably pay close to that. If he or she does pay a premium above the base cost, you can interpret that as indicating the presence of gratitude. If someone is grateful for what you have given, you will desire to give more. If someone is ungrateful, you know that the gift is not being fully received, and you will probably choose not to give to that person again.

Translated into a business relationship, what this means is that you will choose not to do business again with someone who pays you little or nothing above cost, and you will preferentially do business with someone who, using money as token, communicates her high degree of gratitude. This is as it should be. Some people need our gifts more than others. If you have bread, you want to give it to the hungry person. Displays of gratitude help to orient us toward the best expression of our gifts. So, just as today, a business will tend to do business with those who pay the most money (although nonmonetary expressions of gratitude may also come into play). This is different from tending to do business with those who offer the best price. The difference is key. In keeping with the spirit of the gift, the price is not offered ahead of time. The gift is offered first, and only after it is received is a return gift made.

I cannot help but notice a parallel between this approach and various game-theoretic studies of altruism and iterated prisoner's dilemma problems. Look up "tit-for-tat" in Wikipedia for some background on this topic. Essentially, in many situations where there are repeated interactions among discrete entities with varying payoffs for cooperation and betrayal, the optimal strategy is to cooperate first and retaliate only against someone who didn't cooperate last time. Analogous reasoning leads me to think that the business model I have outlined can actually be more financially successful over time than the standard model.[4]

Because gift mentality is so alien to us today, doing business in the gift sometimes requires a bit of education. I've found that if I advertise an event as "by donation," people sometimes treat it as a throwaway, thinking, "It must not be very valuable or very important if he isn't charging for it." They'll come late or not at all, or they'll come with low expectations. Paying a fee is a kind of ritual that sends a message to the unconscious that "this is something valuable" or "I am doing this for real." I and many others are still experimenting to find better ways to invoke the benefits of payment while staying true to the spirit of the gift. We are at the beginning of a new era, so it is going to take some practice and experimentation.

Obviously, at the time of this writing most corporations and business owners are not ready to step into a gift-based business model. That's OK—you can give them a little push! Simply implement it unilaterally by "stealing" their products, for example by illegally downloading or copying digital content like songs, movies, software, and so on. Then, if you feel grateful to the creators of it, send them some money. I would be quite happy if you did the same with this book. It will be hard to do it illegally, though, since I don't claim standard copyrights (I bet you didn't read the copyright page carefully, but it isn't the usual verbiage), and the content

---

4. These principles apply only if the business relationships are happening in a community. In cases where all interactions are one-time transactions with strangers, the gift model is less practicable. In ancient gift cultures this was also generally true; when there was barter, it happened between strangers. However, I have found that most people honor the spirit of the gift even when it is a one-time transaction. Could it be that we sense that we are indeed all part of an all-encompassing community and that our gifts, even our anonymous ones, happen in its witnessing?

is available online without charge. Nonetheless, if you do manage to "steal" this book, I will be pleased to receive an amount from you that reflects your gratitude—as opposed to the amount that I or the publisher presumes reflects its value to you. Each person's experience of reading it is unique: for some it may be a waste of time, for others it might be life-changing. Isn't it absurd to receive an identical return gift from everyone?

THE SACRED PROFESSIONS

The gift model comes especially naturally for professions in which the value delivered is something intangible. Musicians, artists, prostitutes, healers, counselors, and teachers all offer gifts that are debased when we assign them a price. When what we offer is sacred to us, then the only honorable way to offer it is as a gift.[5] No price can be high enough to reflect the sacredness of the infinite. By asking for a specific speaker's fee, I make less of my gift. If you are a member of one of the above professions, you might consider experimenting with a gift model of business—but remember, if you apply that model as a more clever means to "get paid," it won't work. People can detect a phony gift, a gift that isn't a gift but carries an agenda of gain.

In all of the above professions, the intangible rides the vehicle of something tangible, and it is the former, unquantifiable, that naturally wants to abide in the realm of the gift. This is actually true

---

5. Significantly, some of these professions have traditionally operated on the border between payment and gift. Artists and musicians would receive support from a patron, who would basically give them money so that they could work. This allowed people like Mozart to survive at a time before copyrights. Elite prostitutes have long worked on a similar model in which they receive gifts from their regular clients.

of every profession. Always, something is present that is beyond quantification, beyond commodity, and thus beyond price. Every profession is therefore potentially sacred. Consider the example of farming. What makes food—something tangible—a vehicle for the sacred?

- It is grown by someone who cares deeply about its nourishing and aesthetic qualities.
- It is grown in a way that enriches the ecosystem, soil, water, and life in general.
- Its production and processing contribute to a healthy society.

In other words, sacred food is ensconced in a web of natural and social relationships. It is grown with a love for people and earth that is not an abstract love but a love for *this* land and *these* people. We cannot love anonymously, which is perhaps why I've always gotten a somewhat cold feeling from anonymous charity that doesn't create connection. Somebody grew sacred food for *me*!

When we see our work as sacred, we seek to do it well for its own sake rather than "good enough" for something external such as the market, the building code, or a grade. A builder who does sacred work will employ materials and methods that might be hidden in the walls, beyond anyone's notice, for centuries. He derives no rational benefit from this, just the satisfaction of doing it right. So also the business owner who pays an above-market living wage or the manufacturer who far exceeds environmental standards. They have no rational expectation of benefit, yet somehow they *do* benefit, sometimes in ways that are completely unexpected. Unexpected returns accord perfectly with the nature of the Gift: as Lewis Hyde puts it, a gift "disappears around the corner," "into the mystery," and we don't know how it will travel back to us.

Another way to see the unexpected fruits that arise from the mystery is that when we live in the spirit of the gift, magic happens. Gift mentality is a kind of faith, a kind of surrender—and that is a prerequisite for miracles to arise. From the Gift, we become capable of the impossible.

I met a man in Oregon who owns a property management company specializing in low-income elder care facilities. "This," he says, "is an impossible business." Subject to the multiple, conflicting stressors of medical institutions, insurance companies, government regulation, the poverty of the residents, and general financial turmoil, his industry was in a state of crisis. The week I visited him, two of his largest competitors called begging him to take over their money-losing facilities. Yet somehow, this man has built a profitable, growing business, an empowering workplace, and human living environments that are a model for the industry. How does he do it? "Every day," he says, "I walk into the office to face a stack of impossible problems. I cannot imagine any way to solve them. So I do the only thing I can do: I bow into service. And then, like magic, solutions fall into my lap."

The one who bows into service is an artist. To see work as sacred is to bow into service to it, and thus become its instrument. More specifically and somewhat paradoxically, we become the instrument of that which we create. Whether it is a material, human, or social creation, we put ourselves into the humble service of something preexisting yet unmanifest. Thus it is that the artist is in awe of his or her own creation. I get that feeling when I read aloud from *The Ascent of Humanity:* "I could not have written this." That book is its own entity, born through me but no more my creation than parents create a baby, or a farmer a spinach plant. They transmit the impulse of life, they provide a place for it to grow, but they do not and need not understand the details of cell differentiation. I too nourished my growing book with every resource available to me, and birthed it with terrific hardship from its womb in my mind into physical form, and I am intimately familiar with its every nuance, yet I have an abiding sense that it existed already, that it is beyond my contrivance. Can a parent legitimately take credit for the accomplishments of his or her child? No. That is a form of theft. Nor will I take credit for the beauty of my creations. I am at their service.

I have drawn this out to show that the same logic that the Christian fathers, Thomas Paine, and Henry George applied to land applies as well to the fruits of human labor. They exist beyond ourselves—we are stewards at their service, just as we are properly stewards of the land and not its owners. As they are given to us, so we give them onward. That is why we are drawn to do business in the spirit of the Gift. It feels good and right because it aligns us with the truth. It opens us to a flow of wealth beyond the limits of our design. Such is the origin of any great idea or invention: "It came to me." How then can we presume to own it? We can only give it away, and thereby keep the channel open through which we will continue to receive sacred gifts, in diverse forms, from other people and all that is.

As an incentive to make the switch to a gift model of business, observe that for many of the sacred professions, the old model isn't working anymore. Here in the small city of Harrisburg, Pennsylvania, which is not exactly the most progressive place on earth, there are nonetheless literally hundreds of holistic, complementary, and alternative practitioners advertising in the local Holistic Health Networker. Hundreds. And probably at least half of them, upon entering their herbal studies program or yoga therapy program or naturopathy program, or their hypnotherapy, angelic healing, crystal healing, polarity therapy, Reiki, cranial-sacral therapy, holistic nutrition, massage therapy, or other program, had in mind a future career in an office or holistic health center seeing "clients" for "sessions" at $85 or $120 each. It is impossible that more than a handful will realize that dream. Yet the schools and training programs keep churning out new practitioners. Sooner or later, most of them will have to abandon the clients-and-sessions model and turn toward offering their skills as a gift.[6]

What is happening in these professions is starting to happen more generally. We might ascribe it to overcapacity, debt overhang, the "falling marginal return on investment," or some other economic factor, but the fact is that the old profit model is in crisis. Like the holistic practitioners I described, collectively we will soon have no choice but to adopt a different model en masse.

In the old economy, people pursued jobs and careers for the purpose of making a living. From the viewpoint of survival, nothing is too sacred to sell, to charge money for. If you are working for the sake of survival, such as in a lead mine in China, then it probably won't feel wrong to negotiate and demand the best price possible for your labor. Another way to look at it is that the survival of oneself and loved ones is itself a sacred endeavor.

I want to inject a note of gentleness and realism into this discussion. Please do not think I am advocating some saintly standard of altruism or self-sacrifice. You do not gain heavenly rewards for accepting a salary cut. If your main concern right now is survival or security, "work" to you will probably not be an avenue for the expression of your gifts. Your job will feel like just that, a "job"—

---

6. This is a trend toward the universalization of medicine, the migration of healing from the money economy back into the social commons.

something you do primarily for the money and would quit or radically change if you had no financial pressure. And even though you
may feel some sense of being ripped off, of living the life someone
is paying you to live but not your own life, the life of a slave compelled to work or to die, that doesn't mean you "should" overcome
your fears and quit that job and trust you'll be OK. Living in the
gift is not another thing you are supposed to do in order to be a
good person. Fear is not the new enemy in our continuing war
against the self, the successor to the old hobgoblins of sin and ego.
Sacred economics is part of a broader revolution in human beingness: internally, it is the end of the war against the self; externally,
it is the end of the war against nature. It is the economic dimension
of a new age, the Age of Reunion.

So, if you find yourself slaving away at a job, working for the
money, doing it "good enough" rather than "as beautifully as I am
able," I urge you to transition out of that job *when and only when you
are ready.* Perhaps for now you will see your job as a gift to yourself,
giving you a sense of security for as long as it takes for that feeling
to become second nature. Fear is not the enemy, despite what so
many spiritual teachers say. "The opposite of love," says one. "Fro-
zen joy," says another. Actually fear is a guardian, holding us in a
safe space in which to grow; you could even say that fear is a gift.
Eventually, as we grow, the fears that were once protective become
limiting, and we desire to be born. That this will happen is inevitable. Trust yourself now, and you will continue to trust yourself
when your desire moves you to transcend the old fears and enter
a larger, brighter realm. When the moment of birth comes, you
won't be able to stop yourself.

Ending the struggle to be good also means that giving does not
involve a feeling of sacrifice or self-abnegation. We give because

we want to, not because we should. Gratitude, the recognition that one has received and the desire to give in turn, is our innate default state. How could it not be, when life, breath, and world are gifts? When even the fruit of our own labors is beyond our contrivance? To live in the gift is to reunite with our true nature.

As you step into a gift mentality, let your feelings guide you. Let your giving arise from gratitude and not the desire to measure up to some standard of virtue. Perhaps the first steps will be small ones: adding little extras, doing small favors with no agenda of reward. Perhaps if you run a business, you will convert a small part of it to a gift model. Whatever steps you take, know that you are preparing for the economy of the future.

CHAPTER 22

COMMUNITY AND THE UNQUANTIFIABLE

Economics is extremely useful as a form of employment for economists.

—John Kenneth Galbraith

Earlier in this book I described the disconnection and loneliness of a society in which nearly all social capital, nearly all relationships, have been converted to paid services; in which distant strangers meet nearly all of our material needs; in which we can always "pay someone else to do it"; in which the unspoken knowledge *I don't need you* pervades our social gatherings, rendering them vacuous and dispensable. Such is the pinnacle of civilization, the end point of centuries of increasing affluence: lonely people in boxes, living in a world of strangers, dependent on money, enslaved to debt—and incinerating the planet's natural and social capital to stay that way. We have no community because community is woven from gifts. How can we create community when we pay for all we need?

Community is not some add-on to our other needs, not a separate ingredient for happiness along with food, shelter, music, touch, intellectual stimulation, and other forms of physical and spiritual nourishment. Community arises from the meeting of these needs. There is no community possible among a group of people who do not need each other. Therefore, any life that seeks to be independent of other people for the meeting of one's needs is a life without community.

The gifts that weave community cannot be mere superficialities; they must meet real needs. Only then do they inspire gratitude and create the obligations that bind people together. The difficulty in creating community today is that when people meet all their needs with money, there is nothing left to give. If you give someone a product that is for sale somewhere, either you are giving them money (by saving them the expense of buying it themselves) or you are giving them something they don't need (else they would have already bought it). Neither is sufficient to create community unless, in the first instance, the recipient actually needs money. Thus it is that poor people develop much stronger communities than rich people do. They have more unmet needs. This has been one of the greatest teachings of my period of poverty that followed the publication of *The Ascent of Humanity*. Out of necessity, I learned to receive without fear of stepping into obligation. The aid I received reawakened in me the primal gratitude of infancy, the realization that I am utterly dependent for my survival and existence on the web of giving that surrounds me. It empowered me to be more generous, too, having experienced and survived the ignominy of bankruptcy, of losing my apartment and sleeping with my children in other people's living rooms, and learning that it is OK to receive such help. Perhaps one benefit of the hard economic times that are encroaching upon our illusion of normalcy is that they will reawaken in more and more people this primal gratitude, borne of the necessity of receiving gifts in the absence of payment. As in infancy, periods of helplessness reconnect us to the principle of the gift. Other people I know have had similar realizations when severe illness rendered them helpless.

When I realized that the dissolution of community comes from the monetization of functions that were once part of the gift network, I could at first see no other way to recover community than to abandon the money economy and, by extension, the economic and industrial system of mass production. I could see no other way to reestablish community than to resume doing things "the hard way" again: doing things without machines. If community dies when strangers make all the things we need, then to restore it, I thought, we must return to local, and necessarily lower-tech, production—production not requiring a global division of labor.

It would be silly, though, to relinquish the things we have today simply in order to have community. It would be futile, too, because on some level we would sense the pretense. The needs met would not be real needs; they would be artificial. To say, "I could saw these boards in an hour with a table saw, but let's use a two-person handsaw instead and take two days, because that will make us more interdependent," is a delusion. Artificial dependency is not the solution to the artificial separation we have today. The solution is not to meet already-met needs less effectively, so that we are forced to help each other. Rather, it is to meet the needs that languish unfulfilled today.

It is not desire for community that will motivate a renaissance in traditional handcrafts and low-tech production. The cessation of hidden subsidies for energy-intensive centralized production and transport will support this renaissance, but will not force it. We will return to local production from a desire to improve life and meet unmet needs—a desire to become richer. The people who say, "We'd better learn how to use hand tools again because petroleum will become so expensive we'll have to," are indulging in a kind of fatalism. They hope we will be *forced* back into right livelihood. I

421

think we will choose it. The crises borne of separation will nudge us toward that choice with increasing force, but if we really desire as a species to maintain an ugly mass-produced way of life, we probably can for a long time to come, until we exhaust the very foundation of the biosphere. Peak Oil will not save us! Instead, we will *choose* to revitalize local, small-scale, labor-intensive production as the only way to meet important human needs. It is the only way to enrich our lives and to fulfill the New Materialism I describe in the next chapter.

You see, that feeling of "I don't need you" is based on an illusion. In fact, we *do* need each other. Despite being able to pay for everything we need, we do not feel satisfied; we do not feel like all our needs have actually been met. We feel empty, hungry. And because this hunger is present as much in the rich as in the poor, I know it must be for something that money cannot buy. Perhaps there is hope for community after all, even in the midst of a monetized society. Perhaps it lies in those needs that bought things cannot satisfy. Perhaps the very things we need the most are absent from the products of mass production, cannot be quantified or commoditized, and are therefore inherently outside the money realm.

The financially independent person is not bereft of community because he meets all of his needs via money—he is bereft of community because he is not meeting his needs *except* through money. More precisely, he is trying to use money to meet needs that money cannot meet. Money, impersonal and generic, can by itself only meet needs that are the same. It can meet the need for calories, X grams of protein, Y milligrams of vitamin C—anything that can be standardized and quantified. But it cannot by itself meet the need for beautiful food prepared by someone who cares. Money can meet the need for shelter, but it cannot by itself meet the need for a home that is an organic extension of oneself. Money can buy virtually any implement, but not one that is attached to the story of a maker you know personally and who knows you. Money can buy songs, but not a song sung specifically to you. Even if you hire a band to play in your home, there is no guarantee, no matter how much you pay, that they will really sing *to you* and not just pretend to. If your mother sung you lullabies, or if you have ever been serenaded by a lover, you know what I am talking about and how deep a need it fills. Sometimes it even happens at a concert, when the band isn't just putting on an act but is actually playing for that audience, or really, *to* that audience. Each such performance is unique, and its special, magical quality vanishes in recording. "You had to be there." True, we may pay money to attend such an event, but we receive more than we paid for when the band is truly playing to us. We do not feel that the transaction is complete and closed, that all obligations are canceled out, as in a pure money transaction. We feel a lingering connection, because a *giving* has transpired. No life can be rich without such experiences, which might ride the vehicle of money transactions, but which no amount of money can guarantee.

The situation in America, the most highly monetized society the world has ever known, is this: some of our needs are vastly overfulfilled while others go tragically unmet. We in the richest societies have too many calories even as we starve for beautiful, fresh food; we have overlarge houses but lack spaces that truly embody our individuality and connectedness; media surround us everywhere while we starve for authentic communication. We are offered entertainment every second of the day but lack the chance to play. In the ubiquitous realm of money, we hunger for all that is intimate, personal, and unique. We know more about the lives of Michael

Jackson, Princess Diana, and Lindsay Lohan than we do about our own neighbors, with the result that we really don't know anyone, and are barely known by anyone either.

The things we need the most are the things we have become most afraid of, such as adventure, intimacy, and authentic communication. We avert our eyes and stick to comfortable topics. We hold it as a virtue to be private, to be discreet, so that no one sees our dirty laundry—or even our clean laundry: our undergarments are considered unsightly, a value strangely reflected in the widespread American prohibition on hanging laundry outdoors to dry. Life has become a private affair. We are uncomfortable with intimacy and connection, which are among the greatest of our unmet needs today. To be truly seen and heard, to be truly known, is a deep human need. Our hunger for it is so omnipresent, so much a part of our experience of life, that we no more know what it is we are missing than a fish knows it is wet. We need way more intimacy than nearly anyone considers normal. Always hungry for it, we seek solace and sustenance in the closest available substitutes: television, shopping, pornography, conspicuous consumption—anything to ease the hurt, to feel connected, or to project an image by which we might be seen and known, or at least see and know ourselves.

Clearly, the transition to a sacred economy accompanies a transition in our psychology. Community, which in today's parlance usually means proximity or a mere network, is a much deeper kind of connection than that: it is a sharing of one's being, an expansion of one's self. To be in community is to be in personal, interdependent relationship, and it comes with a price: our illusion of independence, our freedom from obligation. You can't have it both ways. If you want community, you must be willing to be obligated, dependent, tied, attached. You will give and receive gifts that you cannot just buy somewhere. You will not be able to easily find another source. You *need* each other.

I have in this chapter circled around the question of what, exactly, are the needs that go unfulfilled in the monetized world. I have given many examples of things that meet a deep need—songs sung to us, homes that are an extension of the self, food prepared with love. But what is the general principle? Whether our needs are for material sustenance or spiritual (e.g., touch, play, story, music, or dancing), none are unassailably free of the money realm. We can buy touch; we can buy stories (e.g., when we go to the movies); we buy music and video games to play; we can even buy sex. But whatever we buy, something unquantifiable (and therefore impervious to monetization) either rides its vehicle, or does not, and it is that unquantifiable thing that we really crave. When it is missing, whatever we have bought seems empty. It does not satisfy. When it is present, then even if we have purchased the vehicle it rides, we know we have received infinitely more than we paid for. We know, in other words, that we have received a gift. The chef who puts extra care into cooking something special, the musician playing her heart out, and the engineer who overdesigned a product just because he wanted to do it right will not directly profit from their extra efforts. They are in the spirit of the gift, and we can feel it—hence the desire to send "our compliments to the chef." Their behavior is uneconomic, and the present competition-based money system weeds it out. If you have ever worked in that system, you know what I mean. I am speaking of the relentless pressure to do things just well enough, and no better.

What is that unquantifiable extra thing that sometimes rides the vehicle of the bought and converts it into a gift? What is this need, mostly unmet in modern civilization? Put succinctly, the essential need that goes unmet today, the fundamental need that takes a thousand forms, is the need for the sacred—the experience of uniqueness and connectedness that I described in the introduction.

Environmentalists often state that we can ill afford to maintain our resource-intensive lifestyles, implying that we would like to if only we could afford it. I disagree. I think we will move toward a more ecological way of life by positive choice. Instead of saying, "Too bad we have to leave our gigantic suburban homes behind because they use too much energy," we will no longer want those homes because we will recognize and respond to our need for personal, connected, sacred dwellings in tight communities. The same goes for the rest of the modern consumer lifestyle. We will put it aside because we can no longer stand the emptiness, the ugliness. We are starving for spiritual nourishment. We are starving for a life that is personal, connected, and meaningful. By choice, that is where we will direct our energy. When we do so, community will arise anew because this spiritual nourishment can only come to us as a gift, as part of a web of gifts in which we participate as giver and receiver. Whether or not it rides the vehicle of something bought, it is irreducibly personal and unique.

When I use the word *spiritual*, I am not contradistinguishing it from the material. I have little patience with any philosophy or religion that seeks to transcend the material realm. Indeed, the separation of the spiritual from the material is instrumental in our heinous treatment of the material world. Sacred economics treats the world as more sacred, not less. It is more materialistic than our current culture—materialistic in the sense of deeply and attentively loving our world. So when I speak of meeting our spiritual needs, it is not to keep cranking out the cheap, generic, planet-killing stuff while we meditate, pray, and prattle on about angels, spirit, and God. It is to treat relationship, circulation, and material life itself as sacred. Because they are.

CHAPTER 23

A NEW MATERIALISM

The appearance of life in space may be compared with some kind
of awakening, almost as if—as it comes to life—space itself, the
very matter, wakes up, awakens, and it is this awakening of space
in varying degrees—indeed in infinitely varying degrees—that we
recognize when we see life in space, when we see life in buildings, in
the mountainside, in a work of art, in the smile upon a person's face.

—Christopher Alexander

Most of this book has been about money, which is the usual subject
of "economics" today. On a deeper level, though, economics should
be about *things*, specifically the things that human beings create, why
they create them, who gets to use them, and how they circulate.

When I drive through American suburbia with its fast food restaurants, enormous boxy stores, and cookie-cutter subdivisions, or
look upon the architecture of modern office buildings and residential high-rises, I cannot help but marvel at the ugliness of it
all. Compared to the charm and the intense vitality that imbues
older objects and structures, ours is a deeply impoverished world. I
marvel, with indignation bordering on outrage, that we can live in
such an ugly world after thousands of years of advances in material technology. Are we really so poor that we can afford no better?
What was the point of all this sacrifice, all this destruction, if we
are poorer in the finer things of life, the beautiful and the unique,

than a Medieval peasant was? Looking at the artifacts of bygone times, I am impressed by their vibrancy, the intense quality of life within them. Today, almost everything we use, even if it is expensive, is cheap, reeking of phoniness, indifference, and salesmanship.

Let's begin with the example of buildings and apply it to other artificial things. Our buildings are generally of two basic types. The first is the unapologetically utilitarian: warehouses, supermarkets, retail outlets, and so on, which aim to serve a function as cheaply as possible. Aesthetics is not a concern. The second type of building does try to incorporate aesthetic elements, but these are either inconsequential add-ons to the underlying functional efficiency, like arches on the porch of a suburban house that serve no structural purpose, or they actually come at the expense of function.

These two types of buildings correspond to two devastating misconceptions about beauty. The first is that beauty is a by-product of devotion to utility and practical efficiency. As the architect Christopher Alexander puts it,

> Because of our still-prevailing 20th-century viewpoint, students are convinced that "beauty" comes about as a *result* of the concern with practical efficiency. In other words, if you make it practical and efficient, then it will *follow* that it becomes beautiful. Form follows function! ... They—often the most rational and most intelligent students—have an almost moralistic passion in their desire to prove that these beautiful things must have been produced by purely functional thinking.[1]

The modern built environment abundantly demonstrates that this is not the case, that beauty does not necessarily arise from the pursuit of

---

1. Alexander, *The Nature of Order*, 423.

efficiency. Yet, neither is it true that beauty is irrelevant to functional efficiency, as the fake-seeming adornment of so many contemporary buildings implies. That is the second misconception about beauty: that it is something extra, something distinct from function. Hence we draw a distinction between the aesthetic and the practical, the fine arts and the applied arts. Art, like mind, like spirit, becomes a rarefied realm not to be sullied with concerns of practicality. Accordingly, the world of art meshes quite poorly with the realm of commerce, and especially with that epitome of worldliness: money.

The first misconception about beauty corresponds to the worldview of Cartesian science; the second to the worldview of Cartesian religion. The first corresponds to the belief that beauty, life, and soul are secondary properties, epiphenomena, not measurable and therefore not real. You take an organism apart, and you get just a bunch of matter, a bunch of elements, some carbon, some nitrogen, some phosphorus . . . where is the ingredient you can call life or spirit? The mentality of religion, on the other hand, appears superficially to contradict science by saying that spirit is a real ingredient in life that science doesn't see. But on a deeper level it agrees: it agrees that spirit does not inhere in matter but occupies a separate, nonmaterial realm. Both agree that *if* there is such a thing as a spirit of life, it is something separate from matter, an extra ingredient. A parallel mind-set makes beauty an extra ingredient on top of function.

And so, even those things that we use today that try to be beautiful as well as functional usually bear a certain inauthenticity. The beauty seems snazzy, gimmicky; it doesn't go very deep. Real beauty, which I might call life or soul, goes to the very heart of an object, and it is inseparable from its function, not secondary to the perfection of function. It evokes the paradoxical feeling, "This is more beautiful than it has to be, yet it could be no other way." It is identical to the feeling I get when I contemplate the beauty of a cell or a sunset or the mathematical object known as the Mandelbrot set. There is no reason for such beauty, such order out of chaos—it seems like a marvelous though gratuitous gift. The world would keep spinning around if sunsets were ugly, or raspberries not quite so delicious, would it not? Yet none of these could be any other way.

It is not that focus on functionality brings about beauty as well; it is that the creative principles and creative spirit that go into making something beautiful are the same that go into making it functional. It starts with the intention to make something the best one can. I was going to use the word *perfect* here, but perfect carries connotations of exactitude and undeviating regularity that have little to do with beauty, life, or soul, and in fact make an object soulless. So let us say the intention is to be a perfectly faithful servant to the creation that is being born through us.

An integrated pursuit of utility and beauty reveals that the same principles often underlie both. Christopher Alexander lays out fifteen such principles in his profound book *The Nature of Order.* These fifteen fundamental properties characterize both natural systems and sublime works of architecture and art. They include levels of scale, strong centers, positive space, local symmetries, deep interlock and ambiguity, boundaries, roughness, gradients, and many others. But the key to his conception of wholeness, order, and life is the concept of centers: entities that, like elements, add up to create the whole but, unlike elements, are themselves created by the wholeness.[2] "The wholeness is made of parts; the parts are created

---

2. As a matter of fact, even physical elements, far from being discrete building blocks of matter, are themselves created by the wholeness even as they create the wholeness. An electron exists only in relationship. This is a universal principle; ugliness results when we pretend otherwise.

by the wholeness." Anything that has the quality of aliveness will be composed of centers within centers within centers, wholenesses within wholenesses, each creating all the others.

The human being is no exception. Just as society is composed of human beings, so also is the human being a product of the society. Remember the truth of the connected self: we *are* our relationships. Moving inward a level, we could say the same for the relationship between ourselves and our organs. This is a universal truth of life. An economy that is alive, that is sacred, that is an extension of ecology, must have the same properties. And each object of that economy, each object that human beings create and circulate, must embody connection to all that environs it. Today, ours is an economy of separation: standard commodities that bear no relationship to the individual user, buildings that bear no relation to the land they occupy, retail outlets that bear no connection to local production, and products made in obliviousness to their effects on nature and people. None of these can possibly be beautiful, alive, or whole.

Although we might describe its properties, beauty, life, or soul cannot be reduced to a formula. It can be found in simplicity, such as Shaker furniture, or in ornateness, such as the Masdi-i-Shah or the Tomb of Mevlana. Alexander offers some powerful ways to recognize it. In comparing objects, we can ask ourselves, "Which of these has more life?" "Which of these is more a mirror of my self?" "Does this object make me feel my humanity is expanding—or contracting?"

Accordingly, to create objects with soul, objects for a rich and beautiful world, we must invest them with life, self, and humanity; in other words, we must invest them with something of our selves. No matter what money system we have, if it does not induce or allow this kind of creative process, then we will not be living in a sacred economy. By the same token, by fostering within ourselves a realization of the sacredness inherent in materiality, and by aligning our work with that sacredness, we lay the social and psychic foundation of an economy in which more and more of the things we make and do for each other are beautiful, personal, alive, and ensouled.

The pursuit of this kind of wealth has not been a public priority for any part of the ideological spectrum for several hundred years. The twentieth-century socialists, for example, rejected any fripperies or indulgences that didn't further measurable material welfare, preferring the squat utilitarianism of rational efficiency in their grand project of maximizing production to bring plentiful, cheap goods to the masses. The same austerity expected of the socialist comrade extends to the progressive activist today, who is supposed to eschew fine living in pursuit of altruistic ideals. And establishment capitalism is little different: it has re-created and perfected the painfully ugly, utilitarian buildings and objects of socialism. I remember as a child hearing of the horrors of life in the Soviet Union. There was supposedly only one kind of store, a gigantic windowless dispensary staffed by listless, surly functionaries selling cheaply made, generic goods. It sounds a lot like Wal-Mart. Oh, and parents had to send their children, as young as two years old, to mandatory state-run day care—even parenting had been abolished. Here today it is nearly the same, with economic exigency replacing state force. In any event, we have created a material world devoid of soul, barren of life and killing of life. All for what? The pursuit of efficiency, the grand project of maximizing the production of commodities, and underneath that, the domination and control of life. This was to be the paradise of technology, life under control, and finally we see it for what it is: the strip mall, the robotic cashier, the endless parking lot, the extermination of the wild, the living, the messy, and the sacred.

A sacred object embodies something of the infinite. It is, therefore, intrinsically antithetical to the commodity, which is defined by a finite list of measurable specifications. And, as we have seen, the homogeneity of money induces the same in everything it touches, dragging all into the commodity realm. The shrinkage of the money realm described in Chapter 14, then, holds the possibility of liberating more and more of our things from the chains of commodity. After all, we have a surfeit of manufactured goods, the result of standardized mass production and efficiencies of scale. Our tremendous overcapacity indicates that we don't need these efficiencies, nor so much mass production. Trapped by the madness of growth-demanding money, we compulsively produce more and more cheap, ugly things we don't need while suffering a poverty of things that are beautiful, unique, personal, and alive. That poverty, in turn, drives continued consumption, a desperate quest to fill the void left by a material environment bereft of relatedness.

Touching on this topic in Chapter 2, I wrote, "The cheapness of our things is part of their devaluation, casting us into a cheap world where everything is generic and expendable." For a long time now, we have cared less and less about our things. We in rich countries don't even bother repairing most things anymore, as it is usually cheaper to buy new ones. However, much of this cheapness is an illusion coming from the externalization of costs. When we must pay the true price for the depletion of nature's gifts, materials will become more precious to us, and economic logic will reinforce, and not contradict, our heart's desire to treat the world with reverence and, when we receive nature's gifts, to use them well.

Ultimately, then, sacred economics is part of the healing of the spirit-matter divide, the human-nature divide, and the art-work divide that has increasingly defined our civilization for thousands of years. In our journey of separation, we have developed amazing creative tools of technology and culture that would never have existed had we not departed from our original wholeness. Now it remains to recover that wholeness and bring it to a new realm, to create with nanotechnology and social media things of the same life, beauty, and soul that the old masters created with adzes and song.[3] Let us insist on nothing less. For what purpose have our forebears sacrificed, if not to create a beautiful world?

We are born creators, here to achieve the exuberant expression of our gifts. The underlying connection between beauty and function suggests a parallel harmony between survival and the expression of our gifts. The old divide between making a living and being an artist will crumble, is already crumbling. So many of us, more and more of us, are refusing that divide. No object will be too insignificant to merit our care, our reverence, and our effort to make it right. We will seek—are already seeking—to embed all things in wholeness. All of the movements I have described in this book are carrying us toward a world that beautiful. The social dividend, the internalization of costs, degrowth, abundance and the gift economy, all take us away from the mentality of struggle, of survival, and therefore of utilitarian efficiency, and toward our true state of gratitude: of reverence for what we have received and of desire to give equally, or better, from our endowment. We wish to leave the world more beautiful than we entered it.

---

3. I am not saying that we should cease using adzes and song but that the entire spectrum of our technology should be turned toward the enrichment of spiritual life.

How beautiful can life be? We hardly dare imagine it. I caught my first glimpse of it at the age of nineteen when I visited the National Palace Museum in Taiwan. It contained objects that, had I not seen them with my own eyes, I would not have believed could exist. I remember in particular a teapot, the emperor's teapot, an object of such beauty and perfection that it seemed to harbor the soul of a god. True wealth would be for everyone to live surrounded by objects like that, objects made by masters in the full flush of their genius. I don't believe that such mastery is available only to a few; rather, it is because our gifts are so suppressed that few achieve such mastery. Thankfully, we have the record of the past to remind us of what is possible. I look at great works such as that teapot and think, "The kind of person who made this does not exist anymore." Such objects are beyond the capacity of any human living in this degenerate age. Yet the possibility lives on in our humanness, and we are on the way to its recovery.

Christopher Alexander tells a story of his visit to the Tofuku-ji temple in Japan, a masterpiece of architecture, in which he wanders up a flight of stone stairs that narrows between two hedges and then stops, leaving him no choice but to sit on the top step—a perfect spot, quiet and breezy after a long climb. A blue dragonfly sits next to him. He writes,

> I was suddenly certain that the people who had built that place had done all this deliberately. I felt certain—no matter how peculiar or unlikely it sounds today, as I am telling it again— that they had made that place, knowing that the blue dragonfly would come and sit by me. However it sounds now, at the time when it happened, while I sat on that stair, there was no doubt in my mind at all that there was a level of skill in the people

who had made this place that I had never experienced before. I remember shivering as I became aware of my own ignorance. I felt the existence of a level of skill and knowledge beyond anything I had ever come across before. (437)

Such skill, transcending what we think is possible, is latent within all of us today. The great project of humanity is to recover it, and build a world upon it.

THE MORE BEAUTIFUL WORLD OUR HEARTS TELL US IS POSSIBLE

It may be that when we no longer know what to do, we have come to our real work and when we no longer know which way to go, we have begun our real journey. The mind that is not baffled is not employed. The impeded stream is the one that sings.

—Wendell Berry

In the introduction, in dedicating my work to "the more beautiful world our hearts tell us is possible," I spoke of the resistance of the mind to the possibility of a world much different from what we have always known. Many centuries and millennia have indeed accustomed us to a world of great and growing inequality, violence, ugliness, and struggle. So used to it are we that we forget that anything else ever existed. Sometimes, an excursion to unspoiled nature, to a traditional culture, or to the sensory richness veiled behind the impoverished modern world reminds us of what has been lost, and that reminder hurts, rubbing salt into the wound of Separation. Such experiences at least show us what is possible, what has existed and can exist, but they do not show us how to create such a world. Facing the enormous powers arrayed to maintain the status quo, our minds quail in anguish. The temporary glimpses of a more beautiful world that we might catch in nature, in special gatherings, at music festivals, in ceremony, in love, and in play are all the more disheartening when we believe that they can never be more than temporary respites from the soul-crushing, money-driven world we are used to.

A primary goal of this book has been to align the logic of the mind with the knowing of the heart: to illuminate not only what is possible but also how to get there. When I use the word *possible*, I don't mean it in the sense of "maybe," as in, "It could possibly happen if only we are very lucky." I mean possible in the sense of self-determination: a more beautiful world as something we can create. I have given great evidence of its possibility: the inevitable demise of a money system dependent on exponential growth, a shift in consciousness toward a connected self in cocreative partnership with earth, and the many ways in which the necessary pieces of a sacred economy are already emerging. This is something we can create. We can, and we are. And given how much of the evil and ugliness of the present world can be traced to money, can you imagine what the world will be like when money has been transformed?

I can't imagine it, not all of it, though I do sometimes get visions of it that take my breath away. Maybe it isn't that I can't imagine it; maybe it is that I dare not imagine it. A vision of a truly sacred world, a sacred economy, makes all the clearer the magnitude of our present suffering. But I will share what I have seen in my visions, even the most speculative parts, the most naive, impractical, dreamy parts. I hope my sharing won't compromise the credibility, if any, that I've built by presenting the concepts of sacred economics in a coherent, logical fashion.

I have given many other examples in this book of ways in which the sacred economy I describe not only is possible but is in fact already starting to emerge. The old ways are still dominant, but they are unraveling at an accelerating rate. I wrote this book between the first stage of this Great Unraveling—the financial meltdown of 2008—and the second, which I imagine will begin within the next year or two. No one can predict how it will unfold. Depending on geopolitical events and even natural disasters, the old regime may be able to maintain a semblance of normalcy for a few more years. But the end of the Age of Usury is near, the end of the story of Ascent, the end of the Age of Separation. The birthing of a new era, the coming-of-age ordeal of the human race, may be a bit messy. It will probably involve the usual accompaniments to economic collapse—fascism, civil unrest, and war—but I think this dark age will be far shorter and mostly more mild than one might reasonably expect.

I think so because of all the enlightened people I keep meeting! We humans have learned a lot in the last half-century, and our consciousness has reached a critical point in its development. It will be the same as it is with transformation on a personal level. In transitioning into a new way of being, we might revisit the old once or twice and try to fit back into the womb; but when we do, we find that it can no longer accommodate us, and a state of being we once inhabited for years becomes intolerable in weeks or days. So it shall be for humanity generally—a few short years of darkness and upheaval. Perhaps this phase of accelerated transition will be what I speculated about earlier as the rapid succession of mini-ages completing the millions-of-years-long age of tools, hundreds-of-thousands-of-years-long age of fire, tens-of-thousands-of-years-long age of symbolic culture, millennia-long age of agriculture, centuries-long machine age, and decades-long information age. The singularity is nigh and then a transition qualitatively more profound than any before it.

Now that I have entered the realm of speculation, I would like to describe a few more aspects of sacred economy that I believe will unfold over the next two centuries. This book has described developments that we can create in the next twenty years, and in some cases the next five. What about the next two hundred years? (I am being cautious—maybe I should think big!)

A corollary to the nonhoarding of gifts and to the social nature of their giving is that wealth in gift cultures tends to be publicly transparent. Everyone knows who has given what to whom, who has how much, who is hoarding, and who is generous. Translated into modern money dynamics, this suggests that all monetary holdings and transactions should be publicly transparent. With the advent of money, a new secrecy came to infect wealth that had been impossible before. When wealth was lands, sheep, and cattle, there was no hiding one's wealth, and therefore no shirking the social expectations incumbent upon it. But money can be hoarded in the basement, buried in the ground, stashed away in numbered bank accounts, kept secret, kept private. To undo the negative effects of money, eventually this characteristic of money must pass.

The transition from physical cash to electronic currency makes this feasible but of course raises the specter of totalitarian control. Do we want the government to be able to survey every transaction, as part of Total Information Awareness? Probably not—unless every expenditure of the government is also available for public view. It will not do for the financial doings of some people and institutions to be public, and others secret. Money must be *universally* transparent.

Obviously, a system in which every transaction and every account balance is available for public view would radically change business practice. If you have ever been in business, imagine if you will that every customer, supplier, and competitor knew your true costs! However, monetary transparency fits in naturally to the gift-inspired business models I explored in Chapter 21, which require that you honestly reveal your costs and invite gifts on top of that. No longer would one be able to lie about one's costs in order to profit from the other party's lack of knowledge.

Many people would find the idea of no financial privacy very threatening. Since money today is so bound up with self, we would feel exposed, vulnerable—as indeed, in today's society, we would be: exposed to envy and judgment and vulnerable to criminal extortion and demands from importunate relatives. In a different context, though, financial transparency is part of a way of being that is open, trusting, unguarded, and generous—being a person who has nothing to fear, who is comfortable in society. Moreover, financial transparency would make many kinds of criminal activity more difficult.

As with the other developments of sacred economy, there are signs we are already moving in this direction, not only with the digitization of currency, but with the new "social currencies" of various online ratings systems that are, by their very nature, public. Ultimately, money is a token of society's gratitude for one's gifts, so it is fitting that the tokens themselves be public as well.

Another basic feature of money as we have known it is its homogeneity: any dollar is the same as any other dollar. Thus money has no history, no story attached to it. In addition to homogenizing all it touches, this feature of money also disconnects it from the material and social world. In former times, though, gifts were unique objects that carried stories. In gift-giving ceremonies, often the entire history of a gift would be recounted (we still do this today, acting on a primal urge; we want to tell about where we bought it, or how Grandma received it as a wedding present).

Money's homogeneity and anonymity (my dollars are the same as yours) therefore make it incompatible with gift principles and with the two features of sacredness I described in the introduction: uniqueness and connectedness.

Therefore, I foresee money eventually losing its homogeneity and gaining the capacity to bear with it its history. With electronic, transparent money, every transaction that a given dollar has ever been used for could be attached to it in an electronic database. In making a purchase, then, you could decide whether to use the money from your salary or the money you were given by a friend, and even if it were in the same bank account, it would be *different money*. The child's intuition that the bank keeps "your money" and returns those same physical bills when you make a withdrawal would become true. (This system does not conflict with credit creation—money could still be born, circulate for a while, and die.)

The history of civilization, of growing separation and its imminent transcendence in a long age of growing reunion, is also a journey from an original abundance, to the extreme of scarcity, and then back toward abundance at a higher level of complexity. I have written herein about the abundance economy emerging via digital media, thanks to disintermediation and the dropping to near zero of marginal production costs for "content." In the long term, this abundance economy, limited in scope today, will become the template for new realms of abundance. One of these will be energy, fulfilling the dreams of atomic-age visionaries who foresaw energy "too cheap to meter."

Today we seem to face the opposite, as petroleum supplies dwindle along with the earth's capacity to absorb fossil fuel emissions. In the short term, energy abundance might arise from recognized eco-friendly sources such as solar, wind, and conservation technologies, but I think that when humanity enters a true spirit of abundance, vast new energy sources will become available that are beyond the purview of conventional science today. These will be the product not of the onward march of technology but of a shift in perception. In fact, "free energy" technologies have been in existence for at least a century, going back to the work of Nikola Tesla.[1] Today there are at least five or ten different energy technologies that seem to violate the Second Law of Thermodynamics. If you research the field, you will find a sordid history of confiscated research, destroyed careers, and even mysterious deaths of researchers. Whether or not there ever was, or still is, an active conspiracy to maintain energy scarcity, on some level humanity has not been ready for the gift of energy abundance, and probably won't be ready for some decades to come, until we have entered deeply and thoroughly the spirit of the gift. When J. P. Morgan destroyed Tesla's career, it may have been, like the record and film industry more recently, an attempt to maintain artificial scarcity and profit from it. But perhaps larger forces were at work; perhaps Morgan was even on some level cognizant that humanity was not ready for Tesla's gift. In any event, our governing paradigms, rooted in separation and scarcity, are constitutionally unable to encompass free-energy technologies, which are dismissed as impossible, fraudulent, or fantastical.

---

1. Significantly, when J. P. Morgan cut off financing for Tesla's wireless energy transmission project (which, according to Tesla, would have provided virtually unlimited energy), he did not question the science. He did not evince the slightest doubt that the invention would work. He rejected it because he saw that it would be impossible to make money from it, saying, "If I can't meter it, I can't sell it." Tesla's earlier inventions, such as AC power, fit into an economy of scarcity and a mentality of control, so they were enthusiastically adopted by the financial powers.

If our outer experience in some ways mirrors our psychology, perhaps the advent of energy abundance for humanity awaits an inventor who lets go of all hope of patenting and profiting from his invention and instead releases it into the public domain. That would short-circuit the usual accusations of charlatanism and the seizure of patents by the Department of Defense. Can a person hope to corral and own what is fundamentally a free gift of the universe?

I do not believe that technology will save humanity. Reading my work, many people have asked me if I know about the Venus Project, a movement that draws from the same basic understanding of the problem with today's money system. While I resonate with its spirit, I find that the Venus Project indulges in the same technological utopianism that has filled us with starry-eyed hope since the age of coal. But in fact, as I described in Chapter 2, abundance has always been available to us. It is our perceptions, and not our means, that engender scarcity.

Let me put it poetically. At the end of Chapter 11 I wrote,

> A vein runs through spiritual tradition that says that we, too, give back to the sun; indeed that the sun only continues to shine through our gratitude. Ancient sun rituals weren't only to thank the sun—they were to keep it shining. Solar energy is the light of earthly love reflected back at us. Here, too, the circle of the gift operates.

Could it be, then, that as we step into the abundance mentality and the generosity of the connected self, the self that connects I and thou through love, the sun will shine more brightly? That new "suns"—new sources of the infinite generosity of the universe—will become available to us, reflecting back our love? We are born into gratitude; it is our primal response to the gift of life itself. As we live from that gratitude, which means to live in the spirit of the gift, and as we open the channels of generosity wider, it is inevitable that the inward flow of gifts should grow as well.

After energy, who knows in what other realms we will express the fundamental abundance of the universe? Matter? Time? Consciousness? All I know is that we humans have only begun to discover our gifts and to turn them toward beautiful purposes. We are capable of miracles—which is good, considering that the state of the planet today requires them.

I cannot predict how the Age of Reunion will unfold in linear time. I do know, however, that by the end of our lifetimes, my generation will live in a world unimaginably more beautiful than the one we were born into. And it will be a world that is palpably improving year after year. We will reforest the Greek isles, denuded over two thousand years ago. We will restore the Sahara Desert to the rich grassland it once was. Prisons will no longer exist, and violence will be a rarity. Work will be about, "How may I best give of my gifts?" instead of, "How can I make a living?" Crossing a national border will be an experience of being welcomed, not examined. Mines and quarries will barely exist, as we reuse the vast accumulation of materials from the industrial age. We will live in dwellings that are extensions of ourselves, eat food grown by people who know us, and use articles that are the best that people in the full flow of their talents could make them. We will live in a richness of intimacy and community that hardly exists today, that we know, because of a longing in the heart, must exist. And most of the time, the loudest noises we hear will be the sounds of nature and the laughter of children.

Fantastical? The mind is afraid to hope for anything too good. If this description evokes anger, despair, or grief, then it has touched our common wound, the wound of separation. Yet the knowledge of what is possible lives on inside each of us, inextinguishable. Let us trust this knowing, hold each other in it, and organize our lives around it. Do we really have any choice, as the old world falls apart? Shall we settle for anything less than a sacred world?

APPENDIX
Quantum Money and the Reserve Question

What is money? In this book I have played with different definitions: it is a medium of exchange, a store of value, and a unit of account; it is a story or agreement; it is a token of gratitude; it is a ritual talisman for the direction of human creativity. All of these definitions are useful, depending on how we are trying to understand money. Ultimately, the conviction that money *is* something, something objective and discrete among a universe of other objective, discrete objects, is a false conviction, part of the story of separation that is ending in our time.

That is why I favor a more fluid, "multi-jective" approach to understanding money. The axiomatic method of understanding, which starts with definitions and reasons from there, is bound to be incomplete. It creates an internally consistent and intellectually comforting system that leaves out important truths. Such is always the case with fundamentalism, economic as well as religious.

It might behoove us, then, to be very cautious in accepting any authoritative statement about what money is and, by extension, about how money is created or should be created. There have been many times that I thought I finally understood money, only to come across new contradictions, sometimes subtle and sometimes flagrant, that showed me that, as in Gödelian logic, the realm of truth is always vaster than my framework for understanding it.

None of the revelations of "what money *really* is" were wrong; they were just partial, useful for certain kinds of reasoning. This is true even of the latest understanding about money to sweep the avant-garde consciousness: that money today is pure credit, created out of nothing—a mere accounting entry—by banks when they write a loan. Upon close examination, however, this definition breaks down. I would like to explore these subtleties of money and credit so that my vision of sacred economy doesn't carry forward the inevitable flaws lurking within any variety of monetary fundamentalism. Some immediate and, to me, surprising conclusions bear on the issue of bank reserve requirements. Fractional? One hundred percent? Zero? Each has its very bright, knowledgeable advocates. As we shall see, much of that debate is based on false (or at least conditionally true) premises.

First, consider the equation of credit with money, as is taught in innumerable explanations today, from the *Zeitgeist* movies to Chris Martenson's *Crash Course* to the Federal Reserve's own manual, *Modern Money Mechanics*. A bank (Bank A) loans John a million dollars, creating it with a few keystrokes. No one's account is debited by a million dollars to do that; it is new money. Now, John probably took out that loan because he wanted to use the million dollars, so it won't stay in his account at the originating bank. Probably he'll spend it, say on a home, and the million dollars will end up deposited in Mary's account at another bank (Bank B). There is still a million new dollars in the system, only now it is in Mary's account, not John's.

However, this is not the only thing that goes on when Mary deposits John's check. The check must also "clear," meaning that Bank A's account at the Federal Reserve (or, more likely, at an intermediate clearing organization, but let's keep things simple) is debited by $1 million and Bank B's account is credited by the same. Typically, though, Bank A will also be receiving checks drawn on Bank B or other banks, so at the end of the day, when all the transactions are settled, it is possible that Bank A's reserve account won't need to be debited at all. It is also possible, especially if Bank A is writing some big loans, that its reserves will fall below zero. That's OK, though—its checks won't bounce. It can simply borrow the necessary reserves from other banks (in the Fed Funds market) or from the Fed itself (from the discount window). These are short-term loans of bank reserves. To meet a longer-term deficit, Bank A would have to attract more deposits or, alternatively, borrow longer term from other banks or sell the loans on the repo markets. If it can show that the loans it has been making are sound, it should normally have no problem acquiring the necessary funds at a favorable rate. This borrowing is fundamentally different from credit creation. When a bank borrows on the interbank lending market, no new money is created. One bank's gain of reserves is another bank's loss. When it comes to reserves, new money can only be created by the central bank (e.g., the Federal Reserve). So already we have two types of money, reserves and credit, corresponding in economic statistics to M0 (or "base money"), M1, M2, and so on.

Something else is going on when bank-created credit is used as a medium of exchange. Keep this in mind over the next few paragraphs as we investigate the idea of full-reserve banking, advocated by many reformers as the key to a sound money system. Full-reserve banking has an illustrious pedigree, supported by thinkers as disparate as Frederick Soddy in the 1920s, Irving Fisher in the 1930s, and numerous reformers today such as Ron Paul, Stephen Zarlenga, Dennis Kucinich, and many economists of the Austrian School. Full-reserve banking eliminates the distinction between credit and reserves. Banks would only be able to lend their own money, or they could lend depositors' money (with their agreement), but that money would be gone until repaid. There would be no lending of demand deposits.

At first glance this system would seem radically different from what we have today. With fractional-reserve banking, a bank can "borrow short and lend long"; that is, it can hold demand deposits, which could be withdrawn anytime, and lend most of them out as long-term loans. With full-reserve banking this is not allowed. Banks could still lend money, but only if that money has been given to them in the form of time deposits. For example, if a depositor buys a six-month certificate of deposit (CD), those funds could be lent out for a term of six months.

One of the main criticisms of full-reserve banking is that it makes financial intermediation—the connection of lenders and borrowers—much more difficult. Instead of issuing loans based purely on creditworthiness, the bank would have to find a depositor willing to commit his money for the term of the loan. However, closer examination reveals this criticism to be for the most part invalid. In fact, banking would be almost the same as it is today.

Let's think about bank deposits first. In a full-reserve system, there would be no interest offered on demand deposits because the bank would gain no benefit from holding them (indeed, there would be a fee). It would only offer interest on time deposits, which it could lend at even higher interest—the longer the time period, the higher it would be. Depositors would do their best to deposit their money for the longest term they could, depending on their projected liquidity needs. A given depositor might put some of his money in a thirty-day CD, knowing he had to pay his bills at the end of the month; some in a six-month CD, anticipating a big purchase then; and the rest in a ten-year CD, planning to save it for college tuition. Taken across all depositors, the bank would have a wide, near-continuous distribution of terms for which it could lend funds. More funds would be available for short-term lending, which would carry a lower interest rate; less would be available for long-term lending.

The main difference is that banks would be limited in making very long-term loans, which today go toward real estate and large capital projects. People might still need a twenty- or thirty-year loan to buy a house, but few savers are willing to part with their money for that long. In fact, this problem is easily avoided, simply by issuing a short-term loan, say one year, and refinancing it every year thereafter. This is basically the equivalent of an adjustable-rate mortgage. I suppose the refinancing rate could be contractually fixed to mimic a fixed-term loan as well.

In principle, all loans could be financed in this way, obviating the need for fixed-term deposits of any specific length at all. One question, then, is, "What constraints on lending would exist in a full-reserve system?" Just as today, a bank could lend any amount (up to its total reserves) for any term, to any borrower. What if a bank had an attractive lending opportunity and wanted to lend beyond its current reserves? It would do exactly the same thing it does today—borrow the necessary reserves from other banks or financial markets.

Now, of course, we must face the very same problem that motivated full-reserve banking proposals to begin with: runs on banks. Even though in theory the full value of short-term deposits would be covered by loans of even shorter term, in practice many of these short-term loans would be intended for periodic refinancing, and thus based on assets that are not very liquid. Just as today, if a bank makes too many of these (de facto) long-term loans from short-term deposits that are indeed quickly withdrawn, the bank will face a liquidity crisis. It could solve that crisis in the same ways banks do today; for example, if its loan portfolio is solid, it could probably find other banks from whom to borrow liquidity. Alternatively, given sufficient lead time, it could issue stock or bonds to investors. In general, liquidity would be no more a restraint on lending than it is today. Random fluctuations in the level of deposits happen every day and are no big deal because banks can cover any shortfall in reserves by borrowing from the Fed Funds market or the Fed's own overdraft facility. Equivalent mechanisms could easily operate in a full-reserve system.

Besides financial intermediation, another apparent difference between the two systems is that in a full-reserve system, banks would supposedly have no capacity to alter the money supply, which would be dependent on the monetary authority. However, this difference too is an illusion. In the present system, the money supply increases when banks lend more, such as during an economic expansion when there are lots of safe lending opportunities. In a full-reserve system, again banks will lend more under such conditions. The total number of dollars won't increase, *but the number of dollars in the hands of people who want to spend them will.* In times of recession, banks won't want to lend, and money will languish in the savings accounts of people who don't need to spend it. Thus, the amount of money actually available to the economy will decrease. It is exactly as it is today.

Proponents of full-reserve banking claim that it would prevent the boom and bust cycle that arises through the excessive expansion of credit. I hope the foregoing makes it clear that this is not the case. The effective money supply depends not on the number of dollars but on the number of dollars being *used as money,* being used as a medium of exchange. No matter whether fractional-reserve banking is allowed, if too many dollars are in the hands of people who don't want or need to spend them, then aggregate demand can collapse, creating a deflationary spiral.

When banks are lending in a full-reserve system, you might say, "The money supply isn't increasing at all—it is the same money in different hands." But what is money? Is it possible that the same thing, in the hands of one person, is not money, while in the hands of another it is? In the hands of one who will never spend it, is money still money? This conundrum has been with us since ancient times. Is the miser's hoard of coins buried under the apple tree money? What is the difference between the Fed decreasing the money supply by selling securities to remove money from the system, and a bank removing money from circulation by hoarding excess reserves? The effect is the same, and the physical reality—bits in computers—is the same too. Richard Seaford, echoing Marx, notes the essential paradox: "Although valuable only in payment or exchange, it [money] can paradoxically only be possessed … by being *withheld* from payment and exchange, as a 'mere phantom of real wealth.'"[1]

Standard economics attempts to resolve this paradox by distinguishing between the supply of money and the velocity of money—how much there is and how fast it circulates. Multiplied together, these two factors determine price levels in the equations. The math works, but do these mathematical formulas truly model reality? So often we see the world through the lens of our symbolic representation of it. The mathematical distinction between the supply and velocity of money conditions and echoes a perception that money is a discrete, objective *thing* existing independently of transactions

1. Seaford, *Money and the Early Greek Mind*, 248.

between human beings. But there is another, post-Cartesian way to view money: as a relationship and not a thing.

I came to this realization thinking about my dear ex-wife, Patsy, who, shall we say, does not count frugality among her many fine qualities. Her motto is, "Money is not yours until you spend it!" From the point of view of an economy, it is the same: money has little effect on economic activity if it is not being used for transactions. In a fractional-reserve system, one way to view what happens is that banks are not creating new money at all, but simply allowing existing money to be *in two places at once.* It is at once in the depositor's savings account and also in the borrower's checking account (and soon thereafter in someone else's savings account, and so on). The same base money (reserves) is in many places at once, yet it can only be used in one of those places at a time: whenever a transaction occurs and a check clears, reserves move from one account to another in the Federal Reserve. When there is high demand for this same amount of money, when it has to be in too many places at once, then interest rates rise unless the Fed provides more of it through open-market operations.

If money is in a savings account, it probably means that someone doesn't need to use it right now. The function of a bank is supposed to be to put that money in the hands of someone who does want to use it. Only then can it be said to "exist" in economic terms, and only then does it have economic effects (e.g., stimulating production). In contrast to a saver, a borrower is someone who does want to use money right now. Therefore, any transfer of money from saver to borrower, whether under a full-reserve or fractional-reserve model, will increase the effective money supply. It will increase the amount of money that is actually being used.

I cannot help but remark on the similarity between fractional-reserve money and the superposition of states of a quantum particle. The matter is therefore more subtle than the same money existing in many places at once, a description that still conceives it as an objectively existing thing. It is that it exists in all and none of those places at once, existing only as a possibility until brought into being by a transaction. Ten people can have $100 each in their savings accounts, based on $100 of base money. Any one of them could withdraw their $100 at any time, but until they do, that $100 cannot be said to exist in any of those savings accounts. Like in a quantum measurement, the money is virtual until brought into reality through an interaction, a transaction. You withdraw your $100 from the ATM and look! There is the cash! It was there all along, right? No. It only appeared there through the act of the withdrawal, or the act of writing a check. Is the money in your savings account "really there" or not? That is the question that bothers "real money" advocates, but ultimately it is not a useful question. Whether or not it is there, it comes into being when a transaction is made, just as an electron comes into being when it interacts with an observer. With money as with matter, existence is a relationship.

"Real money" advocates would seem to want to return us to a Cartesian age, in which existence is not a relationship but a monadic predicate. This desire is inconsistent with the revolution in human beingness that is underway today: the expansion of the discrete and separate self into a larger, connected self. Even in physics, being is no longer an objective property, at least if by "exist" we mean "to occupy a quantifiable point in space and time." Physical location is not an objective quantity. Why, then, should we demand it of our money?

Indeed, perhaps if we are to move with the tide of the times, we should do away with base money entirely and move toward a pure credit system where all money comes into being through a transaction and perishes in its absence. Are reserves even necessary at all? Paradoxically enough, the possibility of a full-reserve system implies that they are not necessary, since a full-reserve system is no different from a reserve-less system. In both cases, there is one kind of money, not two. Moreover, reserve-less systems on a smaller scale have been envisioned and employed—LETS and other mutual-credit system are reserve-free credit-based systems.

Could the present system work without reserves? Why couldn't Bank A create that $1 million credit in John's account and then debit that account by $1 million when he pays Mary, whose account in Bank B is then increased by $1 million, all without reserves? Well, it could, except that we would then face the same problem that all mutual-credit systems face: how to regulate who gets to create how much credit, and how to limit negative balances. The reserve system puts a limit on bank lending. Without it, a banker could lend unlimited amounts to his cronies and then go bankrupt, effectively divorcing money from contribution to society and debasing the value of the money of those who do contribute. Of course, other limiting mechanisms might be employed—for example, the state could determine by fiat who gets credit, or we could use some kind of formula or a social feedback system with ratings and points. To return to the quantum money metaphor, in a quantum system the range of possible quantum states made manifest though a measurement is limited. Just as the probability wave function describes the distribution of particles, we also need some social function that influences the distribution of money. In a single-slit experiment, most of the photons end up in certain small areas. In a credit system, most of the credit should go to those who will put it to good use. The "social function" I describe doesn't dictate to whom it goes; it merely sets the conditions so that it will be most likely to go to a certain area that represents the social consensus of good use. This function can be adjusted, just as a pinhole slit can be made larger or smaller, to "diffract" the creation of money over a larger or smaller domain.

Among such functions, the reserve system offers some important advantages. It is organic and self-regulating; it allows for risk taking; it accommodates both spontaneous grass-roots entrepreneurship and collectively decided direction of the flow of capital. Finally, a credit-based system with decaying currency embodies two cardinal principles of the new world: interdependency and impermanence.

Perhaps most importantly, a credit-based system can accommodate all of the proposals of this book without the revolutionary destruction of the existing financial infrastructure and rebuilding of a new one. Although the effects of negative-interest currency, elimination of economic rents, localization, and a social dividend are indeed revolutionary, the means to achieve them are not. Indeed, they all exist in embryonic form already. While many of us, including at times myself, desire to wipe the slate clean and begin anew, such revolutions have the exasperating tendency to reincorporate the old into the new. The all-or-nothing desire for total revolution can also be dispiriting and paralyzing, since it implies that incremental, doable changes are meaningless. Consequently, today's self-proclaimed revolutionaries sit in their chat rooms doing nothing, cynically assuring each other that when the collapse comes, everyone else will finally see the error of their ways.

I think those cynics are going to be waiting a long time. Where they see a collapse, I see a transformational crisis in which the old is not abandoned but incorporated into something larger. The connected self does not deny the separate self of modernity but adopts it as one of the many ways of being that comprise a larger self. The same is true for the structures of our civilization, all of which ultimately arise from, contribute to, and correspond to our sense of self. We could say, then, that the crises converging upon us today are a kind of identity crisis. The mistake of the collapsist crowd, I think, is to look to that crisis to save us, to do the work of wiping the slate clean. Our own efforts, the thinking goes, are not enough. From 2012 end-time theorists to Christian believers in Armageddon, the underlying thought-form is the same. But while the intuition that "things cannot persist the way they are" is valid, the conclusion is mistaken. It is not that the collapse will do our work for us. It is that the crisis will provoke us into doing the work we need to do. It is work we can start doing right now. As I wrote before, any efforts we make today to "raise bottom" for our collectively addicted civilization—any efforts we make to protect or reclaim social, natural, cultural, or spiritual capital—will both hasten and ameliorate the crisis. It is true that conditions are not yet ripe for the full blossoming of any of the proposals of this book. However, before blossoming can happen, the soil must be prepared, the seedlings nourished. That is the time we are in as I write these words. Soon, these seedlings will grow strong in the soil made fertile by the decay of existing institutions; then they will blossom and finally bear fruit.

BIBLIOGRAPHY

Alexander, Christopher. *The Nature of Order: Book One; The Phenomenon of Life*. Berkeley: Center for Environmental Structure, 2002.

Allen, William R. "Irving Fisher and the 100 Percent Reserve Proposal." *Journal of Law and Economics* 36, no. 2 (1993): 703–17.

Altekar, A. S. *State and Government in Ancient India*. Delhi, India: Motilal Banarsidass, 2002.

Aristotle. *Politics*. Translated by Benjamin Jowett. N.p.: Publishing in Motion, 2011.

Avila, Charles. *Ownership: Early Christian Teaching*. New York: Orbis Books, 1983.

Baker, Dean. "No Way Out: Roadblocks on the Way to Recovery." *Counterpunch*, February 3, 2010.

Brown, Ellen. "Time for a New Theory of Money." Commondreams. org, October 29, 2010.

———. *Web of Debt*. Tempe, AZ: Third Millennium Press, 2008.

Buiter, Willem. "Negative Interest Rates: When Are They Coming to a Central Bank Near You?" *Financial Times Online*, May 7, 2009.

———. "Overcoming the Zero Bound on Nominal Interest Rates with Negative Interest on Currency: Gesell's Solution." *Economic Journal* 113, no. 490 (2003): 723–46.

Buzby, Jean C., Hodan Farah Wells, Bruce Axtman, and Jana Mickey. "Supermarket Loss Estimates for Fresh Fruit, Vegetables, Meat, Poultry, and Seafood and Their Use in the ERS Loss-Adjusted Food Availability Data." EIB-44, U.S. Dept. of Agriculture, Econ. Res. Serv., March 2009.

Caron, Kevin. "Abundance Creates Utility but Destroys Exchange Value." February 2, 2010. http://blog.p2pfoundation.net/abundance-creates-utility-but-destroys-exchange-value/2010/02/02.

Champ, Bruce. "Stamp Scrip: Money People Paid to Use." Federal Reserve Bank of Cleveland, Research Paper, April 1, 2008.

Clark, Stuart. "Absence of Sunspots Make Scientists Wonder If They're Seeing a Calm before a Storm of Energy." *Washington Post,* June 22, 2010.

Cohrssen, Hans L. "Wara." *The New Republic,* August 10, 1932.

Collom, Ed. "Community Currency in the United States: The Social Environments in Which It Emerges and Thrives." *Environment and Planning A,* 37 (2005): 1565–87.

Costanza, Robert, et al. "The Value of the World's Ecosystem Services and Natural Capital." *Nature* 387 (1997): 253–60.

Coxe, Don. "Financial Heroin." *Coxe Strategy Journal,* November 12, 2009.

Dalton, G. "Barter." *Journal of Economic Issues* (1982), 16.1.182.

Daly, Herman. "The Economic Thought of Frederick Soddy." *History of Political Economy* 12, no. 4 (1980).

Deng, Feng. "A Comparative Study on Land Ownership between England and China." Chongqing, China: Chongqing University, School of Economics and Business Administration, 2007.

Dodds, Walter Kennedy. *Humanity's Footprint: Momentum, Impact, and our Global Environment.* New York: Columbia University Press, 2008.

Everett, Daniel L. "Cultural Constraints on Grammar and Cognition in Pirahã: Another Look at the Design Features of Human Language." *Current Anthropology* 46, no. 4 (2005).

Fisher, Irving. *Stamp Scrip.* New York: Adelphi, 1933.

Frank, Robert H., Thomas Gilovich, and Dennis T. Regan. "Does Studying Economics Inhibit Cooperation?" *Journal of Economic Perspectives* 7, no. 2 (1993): 159–71.

Gesell, Silvio. *The Natural Economic Order.* Translated by Philip Pye. Berlin: NEO-Verlag, 1906.

George, Henry. "The Single Tax: What It Is and Why We Urge It." 1890.

Graves, Robert. *The White Goddess.* New York: Farrar, Straus and Giroux, 1948.

Greco, Thomas. *The End of Money and the Future of Civilization.* White River Junction, VT: Chelsea Green, 2009.

Hall, Robert, and Susan Woodward. "The Fed Needs to Make a Policy Statement." *Vox*, April 13, 2009. www.voxeu.org/index.php?q=node /3444.

Handon, Jon D., and David Yosifon. "The Situational Character: A Critical Realist Perspective on the Human Animal." *Georgetown Law Journal* 93, no. 1 (2004).

Hassett, Kevin. "U.S. Should Try Germany's Unemployment Medicine." *Bloomberg*, November 9, 2009.

Holden, G. R. "Mr. Keynes' Consumption Function and the Time Preference Postulate." *Quarterly Journal of Economics* 52, no. 2 (1938): 281–96.

Hoppe, Hans-Hermann. "The Misesian Case against Keynes." In *Dissent on Keynes: A Critical Appraisal of Keynesian Economics*, edited by Mark Skousen. Santa Barbara, CA: Praeger, 1992.

Hudson, Michael. "Deficit Commission Follies." *Counterpunch*, December 6, 2010. www.counterpunch.org/hudson12062010.html.

Hyde, Lewis. *The Gift: Imagination and the Erotic Life of Property*. New York: Vintage Books, 2007.

Jacob, Jeffrey, Merlin Brinkerhoff, Emily Jovic, and Gerald Wheatley. "The Social and Cultural Capital of Community Currency: An Ithaca Hours Case Study Survey." *International Journal of Community Currency Research* 8 (2004): 42.

James, Frank. "Cure for U.S. Unemployment Could Lie in German-Style Job Sharing." NPR.org, December 3, 2009.

Jarvis, Jeff. "When Innovation Yields Efficiency." *Buzz Machine*, June 12, 2009. www.buzzmachine.com/2009/06/12/when-innovation-yields -efficiency/.

Jolowicz, H. F., and Barry Nicholas. *Historical Introduction to the Study of Roman Law*. Dallas: Southern Methodist University Press, 1972.

Keen, Steven. "The Roving Cavaliers of Credit." *Debtwatch*, January 31, 2009.

Keister, Todd, and James McAndrews. "Why Are Banks Holding So Many Excess Reserves?" Federal Bank of New York Staff Report no. 380, July 2009.

Kennedy, Margit. *Interest and Inflation-Free Money*. N.p.: Seva International, 1995.

Keynes, John Maynard. "Alternative Theories of the Rate of Interest." *Economic Journal* 47, no. 186 (1937): 241–52.

———. *Economic Consequences of the Peace*. New York: Harcourt, Brace, and Howe, 1920.

———. *The General Theory of Employment, Interest, and Money*. New York: Harcourt, Brace, and Howe, 1936.

King, F. H. *Farmers of Forty Centuries: Or, Permanent Agriculture in China, Korea, and Japan*. New York: Dover, 2004.

Koenig, Evan, and Jim Dolmas. "Monetary Policy in a Zero-Interest Economy." *Southwest Economy*, issue 4, July/August 2003. The Dallas Federal Reserve.

Kropotkin, Peter. *The Conquest of Bread*. New York: G. P. Putnam's Sons, 1906.

Kuhnen, Frithjof. *Man and Land: An Introduction into the Problems of Agrarian Structure and Agrarian Reform*. Saarbrücken: Deutsche Welthungerhilfe, 1982.

LaSalle, Tim, Paul Hepperly, and Amadou Diop. *The Organic Green Revolution*. Kutztown, PA: Rodale Institute, 2008.

Lee, C. J., Hsien-chan Ho, Shing-Mei Chen, Ya-huei Yang, Soon-joy Chang, and Hui-lin Wu. *The Development of Small and Medium-Sized Enterprises in the Republic of China*. Taipei, Taiwan: Chung-Hua Institute of Economic Research, 1995.

Lee, Richard. *The Dobe !Kung*. New York: Holt, Rinehart, and Winston, 1984.

Laidlaw, James. "A Free Gift Makes No Friends." In *The Question of the Gift: Essays across Disciplines*, edited by Mark Olstein. New York: Routledge, 2002.

Lietaer, Bernard. *The Future of Money*. Post Falls, ID: Century, 2002.

Marx, Karl. *Grundrisse*. New York: Penguin Classics, 1993.

Mauss, Marcel. *The Gift: The Form and Reason for Exchange in Archaic Societies*. Translated by W. D. Halls. New York: W. W. Norton, 2000.

Mankiw, N. Gregory. "It May Be Time for the Fed to Go Negative." *New York Times,* April 18, 2009.

Mumford, Lewis. *Technics and Civilization.* New York: Harcourt Brace, 1934.

Nemat-Nejat, Karen Rhea. *Daily Life in Ancient Mesopotamia.* Westport, CT: Greenwood Press, 1988.

Pakenham, Thomas. *The Scramble for Africa.* London: Abacus, 1991.

Paine, Thomas. *Agrarian Justice.* 1797.

Perkins, John. *Confessions of an Economic Hit Man.* New York: Penguin, 2005.

Piff, P. K., M. W. Kraus, B. H. Cheng, and D. Keltner. "Having Less, Giving More: The Influence of Social Class on Prosocial Behavior." *Journal of Personality and Social Psychology,* July 12, 2010. doi:10.1037 /a0020092.

Reasons, Eric. "Innovative Deflation." July 5, 2009. http://blog.ericreasons .com/2009/07/innovative-deflation.html.

Rösl, Gerhard. "Regional Currencies in Germany: Local Competition for the Euro?" Deutsche Bundesbank Series 1: Economic Studies, no. 43, 2006.

Rousseau, Jean Jacques. *A Dissertation on the Origin of Inequality among Men.* Translated by G. D. H. Cole. 1754.

Sahlins, Marshall. *Stone Age Economics.* New York: Routledge, 2003.

Sale, Kirkpatrick. *Rebels against the Future.* New York: Basic Books, 1996.

Seaford, Richard. *Money and the Early Greek Mind.* Cambridge: Cambridge University Press, 2004.

Senior, N. W. *Outline of the Science of Political Economy.* 1836.

Stodder, James. "Reciprocal Exchange Networks: Implications for Macroeconomic Stability." 2005. http://www.lietaer.com/images/Stodder _Reciprocal_Exchange.pdf.

Temple, Robert. *The Genius of China: 3,000 Years of Science, Discovery, and Invention.* Rochester, VT: Inner Traditions, 1998.

Twist, Lynn, with Teresa Barker. *The Soul of Money.* New York: Norton, 2003.

Vallely, Paul. "How Islamic Inventors Changed the World." *The Independent,* March 11, 2006.

Warner, Judith. "The Charitable-Giving Divide." *New York Times Magazine*, August 20, 2010.

White, Martha C. "America's New Debtor Prison: Jail Time Given to Those Who Owe." *Wallet Pop*, July 15, 2010. www.walletpop.com/blog/2010/07/15/americas-new-debtor-prison-jail-time-being-given-to-those-who/.

Wüthrich, W. "Alternatives to Globalization: Cooperative Principle and Complementary Currency." Translated by Philip Beard. *Current Issues (Zeit-Fragen)*, August 9, 2004. http://www.reinventingmoney.com/documents/BeardWIR.pdf.

Xu, Cho-yun. *Ancient China in Transition: An Analysis of Social Mobility, 722–222 B.C.* Palo Alto, CA: Stanford University Press, 1965.

Yong, Ed. "Fertility Rates Climb Back Up in the Most Developed Countries." August 5, 2009. http://scienceblogs.com/notrocketscience/2009/08/fertility_rates_climb_back_up_in_the_most_developed_countrie.php.

Zarlenga, Stephen. *The Lost Science of Money*. Valatie, NY: American Monetary Institute, 2002.

INDEX

ABOUT THE AUTHOR

CHARLES EISENSTEIN is the author of *The Ascent of Humanity* and frequently writes about civilization, consciousness, money, and human cultural evolution. His writings on the web magazine *Reality Sandwich* have generated a vast online following; he speaks frequently at conferences and other events, and gives numerous interviews on radio and podcasts. Eisenstein graduated from Yale University in 1989 with a degree in Mathematics and Philosophy, and spent the next ten years as a Chinese-English translator. He currently lives in Harrisburg, Pennsylvania, and serves on the faculty of Goddard College.